LEGION O

LEGION OF THE REARGUARD

Dissident Irish Republicanism

MARTYN FRAMPTON
Queen Mary, University of London

IRISH ACADEMIC PRESS
DUBLIN • PORTLAND, OR

First published in 2011 by Irish Academic Press

2 Brookside, Dundrum Road, Dublin 14, Ireland	920 NE 58th Avenue, Suite 300 Portland, Oregon, 97213-3786 USA

www.iap.ie

© 2011 Martyn Frampton

British Library Cataloguing in Publication Data
Frampton, Martyn.
  Legion of the rearguard : dissident Irish Republicanism.
  1. Republicanism—Ireland—History—20th century.
  2. Republicanism—Ireland—History—21st century.
  3. Political violence—Northern Ireland—History—20th
  century. 4. Political violence—Northern Ireland—
  History—21st century. 5. Northern Ireland—Politics and
  government—1994-
  I. Title
  322.4'2'09416-dc22

ISBN 978 0 7165 3055 8 (cloth)
ISBN 978 0 7165 3056 5 (paper)

Library of Congress Cataloging-in-Publication Data
An entry can be found on request

Printed by Good News Digital Books, Ongar, Essex

Contents

Glossary   vii

Map   xi

Acknowledgements   ·   xiii

Introduction   1

1   Origins: The Lighting of the Republican Torch   11

2   The Keeper of the Flame: Timeless Republicanism   43

3   Inferno: The Baton is Passed On, 1997–2002   90

4   A Flickering Flame: The Nadir of Dissident   157
    Republicanism, 2002–6

5   The Flame Reignites: Resurgence, 2006–10   201

Conclusion   279

Appendix Timeline of Violent Dissident Republican Activity   288

Bibliography   320

Index   329

Glossary

32CSM (32 County Sovereignty Movement) – dissident Irish republican political organisation opposed to the peace process. Led by Francie Mackey, it was created in 1997 by republicans unhappy with Sinn Féin's acceptance of the Mitchell Principles on non-violence. It is said to be 'inextricably linked' to the Real IRA

Árd Chomhairle – national executive of an Irish political party, especially Sinn Féin and Republican Sinn Féin

Árd Fheis – annual conference of an Irish political party, especially Sinn Féin and Republican Sinn Féin

CFAD (Concerned Families Against Drugs) – small, Belfast-based organisation opposed to drugs and alleged by the IMC to be 'vigilante' in nature and close to dissident Irish republican circles

'Concerned Republicans' (Ex-POWs and Concerned Republicans against RUC/PSNI) – loose coalition of Irish republicans opposed to Sinn Féin's decision to endorse the PSNI in 2006–7; several candidates took part in the Northern Irish Assembly elections of 2007 under this banner and it was succeeded by the RNU

CIRA (Continuity IRA) – dissident Irish republican paramilitary organisation, created in 1986 by republicans unhappy with (Provisional) Sinn Féin's decision to abandon abstentionism. It became active only after the 1994 Provisional IRA ceasefire. It is opposed to the peace process and held to be closely linked to Republican Sinn Féin

Cumann (Branch) – the smallest unit of organisation within an Irish political party (plural, cumainn)

Dáil (Éireann) – lower house of the Irish parliament

DPP District Policing Partnerships

DUP (Democratic Unionist Party) – Unionist party in Northern Ireland led by Rev. Dr Ian Paisley until May 2008 and currently by Peter Robinson

éirígí – socialist Irish republican political party, created in 2006 by republicans unhappy with the direction in which Sinn Féin was headed. It is led by Brian Leeson

Fianna Fáil – largest political party in the Republic of Ireland

Fine Gael – second largest political party in the Republic of Ireland

FRU (Force Research Unit) – covert military intelligence unit of the British army

An Garda Síochána (known colloquially as the Gardaí) – Irish police force

IICD (Independent International Commission on Decommissioning) – set up by the British and Irish governments in 1997 to facilitate the disposal of paramilitary arms

IMC (International Monitoring Commission) – set up by the British and Irish governments' 'Joint Declaration' of 2003, to monitor paramilitary activity

INLA (Irish National Liberation Army) – socialist Irish republican paramilitary organisation formed in 1974 out of a split within the 'Official' republican movement. Though opposed to the peace process it declared a ceasefire in 1998 and formally decommissioned all weaponry in 2010

IRA (Irish Republican Army) – title claimed by variety of Irish republican organisations

IRLA (Irish Republican Liberation Army) – small dissident Irish republican organisation that, according to the IMC, emerged in the Strabane area

LVF (Loyalist Volunteer Force) – loyalist paramilitary organisation

MI5 (Military Intelligence Section 5) – the British internal security service

MLA – Member of the Legislative Assembly (in Northern Ireland)

MP – Member of Parliament (Westminster)

NICRA – Northern Ireland Civil Rights Association

NIO – Northern Ireland Office

NORAID (Irish Northern Aid Committee) – Irish republican support group based in the United States of America

OIRA (Official IRA) – Irish republican paramilitary organisation, part of the 'Official' republican movement

Óglaigh na hÉireann – 'Volunteers of Ireland' – the title claimed by various forms of the IRA, from the PIRA to ONH itself (it is also the official title of the Irish defence forces)

ONH (Óglaigh na hÉireann) – the acronym ONH is taken to refer to a small dissident Irish republican paramilitary organisation that emerged from the Continuity IRA in the Strabane area in 2006. It is not to be confused with the Real IRA faction that also began using the title 'ONH' from 2009 and is referred to here as Real IRA/ONH

PIRA (Provisional IRA) – Irish republican paramilitary organisation, created 1969–70 after a split with the 'Officials', linked to (Provisional) Sinn Féin. For most of the 'Troubles' it was known simply as 'The IRA'

PSNI (Police Service of Northern Ireland) – successor police force to the RUC, established in 2001

RAAD (Republican Action Against Drugs) – small dissident Irish republican organisation, engaged in paramilitary violence against alleged 'drug dealers' in Derry and the surrounding area

RIRA (Real IRA) – dissident Irish republican paramilitary organisation, opposed to the peace process. It was created in 1997, by those unhappy with Sinn Féin's acceptance of the Mitchell Principles on non-violence

Real IRA/ONH – faction of the Real IRA that began to operate simply under the banner of ONH from 2009 onwards. Not to be confused with the smaller group that used the same name after splitting from the Continuity IRA in the Strabane area in 2006

RNU (Republican Network for Unity) – Irish republican organisation created in 2007 as a successor organisation to the 'Concerned Republicans' movement. Opposed to the direction of Sinn Féin and the Good Friday Agreement

RUC (Royal Ulster Constabulary) – Northern Irish police force, superseded in 2001 by the PSNI

SNH (Saoirse na hÉireann) – small dissident Irish republican splinter group that, according to the IMC, emerged briefly in Belfast

SDLP (Social Democratic and Labour Party) – constitutional nationalist, Northern Irish political party, formerly led by John Hume, currently led by Margaret Ritchie

Sinn Féin – Irish republican political party, led by Gerry Adams. Created 1969–70, after a split with the 'Officials'; linked to the 'Provisional' IRA

Taoiseach – Irish prime minister

TUAS ('Tactical Use of Armed Struggle') – title of the 1994 internal Provisional republican document that outlined the rationale for the first Provisional IRA ceasefire

UDA (Ulster Defence Association) – loyalist paramilitary organisation

UFF (Ulster Freedom Fighters) – loyalist paramilitary organisation (part of the UDA)

UUP (Ulster Unionist Party) – Unionist party in Northern Ireland, formerly led by David Trimble, currently led by Sir Reg Empey

UVF (Ulster Volunteer Force) – Loyalist paramilitary organisation

Northern Ireland

Belfast

Lisburn

Hillsborough

Downpatrick

Castlewellan

Newcastle

Warrenpoint

Antrim

Randalstown

Ballymoney

Bushmills

Largan

Craigavon

Banbridge

Newry

Bessbrook

Jonesborough

Forkhill

Maghera

Stewartstown

Lough Neagh

Portadown

Armagh

Keady

Cullyhanna

Magherafelt

Cookstown

Coalisland

Dungannon

Auchnacloy

Newtownhamilton

Crossmaglen

Draperstown

Newtownstewart

Limavady

Dungiven

Omagh

Clogher

Rosslea

Newtownbutler

Derry

Castlederg

Irvinestown

Lisbellaw

Lisnaskea

Strabane

Enniskillen

Belleek

Garrison

Acknowledgements

This book could not have been written without the advice and assistance of numerous people. While the views expressed herein and any errors contained in the text are entirely my own, there are many to whom I owe a great deal. At the outset I must express my thanks to Lisa Hyde and Irish Academic Press for showing faith in the project. Lisa was unwavering in her support and enthusiasm; and it is testament to her drive that the book was (eventually) finished. I am also enormously grateful to Ruth Dudley Edwards for her willingness to read and comment upon the manuscript. Typically, Ruth went above and beyond the call of duty – and truly this work would never have been completed in the absence of her efforts.

Sean O'Callaghan was another whose contribution to this project has been invaluable. Any conversation with Sean invariably yields a new insight into the world of Irish republicanism. His suggestions as to the shape of the book were always useful and much appreciated. Beyond that, it is a privilege to know him. The same must be said of Henry Robinson, whose passion and dedication is a constant source of inspiration.

Also in this category is Dr John Bew. A great mind and a better person, John possesses a gift for bringing a clarity of analysis to any subject he considers. Always reliable, it is an honour to call him a friend. Throughout the writing process I was fortunate enough to be able to avail of the opinions of an array of people – some of whom doubtless had no idea how much help they were giving! Chief among them were Dr Dean Godson, Professor (Lord) Paul Bew, Professor Brendan Simms, Professor Henry Patterson, Hon. Professor Mitchell Reiss (with thanks too to USIP for funding the London conference, for which some of the material in Chapter 5 was first prepared), Gerry Gregg, Jim Cusack,

Charlie Mitchell, Dr Richard Bourke, Inigo Gurruchaga, Richard O'Rawe and Carrie Twomey.

I am especially grateful to all those who agreed to be interviewed in the course of my research, over a period of years and in different contexts: Danny Morrison, Tony Catney, Brian Leeson, Breandán Mac Cionnaith, Ruairí Ó Brádaigh and Richard Walsh. Special mention must also go to Dr Anthony McIntyre. For a sustained period Anthony has been one of the most perceptive commentators on Irish republicanism. Our analyses may differ, but he has been consistently helpful, indulging me in countless conversations and facilitating key interviews for this project. I am indebted too to Ross Moore and the staff of the Linenhall Library in Belfast for their assistance when collating crucial primary materials.

A special word must go to those who gave of their time to read the manuscript. Jonathan Scherbel-Ball and Matthew Jury availed me of their legal (and intellectual) expertise and for that I am truly grateful; likewise to Ruth, John and Paul for their comments and advice.

I would also like to express my thanks to Professor Adrian Dixon and the fellows and staff at Peterhouse, Cambridge, where I was when this project began; and also to Professor Virginia Davis, Professor Julian Jackson, my fellow colleagues and the staff at the History Department of Queen Mary, the University of London, where the book was completed. I am fortunate to have been blessed with working environments that are both genuinely enjoyable and enriching.

Finally, I wish to thank my close friends in both London and Cambridge and, above all, my family and Rose. I am lucky to be blessed with loving parents and a caring sister; their support is, at all times, appreciated. Rose has been an unyielding source of support during the critical stages of this book. Always reassuring and never ill-humoured (despite the loss of numerous evenings and weekends), she has been a tower of strength. Every day I count my blessings that I met her; she makes everything worthwhile and, therefore, this book is dedicated to Rose.

Introduction

The murder of three men inside forty-eight hours in Northern Ireland in March 2009 called forth an outpouring of commentary within the British, Irish and even American public spheres. Much of the reaction to these events evinced a concerned – at times even bewildered – tone: 'If we are at peace, why are soldiers still dying?' 'Is it the Troubles again?' 'Can Ulster's new politics survive the revival of old enmities?'[1] Many pondered whether the 'Troubles' – the three-decade-long era of violence that had plagued Northern Ireland – were returning to the province; or whether the attacks represented the dying embers of the bygone conflagration. As those groups responsible for the killings made their claims of responsibility, attention also focused on the question of who was behind the attacks.

The 8 March assault on Massereene barracks in County Antrim, which took the lives of two British soldiers – Mark Quinsey and Patrick Azimcar – was claimed by the 'South Antrim Brigade of the Real IRA'.[2] When police constable Stephen Carroll was shot dead in Craigavon on 10 March it was the 'Continuity IRA' that declared culpability. Yet, to many it was far from clear what such labels signified.[3] It was broadly understood, for example, that the two branches of the Irish Republican Army (IRA) referred to were part of a broader phenomenon of 'dissident republicanism'. But beyond this designation, such statements raised far more questions than they answered. What was this 'dissident republicanism' – what were its contours and its manifestations? Who *were* the particular groups in question? Where did they come from? Who precisely was involved with them? From where did they draw their support – and why? And above all, what was it that these 'dissidents' believed in and wanted? On what reasoning and to what end had they resorted to lethal violence?

It is as part of the effort to begin to answer some of these questions that this study will examine the history of 'dissident republicanism' – especially in the years since the Good Friday Agreement (GFA). This is a history that has been all but neglected outside the realm of investigative journalism; or indeed, the columns of some regular commentators on Northern Irish affairs.[4] With regard to the former, the account of John Mooney and Michael O'Toole, *Black Operations: The Secret War Against the Real IRA*, offers a useful – if somewhat limited – synopsis of the Real IRA's history to 2003. There is, though, no broader consideration of dissident republicanism as a political ideology or organisational force. Instead, the focus is firmly on the 'intelligence war' that was waged against the Real IRA by the security services, north and south – particularly on the role of David Rupert, the agent/informer secreted into the group by the American Federal Bureau of Investigation (FBI). While this episode is undoubtedly important and Rupert's insights are an invaluable resource for understanding the Real IRA, the resulting picture is thus a far from complete one. Moreover, there are occasions too in Mooney and O'Toole's analysis where the evidential basis for some of the book's assertions is far from clear.

One of the few academic pieces to have considered dissident republicanism to date was Jonathan Tonge's appropriately named article from 2004, 'They Haven't Gone Away You Know'.[5] However, Tonge limited his analysis to the period prior to 2004; perhaps more importantly, he also focused almost solely on the military progress of groups such as the Real IRA. There was little consideration of the ideological evolution of the dissidents, or developments in organisational expression and political strategy. Significantly more substantial is Ruth Dudley Edwards' account of the 1998 Omagh bombing and the civil case that was launched against the alleged perpetrators. *Aftermath: The Omagh Bombing and the Families' Pursuit of Justice* throws much light on the Real IRA as it emerged in the period after 1997. Though written with a focus more on the relatives of those killed in the Omagh attack, it charts the character and endurance of physical-force republicanism and the lethal consequences of the phenomenon.[6]

Beyond the work of Tonge and Dudley Edwards, however, there has been only fragmentary examination of dissident republicanism, often within works focused primarily on their 'mainstream' republican adversaries.[7] But the nature of this material – as an adjunct to studies that have by-and-large concentrated on the Provisional republican movement (as represented by Sinn Féin and the Provisional IRA (PIRA)) and its apparent journey from 'war' to 'peace' – has ensured that the dissidents have enjoyed only peripheral attention.

Perhaps a key reason for this interest deficit is the conceptual challenge posed by dissident republicanism to the prevailing narrative/prism through which many have viewed the recent history of Northern Ireland. On this reading, the peace process and the Good Friday (or Belfast) Agreement of April 1998 are understood to represent the 'end of history' for the province. After thirty years of conflict, those involved are considered to have settled for a 'historic compromise'. The corollary of this has been an assumption that violence might now be a thing of the past.

This has certainly proved to be a compelling interpretation for some of those involved in the political process over the last decade or more. In November 1998, for example, British prime minister Tony Blair asserted in a speech to the Irish parliament that 'Politics is replacing violence as the way people do business' and 'It is time now ... for the gun and the threat of the gun to be taken out of politics once and for all.'[8] This was a view shared by those who had formerly been fervent opponents of the British state. Only a couple of months earlier, Gerry Adams, leader of the Irish republican party, Sinn Féin, had declared, 'Sinn Féin believe the violence we have seen must be for all of us now a thing of the past, over, done with and gone.'[9] Adams' party stood firmly for an end to what it called 'British rule in Ireland', by way of the reunification of Northern Ireland with its Republic of Ireland neighbour.[10] To this end, it had once been a staunch supporter of the 'armed struggle' waged by the Provisional IRA. Adams himself was widely believed to have been a senior IRA leader for much of the 'Troubles'.[11] Yet, he appeared willing now to commit himself to a future without political violence.

Several years later, Adams clarified this further. In late 2002 he told a Sinn Féin internal conference in County Monaghan that the removal of armed groups from Ireland was the 'aim of every right-thinking republican'.[12] This was followed by an April 2003 speech, in which he declared that Sinn Féin's peace strategy aimed at 'bringing an end to physical-force republicanism'.[13] Later that same year, he was even more explicit:

> Part of our effort was to get the IRA to go away. If you look at the
> history of physical-force republicanism, whether it's Éamon de

Valera or Mick Collins or Kevin Boland or Prionsias de Rossa or
Tomás Mac Giolla or Ruairí Ó Brádaigh or whoever, those people
who left republicanism or tried to develop some alternative all
failed. Physical-force republicanism continued despite attempts to
throttle it or Fianna Fáil-it out of existence. Part of our endeavour
– and it's unprecedented – is to bring an end to physical-force
republicanism ... It's an open secret. I have said within republican
circles that one of the objectives of this process is to see an IRA out
of existence. When I say that we want to bring an end to physical-
force republicanism, that clearly means bringing an end to the
organisation or the vehicle of physical-force republicanism.[14]

And finally, in his 2005 'appeal' to the IRA, Adams made plain his
belief that the time for militancy had past:

I want to speak directly to the men and women of Óglaigh na
hÉireann, the volunteer soldiers of the Irish Republican Army ...
Your determination, selflessness and courage have brought the
freedom struggle towards its fulfilment. That struggle can now be
taken forward by other means. I say this with the authority of my
office as president of Sinn Féin. In the past I have defended the
right of the IRA to engage in armed struggle. I did so because there
was no alternative for those who would not bend the knee, or turn
a blind eye to oppression, or for those who wanted a national
republic. Now there is an alternative. I have clearly set out my
view of what that alternative is. The way forward is by building
political support for republican and democratic objectives across
Ireland and by winning support for these goals internationally. I
want to use this occasion therefore to appeal to the leadership of
Óglaigh na hÉireann to fully embrace and accept this alternative.[15]

By speaking as he did, Adams left no doubt as to the compatibility
between his vision for the outcome of the peace process with that of the
British government. The account of the Northern Irish peace process
produced by Tony Blair's former chief of staff Jonathan Powell confirms
this. Therein, Powell speaks of the British desire that physical-force
republicanism be transformed into a purely political movement, with the
government making peace 'only once' with a united republican movement.[16] What this would lead to had been spelled out unambiguously by
Blair, back in October 2002. In the words of the prime minister, what

the Belfast Agreement offered was the prospect that 'one of the most abnormal parts of the continent of Europe, never mind the UK, would become normal'. On that occasion, Blair had called for 'acts of completion' from the mainstream republican movement, arguing, 'Remove the threat of violence and the peace process is on an unstoppable path.'[17] Three years later, after years of talks, breakthroughs and breakdowns – and a stop-start existence for the institutions created by the Agreement – the promise contained within Blair's 2002 speech appeared to be realised. In July 2005, in response to Adams' above-quoted appeal, the IRA announced the official end of its armed campaign. Several months later, the Independent International Commission on Decommissioning (IICD) confirmed that the IRA had completed the process of weapons decommissioning. The years that have followed have seen the Independent Monitoring Commission (IMC), a body created in 2003–4 to oversee paramilitary ceasefires in Northern Ireland, authenticate the withering of the Provisional IRA as an entity. To give but one example, in October 2006 the IMC reported that the IRA leadership was 'committed to the peaceful strategy and that it was working to ensure full compliance with it'; in line with this it had 'disbanded "military" structures' and consequently, there was 'convincing evidence of PIRA's continuing commitment to the political path'.[18]

In the wake of this winding down of the Provisional IRA, the institutional edifice of the 1998 Agreement was re-established in May 2007. That month saw the return of the Northern Ireland Executive and Assembly – under the joint stewardship of Ian Paisley, leader of the Democratic Unionist Party (DUP), who became first minister, together with Sinn Féin's Martin McGuinness as deputy first minister. Both at the time and subsequently, many remarked on the apparent good relationship that these former political opponents established. Furthermore, a year on and the revived institutions survived the retirement of Paisley and his replacement as first minister by Peter Robinson. True, for a period in 2008 it appeared as if the unresolved question of devolved policing and justice powers might overturn matters, but ultimately that issue too was settled; as of April 2010, the existence of the Northern Irish Assembly and Executive appears relatively secure.

Thus, in light of the objectives ascribed to the peace process by both mainstream Irish republicans and the British government, the view that the peace process was a highly successful endeavour seemed persuasive.

Indeed, there cannot be any doubt that Northern Ireland became a far more peaceable country than it had been in the recent past; nor that it had experienced a remarkable coming together of former political foes. For this reason, there was much to recommend the view that, for all its faults, the peace process and the Agreement arising out of it had consigned violence to the past.

And yet, despite this apparent triumph of the peace process, the hopes contained within it have not been entirely fulfilled. The logical connection contained within Tony Blair's 2002 address has proven somewhat illusory. The peace process – at a political level – might now be on an 'unstoppable path'; but the threat of 'violence' has not been eradicated. That this should have been so is to a significant extent the result of the Agreement's inability to deliver the goal to which Blair, Powell and Adams openly aspired: the end of physical-force republicanism.

Even prior to the lethal attacks in the early spring of 2009, it was clear that there remained a significant minority of Irish republicans for whom the peace process did not represent a satisfactory end to the war. Moreover, it seemed increasingly clear that such people were prepared to use violence in their attempt to challenge the status quo. On 5 November 2008, for instance, the Chief Constable of the Police Service of Northern Ireland (PSNI), Sir Hugh Orde, declared that the level of threat posed by the dissidents was the highest it had been for six years. In evidence to the House of Commons Northern Ireland Affairs Committee, he said, 'Without question, the intensity has increased. The determination of the main groups, Continuity IRA [CIRA] and Real IRA [RIRA], is clear by the evidence of the level of attacks and variety of attacks.' Presciently, Orde claimed that the dissidents' chief objective was to kill a police officer and thereby fuel political instability.[19] These warnings were repeated in March 2009 – on the immediate eve of the murders that were claimed by the CIRA and the RIRA.

It is clear, therefore, that there was a pre-history to the March 2009 attacks; albeit a pre-history that had been largely obscured by an emphasis on the mould-breaking nature of the peace process, which had encouraged a certain degree of myopia. The process – and particularly the Agreement it produced – were founded upon the emphatically liberal principles of a commitment to the rule of law, constitutional means and the primacy of democratic legitimacy. Whatever the divergent aspirations of Irish nationalism and unionism, it was, by some readings, an attempt to displace such tensions to the purely political realm, in which each creed could pursue its own agenda, but in a context in which they 'agreed to disagree'. Yet, this always left open the question of those who did not, and would not, so agree.

Of course, such rejectionists existed on both sides of the political-communal divide in Northern Ireland. The DUP faced its own challenge from a recalcitrant section of unionism. Jim Allister, a one-time senior DUP figure, founded Traditional Unionist Voice (TUV) to represent those who opposed the decision to go into government with republicans. For Allister and his supporters, it was simply unconscionable that a party that had once pledged to 'smash Sinn Féin' should now sit in a shared executive with what it termed 'unrepentant terrorists'; theirs was an ethical objection to the workings of the entire peace process, on the grounds that 'nothing which is morally wrong can be politically right'.[20] That such a stance could gain considerable support was made evident by the electoral achievements of TUV. At its first outing – in a local council by-election in Dromore, County Down in 2008 – the TUV's share of the vote (almost 20 per cent) stopped the DUP from claiming a seat it had looked sure to win.[21] More striking still was its performance in the 2009 European elections. There, the performance of TUV leader Jim Allister prevented the DUP from topping the poll for the first time since 1979.[22] Thus, there remained an indisputable and substantial appetite for unreconstructed rejectionism of the peace process within unionism (though the TUV's performance at the 2010 British general election suggested the tide for this may already be receding).

On the republican side, meanwhile, there were also clearly those who rejected the central tenets of the peace process. As has been described, these were given violent expression in the activities of the CIRA and the RIRA. Alongside these were such pre-existing groups as the Irish National Liberation Army (INLA) – the oft-forgotten, but one-time near-equal of the Provisional IRA. There have also been more obscure formations, with an assortment of factions claiming the title of Óglaigh na hÉireann (ONH). Furthermore, republican rejectionism also ran wider than these purely militant organisations. The last decade has seen the birth of various new entities, all of which claim to embody the 'truest' form of Irish republicanism: from the New Republican Forum, to the Republican Network for Unity, to éirígí.

Should there be any surprise in all this – either that certain strains of Irish republicanism have shown themselves to be unresponsive to the compromises of the peace process or that the result has been a fragmentation and proliferation of republican organisations? The echoes of history suggest not. Irish republicanism has long incubated a belief among some of its adherents that there is a higher calling than that bestowed by elections and democratic mandates. Legitimacy, for some, is not derived from such ephemeral phenomena as ballots; rather it is something eternal and inalienable. Consequently, irrespective of the claims that 'history' was supposed to have been brought to an 'end' in Northern Ireland, there are those who refuse to accept the presumed 'verdict' of that history. For them, there is only one possible terminus for republicanism: the achievement of an independent, united republic encompassing the whole island of Ireland. That the peace process has not delivered that outcome confirms it marks only a false dawn.

What follows is an attempt to map the ideological and organisational world of dissident republicanism. As a phenomenon it includes some who are still committed to the path of violence – but also some who are not. The term 'dissident' is in that sense used as a catch-all, to encompass those of an Irish republican persuasion who have broken with the 'mainstream' movement of Sinn Féin and the Provisionals. It is by their opposition to the peace process and/or the political status quo in Northern Ireland that they have come to be labelled 'dissidents', though many within their amorphous ranks would charge that actually they have stayed true to their beliefs, where others have not. The extent to which this viewpoint self-consciously draws on an older legacy is confirmed by a brief examination of the earlier incarnations of twentieth-century Irish republicanism. In the chapter that follows, a quick overview of the republican movement's history will be provided. Based, for the most part, on existing literature, the purpose of this is not to offer anything radically new, in terms of content, but rather to identify salient features of that history, an understanding of which is often required if the latter day dissidents are to be properly comprehended and contextualised.

Against that background, the remainder of the book proceeds to consider the debates that are convulsing Irish republicanism today in the aftermath of the Belfast Agreement. It draws on analysis of the speeches, documents and publications of contemporary 'dissidents', as well as a series of interviews conducted by the author with leading figures from that world. This was augmented by examination of official documents and existing research on the dissidents (with much valuable work having been done in the field of journalism), in an effort to answer a central, guiding question: Who are the dissidents and what are their arguments?

NOTES

1. D. McKittrick, 'If We Are at Peace, Why are Soldiers Still Dying?', *Independent*, 9 March 2009; J. O'Sullivan, 'Is It the Troubles Again?', *Toronto Globe and Mail*, 13 March 2009; H. McDonald, 'Can Ulster's New Politics Survive the Revival of Old Enmities?', *Guardian*, 10 March 2009.
2. S. Breen, 'The Week the Funerals Returned', *Sunday Tribune*, 15 March 2009.
3. 'Continuity IRA Shot Dead Officer', BBC News Online, 10 March 2009, available at http://news.bbc.co.uk/1/hi/northern_ireland/7934426.stm
4. J. Mooney and M. O'Toole, *Black Operations: The Secret War against the Real IRA* (Ashbourne, Co. Meath: Maverick House, 2003).
5. J. Tonge, '"They Haven't Gone Away, You Know": Irish Republican Dissidents and "Armed Struggle"', *Terrorism and Political Violence*, 16, 3 (2004), pp.671–93.
6. R. Dudley Edwards, *Aftermath: The Omagh Bombing and the Families' Pursuit of Justice* (London: Harvill Secker, 2009).
7. See, for example, R. English, *Armed Struggle: A History of the IRA* (London: Macmillan, 2003). Or the recent article by Lorraine Bowman-Grieve, which examined the dissidents' online presence as an example of a terrorist-supporting 'viral community': L. Bowman-Grieve, 'Irish Republicanism and the Internet: Support for the New Wave of Dissidents', *Perspectives on Terrorism*, 4, 2 (May 2010).
8. Tony Blair, *Address to the Irish Parliament*, 26 November 1998, available at Dáil Éireann Parliamentary Debates, Vol. 497, http://historical-debates.oireachtas.ie/D/0497/D.0497.199811260003.html
9. Gerry Adams, *Keynote Statement on the Current State of the Peace Process*, 1 September 1998, available at CAIN (Conflict Archive in Northern Ireland), http://cain.ulst.ac.uk/events/peace/docs/ga1998.htm
10. For an example of this phrase, see the party's key document at the outset of the peace process: *Towards a Lasting Peace in Ireland* (Dublin: Sinn Féin, 1992).
11. For the foremost account of Adams' career in the IRA, see E. Moloney, *A Secret History of the IRA* (London: Allen Lane, 2002).
12. 'Good Friday Agreement is the Only Show in Town: Keynote Speech Given by Gerry Adams', *An Phoblacht*, 31 October 2002. See also L. Walsh and P. McArdle, 'Government Won't Release Real IRA', *Sunday Independent*, 27 October 2002.
13. 'Adams – We are at a Defining Moment in the Process: Governments and UUP Now Have a Choice to Make (Gerry Adams Keynote Speech from 28 April)', *An Phoblacht*, 1 May 2003.
14. P. Leahy, 'Government, Unionists Can Bring an End to IRA – Adams [Interview]', *Sunday Business Post*, 28 September 2003. See also E. Rice, 'Assembly Elections Key to IRA's Disbanding? Adams', *Sunday Tribune*, 28 September 2003.
15. 'Gerry Adams Addresses the IRA', *An Phoblacht*, 7 April 2005.
16. J. Powell, *Great Hatred, Little Room: Making Peace in Northern Ireland* (London: The Bodley Head, 2008), pp.24–5, 314.

17. Tony Blair, Speech at the Harbour Commissioners' Office, Belfast, 17 October 2002, available at CAIN, http://cain.ulst.ac.uk/events/peace/docs/tb171002.htm
18. *Twelfth Report of the Independent Monitoring Commission* (London: Stationery Office, October 2006), pp.8–12. See http://www.independentmonitoringcommission.org/documents/uploads/IMC%2012th%20Report%20pdf.pdf
19. *Oral Evidence of Chief Constable Sir Hugh Orde OBE, Assistant Chief Constable Judith Gillespie and Chief Inspector Sam Cordner*, House of Commons Northern Ireland Select Committee (HC 1174-i), 5 November 2008, available at http://www.parliament.the-stationery-office.co.uk/pa/cm200708/cmselect/cmniaf/c1174-i/c117402.htm
20. 'About Us', Traditional Unionist Voice, available at http://www.tuv.org.uk/tuv/about
21. *Election Results for District Electorial Area of Dromore*, Electoral Office for Northern Ireland, 13 February 2008, available at http://www.eoni.org.uk/dromore_by-election_result_2008.pdf
22. '2009 European Election Results', ARK Northern Ireland Elections Website, available at http://www.ark.ac.uk/elections/fe09.htm

1

Origins: The Lighting of the Republican Torch

1916: GENESIS

The foundation stone of modern Irish republicanism was laid with the 1916 Easter Rising. This revolt against British rule in Ireland, carried forth by a 'revolutionary elite', was imbued with the spirit of what one historian has called 'sacrificial patriotism', or 'blood sacrifice'.[1] In immediate terms, the failed rebellion did not come close to shaking the edifice of British authority. It brought only the devastation of central Dublin, the death of some 400 people (many of whom were civilians) and the execution of its leading figures. Yet, it bequeathed a powerful legacy – not least in the form of the Proclamation that attended the ill-fated putsch. Signed by seven men, in the name of the 'provisional government' of the 'Irish Republic', this document constituted, in the judgment of Charles Townshend, 'a kind of distillation of nationalist doctrine, a kind of national poem: lucid, terse, and strangely moving even to unbelievers'.[2]

The Proclamation, from the outset, spoke on behalf of Ireland, to 'Irishmen and Irishwomen', 'in the name of God and of the dead generations from which she receives her old tradition of nationhood'. In such fashion, it invoked a mixture of divine right and historical sanctity, to bless the national project it represented. Moreover, it then declared:

> Having organised and trained her manhood through her secret revolutionary organisation, the Irish Republican Brotherhood, and through her open military organisations, the Irish Volunteers and the Irish Citizen Army, having patiently perfected her discipline, having resolutely waited for the right moment to reveal itself, she now seizes that moment, and, supported by her exiled children in

America and by gallant allies in Europe, but relying in the first on her own strength, she strikes in full confidence of victory.

We declare the right of the people of Ireland to the ownership of Ireland, and to the unfettered control of Irish destinies, to be sovereign and indefeasible. The long usurpation of that right by a foreign people and government has not extinguished the right, nor can it ever be extinguished except by the destruction of the Irish people. In every generation the Irish people have asserted their right to national freedom and sovereignty; six times during the last three hundred years they have asserted it to arms. Standing on that fundamental right and again asserting it in arms in the face of the world, we hereby proclaim the Irish Republic as a Sovereign Independent State, and we pledge our lives and the lives of our comrades-in-arms to the cause of its freedom, of its welfare, and of its exaltation among the nations.[3]

With these words, the leaders of the Rising affirmed their right, as an elite, vanguard group, to determine the future of Ireland as a whole. The language deployed was that of legalistically infused moralism, centred on notions of intrinsically held entitlement. In this way, the Proclamation was forged as the legitimising centrepiece of an act of dramatic self-assertion; an act that itself marked the realisation and 'exaltation' of Irish nationhood. The episode represented, in the words of Richard English, a 'non- or pre-mandated gesture', conducted by an elite that 'rather arrogantly identified its own will with the best interests of the people'.[4] In so doing, it consecrated the notion that the enlightened few could act on behalf of the misguided many.

Moreover, the Rising came imbued with a ready-made ideology, which sanctified its place in the Irish national story. Crucial here were the writings of Patrick Pearse. Though not the organisational brains behind the rebellion, it was Pearse who furnished its spirit. In late 1915/early 1916 he had written four pamphlets, which both distilled the nationalist doctrine and reified it for future generations. As Pearse's biographer has observed, the pamphlets fused the national with the religious, depicting the 'four gospels of the new testament of Irish nationality': Wolfe Tone, Thomas Davis, Fintan Lalor and John Mitchel.[5] The labours of these Irish heroes were set against a separatist tradition that was held to reach back to the Norman invasion in 1169. Furthermore, through their invocation Pearse sought to cement the canon for future generations; to 'lay down a book of law for Irish nationalists'. At the core of this was the immutable character of 'the national demand of Ireland', judged to be 'fixed and determined'. As one especially illuminating passage noted,

> Like a divine religion, national freedom bears the marks of unity, of sanctity, of catholicity, of apostolic succession. Of unity, for it contemplates the nation as one; of sanctity, for it is holy in itself and in those who serve it; of catholicity, for it embraces all the men and women of the nation; of apostolic succession, for it, or the aspiration after it, passes down from generation to generation from the nation's fathers.[6]

With the death of Pearse and his fellow conspirators, this vision of Irish nationhood was anointed by its first martyrs. They had left, 'by their words and their actions, a political legacy which could be construed as a defence of the [nationalist] die-hards'.[7] The marginal figures of 1916 received retrospective consecration from those who built the Irish Free State after 1921.

From that time, the smallest minorities have been able to invoke a putative right to act, in the name of the Irish 'people' – without ever requiring a formal mandate from those same people. It is on this philosophical basis that the post-1998 generation of 'dissident' Irish republicans can assert the legitimacy of their rejection of the Good Friday Agreement, regardless of the overwhelming democratic endorsement of that Agreement by the Irish people.[8] The romantic nationalism with which the 1916 Proclamation is imbued – redolent with references to the 'patriot dead' of generations past and the pure authority of Irish nationhood – could scarcely be further removed from the rational and compromising ethos of the 1998 Agreement. The truth of this (and indeed, the implications for the mainstream 'Provisional' Irish republican movement), were captured in the pithy words of one dissident republican writer: 'Good Friday and Easter Sunday are a mere two days apart. But the gap between what Good Friday republicanism achieved and the objectives Easter Sunday republicans died to secure can be understood only in light years.'[9]

And yet, it was the spirit of 'Easter Sunday' (the Rising actually began on the Monday) that entered mainstream Irish national political culture in the years after 1916. There it would remain right down to the

present day, offering nourishment to those who recognised the unfulfilled nature of Pearse's Republic; this, in spite of the de facto acceptance of partition by that same political culture. It was this paradox
which years later would see Taoiseach Bertie Ahern keep a picture
of Patrick Pearse on the wall behind his desk, even as he rebuked the
various IRAs for their ongoing campaigns of violence. As Ruth Dudley
Edwards has noted, 'Children in a free Ireland were nurtured on the
writings and deeds of the men of 1916, and condemned by their own
government when as adults they put into action the logic of force they
absorbed from them.'[10]

It was not merely at the spiritual, or philosophical, level that the
1916 Rising provided subsequent advocates of republicanism with a
potent inheritance. Rather, the modus operandi of the event glorified
the path of insurrectionist violence, in pursuit of the Irish national
dream. This 'lesson' of 1916 was subsequently reinforced by the experience of the entire 'revolutionary period' down to 1923. Both in 1919
and again in 1922, unelected and armed minority groups took upon
themselves the mantle of self-appointed 'liberators' of an 'oppressed'
Irish people. The Irish Republican Army (or IRA, the banner under
which the bearers of that tradition increasingly operated) embarked on
successive military campaigns directed at the removal of what was seen
as Britain's illegal occupation of Ireland. In so doing, they challenged
more moderate groups, which sought to negotiate the future contours
of an Irish state via non-violent means. The point of departure for the
IRA was that no compromise could be brooked. Vistas of a 'home rule'
Ireland, still part of the United Kingdom, or of a partitioned 'Free State'
still within the British Commonwealth were held to be deficient – and
no less intolerable than the perpetuation of unadulterated British rule.
That rule, it was felt, could only be ended via the way of the gun and
it was to this end that the self-proclaimed leaders of the IRA declared
war. Ever since, the shadow of that example has loomed large within
republicanism.

Significantly, though, this was not because it showed itself to contain
an incomparably 'winning formula'. The attempted rebellion of 1916
clearly did not succeed in a direct military sense. Much recent historiog-
raphy has also thrown doubt over the extent to which the IRA 'won' its
campaign against the British in 1919–21. True, the organisation recorded
some spectacular tactical victories (most notably, for example, with

Michael Collins' intelligence strike on 'Bloody Sunday' in November 1920, or the 'Kilmichael ambush' of the same month). And yet, when peace was made, the 'military' initiative seemed to lie squarely with the British. At the very least, the trajectory for the IRA appeared to be one of slow but perceptible decline.[11] Meanwhile, the fact was, as Paul Bew has described, that the terms upon which the conflict was settled were those fundamentally prescribed by the British state. Far from being a unitary thirty-two-county Republic, what emerged (enshrined in the Anglo-Irish Treaty of December 1921) was a twenty-six-county Free State. They got, in other words, 'home rule-plus' rather than independence: 'From an old Sinn Féin point of view, the Treaty was a good deal … But it was not the republican agenda for which a minority had sacrificed so much – and inflicted so much.'[12]

It was for precisely this reason, of course, that the conclusion and acceptance of the Treaty by the majority of republican leaders and the populace as a whole led a minority to reject that decision and launch a civil war. Here again, though, the republican cause suffered an incontrovertible reverse. Moreover, the absolute failure of the republican (or 'irregular') side in that last conflict in 1922–3 confirmed that the Republic, which they worshipped, would remain confined to the realm of imagination.

Simplistic a verdict as it may be, then, it is tempting to suggest that in the decade-long 'Irish revolution' of 1913–23, the volcano of physical-force Irish republicanism had erupted three times into actual violence and three times been defeated. Nevertheless, the final crushing in 1923, of those who pursued an uncompromising vision of the Irish Republic to be achieved primarily by violent means, did not dull the power of that ideal. Neither did it eliminate the IRA, which endured – at least initially in an uneasy, quasi-legal relationship with the newly established Irish state. The symbiosis between the new rulers of the Free State and their republican opposition – sharing, as they did, a common ideological and organisational heritage – ensured that the emergent state was permeated by a culture that venerated the model of romantic, vanguard-driven violence.

Moreover, the leadership of unreconstructed republicanism considered their forces to be bowed but not broken. As the most senior anti-treatyite and president of Sinn Féin, Éamon de Valera, famously declared,

> Soldiers of Liberty! Legion of the Rearguard! The Republic can no longer be defended successfully by your force of arms. Further sacrifice of life would now be in vain and continuance of the struggle in arms unwise in the National interest. Military victory must be allowed to rest for the moment with those who have destroyed the Republic.[13]

The conditionality inherent in de Valera's words, with military reversal accepted only 'for the moment', was very much of a piece with the wider feeling in republican circles. As John Bowyer Bell has described, there was a widespread view that the ceasefire represented merely a hiatus, ahead of a 'second round' against the hated Treaty and Free State. And it was for this reason that defeat was followed not by dispersal, but by military reorganisation.[14]

THE IRA ENDURES I: REPUBLICANISM IN FERMENT

As early as July 1923, less than three months after the IRA leadership had given the order to cease fire and 'dump arms' after defeat in the civil war, a meeting was held in Dublin to restructure the organisation. What emerged was a draft constitution for a new IRA that pledged to 'guard the honour, and maintain the independence of the Irish Republic'.[15] By 1925 that constitution had been accepted at convention.[16] An IRA that remained fiercely opposed to the new states of Ireland was thus signalling that it was there to stay.

From that point, it is possible to trace forward a line of descent that ends with contemporary 'dissident' republicanism. Furthermore, the debates that emerged in the subsequent period foreshadowed some of those which would later ripple through latter day republican circles. Obviously, there are limits to any process of comparative analysis – and there are as many differences as there are similarities between the post-1923 republican world and that of the post-1998 era. And yet, there are certain points of parallel: the fragmentation of republicanism, in a context in which formerly committed republicans had opted to abandon violence; the survival of republican militancy, albeit in weakened form, as a focus for opposition to the new status quo; the subsequent internal debates among would-be militants over the appropriate balance between 'military' and 'political' activity; the discussion of possible political options and the role for 'socialism', however defined; and the question of whether 'reformist' or 'revolutionary' paths provided the best route to the abiding dream of the Republic. For this reason, it is worth considering some key features of the history of recalcitrant Irish republicanism under the Irish Free State.

Even as the process of restructuring the IRA was under way after the 1922–3 Civil War, there were those who counselled that a fresh resort to violence would be unproductive. By late 1923, for instance, de Valera himself appeared to have shifted decisively away from renewed military activity in favour of an effort to build up political support.[17] He faced the problem, though, that his party, Sinn Féin, remained committed to a position of rigid, legalistic opposition to the Free State. The party's view was that the very existence of the Free State frustrated the creation of the Republic; and on this basis, its only policy was 'abstentionism', a refusal to participate in the parliamentary structures of the new state. At general elections in August 1923, this stance had yielded forty-four seats for Sinn Féin in the new, 153-member Dáil (by comparison, the governing Cumann na nGaedheal won sixty-three seats).[18] But thereafter, a belief grew among more 'pragmatic' republicans, such as de Valera and his close ally, Sean Lemass, that a continued refusal to engage with 'everyday', practical politics would lead inevitably to irrelevance and obscurity. The mass of the people, they believed, would ultimately vote for those who could affect their lives in concrete ways. Ultimately, it was for this reason that de Valera resigned from Sinn Féin in March 1926. Unable to convince the party as a whole to shift course, he opted to forsake it in pursuit of a new departure. A couple of months later, he founded a new party, Fianna Fáil, which pledged to work within the existing system and take up any seats it won in parliament, provided the oath of allegiance to the British crown, required of parliamentarians by the 1921 Treaty, was removed.[19] In June 1927, in its first election foray, Fianna Fáil won forty-four seats in the Dáil, just three fewer than Cumann na nGaedheal. It thus became the official opposition within the Free State, proving the appeal of de Valera's more active, relevant republicanism. Sinn Féin, by contrast, found itself reduced to a rump, retaining just five of its seats.[20]

Throughout this time, the IRA, as an organisation, had been reconstituted as an almost wholly military entity, with normal 'politics' (as concerned with everyday social and economic matters) disdained. For a period from April 1924, the IRA did give its support to Sinn Féin, as

the political bearer of its ideals. Yet, by November 1925 even that link
had been severed. A convention in the latter month passed a resolution
that cut ties between the two groups and confirmed that the IRA would
be a purely militarist organisation. (Ironically, the ultimate intention of
the man who proposed the motion, Peadar O'Donnell, had been almost the exact opposite – he had hoped that by freeing the IRA from
the purist dogmas of Sinn Féin it might open the way to political development.[21]) In the run-up to the June 1927 elections, the IRA forbade
any of its members from standing; two men who violated this stricture
were expelled.[22]

Nonetheless, for those who remained outside the 'constitutional',
parliamentary realm it was not true that there was no debate as to the
merits (or otherwise) of political activity – or indeed, over the proper
character of republican politics.

Henry Patterson has traced the origins of inter-war 'social republicanism' to the Civil War period, when the prominent anti-Treatyite
Liam Mellows began to consider the shortcomings of the republicans'
apolitical approach, which 'could only judge of situations in terms of
guns and men'.[23] In making his case, Mellows drew on the thinking of
that other totemic figure from 1916, James Connolly. A signatory to the
Proclamation, Connolly had argued that the national revolution in
Ireland needed also to be a social revolution, if the 'reconquest' was to
be achieved: 'If you remove the English army tomorrow and hoist the
green flag over Dublin Castle, unless you set about the organisation of
a Socialist Republic your efforts will be in vain ... Nationalism without
socialism – without a reorganisation of society – is only national recre-
ancy.'[24] Or, as he put it more succinctly on a further occasion, 'The
cause of labour is the cause of Ireland, the cause of Ireland is the cause
of labour.'

Ultimately, as has been described, it was Pearse and his focus on spiritual nationalism that would come to define the 1916 Rising, rather
than Connolly and social radicalism. Still, the strand of thinking that he
represented was picked up by others, such as Mellows. Though, as
Patterson makes clear, it would be a mistake to overstate the radicalism
of this 'social' thinking. The debate over how to incorporate some kind
of 'leftist' politics within republicanism was one that would continue
into the 1920s – and from there, down to the present day.[25]

From 1926, the republican newspaper *An Phoblacht*, under the

editorship of Peadar O'Donnell, had moved leftwards. It began urging
republicans to engage in social and economic struggles. O'Donnell,
whose own republicanism also incorporated Marxism, fused with an
'instinctive rural socialism', also worked to develop a rural campaign
against land annuities (repayments due to be made to the British
government, of loans made available to finance the purchase of land by
tenant farmers in the late nineteenth and early twentieth centuries).[26] This
campaign, which saw O'Donnell collaborate at a local level with various
Fianna Fáil members, was conducted without official support from the
IRA leadership. The radical activist ethos that underpinned it, though,
offered clear indication of the kind of direction in which O'Donnell
hoped to push the IRA. Moreover, by the early 1930s it was possible to
believe that this vision enjoyed some resonance within the wider ranks
of the organisation.

In May 1931, the IRA leadership endorsed the creation of a new
political front, *Saor Éire*, to pursue an avowedly left-wing political
agenda, under the aegis of leading republican radicals, such as O'Donnell,
Michael Price, David Fitzgerald and Michael Fitzpatrick.[27] The group
declared itself committed to the overthrow of British imperialism and
capitalism, in the name of the Irish working class and working farmers.[28]
In this way, it seemed to mark a firm departure towards more openly
left-wing politics. *Saor Éire*, however, proved a short-lived experiment.
It was declared an unlawful organisation (as was the IRA and a variety
of allegedly 'communist' groups) by the government's Public Safety Act
of 1931.[29] It was also the target of clerical condemnation, with a pas-
toral letter formally excommunicating those affiliated with such 'red'
organisations. And in the face of this pressure, the IRA leadership balked
at following through with the project. The IRA's 1932 convention thus
decided not to pursue the *Saor Éire* initiative any further.[30]

Still, the prospect for a genuinely 'left republican alternative' did
not expire with the passing of *Saor Éire*.[31] O'Donnell and those of a
like mind within the IRA continued to push the case for the adoption
of radical politics. This culminated in a schism in March 1934, when
an IRA convention voted against the creation of any new political party,
with the result that several of the more radically inclined members
walked out, including O'Donnell, Price, George Gilmore and Frank
Ryan. These dissenters soon reassembled and declared the launch of a
'Republican Congress' – a body that explicitly looked to the creation of

a Workers' Republic in Ireland. Ultimately, though, it would prove as ephemeral a phenomenon as *Saor Éire*. Congress was disowned by the IRA army council and its leading protagonists were court-martialled *in absentia* and expelled with ignominy. Moreover, the Congress-istas themselves split in late 1934, between supporters of Price (who wanted to create an openly socialist party), and those of O'Donnell and Gilmore (who preferred to work for a united front of republican forces). And by the following year, this latest initiative had all but ceased to exist.[32]

Even so, within the main body of the IRA, the debate over whether to engage in some kind of political activity had not abated with the rupture that generated Congress. Brian Hanley has demonstrated that the IRA's chief of staff in this period, Maurice Twomey – a man once caricatured as an apolitical militarist – was, in fact, in favour of IRA members being 'more than soldiers'. It was the failure to develop a political strategy, Twomey argued, that had led to the loss of the Civil War and the later stagnation of IRA fortunes. And it was for this reason that Twomey, though not a socialist himself, acquiesced in the leftwards drift of the IRA in the early 1930s.[33] These same instincts probably also explain the renewed interest of the IRA leadership under Twomey, post-Congress, in political activism. Thus, at a convention in the autumn of 1935, a motion was passed that pledged the IRA to contest the next Irish general election. To this end, too, the following March saw the creation of a new party, *Cumann Poblachta na hÉireann*, to fight elections north and south, on an abstentionist basis. In the event, it fought only two by-elections that same year (in both of which it fared poorly), before disappearing in 1937.

This revived interest in electoral avenues was not the only expression of the IRA's impulse to engage in some form of political activity. Earlier, in March 1935, the group had attempted to involve itself in a major bus and tram strike in Dublin. This intervention, though, which saw IRA men engaged in armed clashes with the Irish police and army, proved to be an injudicious one. In its wake came decisive action against the IRA by the government (now led by de Valera), in the form of mass arrests that swept up several senior republican leaders. This move towards the suppression of militant republicanism, brought to an end almost a decade of ambivalence in the association between the IRA and Fianna Fáil; an ambivalence that had complicated the question of the proper place for 'politics' within the IRA's struggle. For despite de Valera's apparent betrayal of the purist path in 1926, the relationship between the IRA and Fianna Fáil had remained far from antagonistic in the years immediately after the party's formation. Indeed, in the run-up to the 1927 election, the IRA had sought a 'pact' with Fianna Fáil, which would see the former give support for the latter in return for concessions in the event of victory. In the event, the prospective deal was rejected by de Valera. Notwithstanding this snub, though, there continued to be close links between the two, which included an overlap of some personnel at local level.[34]

The ambiguous character of the Fianna Fáil–IRA connection even survived de Valera's decision to take the oath of allegiance to the British crown (as demanded by new legislation introduced after the murder of Justice Minister Kevin O'Higgins, by IRA members, in July 1927). And if anything, it appeared strengthened by de Valera's apparent legitimisation of ongoing republican activity in 1929. In March of that year, the Fianna Fáil leader gave a speech in which he acknowledged that those who remained within the IRA could assert their traditional republican inheritance, in much the same way as had Fianna Fáil hitherto. During his address, de Valera described the existing government and parliament as enjoying only a de facto (as opposed to a *de jure*) existence. They were said to suffer from a fundamental moral handicap derived from the circumstances of their creation and de Valera made no secret of his own view of the state's legitimacy:

> I still hold that our right to be regarded as the legitimate Government of this country is faulty, that this House itself is faulty … I for one, when the flag of the Republic was run up against an Executive that was bringing off a coup d'état, stood by the flag of the Republic, and I will do it again. As long as there was a hope of maintaining that Republic, either by force against those who were bringing off that coup d'état or afterwards, as long as there was an opportunity of getting the people of this country to vote again for the Republic, I stood for it. My proposition that the representatives of the people should come in here and unify control so that we could have one Government and one Army was defeated, and for that reason I resigned. Those who continued on in that organisation which we have left can claim exactly the same continuity that we claimed up to 1925.[35]

The Fianna Fáil leader thus appeared unrepentant in his views. His remarks offered no recognition of the Free State's legitimacy; rather, as he went on to aver, this was still seen as a product of a treaty which represented the 'definite betrayal of everything that was aimed at from 1916 to 1922'.[36] And on this point, few within the IRA would have found much with which to disagree.

The fact that the government of the day – that of the pro-Treaty Cumann na nGaedheal – was intent on pursuing the IRA (as reflected in the 1931 Public Safety Act) seemed only to bolster the loose bond between those organisations, both constitutional and otherwise, who remained opposed to the Treaty. It was, for example, partly on this basis that the IRA was spurred to work towards a Fianna Fáil victory in the 1932 Irish general election. However imperfect as his position might be, de Valera and his party were judged preferable to a continuation in power of their opponents. And many in the IRA hoped that Fianna Fáil in government would work to dismantle some of the more egregious aspects of the Treaty.

The wisdom of such a stance, in republican terms, seemed validated in the aftermath of de Valera's assumption of power.[37] Within months de Valera had suspended the tough anti-IRA legislation introduced by his Cumann na nGaedheal predecessors, effectively de-proscribed the group and overseen the release of IRA prisoners.[38] At the same time, his government initiated a series of measures that could be seen as part of a broader republican agenda (such as the removal of the parliamentary oath of allegiance and the launching of an 'economic war' against Britain). That same year, the IRA's annual commemoration of the Easter Rising was attended by some Fianna Fáil TDs.[39] And against this background, when de Valera called another election for January 1933 the IRA again lent its support to Fianna Fáil, helping the latter to achieve an overall majority.

The IRA's assistance for Fianna Fáil in this period was facilitated by the fact that Sinn Féin, divorced from the IRA since 1925, played no part in either the 1932 or 1933 election campaigns. The party instead adopted a hardline abstentionist policy and abjured all involvement. There was therefore no significant alternative for politically-minded republicans. Alongside this, however, support for Fianna Fáil carried a positive draw as well and appears to have sprung from several inter-locking assumptions. The first of these, as described, was that a Fianna

Fáil-led administration was vastly preferable to one under the more hardline Cumann na nGaedheal, which as has been noted seemed intent on suppressing the IRA. Equally, though, there was a belief within the IRA leadership that, sooner or later, republicans would become disillusioned by Fianna Fáil and turn back to them.[40]

The fallacy of this latter notion, though, was doubly exposed in the years that followed de Valera's entry into government. Fianna Fáil proved expert at satisfying the aspirations of most republicans and, indeed, the wider Irish electorate. In particular, the party actively sought to win over many of those who had previously operated within the militant republican milieu. Immediately after the 1932 election, de Valera's close ally, Frank Aiken, had put forward new proposals for a merger between the IRA and Fianna Fáil; though these were rebuffed because of the primacy they afforded the latter.[41] Still, de Valera in power seemed determined to create avenues by which republicans could be given a positive, participatory role *within* the state. This impulse was a key ingredient in the decision to launch a national Volunteer Reserve in early 1934, which effectively constituted a government-funded (and therefore de Valera-controlled) alternative to the IRA. By the end of the following year, the force numbered some 11,000 men and had helped draw many erstwhile refractory republicans into the ambit of the state.[42]

Even more significant, meanwhile, were the steps that de Valera took to revise the Treaty settlement of 1921. As early as July 1932, Fianna Fáil's commitment to a more stridently republican posture was confirmed by the decision to default on land annuity payments to Britain, a move that inaugurated a tariff-based 'economic war' between Ireland and its neighbour. Then, over the course of 1936–7, de Valera moved successively to: abolish the senate (though it was partially reconstituted a year later in much weaker form); remove the British governor-general; and introduce a new constitution for 'Éire', as the country was now to be known (which included a territorial claim on the whole island of Ireland). A year later, de Valera had successfully negotiated an end to the 'economic war' and secured the return of the 'Treaty ports' from Britain.[43] Thereafter, when a snap general election was called for June 1938, it returned a substantial Fianna Fáil majority.[44]

That this should have been so was a product of the fact that de Valera's pragmatic republicanism was complemented by the ability of his party to offer a concrete social and economic programme which connected with the electorate on everyday issues. This vaguely left-wing, populist Fianna Fáil (which nonetheless evinced a Catholic ethos) had found a highly successful political blend – one which could both deliver governance in the here and now *and* claim to be on the road to the Republic.[45] With regard to the latter, de Valera had, by his actions, effectively confirmed the independence of the twenty-six-county Irish state. He had thereby delivered the form (if not the full substance) of a fully sovereign, if still territorially truncated, republic. The experience of the Second World War and de Valera's skilful preservation of Irish neutrality underlined the point. Thus, Fianna Fáil could credibly claim to have delivered on republican aspirations. In the highly pertinent words of one activist, as cited by Richard English, 'There were a lot of people that thought [de Valera] was going slowly, but he was going somewhere – and they were happy with it.'[46]

Against this background, a parting of the ways became inevitable – between on the one hand, Fianna Fáil, and on the other, that diminishing recalcitrant minority who remained committed to militant anti-state republicanism. It was thus noticeable that the once-magnanimous approach of de Valera was superseded by the growing tendency of his party to assert its own credentials as the true bearer of the revolutionary spirit. As Brian Hanley has observed, by the early 1930s Fianna Fáil members could be found making the case that the IRA was no longer the organisation that had fought the British; rather, Fianna Fáil itself laid claim to the mantle of being the 'fighting men' of the revolutionary period.[47] The shift in rhetoric marked a sea change from the generous acknowledgments of the earlier period, as noted above.

Moreover, as the years went by, the points of potential friction be-tween the two organisations had multiplied: from IRA and left-repub-lican critiques of the alleged 'conservatism' of Fianna Fáil in government, to the creation of the Volunteer Reserve, which the IRA rightly perceived as an attempt by de Valera to dilute its hold over its members.[48] Underpinning all of this was the challenge posed to the Irish state by the very existence of an IRA that refused to accept the legiti-macy of that state. In the final analysis, it became increasingly clear that Fianna Fáil, in office, had to definitively confront the challenge of phys-ical-force republicanism.

THE IRA ENDURES II: THE MILITANT FLAME

Throughout the 1920s and 1930s, the flame of armed Irish republican militancy had been maintained. Alongside the IRA's flirtation with radical politics – and whatever about its ambiguous relationship with Fianna Fáil – the organisation's centre of gravity had continued to reside in the espousal of 'legitimist, self-righteous principles'.[49] At root, these principles justified violent action, by an elite minority, in defence of the national ideal. In the decade and a half after the 1923 ceasefire, this was not translated into a sustained and viable campaign against the status quo, but there were sporadic bursts of lethal activity. And between 1926 and 1936 this activity cost the lives of almost forty people.[50]

Though incidents tended to be rooted in certain localities (notably Cork, west Clare, Kerry, Donegal and Tipperary), those targeted included Gardaí who endeavoured to hinder IRA arms seizures, or those policemen who were judged to be too determined in their pursuit of militant republicans.[51] Other victims included informers, jurors (sitting in the trials of IRA men) and, most infamously, the Irish justice minister, Kevin O'Higgins, who was murdered by two IRA men in July 1927.[52] O'Higgins, though, was not the only high-profile casualty of this era. In February 1935, for example, the IRA intervened in a local agrarian dispute by killing Richard More O'Ferrell, the agent of an estate in Edgeworthstown, County Longford.[53] The following year brought two more notorious murders – those of a retired British navy vice-admiral, Henry Boyle Somerville, and of John Egan, who was accused of being a police spy in Dungarvan, County Waterford.[54]

It was this ongoing involvement of the IRA in violence that eventually forced a 'parting of the ways' with Fianna Fáil. A portent of the break to come had been signalled already in 1935 when numerous known IRA leaders were arrested after the IRA's involvement in the transport industrial action in Dublin. Then, in June 1936, in the wake of the Boyle Somerville and Egan murders, the IRA was declared illegal and a fresh round of mass arrests followed. Among those captured was Maurice Twomey, who had served as the organisation's chief of staff over the previous decade. Together with a slew of other leadership figures, Twomey was arrested, convicted and imprisoned.

An indication of the new hardline approach adopted by Fianna Fáil came from the justice minister, Gerald Boland, when he told the Dáil, 'I now give definite notice to all concerned that the so-called Irish

Republican Army or any organisation which promotes or advocates the use of arms for the attainment of its object will not be tolerated.'[55] Ultimately, de Valera's party, having acquired power in the Irish state, had been forced to respond to the threat posed by the IRA. Ideological affinities aside, Fianna Fáil could not allow an armed and active IRA to flourish. By Max Weber's classic definition, the attribute of statehood consists in the assertion of a 'monopoly on the legitimate use of violence'. This being the case, and especially in light of de Valera's forceful upholding of Irish state sovereignty – the central plank of his political platform – the Dublin government had no choice but to confront and defeat the IRA.

Significantly, the IRA quickly realised that in a head-on contest against the Irish state it had little chance of success. In that battle, by the mid-1930s, there could be only one winner. Thus, it was at this stage that the IRA refocused its attention on the British. The result was the launch of an 'England campaign' by the new IRA chief of staff, Sean Russell, in early 1939.[56] A renowned militarist within the movement, Russell had won an internal republican debate over the appropriate way forward. The repeated failure of the IRA to launch a violent campaign in previous years had not diminished the allure of such a prospect for Russell and his supporters. There remained instead a strong desire to confront, through force of arms, the status quo, with resentment now directed increasingly towards 'England'.[57]

It was for this reason that Russell had seized control of the IRA after Twomey's 1936 arrest and steered it towards a bombing campaign on the British mainland – in spite of significant internal opposition to his plans.[58] That he should have done so said much about the militant spirit that continued to animate the IRA. As Bowyer Bell later observed, 'Whether or not the campaign was technically feasible, it was emotionally desirable.'[59] It represented the triumph of the IRA's institutional faith in the viability of the military instrument, even in the face of overwhelming odds.

The idea of a generationally-bequeathed duty of resistance to 'British imperialism', to be acted upon by those who inherited the physical-force republican mantle, seemed to provide the core impulse for what became known as the 'S-Plan' or 'England Campaign'. Furthermore, to establish beyond any doubt that it was indeed Russell's IRA that held the mantle in question, the chief of staff successfully engineered a transfer of 'authority' from the 'Second Dáil' (of 1921) to the IRA's army council. The latter was now to be regarded, so the argument ran, as the *de jure* 'Government of the Irish Republic'. With that legitimating step taken, the IRA then produced an ultimatum on 12 January 1939 calling for the 'withdrawal of all British armed forces stationed in Ireland'. The British were given four days to signal compliance, or the IRA reserved the right to take 'appropriate action without further notice'.[60] Several days later, a further declaration stated:

> The armed forces of England still occupy six of our counties in the North and reserve the right 'in time of war or strained relations' to reoccupy the ports which they have just evacuated in the southern part of Ireland. Ireland is still tied, as she has been for centuries past, to take part in England's wars ... Further weakness on the part of some of our people, broken faith and make-believe, have postponed the enthronement of the living Republic, but the proclamation of Easter Week and the declaration of independence stand and must stand for ever. No man, no matter how far he has fallen away from his national faith, has dared to repudiate them. They constitute the rallying centre for the unbought manhood of Ireland in the fight that must be made to make them effective and to redeem the nation's self-respect that was abandoned by a section of our people in 1923.
>
> The time has come to make that fight. There is no need to redeclare the Republic of Ireland, now or in the future. There is no need to reaffirm the declaration of Irish independence. But the hour has come for the supreme effort to make both effective. So in the name of the unconquered dead and the faithful living, we pledge ourselves to that task.
>
> We call upon England to withdraw her armed forces, her civilian officials and institutions, and representatives of all kinds from every part of Ireland as an essential preliminary to arrangements for peace and friendship between the two countries; and we call upon the people of all Ireland, at home and in exile, to assist us in the effort we are about to make, in God's name, to compel that evacuation and to enthrone the Republic of Ireland.[61]

As with the 1916 Proclamation, it is possible to discern here certain fundamental tenets which underwrote a resort to violence. The historically

validated sanctity of the Republic was made explicit; so too the weight
of the patriot dead. It was the latter that shaped the actions of Irish
republicans, rather than concerns as to the wishes of the present
generation. On this view, legitimacy was inherited, not earned. And in
the face of ongoing 'occupation' from 'England', the North would have
to be freed by force of arms. It was to this end that the declaration's
authors appealed to the people of Ireland, calling them to rally to the
banner of the 'Republic'; for only by so doing could they truly 'redeem
the nation's self-respect'.

These were the words, then, upon which the actions that followed
rested. When the demand for British withdrawal (predictably) went
unheeded, a bombing campaign against the British mainland was initiated. British infrastructure, commercial premises and transport facilities
(including the London Underground) were all targeted. A series of
bombs were detonated in Manchester, London and Birmingham, and
by the middle of 1939 there had been 127 incidents, with one person
killed. Then in August of that year the IRA detonated a bomb in Coventry that claimed the lives of five people and injured some sixty others.[62]
Soon after, tough new legislation was brought in by the British, in order
to interdict the IRA's campaign (notably, the 1939 Prevention of
Violence Act (Temporary Provisions), which facilitated the deportation
of IRA suspects). A hard line was taken too in relation to those found
guilty of involvement in IRA-related activity. Thus, in February 1940,
two men, James Richards and Peter Barnes, were hanged in Birmingham
for their part in the Coventry bomb of six months earlier.

Crucially, British legislation also found parallels on the other side of
the Irish Sea. There again, the Fianna Fáil government understood that
it could not permit the IRA to operate freely from within its territory,
if the Irish state was to be able to claim a genuine monopoly on the
legitimate use of force. Furthermore, de Valera had recognised the
particular danger posed by the IRA *at that time* – lest its campaign of
violence provoke the British to reassess the risks arising from Irish
independence. With renewed world war looming – and de Valera
determined to preserve Irish neutrality – the Fianna Fáil leader was
anxious that IRA activity be curtailed. As a result, a new 'Offences
against the State' was enacted in June 1939, to replace the old one
which had lapsed with the passage of de Valera's new constitution two
years earlier. This was followed by an amendment to the Emergency

Powers Act in 1940, which confirmed the IRA as an illegal entity and created military tribunals, which soon set about imprisoning volunteers. Execution was enshrined as the ultimate sanction against those thereby convicted.

In consequence, by early 1940 the IRA's mainland campaign had petered out. Towards the end of the previous year, Russell had attempted to bolster the morale of his men, in the context of the outbreak of war in Europe, declaring, '"England's difficulty – Ireland's opportunity" has ever been the watchword of the Gael ... Now is the time for Irishmen to take up arms and strike a blow for the Ulster people.'[63] In line with this, Russell had himself sought assistance from the Third Reich, even travelling to Germany to plead his case. His efforts, though, proved to be in vain. And in August 1940, while returning to Ireland aboard a U-Boat, he died.

Russell was succeeded as IRA chief of staff by Stephen Hayes, and under the latter the England Campaign was formally abandoned. In truth, it had never generated the momentum envisaged by Russell and his allies. And in retrospect, the caustic judgment of one of the campaign's instigators, Séamus O'Donovan, seems apposite. In August 1939, O'Donovan recorded that the IRA's effort had been 'hastily conceived, scheduled to a premature start, with ill-equipped and inadequately trained personnel, too few men and too little money ... [and] unable to sustain the vital spark of what must be confessed to have fizzled out like a damp and inglorious squib'.[64]

THE IRA IN THE WILDERNESS: THE FLAME BURNS ON

In the years that followed the 1939–40 campaign, the pressure was kept on the IRA, particularly in Ireland. When those incarcerated by the Irish state attempted to protest against the hardline treatment they faced, by embarking on hunger strikes, they were allowed to die.[65] On the outside, meanwhile, the IRA was squeezed and all but extinguished as a force. Amid failure and under strain from the authorities, the group turned in on itself. In 1941, chief of staff Hayes was accused by northern-based IRA members of being a Garda informer. He was abducted, tortured and forced to confess – a confession he later retracted, but by then the damage had been done. The Hayes affair split the IRA – and one of its most prominent members in Northern Ireland, Sean McCaughey, was arrested and jailed by the southern authorities for the Hayes abduction.

By the time Charlie Kerins, the Kerry-born IRA leader, was executed in 1944 for his part in the murder of a Garda, Denis O'Brien, the organisation appeared to have been defeated. Certainly, Kerins' death seemed to mark the final breaking of the IRA in southern Ireland. Further evidence to this effect could be gleaned from the way in which McCaughey was allowed to die on hunger and thirst strike in Portlaoise prison in 1946. It was against this background that the IRA would bring in its 'General Order No. 8' in 1948, which prohibited acts of aggression against what it termed the '26 Counties'. Henceforth, the IRA was stating, though it might not like the southern Irish state, that there would be no further violent challenge to its existence.

Concurrently, the IRA had engaged in some activity north of the border – with occasionally lethal effect.[66] Again, though, its record of achievement was a far from distinguished one; and in considering this aspect of the IRA's campaign, it is hard to disagree with Richard English's assessment that 'By the end of the war ... the IRA's fitful northern campaign had drawn to an effective close ... the IRA's wartime record in the north was one of low-level brutality and of largely directionless violence.'[67]

More broadly, meanwhile, the IRA was, without question, by 1945 a far weaker body than it had been at the conclusion of the Irish Civil War. From a high point of maybe 12,000 volunteers in 1923, it had experienced a steady fall in numbers and support, with only a brief resurgence in the 1932–4 period (when it had benefited both from its ambivalent relationship with Fianna Fáil and from its role in the anti-blueshirt agitation). Thereafter, the pattern of decline had resumed, exacerbated by bouts of government suppression. Significantly, the growing belief among more pragmatic members as to the unrealistic nature of republican aspirations had brought a succession of splits, most obviously by de Valera in 1926. And the subsequent triumph of Fianna Fáil as a 'catch-all' party, capable of fulfilling the socio-economic needs of a broad section of the populace while retaining a rhetorical commitment to republican objectives, pushed the IRA ever further towards the margins.

And yet, for all this, the contemporaneous defeat of the IRA – in both the British and Irish arenas – did not bring an end to physical-force republicanism. Rather it brought only a shift in focus, with the organisation increasingly concentrating its energies more directly on partition and Northern Ireland itself.

The survival of militant republicanism was signalled by the appointment of Paddy Fleming, a native of Kerry, as the IRA's new chief of staff in 1945. Fleming, having officially ended the 'northern campaign', set about the task of trying to rebuild the movement and slowly gathered those of a like mind around him. A key moment arrived in 1948 when an IRA convention brought the installation of a new leadership based around the 'three Macs': Tony Magan from County Meath (who became chief of staff), Pádraig McLogan from County Armagh and Tomás MacCurtain of County Cork. Together, these men were determined to resuscitate militant Irish republicanism; and to this end, they sought to reinvigorate the political capacity of the movement. In 1948, a new newspaper, the *United Irishman*, was launched in Dublin in order to promote the republican analysis. A year later, meanwhile, IRA volunteers were ordered to join and take over the almost defunct Sinn Féin party. By 1950, McLogan had become Sinn Féin president and plans were being laid for political intervention.[68]

As Hanley and Millar have made clear, republican politics at that time were not distinguished by their sophistication. The problems faced in Ireland, particularly south of the border, were seen almost entirely as being a product of partition. The British presence in 'the North' was held to be the source of all Irish woes. Significantly, such views were of a piece with the broader ethos of state-sponsored anti-partitionism. The 1950s saw the Irish government pursue an anti-partition campaign, which gained the support of all major parties. And Fianna Fáil's newspaper, the *Irish Press*, famously declared, 'there was no kind of oppression visited on any minority in Europe that the Six County nationalists have not also endured'.[69] Not for the first – or indeed last – time, militant republicanism gained succour from the ideological hinterland with which it was endowed by non-violent counterparts. As a result, the possibility that republicans might gain some political traction, both north and south of the border, seemed a viable prospect. In 1955, two republican prisoners, standing as Sinn Féin candidates, won election on an abstentionist ticket in Northern Ireland, in Mid-Ulster and Fermanagh–South Tyrone respectively.

At the same time, preparations began to be made for a new military

campaign. In both Britain and Ireland, raids were carried out in pursuit
of weapons – one of which, in Felsted in Essex in 1953, led to the
arrest of future prominent republicans Cathal Goulding and Seán Mac
Stíofáin. Undeterred by such setbacks, the IRA leadership opted to
launch a campaign (under pressure from belligerent splinter groups), in
late 1956. 'Operation Harvest' looked to the use of 'flying columns' of
IRA men, who would cross the border from the south into Northern
Ireland and strike against Royal Ulster Constabulary (RUC) and British
army targets. The strategy's principal author, Sean Cronin, envisaged the
building of 'liberated areas' which would expand until the final collapse
of Northern Ireland could be achieved.

In the event, such projections for the 'Border Campaign', as it
became more popularly known, proved wildly optimistic. Despite
generating over 500 incidents, the campaign achieved little militarily
other than the deaths of several RUC police constables. Instead, its
greatest success came in the political realm – and in the production of
new republican martyrs. A raid on Brookeborough RUC station in
County Fermanagh on New Year's Day 1957 brought the deaths of
two young IRA men, Fergal O'Hanlon and Sean South. Tens of thousands lined the streets for the respective funerals, as O'Hanlon and
South gained legendary status, the latter remembered in the briskly-
written song, 'Sean South of Garryowen'. Later that same year, another
four IRA members entered the movement's pantheon of heroes when
they were killed at Edentubber in County Louth after a landmine they
were preparing detonated prematurely. Such 'sacrifices' helped generate some sympathy for irredentist republicanism and at the March 1957
Irish general election, Sinn Féin won four seats (Ruairí Ó Brádaigh in
Longford–Westmeath, Eineachan O'Hanlon in Monaghan, John Joe
Rice in South Kerry and John Joe McGirl in Sligo–Leitrim).[70]

Nevertheless, the outburst of pro-republican emotion proved short-
lived – and as IRA violence continued, so support for the movement
ebbed. In 1959, Sinn Féin's vote in Northern Ireland fell to half that
achieved in 1955 and it lost both its seats; two years later, the four seats
won south of the border were gone as well. Republicans also faced
serious pressure from the security services, as governments on both
sides of the Irish border introduced internment. By the end of 1957,
almost all senior IRA figures, including Cronin, had been imprisoned.
That year proved to be the peak of IRA activity, with over 340 IRA

incidents occurring, but after that the organisation's impetus fell away markedly. In 1959, the IRA managed just twenty-seven attacks and a year later there were even fewer. It seemed clear that the campaign was dwindling to a halt.

In 1961, the Fianna Fáil justice minister, Charles Haughey, reintroduced military tribunals, comprising three Irish army officers rather than judges, to hear cases involving alleged IRA men. In the face of this cross-border clampdown, and in the absence of any tangible military momentum, the IRA leadership faced the inevitable. In February 1962, with the campaign seemingly going nowhere, the order was given for arms to be dumped. In an explanatory statement, the IRA stated that, 'Foremost among the factors motivating this course of action has been the attitude of the general public whose minds have been deliberately distracted from the supreme issue facing the Irish people – the unity and freedom of Ireland.' The fault, it was thus argued, lay with 'the people' rather than the IRA itself. That notwithstanding, the organisation declared defiantly:

> The Irish Resistance Movement renews its pledge of eternal hostility to the British Forces of Occupation in Ireland. It calls on the Irish people for increased support and looks forward with confidence – in co-operation with the other branches of the Republican Movement – to a period of consolidation, expansion and preparation for the final and victorious phase of the struggle for the full freedom of Ireland.[71]

Irrespective of such bravado, however, there was little escaping the reality of the IRA's latest military endeavour, which scarcely marked an improvement on the efforts of the 1940s. In a putative six-year campaign, eighteen people had been killed – eleven of whom were republicans. Such political support as had been won early on in the initiative had dissipated by the time the IRA called a halt – and the group seemed more marginal than ever on both sides of the Irish border. In the assessment of M.L.R. Smith, 'the Border Campaign' confirmed the extent to which the IRA was trapped in an 'ideologically elitist prism', which had produced only 'five and a half years of wasted effort'.[72]

TOWARDS THE PROVISIONALS

In the aftermath of the IRA's 1962 defeat, there were prolonged discussions within the organisation as to the appropriate way forward. As Hanley and Millar have noted, 'the failure of the [Border] campaign was a formative experience for the core group who would lead the IRA for the next decade.'[73] That group would come to centre on Cathal Goulding, who became the IRA's new chief of staff in September 1962. For Goulding and those around him, such as president of Sinn Féin Tomás MacGiolla and the young Séamus Costello, it was imperative that republicans now embrace a more political path.

The Wolfe Tone directories (later the Wolfe Tone Society) emerged in 1963, as part of attempts to broaden the appeal of republicanism. Efforts were made to engage with Protestants in Northern Ireland. In addition, the period also saw the IRA drift leftwards in its orientation, under the influence of various radical ideologues such as Roy Johnston, Anthony Coughlan and Jack Bennett. The movement's leadership also paid attention to broader global trends – with the contemporary wave of decolonisation and revolutionary activity in south-east Asia, Latin America and Africa.

In 1964, the movement opted to contest the British general election in Northern Ireland (standing as 'Republicans', as Sinn Féin had been banned there that same year). Though none of its candidates proved successful, it did secure over 100,000 votes. There were other signs too of latent levels of support for republicanism in certain key communities north of the border – with thousands joining republican-led parades and IRA-inspired riots.[74] It was this support that Goulding wished to tap into, as he increasingly urged IRA members to embrace 'social agitation'.[75]

As early as 1965, motions had been put to both an IRA convention and Sinn Féin *árd fheis* (national conference) that republicans should abandon abstentionism and engage in the constitutional sphere, taking seats in the Irish Dáil. At the time, the proposals were defeated, but it became increasingly clear that the leadership favoured a new approach. Equally, it was apparent that the movement was deeply divided as to the best way forward, with prominent figures opposed to the changes being put forward by Goulding and his allies. Unease also soon developed around the leadership style of Goulding, which was felt to be overbearing and autocratic.[76]

The onset of violence related to the push for Catholic 'civil rights' in Northern Ireland in 1968-9 provided the combustion to an already volatile mix. As Richard English and others have pointed out, the genesis for the Civil Rights Movement had come from within republicanism. From the mid-1960s onwards, key republican leaders had been calling for such a campaign in the belief that it would broaden republicanism's base of support and undermine the unionist state.[77] What they had failed to anticipate, however, was the potential for a violent backlash from within unionism more broadly, which saw in the campaign for civil rights merely a subversive assault on the existence of Northern Ireland.

When Goulding continued to push his new departure, regardless of the situation in the North, many traditionalists felt it signalled the leadership's determination to abandon armed violence for good.[78] In reality, as Hanley and Millar have made clear, the IRA leadership had not renounced violence permanently. On the contrary, plans had continued to be laid for a military campaign, and in the late 1960s the IRA remained armed and active in Northern Ireland.[79] Nevertheless, the organisation suffered from a chronic lack of weaponry (in turn linked to its lack of funds), and the leadership's *principal* focus remained on politics. Furthermore, Goulding and his supporters had not foreseen the extent to which the violence flowing from the civil rights agitation would put a premium on the IRA's traditional role as the defenders of the Catholic/nationalist population of Northern Ireland. To many republicans, the leadership was judged to be 'asleep at the wheel' and it was against this background that internal republican discontent erupted into the open.

The precise details of the split that led to the creation of the Provisional IRA have been elaborated at length elsewhere and do not need reiteration here. Suffice to say, an initial coup against the Goulding leadership, by Belfast republicans in September 1969, was narrowly averted, but this proved to be only a stay of execution. At an IRA convention in December 1969, Goulding and his supporters forced through changes to the organisation's policy. This included a pledge to abandon abstentionism, with the IRA now prepared to endorse candidates who would enter Stormont, Leinster House and even Westminster. At this point a faction opposed to the move withdrew to hold a fresh convention, from which would emerge a 'new' IRA. Among the key figures were Ruairí Ó Brádaigh (then thirty-seven years old), Daithí Ó

Conaill, Seán Mac Stíofáin and Joe Cahill. Such people claimed that it
was they, not Goulding and his allies, who represented the 'true' IRA.
The latter had, it was said, by their actions forfeited that title.[80] On 28
December 1969, those with Ó Brádaigh issued the first statement of
the 'Provisional Army Council' of the IRA, declaring 'allegiance to the
32-County Irish Republic, proclaimed at Easter 1916, established by
the first Dáil Éireann in 1919, overthrown by force of arms in 1922 and
suppressed to this day by the existing British-imposed Six-County and
26-County partition states'.[81] In this way, confident of the authority
bestowed upon them by history, the Provisional IRA was born.

    January 1970 brought a corresponding split within Sinn Féin. At the
party's annual gathering in Dublin, when a motion was passed that
committed Sinn Féin to supporting the Official IRA army council
(under the control of Goulding), supporters of the Provisionals staged
a walkout. A new 'Provisional' Sinn Féin was established. By the end of
that year the division had become permanent and the new 'Provisional'
organisation made permanent (though the label stuck as a defining
mark, distinguishing them from their rivals in the 'Officials'). As Agnes
Maillot has emphasised, the identity of this new movement was defined
by its adherence to two pillars of thought: one, which held to the
importance of abstentionism, if republicans were to avoid being corrupted by constitutional politics; the other, which believed 'armed
struggle' to be the only way in which Irish unity could be attained.[82]

    The leaders of the new Provisional movement proceeded to visit
Tom Maguire, the sole surviving member of the 'Second Dáil', in order
to get his blessing for the new departure. Maguire duly declared the
Goulding leadership of the IRA to be illegitimate and stated that 'the
governmental authority delegated in the Proclamation of 1938 now
resides in the Provisional Army Council and its lawful successors.'
Thereby assured of their rightful claim to republican legitimacy, the
Provisional IRA (as distinct from the Official IRA that remained loyal
to Goulding) set about planning for a military campaign against the
'British occupation system' in Ireland.[83] Moreover, it was their determination to launch and prosecute that campaign that proved the single
most important factor in ensuring that Northern Ireland would suffer
three decades of civil conflict from that point.

    Again, the history of what followed has been recounted by others –
and the purpose here is not to re-tell that story other than to make

briefly a couple of key observations. The Provisionals arrived on the scene in Northern Ireland with an established narrative, grounded in traditional republican ideology, for explaining events around them. Moreover, they were prepared to manipulate those events to make them fit their pre-existing narrative. To give but one example, Thomas Hennessey has described how much of the rioting that took place across Belfast in May, June and July 1970 – that did so much to poison inter-communal relations – was pre-planned by the Provisionals with the intention of radicalising the Catholic community.[84] In this way, they sought to prove to the Catholic community the 'bad-mindedness' of the Northern Irish state in which they lived; to 'make real' the injustice that, republicans argued, flowed from partition.

At the same time, the Provisionals were aided by the mistakes of the authorities, both in Belfast and London. The latter's deployment of the army to the streets of Northern Ireland had given insufficient thought to the problems that would flow from the use of troops for the preservation of law and order. As the Catholic population, under Provisional encouragement, grew increasingly hostile to those troops, the army proved an unresponsive, blunt instrument. What followed was a series of incidents that both came to define the early years of the 'Troubles' and generated a surge in support for the IRA: the 'Falls Curfew' of July 1970, when the army sealed off the Lower Falls area of Belfast for seventy-two hours and fired CS gas at Catholic rioters (an incident remembered in republican circles as 'the Rape of the Falls'); the introduction of internment without trial in August 1971; and 'Bloody Sunday' in January 1972, when soldiers opened fire on civil rights marchers in Derry (also called Londonderry, but hereafter simply Derry), killing fourteen unarmed civilians.[85] Anthony McIntyre, the former IRA prisoner, has argued that such events served as highly effective recruiting sergeants for the Provisional IRA. Furthermore, he contends that they endowed it with certain core values, which he summarises as the 'three Ds of Provisional republicanism': 'defence, defiance and dissent'.[86]

According to McIntyre, it was the mistakes of the British state and the extent to which these alienated a large swathe of the Catholic/nationalist community which powered the IRA's campaign. Faced with those mistakes and amid wider inter-communal violence, many sought variously: to protect their local community (to 'defend' their street, or home); to strike back against perceived aggressors (to show their 'defiance' of the security forces); and to show their opposition to a status quo that was judged to be deeply unfair (to demonstrate their 'dissent' against the unionist-led government of Northern Ireland). For McIntyre, it was the impulse to engage in such activities, rather than any deep-seated attachment to republican ideals, that led significant numbers of young Catholics into the arms of the IRA – and in turn made possible the organisation's 'long war' against British rule.[87]

Ultimately, that long war failed to dislodge the British from Northern Ireland, and the Provisionals, under their second generation of leaders around Gerry Adams and Martin McGuinness, slowly opted for the path of pragmatism. The result was, eventually, the calling to a halt of the IRA's armed campaign. Increasingly, Sinn Féin was pushed forward as the primary vehicle for Provisional republicanism, rather than the IRA. The latter was first reduced to a supporting role and then removed from the field altogether. More generally, the Provisional movement was altered out of all recognition. If Maillot's 'twin pillars' are accepted as a useful shorthand for thinking about the identity of the Provisionals at the moment of their creation, by the late 1990s both had been discarded. The commitment to parliamentary abstentionism was forsworn in the mid-1980s, while the IRA ceasefires of 1994 and 1997 showed the readiness of the Provisionals to move beyond 'armed struggle'. Moreover, it was this process of transformation that generated the 'dissident republicans' of today, who are the foci for the rest of this study.

CONCLUSION

What the foregoing hopefully has indicated is the extent to which today's 'dissidents' are able to (and do) place themselves within the context of a long-running history, which in the words of Conor Cruise O'Brien places a premium on 'the language of sacred soil and the cult of the dead'.[88] It is for this reason that the past is consciously evoked as the ultimate source of inspiration and legitimacy. Whether it be with reference to the 1916 Rising, the line of descent from the original IRA, the debates of the 1920s or 1930s or the 'patriot dead' of successive campaigns, Irish republicans live in a world bound and dictated by history. In the course of that history, almost all the central tenets of their version of Irish republicanism were canonised.

Central to this ideology is a belief in the fundamental right of an armed minority to act in the interests of the broader Irish nation. That minority is understood to be the embodiment of 'the people', irrespective of whether those same people actually furnish their support. Herein it is possible to identify a quasi-Marxist notion of 'false consciousness', which is held to afflict the populace at large. Republicans, by contrast, are seen as an enlightened elite, who alone truly understand the situation as it *really* exists in Ireland. They are the guardians of the revealed truth: that the Irish are not free and never can be until British influence is banished from the entire island. All problems can be traced to that influence, and particularly to its foremost expression – partition and the existence of Northern Ireland. The latter is understood to have been imposed by force upon Ireland; the embodiment of occupation and British malignancy, which continues to violate the integrity of the nation. To combat the injustice and oppression flowing from all this, the use of violence is viewed as entirely legitimate and, indeed, necessary. And, here again, history is felt to have sanctified and mandated the republican path. It has ordained the resort to violent methods as the only sure way in which the long 'struggle' against the British can be carried forth, without compromise. Efforts to follow a more political path have repeatedly failed to deliver the Republic. On this view, every generation has played its part; every manifestation of the IRA has delivered its stock of martyr-heroes. From Pearse and Connolly, to Richards and Barnes, from South and O'Hanlon, to Sands and O'Donnell, men have given their lives in the service of Irish freedom. In so doing, they have kept the torch of republicanism alive and ensured that physical force – and indeed, purist, Irish republicanism – has not disappeared.

The advocates of this creed can point to the heritage of their fore-fathers and find solace in the litany of Pearse:

> We have no misgivings, no self-questionings. While others have been doubting, timorous, ill at ease, we have been serenely at peace with our consciences ... We saw our path with absolute clearness; we took it with absolute deliberateness ... We called upon the names of the great confessors of our national faith, and all was well with us. Whatever soul-searchings there may be among Irish political parties now or hereafter, we go on in the calm certitude of having done the clear, clean, sheer thing. We have the strength and peace of mind of those who never compromise.[89]

The reality is that, rather than being eliminated, the long-nurtured vintage of republican militancy has been decanted into other vessels. Those vessels in their own way preserve a commitment to the ideal of a thirty-two-county Irish Republic. Today, in spite of the peace process and the Agreement in Northern Ireland, republican dissident opponents of the status quo remain; opponents who, while widely dismissed as little more than anachronistic avatars of a bygone age, have not disappeared. This is not to suggest that they enjoy as much support as their predecessors. Indeed, one reading of the history of the creed might suggest that militant forms of Irish republicanism are weaker today than at any time since 1916. Certainly, in terms of numbers and the wider ideological encouragement they can solicit, this seems hard to dispute. And yet, the fact is that the bearers of this tradition are not extinct; and neither do they appear to be on the verge of so being.

It is to the contemporary advocates of this republican ideal that this study now turns.

NOTES

1. P. Bew, *Ireland: The Politics of Enmity, 1789–2006* (Oxford: Oxford University Press, 2007), pp.375–7.
2. C. Townshend, *Easter 1916: The Irish Rebellion* (London: Allen Lane, 2005), p.160. For discussion of the character of the Rising, see also R.F. Foster, *Modern Ireland, 1600–1972* (London: Allen Lane, 1988), pp.477–87; R. English, *Radicals and the Republic: Socialist Republicanism in the Irish Free State, 1925–1937* (Oxford: The Clarendon Press, 1994), pp.7–10.
3. *The Proclamation of the Irish Republic* (1916)
4. R. English, *Irish Freedom: The History of Nationalism in Ireland* (London: Macmillan, 2006), p.274.
5. R. Dudley Edwards, *Patrick Pearse: The Triumph of Failure*, 2nd edition (Dublin: Irish Academic Press, 2006), pp.252–60.
6. Cited in ibid., p.253.
7. Ibid., pp.326–7.
8. 'The 1998 Referendums', ARK Northern Ireland Elections Website, available at http://www.ark.ac.uk/elections/fref98.htm
9. A. McIntyre, 'Good Friday to Easter Sunday: 2 Days and Light Years', *The Blanket*, 11 April 2004.
10. Dudley Edwards, *Patrick Pearse*, pp.xxi, 327.
11. Bew, *Ireland*, pp.411, 415. See also P. Hart, *The IRA at War, 1916–1923* (Oxford: Oxford University Press, 2003), pp.62–86.
12. Bew, *Ireland*, p.422.
13. C. Foley, *Legion of the Rearguard: The IRA and the Modern Irish State* (London: Pluto Press, 1992), p.32.
14. J. Bowyer Bell, *The Secret Army: The IRA, 1916–1979* (Dublin: Academy Press, 1979), pp.40–1, 45.
15. T.P. Coogan, *The IRA* (London: HarperCollins, 2000), pp.42–4.
16. English, *Armed Struggle*, p.43.

17. C. Foley, in U. Mac Eoin, *The IRA in the Twilight Years, 1923–1948* (Dublin: Argenta Publications, 1997), p.31.
18. Bew, *Ireland*, p.443.
19. J.J. Lee, *Ireland, 1912–1985* (Cambridge: Cambridge University Press, 1989), pp.150–5.
20. R. Dunphy, *The Making of Fianna Fáil Power in Ireland, 1923–1948* (Oxford: The Clarendon Press, 1995).
21. O'Donnell had hoped to liberate the IRA from the 'formalist' dogma of Sinn Féin, which stressed the enduring legitimacy of the 'Second Dail' of 1921, together with the illegality of both partition and the oath of allegiance to the British crown that was required from Irish parliamentarians. O'Donnell's hope was that this would allow for the development of a more engaged and realistic social and economic policy agenda, a goal he would later pursue via his involvement in the 'left republican' politics of *Saor Éire* and the Republican Congress. For more on this, see English, *Radicals and the Republic*, pp.67–70.
22. B. Hanley, *The IRA, 1926–1936* (Dublin: Four Courts Press, 2002), p.93.
23. H. Patterson, *The Politics of Illusion: A Political History of the IRA* (London: Serif, 1997), p.25.
24. Ibid., pp.13–4.
25. Ibid., pp.25–31.
26. English, *Radicals and the Republic*, pp.80–93. See also Patterson, *The Politics of Illusion*, pp.37–50.
27. Coogan, *The IRA*, p.58.
28. English, *Armed Struggle*, pp.48–9.
29. Commonly referred to as the Public Safety Act, this was actually the Constitution (Amendment no. 17) Act. See Dáil Éireann Parliamentary Debates, vol. 40, 16 October 1931, available at http://historical-debates.oireachtas.ie/D/0040/D.0040.193110160003.html
30. English, *Radicals and the Republic*, p.147.
31. The continuing draw of this notion can be seen from the recent work of advocacy in favour of a 'left republican' vision; E. Ó Broin, *Sinn Féin and the Politics of Left Republicanism* (London: Pluto Press, 2009).
32. Hanley, *The IRA*, pp.106–9; English, *Radicals and the Republic*, pp.181–5; Coogan, *The IRA*, pp.77–8.
33. Hanley, *The IRA*, p.19.
34. Ibid., pp.113–18.
35. Coogan, *The IRA*, pp.56–7.
36. Ibid.
37. Fianna Fáil won seventy-two seats compared to Cumann na nGaedheal's fifty-six.
38. J. Bowyer Bell in Mac Eoin, *The IRA in the Twilight Years*, p.7.
39. Hanley, *The IRA*, pp.113–44.
40. Ibid., p.133.
41. Patterson, *The Politics of Illusion*, p.62.
42. E. O'Halpin, *Defending Ireland: The Irish State and its Enemies since 1922* (Oxford: Oxford University Press, 2000), pp.134–5.
43. Bowyer Bell, *The Secret Army*, pp.17–8.
44. The party won 76 seats in the 138-member Dáil. Fine Gael won 45 seats, Labour 9 and de Valera was thus returned as taoiseach.
45. English, *Radicals and the Republic*, p.158. See also, Patterson, *The Politics of Illusion*, pp.74–5.
46. English, *Armed Struggle*, p.48.
47. Hanley, *The IRA*, pp.25, 142–3.
48. Patterson, *The Politics of Illusion*, pp.56–8, 73–5, 80–4; Hanley, *The IRA*, pp.90–2.
49. English, *Radicals and the Republic*, p.118. See also C. Townshend, *Political Violence in Ireland: Government and Resistance Since 1848* (Oxford: The Clarendon Press, 1983), pp.371–5.
50. Hanley, *The IRA*, pp.78–89, 188.
51. With regard to the former, for example, a series of raids on Garda barracks from late November 1926 saw two men killed. See Bowyer Bell, *The Secret Army*, pp.57–8. For more on the IRA's conflict with the Gardaí in this period, see Hanley, *The IRA*, pp.80–1.

42   *Legion of the Rearguard*

52. For attacks on jurors, police agents and others, see Bowyer Bell, *The Secret Army*, pp.76, 82–6.
53. Bowyer Bell in Mac Eoin, *The IRA in the Twilight Years*, p.11; Coogan, *The IRA*, pp.88–9.
54. Bowyer Bell in Mac Eoin, *The IRA in the Twilight Years*, p.13; English, *Armed Struggle*, p.52.
55. Dáil Éireann Parliamentary Debates, vol. 62, 16 June 1936, available at http://historical-debates.oireachtas.ie/D/0062/D.0062.193606160024.html
56. Bowyer Bell, *The Secret Army*, pp.145–6.
57. Townshend, *Political Violence*, p.388.
58. Coogan, *The IRA*, pp.117–18.
59. Bowyer Bell, *The Secret Army*, p.152.
60. Cited in Coogan, *The IRA*, p.124.
61. Cited in Dáil Éireann Parliamentary Debates, vol. 74, 2 March 1939, available at http://historical-debates.oireachtas.ie/D/0074/D0074.193903020012.html
62. Bowyer Bell, *The Secret Army*, pp.156–63.
63. Cited in M.L.R. Smith, *Fighting for Ireland? The Military Strategy of the Irish Republican Movement* (London: Routledge, 1997), p.64.
64. Cited in P. McMahon, *British Spies and Irish Rebels: British Intelligence and Ireland, 1916–1945* (Woodbridge: Boydell Press, 2008), p.275.
65. For example, Tony D'Arcy and Jack McNeela were allowed to die on hunger strike in Mountjoy prison in April 1940. See Bowyer Bell, *The Secret Army*, p.178.
66. In April 1942 an IRA operation in Belfast had led to the death of an RUC constable, Patrick Murphy; subsequently, Tom Williams, an IRA member found guilty of the murder, was hanged. See English, *Armed Struggle*, pp.68–9.
67. Ibid., p.70.
68. See B. Hanley and S. Millar, *The Lost Revolution: The Story of the Official IRA and the Workers' Party* (Dublin: Penguin Ireland, 2009), pp.2–7.
69. Ibid., p.5
70. R. White, *Ruairí Ó Brádaigh: The Life and Politics of an Irish Revolutionary* (Bloomington, IN: Indiana University Press, 2006), pp.74–5.
71. Ibid., p.107.
72. Smith, *Fighting for Ireland?*, p.72.
73. Hanley and Millar, *The Lost Revolution*, p.21.
74. Ibid., pp.35, 54–6.
75. Ibid., pp.39, 42–4.
76. White, *Ruairí Ó Brádaigh*, pp.117–36.
77. Hanley and Millar, *The Lost Revolution*, pp.44, 60–1, 85–8, 101–5.
78. Ibid., pp.68–9.
79. To give but one example, in May 1967, the IRA bombed Territorial Army centres in Belfast and Lisburn. See ibid., p.63, also pp.66–7.
80. White, *Ruairí Ó Brádaigh*, pp.141–54.
81. Smith, *Fighting for Ireland?*, p.83.
82. A. Maillot, *New Sinn Féin: Irish Republicanism in the Twenty-First Century* (London: Routledge, 2004), pp.17–18.
83. T. Hennessey, *The Evolution of the Troubles, 1970–2* (Dublin: Irish Academic Press, 2007), p.7.
84. Ibid., pp.28–37.
85. For a fuller discussion of all this, see J. Bew, M. Frampton and I. Gurruchaga, *Talking to Terrorists: Making Peace in Northern Ireland and the Basque Country* (London: Hurst & Co., 2009), pp.28–38.
86. J. Bew, 'Defeat, Decommissioning and Dissolution?', *The Cambridge Student*, 28 November 2002.
87. A. McIntyre, 'Modern Irish Republicanism: The Product of British State Strategies', *Irish Political Studies*, 10, 1 (1995), pp.97–122.
88. C. Cruise O'Brien, *States of Ireland* (London: Hutchinson, 1972), p.319.
89. Dudley Edwards, *Patrick Pearse*, p.327.

2

The Keeper of the Flame: Timeless Republicanism

THE ROLE OF HISTORY

The Good Friday Agreement of April 1998 was broadly welcomed around the world as a settlement to the decades-long conflict in Northern Ireland. The then US president, Bill Clinton, described it as a 'chance in a lifetime' for peace and urged acceptance of the accord. Other world leaders 'warmly' welcomed it and commended those who had made it happen.[1] At home, meanwhile, the British prime minister, Tony Blair, described the referendum that approved the deal as marking a 'giant stride along the path to peace, hope and the future'.[2] Blair later added that the Agreement heralded that lifting of the 'burden of history' from Northern Irish shoulders.[3] More generally, the notion that the deal marked 'the end of history' in Northern Ireland became something of a cliché among commentators, with the Agreement described simultaneously as some kind of doorway to the future.

And yet, not everyone was as sanguine as to the outcome of the eight month-long peace talks. From his home in Roscommon, across the Irish border, a 65-year-old Ruairí Ó Brádaigh declared portentously:

> On the exact bicentenary by date (May 23) of the 1798 Rising we answer those commentators who state that Irish Republicanism has run its 200-year course and is at an end. In due course the euphoria will pass as the New Stormont fails to deliver and non-sectarian Republicanism will come into its own again as the last hope for Liberty, Equality and Fraternity with the 'breaking of the connection with England'.[4]

In speaking as he did, Ó Brádaigh took a longer view, centred on his own reading of history. For him, there was nothing to celebrate in the Agreement; rather, he and his supporters saw it as merely the latest step in a process by which Irish republicanism, of the most pure variety, was to be diluted and induced to abandon its central goals. In Ó Brádaigh's eyes, however, far from being consigned to history by that Agreement (as many of its proponents hoped), traditional republicanism would arise again, with history serving as the ultimate testament to its inexorable march.

Ó Brádaigh, the then president of the fringe political party Republican Sinn Féin, had long made clear his opposition to the peace process. In October 1994, in the aftermath of the first Provisional IRA ceasefire (31 August 1994), he claimed that the leadership of the Provisionals had been 'constitutionalised' and, as a result, his party now stood as the only defender of 'the undiluted gospel of Irish Republicanism'.[5] This was a theme to which he returned at his party's annual *árd fheis* in late 1997, at a time when the contemporaneous peace talks in Northern Ireland were inching slowly towards the much-heralded Agreement of 1998. With regard to those talks, Ó Brádaigh maintained that they would lead to nothing but a 'Sunningdale No 2', or an 'up-to-date Stormont', which would include '"reformed" militants' within its ranks. The ongoing peace process would, he argued, 'strengthen and update British rule here – not weaken it'.[6]

The reference here was to the Sunningdale Agreement of 1973–4, a settlement put forward by the British and Irish governments as a possible solution to the emerging conflict in Northern Ireland, but one which had been rejected by both hardline unionists and republicans. Among the latter, the Provisional IRA had been the most significant voice of opposition. Now Ó Brádaigh drew a conscious comparison between that rejectionism and the attitude of the latter-day leadership of the Provisional IRA – and its political arm, Sinn Féin – which was deeply involved in the peace talks and seemed ready to endorse a settlement not too dissimilar from that offered at Sunningdale a quarter of a century earlier. That this should have been the case, Ó Brádaigh averred, was a consequence of the fact that 'a section of our former comrades ... have gone over to constitutionalism and reformism'. By contrast, Ó Brádaigh and his Republican Sinn Féin colleagues 'clung to the revolutionary road forward, rejecting the easy path of constitutionalism'; they remained, he said, committed to the 'historic Irish nation which is entitled to freedom'.[7]

THE FUNDAMENTALIST

Ruairí Ó Brádaigh, born in 1932, first joined Sinn Féin in 1950; a year later, he entered the IRA. From the outset, his commitment to 'the cause' impressed itself upon those who knew him, and within the hermetically sealed milieu of Irish republicanism Ó Brádaigh became something of a rising star. By 1956 he had joined the IRA's leadership body, the army council, and from there, despite being first imprisoned and then interned, he twice served as the organisation's chief of staff during the 'Border Campaign' of 1956–62. Indeed, it was Ó Brádaigh who signed the order terminating that offensive in February 1962.[8]

Outside the closed, conspiratorial world of the 'military' organisation, meanwhile, Ó Brádaigh had become established as perhaps the most prominent public face of Irish republicanism. As early as 1957 he had stood as an abstentionist candidate for the Irish parliament in Longford–Westmeath. And in the context of the military campaign then being conducted by the IRA (which brought the death of Fergal O'Hanlon and Sean South, to much emotional outpouring in southern Ireland), Ó Brádaigh had been one of four candidates elected.[9] Though defeated when he attempted to repeat this feat in 1961, Ó Brádaigh subsequently remained one of the best-known Irish republicans of his generation. Yet, looking back on that period, he has described it as 'largely a period of training and gaining experience for things that would happen later'.[10] For Ó Brádaigh this was only preparatory to the critical phase in republican history that would follow.

During the debates of the 1960s on the proper way forward for republicanism, Ó Brádaigh, who had continued to sit on the IRA's army council, became increasingly disenchanted with the leadership line being put forward by Cathal Goulding and his allies. As a result, he was one of those who led the split in 1969–70 that saw the birth of the 'Provisionals'. Ó Brádaigh was a natural choice to be the first president of (Provisional) Sinn Féin; he also became a member of the first Provisional IRA army council and continued to sit on that seven-man body at various times throughout the next two decades.[11]

That this should have been so was a function of his resolute, uncompromising view of Irish republicanism and its key tenets. His biographer, Robert White, offers a flavour of Ó Brádaigh's temperament in his account of his subject's admiration for Tommy McDermott and the 'irreconcilable' republicans of the 1940s, who had kept the IRA alive.

In Ó Brádaigh's eyes, '[McDermott] went through it all, took all the hard knocks, and in good times and in bad he didn't change his views or his principles to suit the tide of time.'[12] As a 'Tan War man' who refused to renounce the faith, McDermott was an 'inspiring' figure for Ó Brádaigh, whose strength lay in his 'almost religious attitude' to politics.[13]

In such unbending dedication to the Irish republican philosophy, Ó Brádaigh saw a model for himself. At the core of that philosophy, as he understood it, was the belief that the status quo in Ireland was fundamentally illegitimate and needed to be overturned. The Treaty settlement of 1921, which provided for two states on the island, north and south, was, on this reading, an act of 'Original Sin'. It was the fatal point of departure, the act of corruption, from which all the contemporary problems of Ireland flowed. The 'true' Republic of 1916 was judged to have been usurped by that Treaty; its legacy commandeered by partitionist 'entities'. What had emerged at that time could not, it was argued, be reformed, only extirpated. The 'Ireland' then in existence had been contaminated at birth and for this reason, Ó Brádaigh believed that the slate needed to be wiped clean. As he had declared in 1960, on the occasion of his release from prison, 'Sinn Féin aims at abolishing both the Leinster House and Stormont Parliaments, and substituting for them an All-Ireland Republican Parliament.'[14]

Forty-seven years later, at a Republican Sinn Féin Easter 2007 commemoration, Ó Brádaigh drove this point home to his audience: 'Either you accept the existence of the Irish nation or you don't, on this there can be no middle ground.' And if inclined to accept the existence of the Irish nation, then a person also had to recognise that British rule can 'never be either normal or acceptable'. Rather,

> It is our duty now as Irish Republicans to give the lead to that section of the Irish people who will never accept British rule in Ireland ... [1916 remains] unfinished business ... For Irish Republicans the All-Ireland Republic of Easter Week remains the only legitimate state in Ireland, endorsed in the last exercise in All-Ireland democracy in 1918.[15]

For Ó Brádaigh it is the unsullied and ageless character of this vision that defines authentic Irish republicanism. In 2009, sitting in his cramped office in the small Republican Sinn Féin headquarters in

Dublin, he saw his refusal to abandon a single republican precept as the greatest testament to his career: 'the important thing has been to keep the ideology intact – to keep the continuity, with a small "c" – and to maintain a nucleus, towards which people could gravitate in a time of crisis.'[16]

<h2 style="text-align:center">THE PROVISIONALS AND THE 1986 SPLIT</h2>

It was the unconditional commitment to a rigid ideological framework which had ensured that the 'Provisional' republican movement remained united for sixteen years after the divisions of December 1969–January 1970. Its parallel branches, Sinn Féin and the IRA, articulated a 'traditionalist' message, resting on support for the IRA's 'armed struggle' and parliamentary 'abstentionism'.[17] The former meant an unbroken commitment to a violent campaign to force a British withdrawal from Northern Ireland. The latter entailed a refusal to recognise the existing state institutions across Ireland, north and south of the border. These were said to be inherently 'partitionist' in character. While republicans might occasionally participate in elections (as they had done since the 1920s), the belief was that they should not take up any seats won; rather, they would 'abstain' from participation and remain apart from the constitutional realm, in unsullied and splendid isolation. Rigid adherence to this creed established a clear identity for the Provisionals – setting them apart from others (such as the 'Officials') who might also have claimed the republican mantle.

Over time, however, important elements within the Provisional movement came to view abstentionism as more of a hindrance than an asset. The rise of a new generation of republican leaders, centred around Gerry Adams and Martin McGuinness, together with the reorganisation of the IRA and Sinn Féin in the late 1970s, brought a fresh emphasis on attempts to engage in political activity. Adams, in particular, had begun to see the eschewal of politics, implicit within abstentionism, as delivering only stagnation and sterility. What he called for instead, at least initially, was a new 'active abstentionism' that would put an end to 'spectator politics'.[18] As the IRA now geared itself to a 'long war', such rhetoric asked new questions of old certainties. Moreover, as Adams and his supporters gained control of the Provisionals, they initiated the changes they desired within the movement. By 1981, the character of this shift had been captured by Danny Morrison's famous soundbite: republicans, he averred, would pursue the dual approach of 'the Armalite and the ballot box'.[19]

The more vigorous engagement with 'everyday' political life that this emerging strategy entailed brought clear challenges in its wake. In particular, senior republicans began to ask how ever-greater levels of support might be won by Sinn Féin, in light of the party's continuing refusal to recognise existing institutions on the island. The difficulties posed by this conundrum were most keenly felt south of the border, in the Irish Republic. There, general elections held at the time of the hunger strike in June 1981 had appeared to show a reservoir of potential support for Irish republicanism. Two candidates had been elected on a platform of support for the protesting prisoners and their successes had helped to defeat the incumbent Fianna Fáil administration of Charles Haughey. On this basis, the republican leadership of the time had hoped that Sinn Féin might translate such transient (and emotionally charged) gains into a more permanent and solid foothold in southern political life. Such optimism, however, had proven severely misplaced. In the subsequent general elections of February 1982, Sinn Féin stood and secured only 1 per cent of the vote. Thereafter, many of the northern-based republican leaders around Gerry Adams had come to the conclusion that 'abstentionism', as a policy, would have to go if Sinn Féin was to progress in the South.

As early as 1983, Adams spoke of the need for republicans to devise a political strategy which acknowledged that 'most people in the 26 counties see those institutions [i.e. the Dáil] as legitimate.' They could not do this, he argued, 'without taking into account the effects of the acceptance of the State institutions and the effect an abstentionist policy by Republicans is going to have on that strategy'. Although Adams went on to profess 'support' for the existing position of his party, it was clear that he had little affection for it.[20] Furthermore, that same year he moved to consolidate his control of Sinn Féin, replacing Ruairí Ó Brádaigh as party president at the 1983 *árd fheis*.

Still, it would be another three years before the decisive steps were taken to abandon the commitment to abstentionism. Danny Morrison, a close ally of Adams, has since admitted that, 'in order to minimise the size of the split, the abstention debate was stretched out over many years.'[21] And in keeping with this deliberate strategy of procrastination, a 'dress rehearsal' discussion for the effort to persuade the party to alter course was held in 1985.[22] It was only a year later, in November 1986, that motion 162 was finally put before the Sinn Féin *árd fheis*, calling for an amendment to the party's constitution:

> That this Árd-Fheis drops its abstentionist attitude to Leinster House. Successful Sinn Féin parliamentary candidates in 26-County elections:
>> a. Shall attend Leinster House as directed by the Árd Chomhairle ...[23]

Prior to the Sinn Féin gathering it had been announced that a Provisional IRA convention, the first since 1970, had been held in October 1986. There, that group had itself agreed to abandon abstentionism, having been assured that the move into politics would be accompanied by an escalation of the 'war' against the British.[24] And with that crucial endorsement thus secured, republican 'modernisers' such as Adams, McGuinness, Tom Hartley and Jim Gibney felt confident to push the case for change. As has been recounted elsewhere, at the core of their arguments too was an emphasis on militancy, which helped salve the doubts of those whose primary concern was the IRA campaign. The military record hitherto of the Adams faction within the leadership was highlighted, especially their involvement in the 'longest phase ever of resistance to the British presence'; so too was the fact that they had 'led from the front and from within the occupied area'. Simultaneously, the failures of the leadership identified with Ruairí Ó Brádaigh and his supporters (and particularly the IRA's mid-1970s truce) were repeatedly attacked. Finally, Martin McGuinness offered the most uncompromising guarantee that an end to abstentionism would not bring an end to the IRA's campaign:

> Our position is clear and it will never, never, never change. The war against British rule must continue until freedom is achieved ... If you allow yourselves to be led out of this hall today, the only place you're going is home. You will be walking away from the struggle. Don't go my friends. We will lead you to the Republic.[25]

Against this, 'traditionalists' gathered around Ó Brádaigh, who emerged as a totem for those opposed to the changes. They argued that any move to abandon abstentionism would be a violation of core republican principles. Ó Brádaigh himself began by condemning what he believed to be the illegitimate approach of the modernisers. By this argument, he claimed that the Sinn Féin constitution prohibited even a *discussion* of the abstentionism issue. In Ó Brádaigh's view, the prohibition on debate should have been removed first, prior to any substantive consideration as to the merits or otherwise of the policy.

The former Sinn Féin president also then defended abstentionism as 'a fundamental principle ... inalienable, immutable and absolute'. 'If there are fundamentals there,' he declared, 'we either accept them as in the constitution or we go another road, and we disagree with them.' For Ó Brádaigh, it was in 1986, as it had been in 1969–70, a matter of deep-seated ideological belief; Adams and McGuinness were judged to be repeating the mistakes of Goulding and the 'Stickies'. Years later, Ó Brádaigh would reflect on the synergy between events in 1969–70 and those of 1986, seeing in the former the genesis of the latter:

> Both Adams and McGuinness were with the Stickies in the beginning. Gerry Adams was at the *árd fheis* [in January 1970] and he didn't walk out. He says he was at the Springboks game on an anti-apartheid protest – but that was on the Saturday, the walk-out was on the Sunday. And for three months after that he was with the Stickies ... Martin McGuinness was in the Fianna in Derry and they went with the Officials. In fact, he used to say in prison in the Curragh 'Glass house', where I was for six months with him, that he was in the Official movement one year and before the next year was out he was on the Army Council of the Provisional movement ... One wonders about the ideology here. In the late seventies, after Adams came out of prison, he made a remark at an *árd chomhairle* [national executive] meeting, which I found peculiar to say the least ... he said there was nothing wrong with the Stickies except that they wouldn't fight.[26]

Such an appraisal was anathema to Ó Brádaigh. For him, the Stickies had violated the core precept of what it meant to be a republican by their willingness to enter the 'terrible' partitionist parliaments. In other words, the republicanism of Adams and McGuinness was judged to have lacked, from the outset, the purity of his own. The debate over abstentionism cut to the heart of Ó Brádaigh's world view; abstentionism was the *sine qua non* of his republicanism. On this reading, republicanism shorn of such a key tenet would in fact have ceased to be republican-ism – and those who claimed to have revised the creed in such a fash-ion would, in reality, have abandoned the faith.

Constitutional politics, by Ó Brádaigh's reckoning, were simply not an option for would-be revolutionaries. To be part of the status quo, he argued, was to be part of the system; and regardless of intentions, it was judged that the system always corrupted those involved with it. As a self-avowed revolutionary, seeking radical change, Ó Brádaigh felt it to be incumbent upon him to remain on the outside. As he had argued in an internal strategy paper in the early 1980s,

> A revolutionary movement either succeeds or fails badly. There is hardly an in-between position. So many things are put at risk that often failure or the possibility of failure can inveigle some partici-pants into reformism in order to 'save something from the collapse', as it is put.[27]

For Ó Brádaigh, 'reformism' meant being 'sucked into and [becoming] part of the colonial or neo-colonial system'.[28] It was thus to be avoided at all costs. And neither could there be any question of striking some form of compromise with such an approach.

The gap between this kind of outlook and that being increasingly articulated by the pragmatic republican leaders around Gerry Adams was only too clear. At the 1985 Sinn Féin *árd fheis*, Tom Hartley, an ally of Adams, had asserted that 'there is a principle riding above all prin-ciples and that is the principle of success.'[29] Such success, to be achieved through flexible politics in the here-and-now, was considered vastly preferable to the comfortable, but sterile, convictions of long-estab-lished republican dogma. The latter was attacked by Morrison that same year when he urged people not to be 'parading the republican dead' in front of the *árd fheis*.[30] Similarly, in a key speech at the grave of Wolfe Tone in June 1986, Martin McGuinness drove home these very points. There, he evoked the memory of James Connolly and claimed that Connolly had

> … once remarked that the real danger to republicanism was that it might become a commemorative organisation that mourned its martyrs, that lamented its heroic defeats. There is an element of romanticism within our ranks that, while not consciously defeatist, continues to look at the past for legitimacy.[31]

What McGuinness sought instead was a 'winning' formula. More worth was attached to that which might deliver results than that which was ideologically faithful. For Ruairí Ó Brádaigh, by contrast, ideological precision was everything. And it was the 'past', treated so dismissively by Morrison and McGuinness, which guaranteed legitimacy. It was the sacrifices of the 'republican dead' in the name of certain core, unvarying principles which had guaranteed the integrity of republican ideals.

Perhaps not surprisingly, however, Ó Brádaigh's glorification of unbending but heroic failure over imperfect but tangible success proved less appealing to the broader republican constituency. By 1986, a critical mass of republicans had been persuaded of the need for the movement to modify its approach. More important still, in the eyes of Ó Brádaigh, was the fact that people had been persuaded by the militarist emphasis of anti-abstentionist figures such as McGuinness; they therefore failed to see the importance of ideological integrity. When reflecting on that period in 2009, he was able to observe with relative detachment:

> The trouble is that most people aren't swayed by the arguments about the situation, it's only when they see events working out on the stage, as it were, that they realise. And then, often times, it's too late ... With regard to what happened in the eighties, people now say to me, 'well, we were wrong, we were easily deceived!' Now, not much good comes of it, but I like to inquire as to what influenced them and they say things like, 'Ah well, we felt in '86 that the war was the engine that drove everything and as long as the war continued we were satisfied that everything would be alright' ... What they didn't understand is that the vital thing is to keep the idea alive.[32]

Whatever the reason, the motion to end abstentionism was passed by a margin of 429–161 – a margin of eleven in favour of the amendment (given that a two-thirds majority was required to change the Sinn Féin constitution).[33] During the critical debate, Ó Brádaigh had, together with key allies Des Long, Pat Ward and Joe O'Neill, held a private meeting with a group of senior leadership figures who favoured the abandonment of abstentionism – Adams, McGuinness, Kevin Mallon and Michael McKevitt.[34] Their attempts to prevent a parting of the ways, however, proved unsuccessful. The fissures arising from the dispute could not so easily be patched up. Back in 1983, Ó Brádaigh had recommended his own tenure as president of Sinn Féin to party members, with a statement that was half encomium and half warning: 'During my 14 years as head of Sinn Féin there were no splits or splinters – long may it remain so, as it will, provided we stick to basic principles.'[35] It now became clear that, in his mind, the conditionality inherent in that message had been violated. It thus fell to Ó Brádaigh to once more break away and establish a republican vehicle that would stay true to 'basic principles'. Consequently, Ó Brádaigh and his long-time ally, Daithí Ó Conaill, led a walkout of traditionalists, just as they had done in 1970. After exiting the Sinn Féin *árd fheis*, these traditionalists reassembled in the West County Hotel on the outskirts of Dublin and set about forming a new organisation, Republican Sinn Féin.

REPUBLICAN SINN FÉIN

To some extent, the creation of Republican Sinn Féin (RSF) was a replay of events from sixteen years earlier. Of the 1970 'Provisional' Sinn Féin caretaker executive, the only person still involved in politics, but not present at the foundation of RSF, was John Joe McGirl, who chose to remain with the Provisionals.[36] The rest of his erstwhile comrades once more opted to stand with Ó Brádaigh in defence of traditional republicanism. And yet, there were key differences between 1986 and the earlier episode. Most significantly, this time the rebels were not able to tap into a broader hinterland, ready to embrace the republican analysis.

Robert White's analysis of the 1986 split has shown how it was essentially led by 'pre-1969' southern republicans, for whom abstentionism was an issue of paramount importance. These were the same people who had led the walkout in 1969–70, but who on that occasion had been joined by a new generation of 'post-1969' republicans, whose core concern was IRA militancy. The latter, inspired by more immediate concerns such as Anthony McIntyre's 'three Ds' (see above, page 37), had flocked to the Provisional banner and helped tip the republican balance in their favour. Now, by contrast, the founders of RSF could not hope to exploit such disaffection – for the simple reason that the Provisional IRA continued to corner that particular market. Within the existing republican family, meanwhile, most northerners remained loyal to PIRA, save for the odd exception (such as Billy McKee and Leo Martin).[37] Instead, the majority of those present at the creation of RSF were southern-based – people like Ruairí Ó Brádaigh and his brother, Sean (from Roscommon), Des Long (from Limerick), Denis McInerney (from Clare), Tony Ruane (from Mayo) and Frank Glynn (from Galway). Of the twenty-one members of the first RSF *árd chomhairle* (national executive), only two came from north of the border.[38]

By and large these were people who, now entering middle-age, had devoted their entire lives to a purist form of Irish republicanism. Many were close allies of Ó Brádaigh and had stood by him in the increasingly tense struggle with the younger generation around Gerry Adams and Martin McGuinness. Des Long, for instance, who had served as a member of the first 'Provisional' Sinn Féin *árd chomhairle* in 1970, had stepped down from that position in 1982 in protest at changes being made to the party's constitution at the instigation of Adams. So too had other key Ó Brádaigh supporters, Richard Behal, Joe O'Neill and Tom O'Sullivan, all of whom now joined RSF.[39]

In its first public statement, the new party vowed to 'uphold the basic Republican position enshrined in the Sinn Féin Constitution' and pursue 'Republican objectives'.[40] The following year, Ó Brádaigh expanded on these themes in his presidential address to the inaugural RSF *árd fheis*, where he sounded a defiant and obdurate note. On that occasion, he praised his colleagues for having rejected attempts 'to subvert the Sinn Féin constitution'. They had, he claimed, showed 'moral courage' by going 'against the tide', in the face of 'blandishments' and 'threats' from former comrades. The Provisionals, by abandoning abstentionism, were said to have engaged in a betrayal of the true 'Republic', and the lesson of history, Ó Brádaigh argued, was clear:

> For the fifth time in 65 years an attempt was made to depart from that basic Republican and revolutionary position and to accept the British imperialist and colonialist alternative, the 26-County State, the Six-County statelet and the overlordship of Westminster itself. The years of the great breaches of trust – 1922 and 1926, 1946 and 1969, and finally 1986 – with all the disastrous consequences for the faithful Irish Republicans which flowed from them, loom before us today![41]

Defeat during the abstentionism debate in 1986 was attributed to an alleged manipulation of the voting process and the fact that 'the issue of armed struggle was used to cloud and cover over the departure from basic Republican principle'. The truth of the matter, Ó Brádaigh averred, was that those who had voted to accept 'the 26-County neo-colonial state' had 'clearly breached the constitution' of Sinn Féin and thereby put themselves outside the organisation. It was they, not Ó Brádaigh and his followers, who had 'expelled themselves from Sinn Féin'. For this reason, the new RSF president claimed, by way of reference to the well-known republican ballad, that it was *his* organisation, not that of the Provisionals, which could truly claim to carry the mantle of Irish republicanism:

> As the ballad spoke of the flag of the Republic in an earlier and similar episode, we now say of the Sinn Féin constitution and the name Sinn Féin itself: leave it to 'those who intend to defend it, until England's tyranny cease'.[42]

The title of the song in question, *Take it Down from the Mast, Irish Traitors*, made clear the combative nature of Ó Brádaigh's sentiments. And in line with this, he finished his address by declaring, in conscious repudiation of McGuinness's 1986 remarks (see above), 'We have not "gone home". We are here and we are very much in business.'[43]

In the years that followed, the belief in RSF's rightful possession of the republican legacy was expanded upon. Such a stance was under-pinned by their claim to a theoretical heritage that ran back to the early twentieth century and the foundation of the first Sinn Féin party, with its emphasis on abstentionism from Westminster. From there, a lineage was traced down to the present day. The address given by Ó Brádaigh to his party's 2006 Bodenstown commemoration offered a flavour of what this entailed. There, he declared RSF's adherence to the cause of the Republic that was proclaimed in 1916. That Republic, he main-tained, had been, 'ratified by the people in the 1918 election and the deputies assembled in the Mansion House in January 1919'.[44] This lat-ter body was described as the 'First Dáil Éireann', which was in turn succeeded by the 'Second Dáil Éireann'. Both of these were said to have constituted 'the sovereign parliament[s] of the 32 County United Ireland', whose members had sworn 'to defend the Republic against all enemies foreign and domestic'. When, however, the Second Dáil voted by a majority to accept the Anglo-Irish Treaty of 1921, it was judged that supporters of the accord had 'reneged on their oath … and thereby committed perjury'. By contrast, the 'faithful members of the Second

Dáil' were those who refused to accept the Treaty. Despite being 'attacked' by the Free State, these loyal republicans had 'continued to meet and organise' until, in 1938, it was proposed that 'the authority of the Second (All-Ireland) Dáil be passed on to the Army Council of the Irish Republican Army'.[45] In this manner, the shift in the locus of authority was assumed to have occurred. And from there the line of succession ran through the 'Official' republican movement of the 1940s, '50s and '60s (of which Ó Brádaigh had been a member), then transferred to the 'Provisionals' in 1969–70 before finally coming to rest with RSF after the latest split in 1986. As the party's promotional literature declared, this last entity was now the 'only truly Republican political organisation in Ireland'.[46]

On this reading, a belief in abstentionism was not one principle among several for republicans. Rather, it was *the* critical ideological cornerstone of the faith. As one RSF publication explained:

> The principle of Abstentionism is derived from a Republican view of where a State gets its authority to rule: the people. Elected representatives who participate in the institutions of the State effectively accept the authority of that State and its right to voluntarily rule the people they represent. By withdrawing popular support – represented on an official level by withdrawing elected representatives – from the State, it becomes impossible for the State to function. By diverting that popular support to the parallel apparatus of the revolutionary State being formed, the existing State is democratically replaced.[47]

This was what was thought to have occurred in 1918–19 with the creation of the 'First Dáil'. RSF wished to inaugurate a similar process with regard to the modern-day Irish parliament and Northern Irish assembly, which together were perceived to infringe upon 'the sovereignty of the Irish nation'.[48] In the assessment of Ó Brádaigh, these were 'enemy parliaments', which inevitably corrupted those who entered them.[49] History, in his view, dictated this, irrespective of specific circumstance:

> It has all happened before. The question is not the personalities, or the personnel, but the forces, tendencies and trends at work ... Every time one of these crises [over abstentionism] comes to the republican movement there are different personnel involved, and

the journalists have to make it interesting for their readers by dwelling on the personalities involved ... But one has to stand back. Every time this kind of thing happens I lose good friends, I don't enjoy it at all, but [since 1986] the Provisionals have been going down a certain road and there is a logical progression to it.[50]

For this reason, there could be no compromise, or collaboration with 'partitionist' institutions. As self-avowed revolutionaries, proper republicans were to involve themselves in purely oppositional forms of politics – to include support for anti-state violence. As Ó Brádaigh declared, in a critique of the direction in which the Provisionals appeared to be heading in the early 1990s, 'You cannot ride two horses at the same time.'[51] Any engagement in constitutional politics, or a failure to wholeheartedly support the violent campaign of the IRA, was viewed as little more than an act of collusion in the denial of Irish sovereignty. The intensity with which this view was held can be gauged from an interview that Ó Brádaigh gave to an RTÉ Irish-language television documentary, *The Brookeborough Raid*, in 2006. In one notable exchange, the RSF president warned against the dangers of 'the disease of constitutionalism' – a disease to which he felt the Provisionals had succumbed. Ó Brádaigh also went on to dismiss claims that RSF's lack of electoral support in any way served to de-legitimise the party's project. What mattered, he averred, was not the view of the people as manifested in elections but the fact that RSF could claim *'údarás an staire'* – the 'mandate of history'.[52]

The extent to which this reverence for history took on quasi-religious undertones was exemplified by an address given to the RSF-linked prisoner organisation *Cabhair* in 1999. On that occasion the speaker was Marian Price (more of whom below), who, despite her role in the 32 County Sovereignty Movement, remained close to RSF. Price intoned how republicans gathered at Easter 'to draw strength and inspiration' from the events of 1916 and 'to draw allegiance to the legacy which they bequeathed us'. Of the men who died in the aftermath of the Rising, she declared, 'From their sacrifice we receive lessons of history to learn, ideals to espouse and principles of patriotism to uphold.' In language that would later be echoed by Gerry Adams in April 2005 in his appeal to the IRA, Price affirmed 'our appreciation of and our love for those brave Irish men and women who stood in the *bearna baoil* [gap of danger] when it was neither popular, fashionable nor profitable to be an Irish Republican either in the Six or 26 Counties'. Those to whom Price referred specifically, were the 'men and women of the '20s, '30s, '40s and '50s whose fortitude in the face of insurmountable odds and ... horrendous hardship ... sowed the seeds which inspired the free-dom fighters of the past three decades'. The resonance of such a mes-sage for the contemporary dissident cause was only too clear. Price was adamant that the only correct path was to stay loyal to the republican paradigm proffered by history – and to avoid the lure of the 'latest British/Free State initiative' (the Good Friday Agreement). In her as-sessment,

> To suggest that those Republicans and, indeed, nationalists who suffered, fought and died over the past three decades did so in order to walk through the doors of a revamped Stormont, aban-don Articles 2 & 3 of the 26-County Constitution and establish a British/Irish Council which would extend British influence in the 26 Counties, is a *blasphemy* [emphasis added] and a fraudulent assertion.[53]

Price's response to those who would make such an assertion was to quote the famous words of Patrick Pearse:

> I make the contention that the national demand of Ireland is fixed and made by every generation; that we of this generation receive it as a trust from our fathers; that we are bound by it; that we have not the right to alter it or abate it by one jot; and that any undertaking made in the name of Ireland to accept in full satisfac-tion of Ireland's claim anything less than the generations of Ireland have stood for, is null and void.[54]

Though not a member of Republican Sinn Féin, Price had, with such words, effectively captured the spirit of the party; RSF epitomised obe-dience to the maxims of Pearse.

Upon this rigid foundation, the party constructed a political platform rooted in republican history. At the turn of the twenty-first century, RSF was, according to its website, steadfastly opposed to the European Union and a firm advocate of Irish neutrality. Domestically, it claimed to stand for 'social justice based on Irish Republican Socialist princi-ples in accordance with the Democratic Programme and the 1916 Proclamation'. This was allied to a call for 'the complete separation of

Church and State' and a professed belief in the 'central importance of the Irish language to Irish identity'.[55] The synthesis of these rather vague prescriptions was held to be *Éire Nua* – a policy document that symbolised RSF's commitment to an unchanging, almost theological version of Irish republicanism. As a programme, it envisioned a complete transformation of the Irish state. In place of the 'partitionist' status quo, it called for the establishment of a unified, 'four province federal Ireland, with a self-governing parliament in each of the four provinces' – Ulster, Connacht, Munster and Leinster. This new constitution was to be augmented by the complete restructuring of local and regional government, while a national parliament (Dáil Éireann) was to reside at Athlone – 'the geographic centre of Ireland'.[56]

This utopian dream for a refashioned Ireland was little altered from the time that Ó Brádaigh first compiled it, together with Daithí Ó Conaill, in 1971–2.[57] *Éire Nua* had stood as the official policy statement of Provisional republicanism from that time until the end of the decade. Indeed, from 1972, a commitment to implement *Éire Nua* had been written into the Sinn Féin constitution. In his presidential address to that year's *árd fheis*, Ó Brádaigh had declared, 'To all the people of Ireland we say; let us wipe the slate clean and start anew … Éire Nua will restore the wealth of Ireland to the people of Ireland with a more just distribution of the goods of this world, worker-ownership and participation in decision making in industry.'[58]

Ó Brádaigh's fervour notwithstanding, it became clear over the course of the 1970s that not everyone within the republican movement shared his enthusiastic view of *Éire Nua*. Many felt that its millenarian vistas, while understandable amid the maelstrom that engulfed Ireland in the early '70s – when many believed that the Northern Irish state might actually collapse in the face of the Provisional IRA's onslaught – became less relevant as the decade progressed. Again, opposition to the Ó Brádaigh-ite line was led by a group of northern republicans, among whom Gerry Adams was central. As Ed Moloney has described, *Éire Nua* was used by Adams and his supporters as something of a stick with which to beat the Ó Brádaigh faction, in the context of the wider struggle for control of the republican movement in this era. The federal aspects of the scheme were characterised as being essentially partitionist, in that they seemed to perpetuate a divided Ireland. More damaging still was the suggestion, made by people like Danny Morrison, that they constituted a 'sop to loyalism' that rewarded the opponents of republicanism.[59] In the increasingly sectarianised atmosphere of the 'Troubles', such charges helped to discredit the *Éire Nua* brand. By the end of 1979, the IRA had formally removed its commitment to the provisions of *Éire Nua*.[60] Three years later, the federal provisions of the policy were abandoned by Sinn Féin, which instead committed itself to a unitary 'democratic socialist republic'. It was this latter move that precipitated the resignation of Ó Brádaigh's close friend Daithí Ó Conaill as vice-president of Sinn Féin, with Ó Brádaigh himself stepping down as party president (to be replaced by Adams) a year later.[61]

In light of this past allegiance to the cause of *Éire Nua*, then, it was unsurprising that the formation of RSF should have seen Ó Brádaigh and his allies place it once more at the heart of their agenda. In February 2003, RSF issued an 'address to the people of Ireland' which specifically targeted the 'people of Ulster' with their message for a federalist, but united, Ireland. The pamphlet claimed that unionists were experiencing a 'sense of apprehension and insecurity' because Westminster was losing the will to govern Northern Ireland, even as the Irish government showed itself reluctant to accept responsibility for the territory. Demographic trends were said to hang 'like the sword of Damocles' over unionists; and for this reason they were called upon to choose 'a third way, neither London rule nor Dublin rule, but a new democracy in a new Ireland'. Unionists should, RSF maintained, take 'their rightful place, as equals, in the historic Irish nation'. They were thus asked to consider again *Éire Nua* and its federal proposals, which would give them a 'working majority' in a nine-county 'Ulster'.[62]

The jaundiced view of unionism upon which such appeals rested was later encapsulated by Richard Walsh, a director of publicity for RSF, in 2009. One of the more youthful members of the party, Walsh nevertheless demonstrated the amaranthine character of its ideology. Seated alongside an Irish tricolour in RSF's smoke-ridden Belfast office, the hirsute Walsh declared:

> The fact is the overwhelming majority of the Irish people have always supported national liberation and the fact is that the Unionists on this side of the border have an entirely artificial majority. The border was drawn around them to give them that majority in a created area.[63]

When asked about the possibility of some kind of violent 'unionist backlash' in the event that the British government did announce a departure from Northern Ireland, Walsh was little moved:

> I don't think so, because we have a policy, *Éire Nua*, in which we propose a federal Ireland, which would give the unionists – well, the former unionists – a working majority within Ulster ... they would come to realise that everyone's interests would be protected within the new Ireland ... [The unionists'] interests aren't in England being here ... The unionist position is not going to do them any favours in the long term.[64]

In its twenty-first-century format, then, *Éire Nua* was underwritten by the enduring belief that Ireland had 'enormous problems, two failed states, and a political system that perpetuates our plight'; all of which was said to be the legacy of a history dominated by the 'invasion and colonisation' of the historic 'Irish nation' by England.[65] At various points over the previous eight hundred years, this oppression had been 'heroically resisted' and 'each generation handed on the torch of liberty to the next'. Clearly again, the message was that RSF was to be seen as the rightful inheritor of this mantle. By contrast, the Good Friday Agreement, which was then in place, was viewed as merely another 'failed arrangement' that did not address 'the basic problem of English rule in Ireland'. In this respect, it was described as being no different from the 'Treaty of Surrender in 1921'.[66]

Elsewhere, *Éire Nua* railed against the 'commercialised Anglo-American pop culture' that had helped to downgrade authentic 'Irish identity and the Irish language'.[67] The European Union, meanwhile, was described as a 'modern form of imperialism', which was corrupt, undemocratic and run solely in the interests of big business.[68] To remedy all such problems, RSF encouraged an embrace of *Éire Nua* – federalism and all – as the only basis for the achievement of a 'new beginning', and the building of a 'pluralist participative democracy'.[69] What had been judged appropriate to 1971 was held to be no less appropriate for the post-2000 world. Rather than dispense with *Éire Nua*, there was merely some embellishment of its terms – and the addition of a separate, but supposedly compatible, 'social and economic programme'.

RSF's November 1991 *árd fheis* had instructed the incoming *árd chomhairle* to develop just such a programme for the organisation.

What emerged was christened 'Saol Nua' and adopted by the party a year later. Subtitled 'a new way of life', Saol Nua declared 'conventional' economics to be 'an unsustainable discipline which must be subordinated to social, environmental, ethical and spiritual values'. What was required, it declared, was 'a new system of economics which would put human beings and human development before the interests of finance and maximisation of profits'.[70] To this end, Saol Nua was said to represent a 'vision of Ireland based on Republican, Socialist, Self-reliance and Ecological principles'.[71]

As to what all of this meant in practice, much of Saol Nua offered little more than platitudes and nebulous prescriptions. A key aim was thus described as ensuring that 'people come first'; while a central criticism of existing conditions was the fact that 'Selfishness and individualism are replacing the old Irish traditions of neighbourliness and social responsibility.'[72] The solution laid out was to include the abolition of national debt, the bringing of 'banking and all key industries' under 'public, democratic or social control' and the development of national resources in a 'sustainable, non-polluting manner'.[73] 'Neo-colonial' multinational companies were to be removed, in favour of 'local small-scale enterprise'.[74] Taxes were to be 'progressive and redistributive' and to be used to fund both a 'comprehensive national health service' and 'a comprehensive network of public transport'. And a new education system was to be created with a focus on 'moral responsibility' and 'social ethics'.[75]

The end goal was said to be a 'social and economic system which would seek to make it possible for every citizen to own an economic unit of production'. That this should be so, it was argued, was because

> It is only in small, distinct and comprehensible groups that people can be themselves and achieve self-esteem, dignity and fulfilment. The Irish Comhar na gComharsan is an example of the kind of local or community development in which each worker owns a unit of production.[76]

Significantly, the reference here to 'Comhar na gComharsan' was to a philosophy developed by Ó Brádaigh and others decades previously. Roughly translated as 'neighbourliness', this was said to embody a form of indigenous socialism, suited to rural Irish needs, which would be the most appropriate form of social organisation for the country.[77]

In some respects, notions such as 'Comhar na gComharsan' were symptomatic of republican efforts to square the circle between revolutionary leanings – usually expressed through a left-wing discourse – and a Catholic belief system that was customarily antagonistic to Marxisant modes of analysis. Ó Brádaigh's rhetoric, for instance, could on occasion veer from an enthusing for 'socialism' to an acclamation of 'the re-birth of Christian idealism', which was what 1916 was said to have brought about.[78] The appearance of a doctrine such as Comhar na gComharsan within *Saol Nua* thus typified what Henry Patterson has described as Ó Brádaigh's affinity for a moderate conception of a specifically 'Irish' brand of socialism, which drew much on loosely defined notions of corporatism and 'Christian values', and owed a great deal to mid-twentieth-century papal encyclicals.[79]

At the same time, what *Saol Nua* and *Éire Nua* both evinced was a reverence for a mythic Irish past in which 'everything had been better'. As Tom Garvin has described, concerns as to the corrupting effect of the modern world and an antipathy for 'the long present' were staples of Irish separatist thought from the late nineteenth century onwards. For men such as Ó Brádaigh, salvation was to be found in a romantic vision of a Gaelicised Ireland that would somehow recapture its authentic character. On this view, the egocentric individualism of modern (and liberal) society was to be replaced by an ethos of co-operative communalism (or 'neighbourliness'). Private property would survive, but be divorced from the seemingly rapacious thrust of capitalism. Central government would deliver wide-ranging public services, even as power was fundamentally de-centralised. Above all, the 'Irish nation' would be resurrected through the harmonious exertions of its people; the Republic would be realised.[80]

PRACTICAL POLITICS?

Against this idealistic background, it is perhaps unsurprising that Republican Sinn Féin's attempts to construct a practical political message have remained confined to the realm of abstract postulation. In this regard, the positions adopted at the party's 2000 and 2001 *árd fheiseanna* are highly instructive. There, it was decreed variously that: 'the problems of the homeless, the disadvantaged and marginalised in society be tackled'; that 'in the future All-Ireland Republic it will be mandatory for employers to negotiate with trade unions'; and that 'this Árd-Fheis support the rights of Irish fishermen'.[81] All of which was indicative of the somewhat intangible character of the RSF message. Where greater detail was provided, it was often in the form of equally quixotic pledges, such as that which demanded not only that 'no planning permission for the erection of houses will be granted unless the proposed names of these housing estates be approved by the elected councillors' but also that 'these estates and street names must have cultural and/or historical significance to the area where they are to be situated.'[82]

The broader worldview of RSF's members, meanwhile, can be gleaned from the party's declarations of 'solidarity' with Basque and Breton prisoners, as well as the hunger strike then underway in Turkey by Kurdish prisoners. Alongside this were calls for the removal of the US embargo on Cuba and UN sanctions on Iraq; and pronouncements of support for the Palestinians in their 'ongoing struggle to regain their homeland'.[83] Less tangible were Ó Brádaigh's attempts to link RSF to a wider global context, stating, 'Our cause is the cause of humanity, which is why we oppose the forces of imperialism not only in Ireland but internationally as well.'[84]

Predominant, though, was a kind of unbending, 'traditional' form of republicanism that rarely departed from an established script. This interpreted the present through the kind of lens already described, which simultaneously poured scorn on existing conditions, while also looking to a hazy vision of imagined redemption. The 2003 presidential address given by Ruairí Ó Brádaigh to his party's *árd fheis* stood as a typical example of this. Therein, Ó Brádaigh deployed a stream of familiar themes, which highlighted both the malign character of British rule in Ireland and the wider shortcomings of the status quo. Reference was thus made to: the alleged harassment of republicans by the 'RUC' (not the PSNI, despite the fact that it had now replaced the RUC); the terrorising of the nationalist community by 'loyalist gangs'; the fact that the 'nightmare of the Nationalist community' in Northern Ireland still endured; the iniquitous nature of the Stormont Agreement, which was described as essentially 'sectarian in nature'; the 'horrific war of conquest on the people of Iraq' (in which Britain had been involved); and the dangers of the 'emerging EU nuclear armed superstate'.[85] As an assessment of the status quo, Ó Brádaigh's views were almost wholly negative, and mixed sweeping generalisation with a clear lack of nuance. Neither did they entail any meaningful engagement with the existing situation, other than to reject it. The policy prescriptions put forward as remedy were no more thought-out: a commitment to the updated version of *Saol Nua*, to be embraced in full; an appeal for all people to 'consider again' the RSF proposals of *Éire Nua*; and the launching of the party's 'initiative to Unionists' based on that message.[86] Here again, then, the binary character of such a worldview can be discerned. The present is judged worthy only of denigration; deliverance is envisaged through the embrace of some ill-defined but incontestably 'better' future. In this respect, Ó Brádaigh's speech was typical of the outlook he had embraced back in the 1950s, and it could, by-and-large, have been given at any point over the previous five decades. It embodied classic, unreconstructed republicanism, replete with archaic interventions about fisheries policy and wind power.

Aside from anything else, it is hard to see how a set of policies framed in this way could have hoped to appeal to anyone outside the closed circle of the republican faithful. Ó Brádaigh spoke to the initiated alone and laid out an oppositional, vaguely left wing, anti-the-status-quo form of politics. As his brother Seán Ó Brádaigh asserted in his Bodenstown address of the same year, Ireland as a whole was thought to be afflicted with 'rampant capitalism'. The political system was held to be nothing more than a 'travesty of democracy' which could be compared with the situation in Zimbabwe or Burma. North and south of the border, according to Seán,

> Both states are in hock to English imperialism and neo-liberal capitalism and its free market and culture of greed ... There is a moral and spiritual vacuum in the Ireland of today.

To fill that vacuum, he argued, republicans should work to 'restore the historic Irish nation'.[87] And again, it is noteworthy that the moral component of this brand of republicanism was as much to the fore as the more straightforwardly 'political' aspects of the message.

As to how that message might translate into practice, in terms of the 'everyday' political activities of RSF, the 2000 *árd fheis* made it clear that the party divided its work into two spheres: 'annual events', such as the *árd fheis* or the commemorations that were held at various locations at Easter, or at Edentubber and Bodenstown; and also 'political campaigns' such as those around prisoners, policing, Europe and elections.[88] With regard to the former, it is perhaps no surprise that RSF should attach such importance to the regular cycle of commemorative events that were spread across the republican calendar.[89] This was a party, after all, for which the shadow of history loomed large; the present was forever interpreted through the prism of the past (and judged inherently inferior as a result).

To give but one illustration, this readiness to evoke history, with a clear eye to the message it could impart to the contemporary world, can be seen in the fifty-two-page glossy booklet produced by RSF in 1994 to celebrate the fiftieth anniversary of former IRA leader, Charlie Kerins, 'the spirit of Kerry'. At a time when the peace process appeared to be moving forward (with the first Provisional IRA ceasefire in August of that year), it was telling that the party should invoke the memory of Kerins – a 'forties' man, whose intransigent republicanism eventually cost him his life. To commemorate that life, the RSF publication was replete with poems and ballads about Kerins. Alongside this were 'impressions' of him from those who knew him, accounts of his death, a copy of the 1916 Proclamation and 'rolls of honour' of deceased IRA volunteers. Significantly, in his introduction, Ruairí Ó Brádaigh intoned how the 'Republican soldiers of 1938–44' had maintained the cause in spite of the huge odds they faced, 'at a time when the collaboration of Westminster, Stormont and Leinster House had almost strangled the Cause of Irish Freedom'. Kerins' core concern as he faced death, according to Ó Brádaigh, was that 'the ideals and principles for which I am about to die ... be kept alive until the Irish Republic is finally enthroned'. The lesson for any reader was clear: purity in death, over compromise in life, was Kerins' greatest achievement. By remaining true to his beliefs, he 'did not evade his responsibilities' but rather 'sacrificed his noble young life to seal a pact with Republicans of succeeding generations'. In this way, Kerins was said to embody 'the noble and unyielding spirit of Republican Kerry'; a spirit that was doubtless judged to be in short supply among those present-day republicans now considering peace.[90]

For whatever the occasion, the dominant theme for RSF in the period after 1994 was the alleged iniquity of the peace process and the path taken by the Provisional movement. At a hunger strike commemoration in Bundoran, County Donegal, in August 2000, one member of the party claimed that the ultimate lesson of the 1981 hunger strike was 'to never, ever give up the struggle for freedom, no matter what the odds are against us. They died rather than submit to British rule!' Such determination was contrasted starkly with the 'Provos' who were said to be 'indistinguishable from their British master'. In the eyes of RSF they were 'willing paid traitors'.[91] Similarly, in his 2008 address to the RSF *árd fheis*, Ó Brádaigh derided the Provisionals as 'turncoats' and 'renegades'. Only RSF, he maintained, could claim to stand 'in direct lineal succession to the United Irishmen of 1798, the Young Irelanders of 1848, the Fenians of 1867, the 1916 Rising and the First (All Ireland) Dáil'.[92]

In this, there was perhaps a conscious echo of Patrick Pearse's narrative of the 'four gospels' of Irish nationalism, with RSF the repository for that sacred canon.[93] Those who had abandoned it were viewed as having taken on the role of 'Judas'.[94] By comparison, RSF declared itself to follow 'in the tradition of Tone, Emmet, the Fenians and Pearse'; it accepted nothing less than 'the programme of previous generations of Republicans: Ireland free. No compromising "interim" settlement is acceptable.'[95]

The accusation of Provisional treachery reached a crescendo in the wake of the March 2009 murders, when Martin McGuinness accused the perpetrators of being 'traitors to the island of Ireland'. In response, Richard Walsh, the RSF publicity director, charged McGuinness himself with being guilty of 'severe treachery' and insisted that the Provisionals had abandoned republicanism altogether and in fact had become unionists.[96] They were, according to Walsh, merely 'people who are claiming to be nationalists, but who are helping to administer the British presence'.[97]

Elsewhere, the line of attack deployed by RSF invariably focused on the failings of the Provisional movement's leadership who had led their followers astray: 'The English regime in Ireland never had as close a call as it had in the 1970s and '80s. As in 1921 the resistance collapsed due to a failure of leadership.'[98] Inevitably, that failure of leadership was assumed to have begun with the decision by Sinn Féin in 1986 that it would henceforth take up any seats won in the southern Irish parliament. At a commemoration for the Derry republican Sean Keenan in early 2009, the then RSF vice-president, Des Dalton, made this link explicit: 'Today Provos are taking the next step in logical progression from collaborating with the British to actually taking part in enforcing British rule on the ground.'[99] What was required, Dalton contended, was a return to a purist conception of republicanism; one shorn of the accretions of the post-1986 period:

> Accordingly the rebuilding of our movement must continue on the firm and sure basis of the principles of Irish Republicanism. There is no short cut, only the hard road of people's struggle. These alleged short cuts lead only to division in the ranks and to disaster, as we have seen to our cost. Let us renew our pledges, then, and bend ourselves to our hard task in the sure and certain knowledge that this is the only road to success.[100]

Interestingly, such vitriolic criticism as was directed at the Provisionals was also, from time to time, balanced by RSF attempts to 'reach out' to potentially disaffected Provisional members. The 1997 *árd fheis*, for example, saw the party pass a motion that urged 'all republicans including those who have been misled in the past' to join RSF. Des Long, the party's vice-president, confirmed that this could extend to former Provisionals, stating that RSF was prepared to 'extend the hand of friendship' to such individuals.[101] Nevertheless, while some consideration could be offered to those Provisionals willing to recant the error of their ways, the movement as a whole continued to be viewed with utter contempt. Its position was viewed as being intrinsically and irredeemably wrong and to be challenged at every opportunity.

In this regard, as the reference to 'political campaigns' at the 2000 *árd fheis* had made clear, RSF was, in some circumstances, prepared to challenge mainstream Sinn Féin electorally. The party's official publication on the subject of abstentionism noted that this policy did not apply to local government assemblies, because they did not claim 'sovereignty over the territory they administer'. As a result, RSF was prepared to contest local elections south of the border and also participate in the councils if elected. The same approach, though, did not pertain in Northern Ireland because of the 'anti-violence' declaration required from potential candidates, which was felt to prohibit support for 'the struggle for Irish freedom' and require 'a repudiation of the right of the Irish people to use force of arms to end British occupation'.[102] Still, this self-denial in relation to local elections in the North did not extend to other levels of government there, where RSF felt it *could* stand for election on an abstentionist basis. As the party stated, the principle did not 'preclude contesting elections on a selective basis under certain preconditions'.[103]

Unfortunately for RSF, however, the political appeal of the party proved highly limited on those occasions where it did participate in the electoral process. Consequently, the party was unable to mount any meaningful challenge to Sinn Féin, which attained hegemonic status over not just the republican community but also northern nationalism as a whole, in this period. The 2001 local and British general elections provided a case in point as to the disparity between the two parties. In that contest, RSF selected the Continuity IRA prisoner Tommy Crossan as a 'POW Candidate' for the West Belfast constituency. Crossan's nomination papers were subsequently refused by the authorities on the basis that he was serving a jail sentence at the time; instead, therefore, RSF asked people to 'come out and register a spoilt vote for political status in both the Westminster and Council elections'.[104] Jonathan Tonge has pointed out that 1,500 people did precisely that, a figure significantly above the average of 300 spoiled votes per constituency – suggesting there had been some support for the RSF message. This 'success', though, was dwarfed by the fact that Sinn Féin's president Gerry Adams secured three quarters of all the votes cast in West Belfast.[105] It was thus only too clear where the 'balance of power' lay between RSF and its Sinn Féin rivals.

Even more stark were the results of the 2007 elections to the Northern Ireland Assembly, a contest which in many ways underscored the shortcomings of RSF as a political vehicle. The abstentionist manifesto upon which the party fought the poll stated boldly, 'For close on four decades Republican Sinn Féin has adhered to the noble concept of Éire Nua', a message of rigidity that seemed unlikely to transform its fortunes. Indeed, the extent to which RSF occupied a political realm far removed from the wider population was indicated by the promise that any candidates elected would not take part in the Assembly, but would instead 'make themselves available to sit in an All-Ireland parliament of the future'.[106] The question of how the RSF approach of remaining detached from contemporary issues would 'strengthen' the cause of 'national liberation' was left open to interpretation. Meanwhile, the 'Dad's Army' stereotype of the party, with which it was frequently labelled by opponents, was scarcely challenged by the respective profiles of its electoral candidates. In East Derry, for instance, it was represented by Michael McGonigle, the treasurer of the party's Ulster Executive. McGonigle had been part of the original split from Sinn Féin in 1986 and had served as a local councillor in the mid-1980s. Other candidates who had been with RSF since the 1986 split included Geraldine Taylor (standing in West Belfast), Michael McManus (Fermanagh-South Tyrone) and Joe O'Neill (West Tyrone). The latter was said to have been a member of the republican movement since 1955 and had served time in prison during the early 1970s. Another former prisoner representing the party was Brendan McLaughlin, who stood in Mid-Ulster. McLaughlin had taken part in the republican prison protests of the late 1970s/early 1980s, even joining the hunger strike (when he replaced Francis Hughes after his death, before being forced off the protest by a stomach ulcer).[107]

With this line-up, RSF proved unable to capture a seat. Across the six constituencies in which it stood, it won an average 420 votes; and some 2,500 in total, representing 0.4 per cent of those who voted.

Table 2.1:
Performance of RSF Candidates in Northern Ireland Assembly Elections, 2007

CONSTITUENCY	CANDIDATE	VOTES CAST
West Belfast	Geraldine Taylor	427
East Derry	Michael McGonigle	393
Mid-Ulster	Brendan McLaughlin	437
Upper Bann	Barry Toman	386
Fermanagh-South Tyrone	Michael McManus	431
West Tyrone	Joe O'Neill	448

By comparison, Sinn Féin maximised its level of support, taking some 180,000 votes (26.2 per cent of the total cast), winning twenty-eight seats in the Assembly and gaining the right to put forward Martin McGuinness as co-premier of the new Executive that emerged from the election.[108] In the aftermath of the poll, Ruairí Ó Brádaigh claimed that the results were a function of the 'media blackout' and predicted that 'The Provos ... will go on to consolidate English rule here.'[109] On this latter count, he was, by his own assessment, correct, as Sinn Féin entered a power-sharing arrangement with Ian Paisley's Democratic Unionist Party. There could be few doubts, though, that McGuinness and Sinn Féin had won an overwhelming mandate for acting as they did. RSF's hopes of forming an effective alternative to Sinn Féin had ended in near total failure; and that failure seemed to serve as an indictment of the party's broader irrelevancy in the eyes of most voters.

Beyond the electoral arena, moreover, it was apparent that, in many places, RSF enjoyed little more than a shadow existence. The reality of this was reflected in the party's publicity organ, *Saoirse: Irish Freedom – The Voice of the Republican Movement*. Not only did this newspaper continue to have a very dated feel to it, which made it a less than well-designed publication, but also its principal focus seemed to be the launching of invective against the British and/or the Provisionals. There was often little in the way of RSF 'activism' to report, as evinced, for example, by the paper's August 2008 edition. This contained criticism of loyalist violence associated with the annual twelfth of July celebrations and also condemnation of the 'RUC' for its arrest of three men (one of whom was an RSF *árd chomhairle* member) in connection with what was described as 'the attempted execution of two RUC men near Roslea'.[110] Another article outlined the importance of *Éire Nua* as being the best way to 'abolish the failed, undemocratic system of Partition rule'; while additional pieces highlighted the 'Shell 2 Sea' campaign and opposition to the M3 motorway near Tara.[111] But these were all relatively small stories and none appeared to demonstrate that RSF was a vibrant political force. Far more attention was devoted to the latest commemoration in the republican calendar: that of Patrick McManus, James Crossan and John Duffy – 'three IRA Volunteers who died during the 1950's [sic] Resistance Campaign against British Occupation'.[112] Again, as a sign of where the party's heart lay, the fact that more space was devoted to the celebration of three 1950s 'martyrs' than any contemporary political event was highly instructive.

One current issue on which RSF did at least attempt to maintain a reasonably high profile – another of the 'political campaigns' specifically referred to by RSF in 2000 – concerned the conditions faced by republican prisoners. Here, a key focus down to 2003, was the situation faced by the above-mentioned Tommy Crossan. The 2000 *árd fheis* saluted him and his 'continuing struggle for political status'.[113] Thereafter, there was some effort to turn Crossan's case into a cause célèbre – albeit without much success – as reflected in the relatively small support given to him at the 2001 elections.

That fact notwithstanding, RSF did continue to campaign on the prisoners' issue, staging protests outside Maghaberry prison in 2006 which urged people to 'remember the 1981 hunger strikes!' and support the latest insistence that 'five demands' be granted to republican prisoners. As on other issues, such activity was symptomatic of RSF's attempts to take possession of key facets of the republican heritage – this time related to the most recent 'Troubles'. The imputation here was that a continuum could be drawn between the republican prisoners of the late 70s and early 80s, and those of the post-Agreement era. The struggle of the former was held to be also that of the latter. A key subtext here was the alleged contradiction in the position of the Provisionals. While they had stood foursquare behind the earlier generation of protests, which included the 1980–1 hunger strikes, they were now said to be indifferent to the plight of republican prisoners. In line with this, the Sinn Féin-supported Agreement was condemned for having 'removed political status from Republican prisoners'. The result was said to be that those incarcerated faced prolonged periods of being locked in their cells, as well as regular strip searches, restrictions on movement and visits, a loss of remission and denials of compassionate parole. In other words, they faced precisely the kinds of conditions to which Sinn Féin had once objected so vocally – all of which stemmed from the denial of their rights as political prisoners.

Nevertheless, at times the grievances identified by RSF seemed almost to verge on an exercise in parody. Thus, under the banner of being 'made to choose between daily exercise and education', it was noted that 'Hankies made by the POWs were either destroyed or confiscated by prison staff.' By the same token, the measures taken by the prisoners to protest their plight exuded a faint note of absurdity – at least in the manner they were described by the RSF literature: 'They are refusing to eat their meals in their cells and are only taking food, purchased in the tuck shop, during unlock. As a result their health is suffering.'[114] The image of republican prisoners as reduced to eating only confectionary seemed to be a somewhat less emotive draw than their predecessors' resort to self-starvation in pursuit of their goals. Certainly, whatever the reason, it seems clear that the prisoners' campaign generally failed to resonate with a wider audience.

'CONTINUITY' REPUBLICANISM: A NEW IRA?

For all its shortcomings, the support lent to republican prisoners by RSF *was* significant as the public symbol of one crucial facet of the party: its subterranean and murky relationship with physical-force violence. At various points, Ruairí Ó Brádaigh did make declarations to the effect that 'Republican Sinn Féin has no military wing nor is it the political wing of any other organisation.'[115] And yet, from the beginning, there had been hints from RSF that abstentionism was not their only interest. That this should have been so was, to a large extent, inevitable. After all, much of the party's concern over that issue stemmed from the belief it constituted the 'thin end' of a much larger, compromise-inducing wedge. Those who abandoned abstentionism were held to be on a path that would end with a wider rejection of key republican tenets – including the 'armed struggle' of the IRA. It was this synthesis of principles which had underlain the 1969–70 split that created the Provisionals. In the same way, it was implicit within the schism of 1986. As the statement announcing the existence of RSF had stated, 'We uphold the historic right of the Irish people to use whatever degree of controlled and disciplined force is necessary in resisting English aggression and bringing about an English withdrawal from our country for ever.'[116]

In line with this, in another echo of 1969–70, it would appear that, alongside the emergence of RSF, plans were also laid for a new military organisation. In the wake of the Provisional IRA's October 1986 convention, at which it had endorsed support for candidates who entered Leinster House, Tom Maguire, the surviving member of the 'Second Dáil', had issued a statement to the effect that, in his view, 'There is no difference between entering the partition parliament of Leinster House and entering a partition parliament of Stormont.' He went on to state:

> I do not recognise the legitimacy of any Army Council styling itself the Council of the Irish Republican Army which lends support to any person or organisation styling itself as Sinn Féin and prepared to enter the partition parliament of Leinster House.[117]

In Maguire's eyes, then, the Provisionals were felt to have forfeited their claim to legitimacy, in just the same way as had Goulding's 'Officials'; that legitimacy now devolved to those who were prepared to remain true to abstentionism.

At around the same time, therefore, it would appear a 'Continuity Army Council' was formed by many of those who took the lead in creating Republican Sinn Féin – with a crossover of key personnel between the two organisations. Sean O'Callaghan, the ex-IRA informer, states that the formative gatherings for the new body occurred in late 1986, in a house in Dublin; at which time it was agreed that a skeletal hierarchy for a new IRA would be created.[118] Leading members of RSF, such as Ruairí Ó Brádaigh, Des Long and Tom O'Sullivan, were all believed to have been present on the new army council. In the years that followed, that new group remained dormant – mainly through concerns that the Provisional IRA would act to destroy any possible rival to its hegemony within republicanism. From 1996, however, with the Provisional movement becoming more engaged with the peace process, the Continuity IRA (CIRA) announced itself as an active military force (though interestingly, at the moment that the CIRA announced itself to the world, the Provisional IRA had reignited its violent campaign after the February 1996 collapse of its ceasefire). In July of that year, a CIRA spokesman claimed responsibility for the bombing of a hotel in Enniskillen. Further acts of violence and attempted attacks followed over subsequent years – with major bombs uncovered, for example, in Belfast (September 1996), Derry (November 1996), Lisbellaw in County Fermanagh (July 1997) and Markethill in County Armagh (September 1997).

It was against this background that the senior RSF member Des Long spoke to a motion at the party's November 1996 *árd fheis* approving a statement from Tom Maguire that 'recognised the Continuity Army Council as the legitimate leadership of the Irish Republican Army Council'. Long told the assembled delegates that he had been 'delighted' by Maguire's recent statement. And he contended that, while RSF 'neither directs or is controlled by the Irish Republican Army',

> ... we as Republicans recognise that while there is an armed British presence in part of our country, it is only logical that Irish men and women will always be prepared to offer armed opposition to that presence.

Long also went on to remind his audience of Maguire's concluding statement:

> I thereby declare that the Continuity Executive and the Continuity

Army Council are the lawful Executive and Army Council respectively of the Irish Republican Army and that the Governmental Authority delegated in the proclamation of 1938 now resides in the Continuity Army Council and its lawful successors.[119]

The integrity of the new group's republican ancestry was thus confirmed. For Ó Brádaigh, Maguire had successfully 'adjudicated' between rival claimants: 'the Provisionals had let things down and it was the Continuity that stepped into the breach.'[120] The RSF leader placed great weight by Maguire's intervention. He would later publish a short biography of Maguire entitled *Dílseacht*, translated as 'fidelity, loyalty, sincerity, love'.[121] Maguire had, Ó Brádaigh argued, 'served the All-Ireland Republic for 80 years of his life and the outstanding characteristic of his career, in both its military and political aspects, was his *dílseacht*, his unswerving fidelity to the Republic'.[122] With such a figure having declared in favour of the CIRA, its legitimacy was judged to be beyond question. In keeping with this, the motion to which Long was speaking was passed. RSF thereby committed itself to playing, in the words of Long, 'a full part in this struggle ... [to] force the British to withdraw from Ireland for ever'.[123]

A year later, at the 1997 *árd fheis* (attended, interestingly, by the Price sisters, more of whom below), a motion was passed which affirmed RSF's position as one of support for 'the historic right of the Irish people to use controlled and disciplined force if necessary to defend the nation's right to freedom and democracy against colonial occupation of any part of the national territory'.[124] This dedication to a belief in the fundamental legitimacy of physical-force republicanism remained an enduring feature of the RSF platform. At the party's 2000 gathering, a motion was passed endorsing 'continued resistance to British rule in Ireland' and in 2001 this was refined to a commitment to support 'the right of the Irish people to use all and every means at their disposal to achieve Irish freedom'.[125]

Thereafter, RSF continued to give rhetorical and ideological support to the Continuity IRA and its cause. In his 2003 address to the party's *árd fheis*, Ruairí Ó Brádaigh declared that there could be no 'full and final closure to the conflict' (an objective famously set by Gerry Adams in relation to the end of the 'Troubles') 'until the British government signals to the world its intention of leaving Ireland forever'.[126] For RSF, it seemed clear that the only way such a withdrawal could be achieved was by violence. It was for this reason that the party was prepared to promote those engaged in such violence. The front page of *Saoirse* for July 2008, for example, acclaimed a recent 'CIRA landmine attack on Brits' and described a 'bomb attack on the British colonial police on the Rellan Road outside Roslea'. Responsibility for the action was said to have been claimed by the 'Fermanagh Command of the Continuity IRA'.[127] Later the same year, *Saoirse* also reported, in approving tones, further CIRA attacks and serious rioting in Belfast and Craigavon. The latter was said to be the work of 'a new generation of young Irish republicans' who had shown that they were 'prepared to take on the forces of British occupation' and had 'intensified [their] resistance'. What the disturbances had shown, RSF declared, was that 'the spirit of resistance has not been quenched despite the efforts of Westminster, Stormont and Leinster House'.[128]

At a hunger strike commemoration in August 2008, a Fermanagh member of RSF, Michael McManus, declared, in an echo of his party president, that their movement would 'continue the struggle until the Brits are gone from our shores'. The Provisionals were criticised for having set aside a key part of the republican armoury: 'they forgot the Armalite and opted for the ballot box only. They sold out to the English.'[129] That same year's *árd fheis* saw RSF unanimously pass a motion 'commending the Continuity leadership of the Republican Movement', while another pledged 'unremitting hostility against the British forces of occupation in Ireland'.[130] In his address to that conference, Ruairí Ó Brádaigh described 'acts of resistance' as 'inevitable in Irish history'.[131]

This line of argument was later replicated by the party's director of publicity, Richard Walsh, after the March 2009 murders, which he described as 'acts of war'.[132] Wearing green camouflage fatigues and a replica Castro beard, Walsh claimed that RSF had

> ... always upheld the right of the Irish people to use any level of controlled and disciplined force to drive the British out of Ireland and secure the all-Ireland Republic. Ireland is no different from any other country in that it has a right to defend itself ... Our history shows that while the British are here, it is inevitable that there will be resistance including obviously armed resistance.[133]

When asked whether the killing of the soldiers and policeman was likely to advance the cause of Irish unity or be counterproductive, he was adamant: 'I wouldn't agree that its counterproductive ... I think for as long as there's a [British] presence then you're going to have resistance. I wouldn't criticise people for that.'[134]

In adopting such a line, Walsh was clearly speaking for his party. The truth of this was further confirmed by the fact that available for purchase from RSF were laminated posters bearing pictures of masked and armed gunmen; so too was a poster that again laid claim to the legacy of Bobby Sands and quoted him under the headline 'Resistance', to the effect that

> There can never be peace in Ireland until the foreign, oppressive British presence is removed, leaving all the Irish people as a unit to control their own affairs and determine their own destinies as a sovereign people, free in mind and body, separate and distinct physically, culturally and economically.[135]

In similar fashion, RSF's 'Republican Resistance calendar' for 2009 offered additional evidence as to the militancy of the party. February, for instance, carried a picture of three masked men holding guns aloft, together with a quote from 'Óglaigh na hÉireann' that read: 'The Irish Republican Army cannot be beaten ... When we put away our guns, Britain will be out of Ireland.' Masked and armed men also made an appearance in April, while September had a photo of young rioters in Craigavon, with the caption referring to 'local people ... resisting British colonial police (RUC) attacks on their homes on August 26, 2008. A new generation takes on the Brits.'[136]

KEEPING THE IDEAL ALIVE

For all the talk of a new generation 'taking on the Brits', one of the most pressing issues facing RSF was the question of whether the party could regenerate itself beyond its founders. The subject of how this might be achieved was one that was addressed in an RSF publication that examined the 'importance of youth' in this period. The document began by pointing to the crucial role of young people in poster-ing/leafleting, selling newspapers and various other activities at '*cumann* level'. It was also claimed that 'at rallies and demonstrations our younger members are always at the forefront' – an assertion that might well be challenged by opponents of the party. Irrespective of the truth of such claims, the pamphlet went on to declare RSF's desire to recruit more young people – whether from other republican groups such as music bands and *Na Fianna Éireann*, or in the form of new people who might be attracted by a 'poster/leaflet campaign'. Furthermore, the same pamphlet acknowledged that

> ... in the modern culture in which we live it seems that image is everything. Many young people believe that what looks good must be good and what looks bad must be bad. While attempting to recruit younger members Sinn Féin Poblachtach [RSF] should not forget this. We should be conscious of our image and attempt to improve it should we find it lacking.

With this in mind, the author went on to note that 'there are also several tee shirts available that our youth members could wear', which would 'stimulate conversation and curiosity about Sinn Féin Poblachtach'. The internet was also (belatedly) recognised as important, though the party felt it already made 'good use of this medium' – again, a not uncontroversial claim to anyone who has visited the RSF website.[137]

In an effort to inject a new vitality into its performance, the party did undergo some changes in leadership in this period. The appointment of Richard Walsh as the party's new publicity officer in 2007 did at least suggest there might be some possibility for a younger cadre to emerge. Even more significant was the 2009 decision of the 76-year-old Ó Brádaigh that he would step down as RSF president, 'for reasons of age and health'. At that year's *árd fheis* he was succeeded by the much younger Des Dalton, from Kildare, who defeated a near-contemporary of Ó Brádaigh's, Des Long, in a run-off for the post.[138]

Still, the extent of change underway within RSF should not be overstated. For one thing, Ó Brádaigh may have stood down as party president, but he moved into a new position as 'patron' of the organisation – a move which suggested he remained unwilling to relinquish all authority over the trajectory of RSF.[139] At the same time, the party's hierarchy continued to be populated by such longstanding republicans as Josephine Hayden, Líta Ní Chathmhaoil and Cathleen Knowles McGuirk. In spite of Ó Brádaigh's resignation, therefore, there seemed unlikely to be any broader transformation in the party's age profile.[140]

Furthermore, the reality of RSF has been that it remains committed to an unchanging vision of what constitutes Irish republicanism. Des

Dalton, soon after his election as RSF president, had delivered an uncompromising message as to his party's view of the Police Service of Northern Ireland, stating that 'while the cap badge might change [from the RUC], the essential point of these forces remains the same. They are to uphold British rule, they are an integral part of the British state forces.' On this basis, he affirmed that RSF continued to 'uphold the right of the Irish people to resist British rule in any way they can, including armed resistance'.[141] Such obduracy was also in evidence as regards the rest of party policy. In November 2008, the party's *árd fheis* had reasserted its commitment to the *Éire Nua* and *Saol Nua* policy documents and the task of building a 'Worker's Democracy in Ireland, free of foreign control'.[142] In his first public address as RSF president in January 2010, Dalton restated his faith in the 'radical programmes for real political and economic democracy', as contained in both *Éire Nua* and *Saol Nua*.[143] The limitations of such political programmes, in terms of their inability to mobilise support, did not appear to deter RSF from remaining loyal to the faith. In 2009, those limitations were once more exposed during local government elections in southern Ireland. At the previous year's *árd fheis*, the party had committed itself to involvement in the contest.[144] In the event, its nine candidates secured a total of 2,473 first preference votes – out of almost 1.9 million cast (or 0.01% of the total). It did succeed in having Tomás Ó Curraoin elected for the Connemara electoral area of Galway County Council, but this represented just 0.1% of the 883 local council seats available in the country. Remarkably, this result was nevertheless hailed by both Ruairí Ó Brádaigh and Richard Walsh as a symptom of the party's vitality, the latter maintaining that it showed 'there is a constituency for us.'[145] In truth, it appeared to mark just the latest milestone on RSF's road towards total political oblivion.

And yet, even if that were the case, it is far from clear that this would be a cause for great concern for Ó Brádaigh. As has been described, he has long been of the view that defeat is preferable to compromise; for him, it is always better to remain pure than to adjust one's views. The outlook of someone like Ó Brádaigh can be gauged from his comment that 'if Sinn Féin gets sucked into the constitutional line, who else is there to speak up?'[146] Ó Brádaigh's self-articulated position has increasingly been that of 'defender of the faith'. Viewed from this perspective, the purpose of RSF is simply to maintain fidelity to a canon of principles that it believes would otherwise be abandoned. In November 2007, following the death of the 105-year-old RSF patron Dan Keating, the front page of *Saoirse* made this point with its affirmation that the 'Republican ideal still burns bright'.[147] Significantly, two months later the Continuity IRA fired shots over Keating's grave in County Kerry and pledged that 'the armed struggle against British occupation continues despite the sell-out and surrender by some former Republicans who now administer British rule in Ireland.'[148]

For RSF (and, indeed, CIRA), it is about keeping the flame going – with the organisation, by its very existence, proving the lie of any claim that the conflict in Ireland might now be closed.[149] In this regard, a useful summation of the party's position can be gleaned from the oration given by Des Dalton, when still vice-president, at an RSF commemoration in August 2008, in honour of two republicans from the 1940s, Richard Goss and Liam Gaughran – the former of whom was executed by the Irish state. Dalton's address was infused with the parallels that were imagined to exist between republicans then and the situation in the here-and-now. Republicans of the 1940s, according to Dalton, had faced death in pursuit of an ideal, even though 'that ideal had been robbed of popular support'. In this context, the question was posed, 'Have they [who were killed] died in vain?' To which Dalton himself had a clear answer: 'Most categorically no ... those men have helped to ensure the continuity of the struggle ... Their sacrifice ensured the survival of the Irish Republican ideal.' Men such as Goss and Gaughran had played their 'part in the historic and ongoing struggle'; and they had demonstrated that 'another generation of Irish Republicans were determined to resist British rule'.[150]

A few months later, when speaking to yet another commemoration (this time for the Derry republican, Sean Keenan), Dalton confirmed that the role of RSF was indeed akin to that which he had outlined for Goss and Gaughran: 'We take up the banner from the generation which passed before us, just as they took it up from the preceding generation. The road ahead is a difficult one but no more difficult than that travelled by Sean Keenan and his comrades.'[151]

In this context too it was apparent that 1986 and the debate over abstentionism – arcane though it might seem to broader developments remained the defining point of departure for those within RSF. Everything else that the Provisionals had been involved with since that point

– whether the peace process, the Good Friday Agreement or IRA decommissioning – was judged to have stemmed from the decision to abandon abstentionism. As *Saoirse* stated in its account of the 2008 RSF Bodenstown Commemoration,

> Since 1922 there have been betrayals by former comrades of the Republican struggle but the latest in 1986 could be viewed as the worst. Erstwhile Republicans had not alone taken their place in a Stormont parliament but had destroyed the weapons which had been acquired for the freedom of Ireland.[152]

The elision here of the events of the peace process and the signal shift in Sinn Féin policy on abstentionism in 1986 was particularly evident. The latter was held to be the critical deviation, from which all the other follies of Provisionalism originated. As Ó Brádaigh stated in his 2008 address to the RSF *árd fheis*, the Good Friday Agreement was to be viewed as merely 'another chapter in the "normalisation" which began formally with the perversion of a majority of the Republican Movement to constitutionalism in 1986'.[153]

It was doubtless because of this outlook that RSF remained resolutely opposed to any concept that the various strands of 'dissident republicanism' might unify to form an alliance opposed to the Provisionals and the peace process. At the September 2008 commemoration for Goss and Gaughran, Des Dalton had declared:

> We hear calls for unity from many disparate elements: Irish Republicans are described as 'elitist' and 'backward' if they are not willing to dilute their programme in the interest of this so-called 'unity'. Irish Republicans want unity. In 1969/70 and in 1986 Republicans resisted those who sought to divert the Republican Movement down the cul de sac of reformism. Many of those most vociferous now in their calls for 'unity' ignored the leadership given by Republicans such as Ruairí Ó Brádaigh and Daithí Ó Conaill who charted a path of unity based on the sure foundations of basic Republican principle. It is true [that] unity is required to achieve the goal of Irish freedom. But it must be a real unity based on a common programme, cohesive and coordinated and based on unequivocal Republicanism. The Republican Movement provides such a programme, it is the only vehicle which can deliver direction and leadership ...[154]

What was required, in Dalton's view, was 'strict adherence to principles'. As for the message of past republican history: 'The lessons are simple; by sticking to the basic fundamentals of Irish Republicanism is the only means to ensure unity of purpose while delivering a clear and coherent message to the Irish people.'[155] The language here was itself striking – pointing as it did to the fundamentalist nature of the republicanism that Ó Brádaigh, Dalton and RSF, as a party, represented.

Clearly, one consequence of this was that RSF could only contemplate working with those who were in total agreement with its policies. There was to be no 'broad church' or umbrella movement for all republicans opposed to Sinn Féin's trajectory or the wider peace process. Rather, those looking for unity would have to accept RSF's outlook in its entirety. In keeping with this approach, the post-1999 RSF 'code of conduct for members' prohibited them from taking part 'in political activities with political groupings such as the IRSP [Irish Republican Socialist Party] or the 32-County Sovereignty Movement or any other body which recognises the Six or 26-County States'.[156] This message was reiterated in 2000, when the party's *árd fheis* confirmed that it was 'not aligned to any political group or groupings which do not share our allegiance to the All-Ireland Republic'.[157] And that same year, one RSF spokesperson declared, with a clear eye on the 32 County Sovereignty Movement (see below),

> ... we are not to be confused with an organisation which has been set up lately, half Provo and half Free State, the two halves adding up to 32. We are the rightful inheritors of the United Irishmen, the Fenians, the patriots of the 1916 Rising, and in our own time the Hunger-Strikers. History will record our faithfulness to the cause of Irish Freedom.[158]

For RSF, the crucial issues remained those upon which it had been founded in 1986. If an individual had stayed with the Provisionals at that point, then they were indelibly tarred with that betrayal. While, as was noted earlier, there obviously was some scope for people to 'come over' to the RSF side after that point (Des Long's 'hand of friendship'), it was equally clear that this required an act of contrition and conversion; an acceptance that Ó Brádaigh and his colleagues had been right all along.

In reality, there was an extreme aversion on the part of the RSF leadership to any link with those who had stayed with the Provisionals in

1986. This much can be gauged from a split that occurred within RSF in November 2008. In that instance, the east Tyrone *comhairle ceantair* (district executive) announced it was breaking away, after the Dublin leadership had ordered it to change the name of a *cumann* (branch) of the party. The *cumann* in question had been named after Jim Lynagh, who was shot dead during an SAS ambush of Provisional IRA men at Loughgall in 1987. The dispute had arisen over the fact that, because the Loughgall killings had occurred after the split that created RSF, the leadership had judged him to be unworthy of veneration. East Tyrone RSF members were thus ordered not to name their *cumann* after Lynagh who, although a renowned IRA militant, had not abandoned the Provisionals over the abstentionism issue. The situation had come to a head when east Tyrone RSF members were told that they would be banned from attending the party's *árd fheis* if they ignored the ruling.[159] In response, they had resigned en masse. At the subsequent gathering, a motion was passed stating that 'Cumainn shall be named solely after persons who have been faithful to the All-Ireland Republic until death.' Typically, during the debate in question, Ruairí Ó Brádaigh had spoken out strongly in favour of the motion. With regard to the men killed at Loughgall, he stated simply, 'with all due respect to them, [they] allowed themselves to be used as cover from 1986 onwards to subvert a large section of the Republican Movement into a constitutional party.'[160] A fellow member of the RSF *árd chomhairle*, John Joe McCusker, likewise stated that the 'Loughgall martyrs', though commendable men, were 'members of an organisation which had accepted the partitionist assembly at Leinster House'.[161]

CONCLUSION

The essence of Republican Sinn Féin was thus again confirmed. This was a party which had taken a stand on what it considered the inviolable principles of Irish republicanism in 1986, and not moved since. Other individuals and groups might have betrayed and corrupted their beliefs, but RSF had not. Its members felt themselves to be *the* irreducible core, whose republican faith could not be distorted by the passage of mere events. Viewed from this perspective, political 'success' was seen as ephemeral and shallow; integrity and intransigence were the only virtues that mattered. The endorsement of the contemporary electorate, such as that attained by Provisional Sinn Féin in the years of the peace process, was judged to be inconsequential when compared with the deeper legitimacy of the RSF position – a position forever sanctified by the 'authority of history'.

Moreover, it was not merely authority that was conferred by history, but also the guarantee of ultimate vindication. Just as Pearse and his comrades had received retrospective sanction from their political successors, so Ó Brádaigh expected the same to occur for RSF:

> In the early days of the twentieth century, republicanism was at a low ebb ... and yet within twenty years it became a dominant force. There was a nucleus there, which in time would take advantage of the situation ... We'll continue to educate ourselves and our followers and build and renew ourselves. But so much will depend on circumstances. We don't believe the situation, as it is, in Stormont, will go on forever ... And as the situation clarifies it will be that much easier to go forward.[162]

To prove his point, he could draw on his own experience of the 'ups-and-downs' of Irish republicanism. When asked if his brand of politics could recover, he was unequivocal:

> Oh yes it will ... I don't think it's a question of if it will; the question is, how long will it take? I often remember being back in Roscommon after the '56-'62 campaign and the year afterwards we were out and had done our rounds selling the [republican] paper ... It was raining and we were sheltering in front of a butcher's shop – it's very clear in my mind – and one of the other lads said to me, 'Will there be another campaign?' And I began to laugh and I said, 'Don't worry about that ... Of course, there'll be another campaign. That isn't the question. The question is, will it be successful? That's what we've to worry about, not whether it will happen or not ...'[163]

The RSF president was in no doubt, in other words, that the wheel would turn again. As long as the Republic remained unfulfilled, there would always be an active Republicanism ready to pursue it.

Surrounded by history books and party papers in his somewhat ramshackle Dublin office in 2009, the 76-year-old Ó Brádaigh was as convinced as ever that there was a future for those, such as himself, who clung to the unadulterated republican faith:

> The real question is, 'Will the idea of the Irish nation survive?' We believe that it will and since we're the people that have upheld that idea through thick and thin, if it does remain and is an important one, then we will be attached to it.[164]

NOTES

1. 'World Leaders Back Stormont Agreeement', BBC News Online, 16 May 1998, available at http://news.bbc.co.uk/1/hi/special_report/1998/05/98/g8/94879.stm
2. 'Huge Yes Vote Welcomed', BBC News Online, 23 May 1998, available at http://news.bbc.co.uk/1/hi/events/northern_ireland/reaction/99329.stm
3. Tony Blair, *Address to the Irish Parliament*, 26 November 1998, available at Dáil Éireann Parliamentary Debates, vol. 497, http://historical-debates.oireachtas.ie/D/0497/D.0497.19981 1260003.html
4. 'Campaign for British Disengagement Continues', *Saoirse – Irish Freedom: The Voice of the Republican Movement* [hereafter simply *Saoirse*], June 1998.
5. V. Kearney, *Belfast Telegraph*, 12 October 1994.
6. Ruairí Ó Brádaigh, *A Permanent Peace Depends on Ending British Rule, Not Updating It: Presidential Address to the 93rd Árd Fheis of Sinn Féin Poblachtach*, Dublin, 9 November 1997.
7. Ibid.
8. See above, page 33. See also, White, *Ruairí Ó Brádaigh*, pp.36, 57, 70–8, 83, 98–9, 106–7.
9. White, *Ruairí Ó Brádaigh*, pp.74–8.
10. Ruairí Ó Brádaigh, interview with the author, Dublin, 24 June 2009.
11. Moloney, *A Secret History of the IRA*, p.79; White, *Ruairí Ó Brádaigh*, pp.152, 162, 203–4.
12. White, *Ruairí Ó Brádaigh*, p.45.
13. Ruairí Ó Brádaigh, interview with the author, Dublin, 24 June 2009.
14. White, *Ruairí Ó Brádaigh*, pp.95–6.
15. Ruairí Ó Brádaigh, *Stormont an Obstacle to Realising Ideals of 1916: Speech Given at the GPO*, Dublin, Easter Monday, 9 April 2007.
16. Ruairí Ó Brádaigh, interview with the author, Dublin, 24 June 2009.
17. Maillot, *New Sinn Féin*, pp.17–18.
18. For a brief discussion of this, see M. Frampton, *The Long March: The Political Strategy of Sinn Féin, 1981–2007* (Basingstoke: Palgrave Macmillan, 2009), pp.10–11.
19. Morrison, cited in 'By Ballot and Bullet', *An Phoblacht/Republican News*, 5 November 1981.
20. '"We Have Now Established a Sort of Republican Veto": Michael Farrell Interviews Gerry Adams, MP, Vice-President of Sinn Féin', *Magill*, July 1983, p.17.
21. Danny Morrison, interview with the author, London, 12 March 2005.
22. See B. Lynn, 'Tactic or Principle? The Evolution of Republican Thinking on Abstentionism in Ireland, 1970–1998', *Irish Political Studies*, 17, 2 (2002), pp.74–94; Moloney, *A Secret History of the IRA*, pp.287–97.
23. Sinn Féin, *The Politics of Revolution: The Main Speeches and Debates from the 1986 Sinn Féin Árd Fheis* (Dublin, 1986).
24. Moloney, *A Secret History of the IRA*, p.288.
25. Sinn Féin, *The Politics of Revolution: The Main Speeches and Debates from the 1986 Sinn Féin Árd Fheis* (Dublin, 1986).
26. Ruairí Ó Brádaigh, interview with the author, Dublin, 24 June 2009.

27. White, *Ruairí Ó Brádaigh*, p.289.
28. Ibid.
29. Hartley cited in 'Electoral Strategy', *An Phoblacht/Republican News*, 7 November 1985.
30. White, *Ruairí Ó Brádaigh*, p.297. It is unclear whether Morrison recognised the parallel with fifteen years earlier. In a report on the 1970 *árd fheis*, one supporter of Cathal Goulding had written how 'The Republican dead were paraded before the assembled delegates and their names invoked infrequently in defence of abstention'. See White, *Ruairí Ó Brádaigh*, p.155.
31. Martin McGuinness, *Oration to Annual Wolfe Tone Commemoration*, Bodenstown, 22 June 1986.
32. Ruairí Ó Brádaigh, interview with the author, Dublin, 24 June 2009.
33. Moloney, *A Secret History of the IRA*, pp.294–6. See also Lynn, 'Tactic or Principle?'
34. White, *Ruairí Ó Brádaigh*, p.302.
35. Ibid., p.293.
36. Ibid., p.308.
37. R. White, *Provisional Irish Republicans: An Oral and Interpretive History* (London: Greenwood Press, 1993), pp.147–63.
38. Ibid., p.157.
39. White, *Ruairí Ó Brádaigh*, p.288.
40. Ibid., p.309.
41. Ruairí Ó Brádaigh, *Address on behalf of the National Executive to the 83rd Árd Fheis of Sinn Féin in the Spa Hotel, Lucan, Co. Dublin, October 24 and 25 1987*.
42. Ibid.
43. Ibid.
44. Ruairí Ó Brádaigh, *Participation in Partition Parliament Denial of Sovereignty: Wolfe Tone Commemoration 2006*, Bodenstown, 11 June 2006, available at http://www.rsf.ie/boden06.htm
45. Ibid.
46. 'Where We Stand: Lecture Delivered by Des Dalton, Árd Chomhairle, in Dundalk, Co. Louth, February 20, 2000', in Republican Sinn Féin, *Where We Stand: Republican Education 1* (Dublin, April 2000).
47. Republican Sinn Féin, *Elections and Abstentionism: Republican Education 3* (Dublin, 2000).
48. Ibid.
49. Ruairí Ó Brádaigh, interview with the author, Dublin, 24 June 2009.
50. Ibid.
51. Cited in Smith, *Fighting for Ireland?*, p.171.
52. 'Léargas: The Brookeborough Raid', RTÉ, 9 July 2006.
53. 'By Principle and Sacrifice Will Ireland Be Free: 1999 Easter Oration in Belfast by Marian Price', cited in *Cabhair Testimonial Journal* (Dublin, 1999).
54. Ibid.
55. Ibid.
56. *Éire Nua: A New Democracy* (Dublin: Republican Sinn Féin, March 2000), pp.15–24.
57. Ibid.; White, *Ruairí Ó Brádaigh*, pp.165, 187.
58. White, *Ruairí Ó Brádaigh*, p.194.
59. 'Federalism Rejected, Positive Electoral Policy Adopted', *An Phoblacht/Republican News*, 5 November 1981.
60. Moloney, *A Secret History of the IRA*, p.183.
61. Ibid., pp.190–1.
62. *An Address to the People of Ireland from Republican Sinn Féin Poblachtach* (Dublin: Republican Sinn Féin, 2003)
63. Richard Walsh, interview with the author, Belfast, 23 June 2009.
64. Ibid.
65. *Éire Nua*, p.3.
66. Ibid., p.11.
67. Ibid., p.12.
68. Ibid., pp.13–15.
69. Ibid., pp.15–24.

70. *Saol Nua: A New Way of Life* (Dublin: Republican Sinn Féin, 2004), p.2.
71. Ibid., p.3.
72. Ibid., pp.5–6.
73. Ibid., p.7.
74. Ibid., p.8.
75. Ibid., pp.8–10.
76. Ibid., p.6.
77. For a discussion of this see P. Walsh, *Irish Republicanism and Socialism: The Politics of the Republican Movement, 1905–1994* (Belfast: Athol Books, 1994), pp.41–2, 103–4.
78. Ruairí Ó Brádaigh, *Stormont an Obstacle to Realising Ideals of 1916*.
79. Patterson, *The Politics of Illusion*, p.186.
80. T. Garvin, *Nationalist Revolutionaries in Ireland, 1858–1928* (Dublin: Gill & Macmillan, 2005), pp.108–41.
81. See Motion 30, *Programme of Motions for RSF Árd Fheis/National Conference, October 13–14 2001*; Motion 28, *Programme of Motions for RSF Árd Fheis/National Conference, 2000*; Motion 47, *Programme of Motions for RSF Árd Fheis/National Conference, October 13–14 2001*.
82. See Motion 25, *Programme of Motions for RSF Árd Fheis/National Conference, 2000*.
83. See Motions 26–9, *Programme of Motions for RSF Árd Fheis/National Conference, October 19–20 2002*.
84. Ruairí Ó Brádaigh, *Stormont an Obstacle to Realising Ideals of 1916*. For more on the 'foreign policy' of RSF see 'Bush Stopover at Shannon en Route to Afghanistan', *Saoirse*, April 2006; 'Shell Protest Escalates', *Saoirse*, December 2006; 'Clarification of Corrib Gas Route Changes Sought', *Saoirse*, January 2009; '"The More the State is Repressing the More the People are Resisting"', *Saoirse*, January 2009; 'Maura Harrington's Jailing Indictment of State', *Saoirse*, April 2009.
85. 'Republican Sinn Féin Must Lead Opposition to British Rule', *Saoirse*, December 2003.
86. Ibid.
87. Seán Ó Brádaigh, *Oration at Bodenstown, 15 June 2003* (Dublin: Republican Sinn Féin, 2003).
88. See Motion 51, *Programme of Motions for RSF Árd Fheis/National Conference, 2000*.
89. See, for example, 'Na Fianna Members Commemorated in Co. Tyrone', *Saoirse*, April 2006; 'Parle, Crean and Hogan Remembered in Wexford', *Saoirse*, April 2006; 'Charlie Kerins Commemorated in Kerry', *Saoirse*, December 2006; 'Edentubber Martyrs Honoured in Wexford', *Saoirse*, October 2007; 'Seán Sabhat Commemorated', *Saoirse*, January 2009; 'Liam Mellows Commemoration in Wexford', *Saoirse*, January 2009; 'Daithí Ó Conaill Remembered', *Saoirse*, January 2009; 'Feargal Ó hAnluain Remembered in Monaghan', *Saoirse*, February 2009.
90. *Charlie Kerins: 50th Anniversary* (Dublin: Republican Sinn Féin, 1994).
91. S. Murphy, *Address Given at Bundoran Hunger Strike Commemoration, August 2000* (Dublin: Republican Sinn Féin, 2000).
92. Ibid.
93. See above, pages 12–13.
94. For an example of this rhetoric, see the Easter Oration given by John Joe McCusker in Fermanagh in 2009, in which he referred to Martin McGuinness as an 'imposter' and 'a Judas goat'. See '1916 Easter Commemorations 2009', *Saoirse*, May 2009.
95. *Beir Bua: The Thread of the Irish Republican Movement from the United Irishmen Through to Today* (Dublin: Republican Sinn Féin, n.d.).
96. D. Sharrock, 'PC's Killing an Act of War, not Murder, Says Republican Sinn Féin', *The Times*, 26 March 2009.
97. Richard Walsh, interview with the author, Belfast, 23 June 2009.
98. Ibid.
99. 'Eternal Hostility to British Rule', *Saoirse*, March 2009.
100. 'No Short Cut, Only the Hard Road of People's Struggle', *Saoirse*, December 2008.
101. Cited in S. Breen, '"Misled" SF Members Urged to Join Former Colleagues', *Irish Times*, 10 November 1997.

102. *Elections and Abstentionism: Republican Education 3* (Dublin: Republican Sinn Féin, 2000)
103. Ibid.
104. *Support Crossan, The POW Candidate: Spoil Your Vote for Political Status*, Leaflet, Republican Sinn Féin, 2001.
105. Tonge, '"They Haven't Gone Away You Know"'.
106. *Stormont Election Manifesto, 2007*, Republican Sinn Féin, February 2007.
107. Ibid.
108. All figures drawn from 'Northern Ireland Assembly Elections 2007', ARK Northern Ireland Elections Website, available at http://www.ark.ac.uk/elections/fa07.htm
109. Cited in *Irish Republican Information Service* (no. 98), March 2007.
110. 'Violence Erupts for Loyalist Twelfth' and 'RSF Condemn Raids and Arrests in Co. Fermanagh', *Saoirse*, August 2008.
111. 'Eire Nua: A New Beginning', 'Shell to Sea Protestors Arrested' and 'Tara's World Heritage Significance', *Saoirse*, August 2008.
112. 'True Republicans are Successors of McManus, Crossan and Duffy', *Saoirse*, August 2008.
113. Motion 47, *Programme of Motions for RSF Ard Fheis/National Conference, 2000*.
114. *Maghaberry Prison Protest*, Leaflet, Republican Sinn Féin, 2006.
115. See, for example, the leaflet entitled *Protest Against US State Department*, Republican Sinn Féin (n.d.)
116. White, *Ruairí Ó Brádaigh*, p.309.
117. Ibid., p.327. See also *Beir Bua: The Thread of the Irish Republican Movement from the United Irishmen Through to Today* (Dublin: Republican Sinn Féin, n.d.).
118. Sean O'Callaghan, interview with the author, London, 12 December 2009.
119. *Speech of Des Long on Motion 16, Dublin, 31 November 1996* (Republican Sinn Féin, 1996).
120. Ruairí Ó Brádaigh, interview with the author, Dublin, 24 June 2009.
121. R. Ó Brádaigh, *Dílseacht: The Story of Comdt. Gen. Tom Maguire and the Second (All-Ireland) Dáil* (Dublin: Irish Freedom Press, 1997), p.1.
122. Ibid., p.3.
123. *Speech of Des Long on Motion 16, Dublin, 31 November 1996* (Republican Sinn Féin, 1996).
124. S. Breen, '"Misled" SF Members Urged to Join Former Colleagues', *Irish Times*, 10 November 1997.
125. Motions 3 and 4, *Programme of Motions for RSF Ard Fheis/National Conference, 2000*; Motion 2, *Programme of Motions for RSF Ard Fheis/National Conference, October 13–14*.
126. 'Republican Sinn Féin Must Lead Opposition to British Rule', *Saoirse*, December 2003.
127. 'CIRA Landmine Attack on Brits', *Saoirse*, July 2008.
128. 'Resistance Flares Up', *Saoirse*, September 2008.
129. 'Follow the Cause, Not the Man – The Cause Will Never Let You Down', *Saoirse*, September 2008.
130. '104ú Ard-Fheis of Republican Sinn Féin held in Dublin', *Saoirse*, December 2008.
131. 'No Short Cut, Only the Hard Road of People's Struggle', *Saoirse*, December 2008.
132. D. Sharrock, 'PC's Killing an Act of War, Not Murder, Says Republican Sinn Féin', *The Times*, 26 March 2009.
133. Richard Walsh, interview with the author, Belfast, 23 June 2009.
134. Ibid.
135. Posters available from Republican Sinn Féin, in possession of the author.
136. *Republican Resistance Calendar 2009*, in possession of the author.
137. *Youth in Republican Sinn Féin: Republican Education 5* (Dublin: Republican Sinn Féin, 2000).
138. 'New Leader for RSF', *Saoirse*, December 2009. See also V. Gordon, 'Ó Brádaigh Quits as Republican Sinn Féin Chief', *Belfast Telegraph*, 28 September 2009; A. Morris, 'Republican Sinn Féin Elects Leader to Replace Ó Brádaigh', *Irish News*, 16 November 2009.
139. 'New Leader for RSF', *Saoirse*, December 2009.
140. Archive webpage from 2006 of 'Leadership', Republican Sinn Féin, available at http://web. archive.org/web/20060718000138/http://rsf.ie/intro.htm; 'Leadership', Republican Sinn Féin, available at http://www.rsf.ie/intro.htm

141. H. McDonald, 'Catholics Who Join Devolved PSNI "in Line of Fire" Says Republican Sinn Féin', *Observer*, 7 February 2010.
142. '104ú Árd-Fheis of Republican Sinn Féin Held in Dublin', *Saoirse*, December 2008.
143. 'Revolution Not Reform', *Saoirse*, January 2010.
144. Ibid.
145. Ruairí Ó Brádaigh, interview with the author, Dublin, 24 June 2009; Richard Walsh, interview with the author, Belfast, 23 June 2009.
146. Cited in English, *Armed Struggle*, p.315.
147. 'Republican Ideal Still Burns Bright', *Saoirse*, November 2007.
148. 'Provisional IRA Urged to Disband', *Irish Republican News* (available online by subscription), 24–30 January 2008.
149. With regard to the CIRA, there were even reports by late 2009 that many within the organisation's leadership no longer believed a violent campaign to be appropriate, but nevertheless remained reluctant to terminate it for fear of relinquishing their position. See J. Mooney, 'Real IRA May Be the Winners of Continuity's Big Split', *Sunday Times*, 4 October 2009. This was later augmented by suggestions of internal division within the group. See G. Moriarty, 'Divisions in CIRA After Meeting of Dissenters', *Irish Times*, 9 June 2010.
150. 'Republicans Must Deliver a Clear and Coherent Message', *Saoirse*, September 2008.
151. 'Eternal Hostility to British Rule', *Saoirse*, March 2009.
152. 'Join the Republican Movement', *Saoirse*, July 2008.
153. 'No Short Cut, Only the Hard Road of People's Struggle', *Saoirse*, December 2008.
154. 'Republicans Must Deliver a Clear and Coherent Message', *Saoirse*, September 2008.
155. Ibid.
156. 'Code of Conduct for Members of Republican Sinn Féin', in *Where We Stand* (Dublin: Republican Sinn Féin, n.d.).
157. Motion 5, *Programme of Motions for RSF Árd Fheis/National Conference, 2000*.
158. S. Murphy, *Address Given at Bundoran Hunger Strike Commemoration, August 2000* (Dublin: Republican Sinn Féin, 2000).
159. 'East Tyrone Members Split from Republican SF', *Tyrone Times*, 4 November 2008, available at http://www.tyronetimes.co.uk/2617/East-Tyrone-members-split-from.4652871.jp
160. '104ú Árd-Fheis of Republican Sinn Féin Held in Dublin', *Saoirse*, December 2008.
161. Ibid.
162. Ruairí Ó Brádaigh, interview with the author, Dublin, 24 June 2009.
163. Ibid.
164. Ibid.

3

Inferno: The Baton is Passed On, 1997–2002

THE REAL IRA

After the split that created Republican Sinn Féin and the Continuity IRA, the mainstream republican movement remained united for a further eleven years. As the Northern Irish peace process developed during the 1990s, however, it became apparent that many Provisionals were less than pleased with the direction in which their leadership was taking them. Discontent focused, in particular, on the not insignificant matter of the IRA ceasefires. Ed Moloney has described the development of increasingly insuperable tensions within the ranks of the Provisionals after the first cessation in 1994. Those who dissented from the 'peace strategy' being pursued by Gerry Adams and Martin McGuinness lined up behind members of the IRA's 'executive' (the internal body that selected the seven-man 'army council' that led the IRA, of which Adams and McGuinness were members). Within that body, the organisation's 'quartermaster general', Michael McKevitt, emerged as a firm critic of the peace process, as did Séamus McGrane, the chairman of the executive. For a period after the collapse of the first ceasefire in February 1996, it appeared as if the McKevitt–McGrane faction might displace the Adams–McGuinness leadership. And yet, as lucidly detailed by Moloney, Adams and his supporters were ultimately able to outmanoeuvre their opponents. By the time of the second IRA ceasefire in July 1997, the truth of this had become increasingly evident. Indignant and marginalised, it thus became clear to those opposed to the peace process that they would have to take their resistance outside of the Provisional movement.

In this way, the Provisional IRA moved towards a second significant split. The actual point of rupture arrived with the decision of Adams and McGuinness to have Sinn Féin endorse the Mitchell Principles on non-violence, so that the party might join the talks process in September 1997. The Mitchell Principles were seen by many on the IRA executive as an infringement of the organisation's constitution and the negation of the IRA's claim to be fighting a legitimate 'war' against British 'colonial' occupation in Northern Ireland. At the same time, concerns over the principles had come to symbolise the broader sense of disquiet over the trajectory of the Provisional IRA. For this reason, opponents of the Adams–McGuinness leadership attempted to engineer a *post-facto* rejection of their endorsement.

In October 1997, an IRA convention was held in Gweedore, County Donegal, to decide which faction was in the right – Adams–McGuinness or McKevitt–McGrane. It was Adams and his allies that won. Thereafter, the dissidents around McKevitt and McGrane resolved to leave the Provisionals and form a new group that would remain committed to the prosecution of an 'armed struggle' against British rule.[1]

Later that same October, a founding 'convention' for what would become known as the 'Real IRA' (RIRA) was held at Falcarragh in County Donegal. John Mooney and Michael O'Toole have claimed that McKevitt and McGrane were joined in the endeavour by others, such as Liam Campbell from Upper Faughart in County Louth and the Dubliner, Pascal Burke.[2] Campbell, in particular, would later be portrayed by McKevitt as a 'real power house of energy' and 'very key' to the new group's emergence.[3] From the outset, the organisation's centre of gravity lay south of the border, with leading members drawn from Cork, Dublin and the border counties. The immediate aim was to initiate a campaign that could put serious pressure on the peace process and reduce the mainstream republican movement's room for manoeuvre. With Sinn Féin party to the negotiations then under way, the hope was that a fresh surge in republican violence would place intolerable pressure on their unionist interlocutors. The expectation was that this would force the latter to withdraw, thereby collapsing the process. (Interestingly, suspicions remain that such an objective may have been to some extent shared by Sinn Féin itself – the difference being that where the dissidents hoped this would bring an end to the peace process altogether, their mainstream rivals felt that republicans could then conclude a deal, in the absence of unionist representation, with the British government.)[4]

The Real IRA joined other militant republican groups that were similarly opposed to both the peace process and any notion that there should be an end to anti-British violence. The Continuity IRA, as has been noted, had been in existence since 1986 and had taken on a more active public persona from 1994. A more long-established group still was the Irish National Liberation Army (INLA), which had prosecuted its own campaign for Irish unity since the mid-1970s.

The INLA had emerged from the 'Official' wing of republicanism in the years after the split that created the Provisionals. In 1972, the Official IRA had called a ceasefire (though thereafter it had continued to engage in 'defensive' operations in Catholic areas of Northern Ireland). By late 1974, several senior members had become disillusioned with the decline in violent activity and moved to establish a new breakaway group. The Dublin-based militant Séamus Costello proved to be a key figure in this departure – playing a central role in the founding of both the INLA and the associated political party, the Irish Republican Socialist Party (IRSP). From the beginning, the INLA became involved in a bitter feud with the Official IRA, a feud which would eventually cost the life of Costello in October 1977.[5] Thereafter, the organisation exhibited a tendency towards factionalism and bloody fragmentation – and in the late 1980s spawned its own splinter group, the short-lived Irish People's Liberation Organisation (IPLO). At the same time, the INLA also showed itself to be capable of serious terrorist violence. It gained notoriety when it assassinated Margaret Thatcher's shadow secretary of state for Northern Ireland, Airey Neave, in March 1979.[6] And in December 1982, the INLA was responsible for one of the worst atrocities of the entire 'Troubles' when it bombed the Droppin' Well Bar in Ballykelly, County Londonderry, killing eleven British soldiers and six civilians.[7]

In subsequent years, though, the group was significantly weakened by the 'supergrass' trials of the mid-1980s, the arrest of its chief of staff, Dominic McGlinchey, and the feud that attended the birth of the aforementioned IPLO. The latter brought the murder of key INLA leaders Thomas 'Ta' Power and John O'Reilly.[8] Prior to his death, Power had sought to define the character of the 'Republican Socialist Movement' in two extended essays, 'An Historical Analysis' and 'Contradictions'. The former, for example, emphasised Costello's ideological legacy and his belief in 'the unity of the National Liberation Struggle and the Class Struggle'. To this end, Power wished the IRSP to engage in 'Revolutionary politics' in an effort to achieve the '32 County Socialist Republic with the working class in control of the means of production, distribution and exchange'.[9] Such ideological reflections, however, were lost amid the violent feuding that characterised the INLA's existence.

By the time of the Provisional IRA ceasefires, the INLA was in a much weakened state as compared to its heyday in the early 1980s. Nevertheless, it retained a capacity for individual acts of violence that carried the potential to derail the peace process. This point had been underlined when several of the group's imprisoned members murdered a fellow inmate at Northern Ireland's Maze prison, the notorious loyalist Billy Wright, in late 1997. In the wake of the killing, the loyalist paramilitaries had come close to abandoning the (imperfectly observed) ceasefires they had called in 1994. Though the government prevailed upon the organisations in question to desist from a full-scale return to violence, the episode had certainly shown the INLA's capacity to intervene in the political sphere.[10] Few could doubt that it continued to pose a serious threat. The Real IRA was therefore far from alone in its belligerent opposition to the fledgling peace process.

In January 1998, the RIRA announced its appearance with an attempted 500-pound bomb attack in Banbridge, which was thwarted by the Royal Ulster Constabulary (RUC). Other more successful operations followed, with the immediate focus on the destruction of urban centres within Northern Ireland. February brought the devastation of Moira and Portadown in Counties Down and Armagh respectively. On each occasion, people were injured (some seriously), but there was no loss of life. In the months that followed, a west Belfast public house was bombed, an explosive device was thrown at a bank in Derry, and there were mortar and bomb attacks on various RUC stations in Armagh city, Forkhill (south Armagh), Belleek (Fermanagh), Kinawley (Fermanagh), Newry (Down) and Belfast. Elsewhere over the same period, police in both jurisdictions on the island uncovered huge bombs, at least one of which (seized in Dun Laoghaire in April 1998) was believed to be destined for central London.

From the moment of the Real IRA's inception, there appeared to be a strong degree of cross-fertilisation and collaboration between the different militant republican groupings. The major bombings mentioned – in Moira, Portadown, Newtownhamilton and Banbridge – were claimed by, or attributed to, variously, the CIRA, the RIRA and the INLA. Irrespective of the strictures against co-operation with other republican groupings adhered to by CIRA-aligned Republican Sinn Féin, CIRA itself (or at least key elements within it) seemed more than willing to liaise with others towards a common goal. RIRA leader Michael McKevitt, for instance, would later describe to an associate how in May 1998 his group had worked alongside the CIRA (after it had approached McKevitt) to exploit an arms smuggling route from eastern Europe. On that occasion, under the terms of a deal reached between the two organisations, each was meant to pay half the overall cost and the RIRA, drawing on McKevitt's long experience as quarter-master-general of the Provisional IRA, was given responsibility for land-ing the weapons in Ireland. However, when the CIRA was unable to come up with its share of the money, the Real IRA kept the entire con-signment of weaponry, which were imported after McKevitt himself made a personal visit to Croatia.[11]

In spite of this abortive effort at co-operation, the Real IRA contin-ued to work with both the CIRA and INLA, as the situation demanded. According to Mooney and O'Toole, the result was an informal *modus vivendi* comprised of three parts: 'The INLA would provide stolen ve-hicles, which the RIRA would transform into car bombs. A mixture of RIRA and CIRA men would oversee the third stage of the strategy by delivering bombs to targets.'[12] More broadly, it would seem that mem-bership of these different groups was not rigidly defined and the bound-aries between them were permeable. Mooney and O'Toole quote one Real IRA army council member as admitting:

> There was a floating membership between the Continuity and the RIRA. Sometimes we didn't know who was in what group. Lads from Continuity would often be asked to take part in an operation for the RIRA. I suppose they took the attitude that they were fight-ing the British and it didn't matter what organisation they belonged to.[13]

The goal of these dissidents was clear: to disrupt the peace process. By their attacks, these 'rejectionist' republicans hoped to create and main-tain a state of instability in Northern Ireland. Much as the Provisionals had done in years gone by, they sought to apply what Gerry Adams had once described as a 'republican veto', which would prevent a perma-nent settlement to the conflict.[14] Ongoing violence, it was believed, would ensure a continuation of repressive legislation, the presence of

British army soldiers on the streets and thereby prove that Northern Ireland was not an 'ordinary' country/state. The impression would instead be sustained that the province was a 'failed entity'.

The advent of the Good Friday Agreement on 10 April 1998 and its endorsement at referendum a little over a month later did little to discourage the new dissidents. On the contrary, it appeared to make them all the more determined to apply violent pressure to the still-fragile political process. On 30 April, a 600-pound car bomb was defused at Lisburn in County Antrim; in the week before the Agreement referendum on 23 May, a similarly large attack was prevented in Armagh city. Earlier that same month, the Real IRA had gained its first 'martyr' when an attempted armed robbery near Dublin had been intercepted by Gardaí and a member, Ronan MacLochlainn, was shot dead. At the funeral in Glasnevin cemetery, MacLochlainn was buried in full paramilitary regalia. Present at the graveside were leading figures from the dissident world, including McKevitt himself – a moment famously caught on tape by a BBC cameraman. The atmosphere was subsequently described in vivid fashion by the writer Kevin Toolis:

> The funeral was supposed to be a republican celebration, a prayer ceremony for the renewal of arms, and an evocative link to Pádraig Pearse who stood at the self-same spot and vowed that from the graves of Irish patriots new nations would spring. The symbolism could have been shovelled on with a wheelbarrow. On the day, the glorious internment of [the] Real IRA's first dead volunteer was a bit more tawdry. McKevitt's small band of supporters looked more like the last dregs of an old army as they gathered outside the run down Dublin council house, peeling with paint. Their faces, men and women, were exhausted, wracked by fags and poverty. Inside in the front sitting room in an open coffin lay McLaughlin. Beside his IRA beret lay a card written on the back of a cornflakes packet. On the front of the card were three letters, I-R-A, coloured-in. Inside in childish handwriting: 'Bye, bye, Daddy' … It was a scene of pitiful sorrow, of abject human folly.[15]

Needless to say, the death of MacLochlainn was not viewed in such caustic light by the leaders of the RIRA. On the contrary, he was held up as inspiration – to be celebrated in verse as had been previous IRA 'heroes':

> A rebel by nature,
> Yet gentle and caring:
> And heir to a conscience
> That would not be sold ...
> He lies where the heroes
> Of Ireland are sleeping ...[16]

The 'Ballad of Ronan MacLochlainn' was testament to the enduring, romantic power of the Armalite. MacLochlainn's death was interpreted by his militant contemporaries as analogous to that of Sean South some half a century earlier (see page 32). Certainly, his passing did nothing to convince the Real IRA's leaders that their campaign was a non-starter. On 22 June a landmine was detonated near the village of Drumintee in south Armagh. Two days later and less than ten miles away, a large car bomb destroyed the centre of Newtownhamilton, injuring six and causing over £3 million worth of damage. By this point, the RIRA appeared to have established something of a rhythm. July began with the blowing up of the Belfast–Dublin railway line near Newry. A 1,400-pound bomb, believed to have been intended for Portadown (to coincide with the ongoing Drumcree parade dispute) was then found abandoned between Moy and Blackwatertown in County Armagh. That same month, the RIRA suffered a further setback when police in London arrested three men (Liam Grogan, Anthony Hyland and Darren Mulholland), who comprised a RIRA active service unit that was planning a range of attacks on the British capital.[17] Notwithstanding this failure, though, the group continued to plan and carry out operations. A 500-pound car bomb was defused outside the Newry courthouse on 13 July and then on 1 August a massive device exploded in the centre of Banbridge, the town the RIRA had tried and failed to hit when commencing its campaign.

In this last incident, the bomb had detonated as police were still in the process of evacuating the area and over thirty people were injured; that no-one was killed was considered by many to be a matter of luck alone. Few now doubted that the Real IRA constituted an increasingly deadly threat to the precarious peace that had been established in Northern Ireland. Through its endeavours, the flame of militant republicanism had been passed on, beyond both the Provisional IRA ceasefire and the Good Friday Agreement. In the late summer of 1998, there appeared little prospect that it could be quenched any time soon.

THE 32 COUNTY SOVEREIGNTY MOVEMENT

Alongside the effort to unleash a campaign of violence, those who led the creation of the Real IRA also sought to open a political front against the peace process. Initially, this took the form of the '32 County Sovereignty Committee' (32CSC), which was 'founded in Fingal, County Dublin, in December 1997' by those Provisional republicans who felt they had been 'marginalised'. Their response was to create a committee to unify them as a bloc, which could also act as a pressure group *within* Sinn Féin.[18] However, the members of this new outfit were soon expelled from the party – on account of their opposition to the Adams–McGuinness leadership. They were physically barred from entering a Sinn Féin *árd fheis* in early 1998.[19] And a formal parting of the ways followed. The 32CSC then reconstituted itself as an independent organisation, subsequently renamed the 32 County Sovereignty Movement (32CSM).

Bernadette Sands-McKevitt, the wife of Michael McKevitt and a sister of the dead hunger striker Bobby Sands, from the start emerged as a central figure in the new grouping. In an interview with the US-based 'Radio Free Éireann' in late December 1997, she discussed at length the formation of the 32CSC and what it hoped to achieve. The ongoing peace process, she said, was 'flawed' and likely to produce only a 'partitionist solution', which would 'pump the life force back into the rotten 6 county corrupt state'. As with the creation of the RIRA, the Mitchell Principles were cited as a key point of contention: 'The acceptance of the Mitchell principles was perhaps the straw that broke the camel's back. We would view the Mitchell document as a partitionist document which guarantees the unionist veto and this in turn undermines Ireland's sovereignty.'[20]

In response to this, the 32CSC had been formed by those concerned 'about the direction in which the peace process is going'. Their aim, according to Sands-McKevitt, was to 'lobby the Nationalist parties' and persuade them to refocus on the 'core issue' of national sovereignty. While claiming to support the Provisional IRA's second ceasefire, she also warned that unless the problems of Ireland were properly addressed, 'there will be further insurgencies in the future.' To indicate what she saw as the only *true* solution, Sands-McKevitt ended the interview by reading a section from Bobby Sands' diary (his final entry, on day seventeen of his hunger strike):

I'm standing on the threshold of another trembling world … I am a political prisoner … I believe in the God given right of the Irish nation to sovereign independence and the right of any Irish man or woman to assert this right in armed rebellion … there can never be peace in Ireland until the foreign oppressive British presence is removed …[21]

There was, therefore, little ambiguity as to where Sands-McKevitt and the 32CSC stood. This was not a political party in the traditional sense, but rather, its members viewed themselves, in the formulation of Sands-McKevitt, as 'watchdogs over Ireland's sovereignty'. This latter point was subsequently underscored in the group's mission statement, which averred, 'We do not claim to be the "Real Sinn Féin" and we are not trying to steal the thunder from any group that does.'[22] Instead, its central impulse was to try and force the Provisional movement to withdraw from what it felt was a defective and dangerous peace process. It set itself in opposition to the foundational parameters of that peace process, which were judged to be inimical to Irish sovereignty, because of their emphasis on the 'consent principle' for Northern Ireland (the notion that the constitutional status of the province could only be altered with the 'consent' of a majority of its people).

Alongside Sands-McKevitt, other prominent members of the 32CSC/32CSM included Joe Dillon, Rory Dougan, Ciarán Dwyer, Michael Burke, Francie Mackey and Marian Price. Dillon was a republican from north Dublin and Dougan a former member of Sinn Féin from Dundalk who had resigned from the party in 1997.[23] Dwyer and Burke were similarly known as hardline, southern-based republicans, the former from Limerick, the latter from Cork; both had previously served prison sentences for Provisional IRA activity (Burke convicted in connection with the 1983 kidnapping of Don Tidey).[24]

Mackey, meanwhile, was a psychiatric nurse at the Tyrone and Fermanagh Hospital, who had also been a Sinn Féin district councillor in the town of Omagh since the mid-1980s.[25] In December 1997, he gave an interview to RTÉ in which he declared his support for the views of the fledgling 32CSC and called on the Sinn Féin leadership to pull out of peace talks. Those talks, in his view, seemed destined to produce an 'internal settlement and thereby copper-fasten partition'. Mackey also said he was specifically opposed to the Mitchell Principles, because of the absolute commitment these required to 'democratic and exclusively peaceful means of resolving political issues'. The unacceptable logic of this, for him, was that 'in effect for Sinn Féin and the IRA [it] should mean the armed struggle is over.'[26] In the wake of those remarks, Mackey was warned by Sinn Féin to end his involvement with the 32CSC or risk expulsion from the party. When he refused to comply, he was forced out.[27] The dismissal, though, did little to dampen Mackey's militancy. In May 1998, it was he who delivered the funeral oration at the grave of Ronan MacLochlainn in Dublin. During his address, he praised the dead man for having 'remained loyal and true to the IRA constitution when others have used and usurped it'. Republicans, he said, had a duty to do 'whatever is necessary' to defend Irish national sovereignty.[28] Mackey's uncompromising message of support for 'armed struggle' and his undiluted vision of Irish 'sovereignty' came to define the 32CSC/32CSM, of which he became chairperson. Alongside him, Sands-McKevitt became vice-chair and Dillon the press officer.[29]

The deep-seated commitment to Irish republicanism that such people brought to the new organisation was best exemplified by the figure of Marian Price. On her own admission, republicanism was, for Price, a 'family tradition'. Her father had been involved in the IRA of the 1940s, while her mother and aunt had both been members of *Cumann na mBan* (the IRA's female wing). The latter had even lost her hands and sight when a bomb she was transporting exploded prematurely. Of her own decision to get involved in the early '70s, Price told one interviewer, 'I made an ideological choice to join. It wasn't a reaction to Bloody Sunday, internment or anything else.'[30] She was, in other words, a natural, true believer when it came to republicanism; for her, there was little sense of the more practical considerations that led many to join the IRA in that era.

After joining the Provisionals, Price was part of a unit that bombed London in 1973 – an episode that led to her arrest and imprisonment. In jail, she spent some 200 days on hunger strike being force-fed. She was freed early, in 1980, because of health problems, but thereafter abjured political involvement because of her conviction that 'to be a politician, you must be a liar and a hypocrite.' Unsurprisingly, for one imbued with such views, over the course of the 1990s she became concerned at the direction in which mainstream republicanism was headed. Eventually, a parting of the ways seemed inevitable. As has been described, by 1997 she and her sister Dolours could be found attending Republican

Sinn Féin *árd fheiseanna*. In 1999, she joined the 32CSM. From there, she refused to condemn violent republican activity, both because of her own past involvement in it and because she viewed it as morally legitimate, on account of the ongoing British occupation. What such activity confirmed, she declared, was that 'there are people out there who don't accept the status quo.'[31] The fact that such people might be in a minority was, in her view, utterly irrelevant. As Price told *The Guardian* in 2003:

> The majority of Irish people have never supported the republican cause ... Most are not willing to make the sacrifices it requires. But as long as there is a British presence in Ireland there will always be justification. Republicanism will never fade. My principles and ideals will never be crushed. I didn't make the choices I did for individuals within the republican movement or Sinn Féin. The fact they've sold out does not belittle me.[32]

Through such words, she confirmed her adherence to an intransigent form of republicanism that gloried in being elitist. For Price, this was a timeless faith – one kept alive by the resort to arms, however limited support for such actions might be.

From the outset, then, the 32CSC/32CSM was close ideologically – and personnel-wise – to the RIRA. Indeed, the founder of the Real IRA, Michael McKevitt, would at one point confide to the FBI agent David Rupert that '32 were all military people and were put there for that purpose to keep army politics in the hands of the military.' McKevitt, according to Rupert, was anxious that all of the '32 people' should be members of the army, because he feared the extent to which political considerations could impede the prosecution of an armed campaign.[33] As he put it on a separate occasion, 'the game at this time is a military one, politics has no place in the military and will not be tolerated.'[34]

Whatever the truth of this assertion – and it should be noted that leading members of the 32 County Sovereignty Movement, including Francie Mackey, have denied membership of the Real IRA – there can be little doubt that the two groups did share a similar worldview. As the 32CSM's website later stated, under a section entitled 'support for the army', it viewed the 1997 split within the IRA in the following way:

> ... a small but significant section of the Army leadership ... [decided] to reorganise Óglaigh na hÉireann along traditional

Republican lines, in the spirit of the Constitution and outside of the Provisionals remit ... the 32CSM understood and agreed with the IRA in its decision to re-organise, this is still our position.[35]

On this basis, the brief for the 32CSM was, in effect, to publicise the cause that united the two organisations – and in the process to create a hinterland of support for the Real IRA and its violent campaign.

Much of the initial energy of the 32CSM was deployed in attacks on the Provisional republican movement, which was said to be in the process of abandoning republican principles. This critique gained added vehemence after the Good Friday Agreement was approved in April/ May 1998. Sinn Féin, it was argued, had settled for far less than was acceptable given the sacrifices of the war. In so doing, the Provisionals were said to be dishonouring and de-legitimising the entire concept of physical-force republicanism. As Marian Price noted acerbically:

> To suggest that a war was fought for what they have today, it diminishes anybody who partook in that war ... It diminishes all that to suggest that this is what it was fought for ... When Séamus Mallon said that the Good Friday Agreement was Sunningdale for slow learners, he hit the nail on the head. It wasn't: it was Sunningdale for retards.[36]

Similar to Republican Sinn Féin, the 32CSM viewed the Provisionals as engaged in a collective act of gross betrayal and stressed the impossibility of there being any end to the conflict in Northern Ireland, short of a British commitment to withdraw. In the face of criticism about their lack of support, as the above-quoted words of Price reflect, the group claimed a natural and innate 'mandate' – of the kind once claimed by the Provisionals themselves. Again, this was not held to be a product of anything so prosaic as electoral support, but rather, was thought to flow from the 1916 Proclamation and the inherent right of the Irish people to national self-determination.

On this basis, the self-ascribed purpose of the 32CSM was to maintain the issue of the allegedly 'illegal' British presence in Ireland on the international and domestic political agenda. To this end, the group lodged an appeal to the United Nations in April 1998 against the continuation of partition through the Good Friday Agreement. The submission drew heavily on the writings of the former Irish government minister and Nobel Prize winner (and one-time IRA chief of staff) Sean

MacBride to condemn Britain's 'colonial policy' and its 'continued military occupation of the six north-eastern counties of our country'. It embraced McBride's assertion that 'For over seven centuries, Britain has sought to conquer Ireland to treat it as a colony'; so too his belief that Northern Ireland had been a 'police state', operating 'a regime of wholesale discrimination'. Space was also given over to a historical analysis of why the Dáil's acceptance of the Treaty in 1921 was illegitimate. By acting as it did, the Dáil was said to have usurped the sovereign decision of the people, when in fact it was 'not within their remit to disestablish the sovereignty of the people'. The 32CSM declared its objective as being

> ... to uphold Ireland's Declaration of Independence as declared by Dáil Éireann on January 21st 1919. We reject Britain's right to occupy any part of our country and to involve itself in any make, shape or form in the affairs of the Irish nation ... Partition perpetuates the British Government's denial of the Irish people's right to self-determination.[37]

That right to self-determination, it was maintained, was enshrined in international law. And to prove the point, the 32CSM evoked the International Covenant on Civil and Political Rights (1966), the International Covenant on Economic, Social and Cultural Rights (1966) and the Declaration on Principles of International Law Concerning Friendly Relations and Co-operation Among States in Accordance with the Charter of the United Nations (1970). In addition, Britain's 'repression and partition of Ireland' was said to contravene the United Nations' Declaration on the Granting of Independence to Colonial Countries and Peoples (1960). For these reasons, the 32CSM asked the UN to investigate British infringements and issue 'an appropriate ruling'.[38]

Overall, the submission was a curious mix. It articulated the standard republican narrative, which stressed historical continuity and the enduring character of Ireland's struggle against *perfidious albion*. At the same time, this was partially re-worked to accommodate an international 'rights-based' discourse, based on the claim to self-determination. While the 32CSM claimed to be not naïve enough to think that its initiative would succeed, it was judged valuable in that it kept the question of 'Irish sovereignty' alive.[39] To publicise their case, Mackey and Bernadette Sands-McKevitt hoped to visit the US in April 1998.

Mackey, though, found that his visa had been refused – a decision he attributed to 'political reasons' arising out of his opposition to the Good Friday Agreement.[40] That setback notwithstanding, Sands-McKevitt did enter the United States and was even able, with the assistance of representative Peter King, to address the 'Ad Hoc Committee on Ireland' in Congress.[41] There, she took the opportunity to denounce the recently made Agreement and put across the arguments of the 32CSM.

In part because of such high-profile events, the 32CSM had clearly generated some concern within official circles, on both sides of the Irish border, by the middle of 1998. What really made the governments take note of the group, however, was the fact that its political initiatives came against the backdrop of ongoing Real IRA violence. It was as a result of this that the Irish government reached out for talks with the group in May of that year. Martin Mansergh, special adviser to the taoiseach, Bertie Ahern, was entrusted with the task of making contact. Fr Alec Reid, the Redemptorist priest who had played such a key role in building dialogue between the Irish state and the Provisionals, was once again the conduit.[42] At Reid's instigation, talks were held in a Dundalk monastery. Present for the 32CSM were Sands-McKevitt, Mackey, Dillon and Dougan; Mansergh was accompanied by an Irish civil servant, in what was described as a 'quite civilised', if unproductive, encounter.[43] As Mooney and O'Toole have described, Mansergh was keen to establish that his interlocutors were representatives of the Real IRA and urged them to abandon the path of violence. Mackey, though, insisted that they were only members of the 32CSM and represented no-one else; his delegation also pressed the arguments as laid out in the group's UN submission.[44] As might have been expected, there was no meeting of minds and the meeting broke up without agreement.

Mansergh did subsequently feel moved to respond formally to the substance of the 32CSM case, sending a letter that stated, 'No breach of international law existing at the present time can be established that would ... now justify further or continued armed insurgency.'[45] That message, however, was not the one imbibed by the RIRA–32CSM. On the contrary, what *had* impressed them was the fact that Mansergh had opted to meet with them at all and on doing so had pressed keenly for a ceasefire. As one 32CSM representative told Mooney and O'Toole:

> Some people in the army got the impression that, because the Government was concentrating on ending the war; that was all

that counted. It made some army people believe that war was the only thing the Irish government would listen to.[46]

Armed with this insight, the Real IRA pressed on with its campaign; alongside it, the 32CSM continued to argue the legitimacy of continued violence in pursuit of Irish 'freedom'.

OMAGH

By the summer of 1998, then, there were grounds for believing that the RIRA–32CSM grouping had the capacity to cause serious problems for the peace process. On the political front, Sands-McKevitt and her allies were putting across a series of arguments, grounded in traditional republican ideas, which seemed likely to cause Sinn Féin severe difficulties. More significantly still, the Real IRA, in conjunction with elements of both the CIRA and INLA, had shown itself capable of posing a considerable militant threat.

All of this was changed, though, by the events of 15 August 1998. On that day a 500-pound car bomb left in the small County Tyrone town of Omagh took the lives of twenty-nine people, including the mother of unborn twins. Among those who lost their lives were eleven children, twelve women and six men. The purpose here is not to delve into the detail of what occurred that day; this has been expertly laid bare elsewhere.[47] The fact that women and children were so heavily represented among the dead, came from across Northern Ireland's sectarian divide and were drawn from all walks of life magnified the impact of the atrocity; so too did the timing of the bombing – coming as it did just a few months after an Agreement that was meant to have ended the province's long-running conflict. Omagh was perceived as unique; the effect it had was profound.

It is not entirely clear which of the dissident groups were involved in the atrocity, but it seems likely that all three may have had some hand. McKevitt would later tell the FBI/MI5 agent David Rupert that, prior to Omagh, the Real IRA had been 'equipping, arming and training' the CIRA who, as an outfit, were 'in a terrible state of readiness'. Omagh had then been a 'joint Op', that was in fact 80 per cent CIRA. On McKevitt's account, the RIRA had stolen the car and built the bomb, but the CIRA had driven it in.[48] Whatever the truth of this assertion, it was upon the Real IRA–32CSM nexus that public attention and opprobrium settled (though the organisation would, in later years, attempt to distance itself from the bomb and claim that the CIRA was more culpable). Soon after the attack, the RUC Chief Constable, Ronnie Flanagan, singled out those linked to the 32CSM as the likely perpetrators and this intensified the pressure on leading figures within the movement. The local priest in Dundalk – where the McKevitts lived – later recounted conversations with a hysterical Sands-McKevitt on the day of the bombing, in which she pleaded her and her husband's innocence in respect to Omagh, saying they had 'neither hand, act nor part' in it.[49] More formally, the 32CSM was quick to issue a statement, in response to Flanagan's allegations, in which it ruled out any connection with the 'terrible tragedy' and stated that the 'killing of innocent people cannot be justified in any circumstances'.[50] Thereafter, the 32CSM emphasised that it was a 'legitimate political group' that was 'completely separate and distinct from any military organisation'.[51]

Such apologias, though, failed to head off the wave of vitriol and harassment now directed at the group and its leaders. After Omagh the Irish prime minister, Bertie Ahern, told the Dáil that he intended to 'crush' the Real IRA and those associated with it. In the first days of September 1998, emergency legislation was introduced by the two governments across Ireland. South of the border, Ahern's government amended the Offences against the State Act with a new set of practices that it, itself, billed as 'draconian'.[52] In terrorism-related trials, courts were now permitted to draw inferences from a suspect's silence when questioned by police. The length of time for which a person could be held, without charge, was extended from forty-eight to seventy-two hours; and a range of new offences were created. The most significant of these was the felony of 'directing an unlawful organisation', which was designed to tackle the leaders of paramilitary groups.[53]

The British government, meanwhile, had recalled both houses of parliament from summer recess in the wake of the attack and secured the passage of the Criminal Justice (Terrorism and Conspiracy) Act 1998. This made changes similar to those introduced by the Irish authorities. Inferences could thus be drawn from a suspect's silence. In addition, in an echo of longer-established practice in the Irish Republic, the opinion of a senior police officer was now to be judged admissible as evidence in cases where suspects were accused of membership of a proscribed organisation.[54]

The crackdown was not confined to Ireland. In contrast to a few months earlier, Sands-McKevitt now found herself refused a visa to enter the US.[55] Even Peter King, her erstwhile patron, described himself as 'appalled and sickened' by the Omagh attack and called on both the Real IRA and 32CSM to 'disband immediately'.[56]

In spite of such criticism, though, the confidence of the 32CSM did not take long to recover. Within days of the bombing, Francie Mackey had felt able to attend a local council meeting in Omagh itself. Not only did he take the opportunity afforded him there to deny any role in what had occurred, but also he asked the council to help him and his family deal with the trauma *he* had experienced since the attack. By the end of August 1998, the 32CSM had issued a further statement demanding that 'those journalists who publicly vilified Bernadette Sands McKevitt and Michael McKevitt by name retract those articles and where appropriate ... issue an outright apology'.[57] The same period also saw the group condemn the introduction of what it termed 'cross-border repression'. The legislation brought in by the governments was said to be designed to 'outlaw all Republicans who will not accept British sovereignty'. It was portrayed as an attempt by the authorities to move against 'legal political organisations like the 32 County Sovereignty Movement, which are clearly separate and distinct from the Real IRA in exactly the same way that Sinn Féin differs from the IRA'.[58] In making such a case, it would seem likely that the 32CSM was being deliberately provocative, drawing attention to what it perceived to be official hypocrisy. The group's leaders would have known, as well as anyone, just how intertwined were the two arms of the Provisional movement. As British prime minister Tony Blair had put it in 1997, 'No one should be naïve about the IRA and Sinn Féin. The two are inextricably linked. One cannot claim to be acting independently from the other.'[59] Yet, in spite of such rhetoric, Blair's government (and that of Ahern) had worked with Sinn Féin throughout the peace process. And in this respect, the case being made by the Sovereignty Movement seemed particularly pointed.

Such defiance notwithstanding, however, there was some recognition within the world of militant Irish republicanism that Omagh had decisively altered matters. In the immediate aftermath of the bombing, the RIRA released a statement accusing the police of failing to heed warnings as to the location and time of the bomb.[60] Nonetheless, on 18 August 1998, the group declared a suspension of 'all military operations' while it conducted a 'process of consultation on our future direction'.[61] A few days later, on 22 August, the INLA announced the cessation of its own (already sporadic) campaign, stating that 'the conditions for armed struggle do not exist'. The 'political situation' was said to have changed and as a result, while

> … the Good Friday agreement was not worth the sacrifices of the past 30 years and [we] are still politically opposed to it, the people of the island of Ireland have spoken clearly as to their wishes … We recognise their desire for a cessation of violence expressed through the referendum and for a peaceful future.[62]

In speaking as it did, the INLA had appeared to acknowledge that the path of 'military' struggle was simply no longer available. The Real IRA soon followed suit. On 7 September 1998, it announced a 'complete cessation of violence'.

Interestingly, the Provisional movement may well have played a critical role in bringing about this move from the RIRA. Post-Omagh, Gerry Adams had stated that, as regards the dissidents, 'We are saying they should stop and stop now.'[63] This was followed by an article in Sinn Féin's newspaper *An Phoblacht/Republican News* which denounced the RIRA as lacking either strategy or credibility.[64] Subsequently, according to Dean Godson, Martin McGuinness had told David Trimble that the Provisionals had stepped in and forced the RIRA to call a halt: 'It was Sinn Féin and republicans who stopped the Real IRA, not British or Irish legislation.'[65] In similar vein, Jonathan Powell's narrative of the peace process contains an intriguing reference to Powell being told by Gerry Adams in April 2000 that the Provisional leadership was 'relying on their supporters in south Armagh to keep the RIRA in check in the pubs and clubs.'[66]

Irrespective of the precise factors at work, it was clear that the various dissident organisations had been forced to reassess the viability of continued 'armed struggle'. Omagh had seemed to show the self-defeating character of such an approach. For a period thereafter, it was tempting to believe that the physical-force tradition in Irish republicanism had finally been extirpated. And yet, those holding to such expectations were to be bitterly disappointed.

REGROUPING: TOWARDS A NEW IRA

Even after the catastrophe of Omagh, militant Irish republicanism did not wholly disappear. The CIRA, for instance, pledged in December 1998 that it would not end its campaign, but would instead try and recruit those disaffected by the RIRA ceasefire.[67] Moreover, it soon resumed its sporadic attacks, as evinced by a series of abortive attacks on RUC patrols and the May 1999 assault on a police station in Lisnaskea, County Fermanagh. The CIRA had always refused to countenance any cessation so long as the British remained in Ireland. Continuity obduracy was held to illuminate the fact that the Provisionals (and now the 'Reals') had ended their campaign short of a British declaration of intent to withdraw – for so long, the PIRA bottom line. In keeping with this, when a political deal appeared to have been reached between republicans and unionists for Sinn Féin's entry into a power-sharing government in Northern Ireland, in return for IRA weapons decommissioning, in December 1999, the CIRA issued a statement calling for PIRA weaponry to be transferred to them:

> Recent events at Stormont and elsewhere have now confirmed our constant warnings of imminent treachery. Any lingering doubts or confusion should now dissipate. Those who for 30 years fought the Crown Forces are now paid Crown agents. Óglaigh na h-Éireann (Continuity) are committed to the cause of Irish Independence and are fully resolved to carry on the struggle. We hereby call on all Republicans to do all they can to assist us in that noble objective. We are aware of a large amount of weaponry and ancillary items under the control of a number of individuals – all that material was procured to defend the Republic and make that Republic a living reality. These arms belong to the Republic and must be under the control of those who will defend the Republic ... all such material should be immediately transferred to the custody of the CIRA to be used for the purpose for which they were acquired.[68]

The contours of CIRA–RSF ideology were again apparent here. The organisation spoke of defending an Irish Republic that was presumed to be already in existence, having been enacted in 1916. The existing states of Ireland, by their very being, were deemed to subvert that Republic; it thus fell to 'Óglaigh na hÉireann (Continuity)' to make it 'a living reality'.

As the new millennium dawned, the CIRA ploughed on. In March 2000, it bombed a hotel in Irvinestown, and a couple of months later it was judged responsible for a failed mortar attack on the RUC station in Rosslea. What such incidents indicated was the extent to which the group's organisational hub lay within County Fermanagh. Nevertheless, it was occasionally able to reach further afield. The CIRA thus continued to pose a genuine threat to the lives of those serving in Northern Ireland's security forces.

With that said, though, 'Continuity' republicanism did not represent the most dangerous of the dissident movements in the post-1998 era. Instead, that 'accolade' belonged to a new group that emerged bearing the title deeds of the Real IRA. Whether going by that label, or simply operating under the banner of 'Óglaigh na hEireann', it was this group, led once more by Michael McKevitt, that was to exercise the authorities most in the first years of the new century. McKevitt, who was subsequently arrested by Gardaí, found guilty at the Special Criminal Court of directing terrorism and given a twenty-year prison sentence, had never renounced the path of militant republicanism. True, he had bowed to the inevitable post-Omagh pressure, which demanded a ceasefire. But McKevitt had always viewed this as an expedient, 'tactical manoeuvre' rather than a permanent shift to a new outlook.[69]

In December 1998, Martin Mansergh had returned to Dundalk to try and get the disbandment of the Real IRA. In a meeting with McKevitt, however, he was rebuffed.[70] Far from being ready to walk away, McKevitt was determined, as soon as the time was ripe, to re-commence a violent campaign. According to Mooney and O'Toole, the groundwork for such a move was laid in July 1999 at a meeting on the Inishowen peninsula, in the Irish Republic, to which former members of the RIRA, CIRA, INLA and PIRA were invited. Under the auspices of McKevitt, it was decided that a new IRA, or second Real IRA, should be created; and to this end, as was customary on such occasions, a new army council and executive were established. McKevitt, it would seem, did not officially join the former body, but in his ongoing capacity as 'quartermaster general', *his* was the real authority within the group.[71] In fact, according to David Rupert, he would later claim that the 'chain of command' ran from him to Liam Campbell, who was once more centrally involved, and thence to Bernadette Sands-McKevitt.[72]

Doubtless such developments were of major concern to the security services on both sides of the border. From the outset, though, they were given a close insight into the workings of this new IRA by the efforts of David Rupert, a paid agent of the FBI who was also working in close liaison with MI5. Rupert, posing as a fervent American supporter of unreconstructed republicanism, had gained access to militant groups on both sides of the Atlantic. Ultimately, this culminated in an unlikely relationship with McKevitt, of whom Rupert noted, 'he and I are very similar on a lot of things' and if circumstances were different, he felt they might have been friends.[73] This remarkable relationship was laid bare in the course of McKevitt's 2003 trial – and again during the 2008–9 civil action taken against the alleged perpetrators of the 1998 Omagh bombing. It offers an extraordinary insight into what McKevitt was thinking and doing, as he attempted to re-launch Irish republican 'armed struggle' in this period. During McKevitt's trial, a substantial element in the defence team's strategy was to target Rupert's credibility and the consistency of his testimony. The judges at the Special Criminal Court, however, concluded that he had been a 'very truthful witness', giving a significant endorsement of his reliability as a source.[74]

In August 1999, Rupert reported to his security force handlers that a member of McKevitt's new organisation, Paddy Fox, had been dispatched on a mission to, variously, the Middle East and Paris, in an effort to build links with other groups abroad. Through such endeavours, the new IRA was said to be keen to work with four groups in particular: hardline Serbs, the Tunisian branch of the PLO (Palestinian Liberation Organisation), Basque militants and radical Cypriots.[75] Also mentioned by McKevitt as possible allies were the Palestinian PFLP (Popular Front for the Liberation of Palestine) (with McKevitt looking to exploit a Cypriot contact to arrange a liaison), the Tamil Tigers of Sri Lanka, and Chechen militants – the latter to be contacted via a gathering of 'liberation groups' in Georgia.[76] As a mark of violent republicanism's ideological promiscuity in the search for assistance, the list of possible allies is highly instructive. A reprise of the Libyan connection, which had proven so beneficial to the Provisional IRA in the 1980s, was said by McKevitt to be now no longer an option, as the regime of Colonel Qadhaffi looked to rebuild relations with the western world.[77] Instead, in the search for funds and material, he found himself drawn to the various non-state actors identified above, as well as the black markets of eastern Europe. The latter was said to be 'awash' with weaponry, as a consequence of the Balkan wars of earlier in the decade. For this reason, McKevitt's initial philosophy was to attempt to buy 'cheap disposable weapons of the most destructive capacity' on the European market. His attitude was that even if these were intercepted, it would be 'no great loss', though if they got through, so much the better.[78]

Alongside this, McKevitt also appeared to expect that Rupert could source more hi-tech equipment for the new group from the United States. During the informer's trips to Ireland, he more than once met members of the new RIRA's 'engineering department' and was furnished with shopping lists of equipment to pursue on his return home.[79] More broadly in the United States, McKevitt was determined to secure the backing of the most militant Irish-American republican support groups.[80] These had the potential to deliver substantial financial resources. One estimate, for example, of the amount raised for militant republicanism in Chicago alone, in this era, gauged it to be between $20,000 and $40,000.[81] It was as part of the effort to tap into such funding that McKevitt had embraced Rupert as both genuine and reliable: he hoped that Rupert might deliver 'unity of all support' within Irish America for his group.[82] The American had come to the attention of McKevitt as a Chicago-based member of the Irish Freedom Committee (IFC). Over time, Rupert had risen to become a member of the board of directors of that group, which ostensibly raised money to support the dependants of republican prisoners, through such events as the annual 'Michael Flannery Testimonial Dinner'.

The IFC had been set up in 1987, by Flannery and another American republican veteran, George Harrison, as a solely US-based and organised entity.[83] It counted within its ranks many former members of NORAID, the group that had for much of the 'Troubles' worked to raise funds for the Provisional republican movement. In similar vein, the IFC set its mission as being a mixture of education and fundraising. From the beginning, while it declared itself to support fully the political analysis of Republican Sinn Féin, it remained a US-controlled entity, unlike NORAID, which was felt to have fallen wholly under the direction of the Provisionals. In this way, the IFC was the creation of those, like Flannery, who had grown concerned about the trajectory of both NORAID and the Provisional movement. In the years after its formation, it worked independently to proselytise a traditional republican message, analogous to that of RSF in Ireland.[84] In 1998 though, efforts were made to broaden the character of the IFC and transform it from being a purely east coast entity, which was effectively an RSF support group, into a 'national umbrella organisation'. An attempt was made to re-orientate the group away from exclusive support for RSF–CIRA and towards support for all Irish republican prisoners who were opposed to the Good Friday Agreement. It was the taking forward of this agenda that was pursued by David Rupert, after he had entered the labyrinthine world of Irish America, via the Chicago IFC; at least that was the *prima facie* view of his activities. And it was, in turn, this that allowed Rupert to ingratiate himself with McKevitt.

Rupert won over the RIRA leader with promises that he would help move the IFC away from its pre-existing sponsorship of Cabhair (the RSF–CIRA-linked prisoner organisation), and towards patronage of the 32CSM–RIRA-aligned Irish Republican Prisoners Welfare Association (IRPWA). According to Rupert, he was assured by McKevitt that this latter entity was under 'complete control' of the RIRA.[85] Moreover, McKevitt would also later tell Rupert that all IFC money sent to Ireland went to 'military use'; the only exception being if the IRPWA was in need of assistance, when they would 'help them out'.[86]

In all of this, a key assumption was that the Irish group offering the most militant outlet for American funds would be likely to secure the vast majority of the available financial support; certainly, this was the basis upon which Rupert, in his public persona of hardline RIRA supporter, set about trying to shift the allegiance of the IFC. In this endeavour, he was aided by Martin Galvin, a former publicity director at NORAID and a vocal champion of the Provisional IRA. Galvin had broken with the Provisionals over the 1994 ceasefire and remained committed to the notion of 'armed struggle'. As such, he was considered an influential figure in hardline Irish American circles. Despite such backing, though, Rupert found that he faced opposition to his proposed changes from the New York City branch of the IFC. By the spring of 2000, the result was a split within the organisation. Rupert and his allies were charged with being under foreign control (that of McKevitt in Ireland). Ironically enough, of course, there was more than an element of truth in the accusation: Rupert *was* trying to bring the IFC under the ambit of the Real IRA, as desired by McKevitt. In keeping with the Machiavellian atmosphere present in US-based Irish republican circles, though, such claims were met with strenuous denials from Rupert and his supporters.

Ultimately, a significant section of the IFC was persuaded to follow the Rupert line – in large part because they were impressed by his assertion that he could speak for the 'army' back in Ireland. At one stage, it appeared that McKevitt wanted this to be literally the case, with the suggestion being that Rupert should occupy a de facto position on his new army council, thereby allowing him to act as a guarantor for the disbursement of US funds.[87] Ultimately, it would seem that this proposal came to nothing. Still, Rupert felt that McKevitt had given him a 'kind of blanket authorization', which meant he was to be viewed as the American 'spokesman' to the army council.[88] He later reported that, to bolster this image, at least one hardline republican, Thomas Noel Abernathy, was dispatched to meet him in the US in April 2000.[89]

The very fact that McKevitt was willing to sanction such an expedition by an important lieutenant was a sign of the importance he attached to the effort to secure the American support base. Access to US financial aid was clearly considered a prerequisite for any sustained campaign of violence. This much was confirmed too by Rupert, who noted of McKevitt that his 'philosophy' on running the RIRA came down to two things: discipline and finance.[90] The conduit to the United States promised to go a long way to ensuring the latter was in place. Along with bank robberies, extortion, smuggling and other illegal fundraising, it was an indispensable source of income to the group. With it in place, McKevitt could focus on matters within Ireland.

PREPARING FOR A CAMPAIGN

Towards the end of 1999, the RIRA leader appeared confident that his revitalised Real IRA was increasingly well organised across Ireland. By his estimation, it had taken some '98%' of Continuity IRA members and supplanted the RSF–CIRA faction as the leading expression of dissident republicanism.[91] Such an assessment accorded with Rupert's own estimation of RSF vitality. He had previously attended the 1999 *árd fheis* of Ó Brádaigh's party and reported that it was an organisation in its 'death throes'. Still, at one point McKevitt did appear to envisage a potential use for RSF, with it possibly providing political cover to his new IRA. The 32CSM was described at this time as possessing only a 'lobbying' function and consisting of no more than four people: Joe Dillon, Bernadette Sands-McKevitt and two others. Perhaps because of this, McKevitt had explored the option of an alliance with RSF and he even detailed Rupert to explore possibilities for co-operation. It was suggested that a secret 'co-ordinating council' might even be set up to link the RIRA, 32CSM, RSF and various support groups in the United States.[92]

In the end, though, efforts to establish some form of collaboration were to prove in vain. By Rupert's account, the stumbling block was McKevitt's relationship with Ó Brádaigh. Disagreement between the two men was said to reach back to the time of the 1980–1 hunger strikes, when McKevitt had allegedly wanted to kidnap four members of the British House of Lords, together with one each of their sons, and hold them captive in a cave where they could be starved in parallel with the fasting of the hunger strikers. This audacious/hair-brained scheme had apparently been vetoed by Ó Brádaigh, much to the lasting chagrin of McKevitt.[93] Neither was this the last occasion on which the two found themselves at loggerheads. As mentioned previously, during the 1986 debates on abstentionism within the Provisionals, they had taken different sides, with McKevitt supporting the Adams–McGuinness leadership. Thereafter, he appeared to have been unimpressed with the stance taken by Ó Brádaigh. Indeed, McKevitt would later tell Rupert that, in his view, Ó Brádaigh was not all that different from Gerry Adams, in that his interests were 'personal', rather than for Ireland.[94]

More broadly, there appeared to be enough hostility to any rapprochement, within both the new IRA and RSF, to ensure that co-operation between the two would not be forthcoming. On the one hand, there was an enduring animosity dating from the aftermath of the Omagh bombing. Many within the Real IRA's senior ranks felt that the Continuity IRA had betrayed RIRA when it denied all responsibility and even condemned the attack.[95] At the same time, one aging member of RSF reputedly told Rupert that an alliance would occur only over his dead body; elsewhere, it was suggested that Ó Brádaigh's son, Ruairí Óg, was a leading voice of opposition against any inter-group affiliation. It was in part because of this resistance that McKevitt's enthusiasm for the venture soon diminished. Of greater significance, though, was the fact that he had come to believe he could achieve his objectives without the RSF link-up. As has already been mentioned, McKevitt reckoned his new organisation to have all-but swallowed up the CIRA.

By November 1999, he had come to see the latter as a 'joke', while also feeling that RSF would 'die a slow death'.[96] Increasingly, McKevitt's only concern for the CIRA was that it might attempt an attack, to prove it was still in existence, and risk making a mistake – worsening the atmosphere in which a forthcoming RIRA campaign would be launched.[97] This was an outlook shared by his close associate, Séamus McGrane. In conversation with Rupert, he dismissed the CIRA as incompetents, who had even conspired to lose a bomb built for them by Real IRA engineers (the car in question was allegedly stolen).[98] With such an attitude prevailing among the RIRA leadership, it was scarcely surprising that prospects for co-operation seemed negligible.

Irrespective of any half-pursued liaisons, it would seem that by the autumn of 1999, McKevitt was looking towards a six-month period of preparation before the launch of a full campaign of violence. The focus was to be on a military push, targeting the British state, with it envisaged that an initial strike would be directed at the British military presence or London's financial district.[99] A key aim here for McKevitt was to ensure that it would 'overshadow' what had happened at Omagh.[100] The 1998 atrocity clearly loomed large in his thinking. It was for this reason that he told Rupert that they would avoid issuing claims of responsibility for attacks. The aftermath of the Omagh bombing – which had involved both the CIRA and INLA, but which would forever be associated with the Real IRA – had convinced him that such admissions were counterproductive. McKevitt's new approach was largely one of 'no claim no blame', on the basis that 'it was better to let the press have it and make their story as big as they wanted'.[101] With that said, the RIRA leader did appear ready to make occasional use of the 'Continuity IRA' label as well. In one encounter with Rupert, McKevitt told him that this was a tactic used by his men to spread some of the 'heat' after an attack – even though, in reality, the CIRA 'for all intents and purposes does not exist.'[102] Eventually, McKevitt maintained, his group would take full responsibility for their actions – but only when they were strong enough and had definitively put Omagh behind them. Initially, though, he felt they would be best served by the confusion that would follow a failure to claim attacks, particularly among the security services.

Similar concerns over the legacy of Omagh ensured that McKevitt had also ruled out a return to the use of car bombs in Northern Ireland.

He did so because of a fear that the security services would intercept one and redirect it to kill civilians.[103] The RIRA leader claimed that the only suitable target for the use of car bombs was central London.[104] The overriding aim was to 'raise absolute havoc with the Brits but [to] do it in a way that would absolutely minimise the chances of loss of civilian life'.[105] In arguing thus, McKevitt displayed not only his concern that there be no 'new Omagh', but also his belief in the sinister omnipotence of the security services (a characteristic which made it all the more surprising that he so readily accepted Rupert's *bona fides*).

Alongside this, McKevitt also spoke of his desire to practise 'cyber terrorism', which he envisaged as taking place, not as a substitute for conventional bombing, but as a complementary tactic.[106] McKevitt was keen to impress on Rupert the capabilities of his new group, which he claimed exceeded those of the Provisionals. In time, he would boast of their technical sophistication, especially in the form of 'clean skins' who were unknown to the security services.[107]

In all of this, there was little consideration of more 'political' avenues – at least in the sense of electoral, party politics. As McKevitt told Rupert, 'the game at this time is a military one, politics has no place in the military and will not be tolerated.'[108] In line with this outlook, McKevitt was vehement in his denunciation of Gerry Adams and Martin McGuinness as 'sell-outs'. At the same time, though, he was equally adamant that they would not be targeted by the RIRA, as they were not the real enemy; that status being accorded to the British only. Instead, the hope of McKevitt and his followers was that the betrayals of the Provisionals would speak for themselves – especially with regard to weapons decommissioning. On this issue, Rupert would report that both McKevitt and Liam Campbell felt that if the Provisionals carried out any actual decommissioning, then it would create serious opportunities for RIRA recruitment. The strategy was to give Adams time to 'hang himself', to give him the space to 'tighten the noose around his neck'.[109]

Moreover, it was on this basis that the Real IRA deliberately sought to avoid a direct confrontation with the Provisionals. Such a conflict had, according to McKevitt, almost taken place several times, and to some degree the two sides were both 'girding' for that. Indeed, it was to this end that McKevitt had instructed one of his subordinates to prepare 'dossiers' on senior Provisional republicans, which would prove useful in the event of a feud.[110] Nevertheless, he feared that his new organisation could not survive a full-frontal clash. It was his hope simply that decommissioning would foment disarray in the ranks of his rivals – and eventually generate a steady slew of recruits to the RIRA. Such a process of gradual erosion, it was felt, would only be stalled by a head-on collision between dissidents and mainstream republicans. Instead, the key was for McKevitt and his group to bide their time and, little by little, establish themselves as a 'viable alternative' to the Provisionals.[111]

Elsewhere, preparations for the launch of the new campaign were hampered by the arrest, in October 1999, of the key RIRA figure Séamus McGrane at a training camp in County Meath. In that incident, it was later thought that McKevitt himself had come close to being detained. Whatever the truth of this, he subsequently attempted to play down the seriousness of McGrane's capture. It was, he told Rupert, a 'bruise', but one from which the group could 'easily' recover. Thereafter, the Real IRA's planning went forward and in early February 2000, Rupert was told by McKevitt that they were 'ready to go'. By this stage, the RIRA leader claimed that a 'shadow council' had been set up, 'to run things in case the main players went inside'. They could, McKevitt contended, withstand arrests and still maintain violent activity. The only thing holding them back was their perception of where the peace process was headed at that time. Significantly, McKevitt indicated that what he wanted was for a new deal to be achieved (between Sinn Féin and David Trimble's Ulster Unionists), which would allow for the re-creation of the Stormont institutions, alongside IRA weapons decommissioning. In the event of such an outcome, the Real IRA was set to issue a statement denouncing the Provisionals' latest capitulation, and then launch a formal campaign.[112]

The belief was that, in this context, a large number of Provisionals could be persuaded to switch allegiances – including several who had previously been sent to warn off the Real IRA post-Omagh. Already, by early 2000, McKevitt was pointing to recent membership 'coups', both in terms of ex-Provisional recruitment in the Tyrone area and the coming over of former CIRA people from Fermanagh (the latter development was judged by him to be the cause of the bombing of a hotel in Irvinestown on 6 February 2000, as the CIRA leadership unsuccessfully tried to 'woo back' its members).[113] The outworking of the peace process

– and the restoration of Northern Ireland's institutional framework – was expected to reap further dividends for the dissident cause.

During a meeting with Rupert in February, McKevitt gave the impression that he thought a resolution at the political level might take a further two months. He had, however, perhaps failed to anticipate the insurmountable nature of the crisis in the process, which had led to suspension of the Northern Irish Executive and Assembly (after just six weeks). As the depth of the problems became apparent, it would seem that the campaign start date was brought forward. That this should have been so was a function of McKevitt's analysis as to why the Real IRA had failed previously. When reflecting on the earlier campaign of 1997–8, McKevitt told Rupert that they had made two mistakes: working with the CIRA; and allowing their agenda to be dictated by 'political reasons', as opposed to 'military strategy'. The RIRA leader was now determined that their actions would be governed solely by military considerations.[114]

There was, in other words, to be an autonomous impulse to the activity of the resurgent Real IRA. For all that McKevitt and his associates were conscious of the wider political issues, they did not ultimately feel bound by them. The campaign was emphatically not to be contingent on a broader context; and in the event it commenced regardless of that context.

BACK IN BUSINESS

In January 2000, the Real IRA leadership released a statement under the banner of 'Óglaigh na hÉireann'. It noted the 'tremendous sacrifices' of the previous century and affirmed, with pointed intent: 'In every generation the Irish people have rejected and challenged Britain's claim to interfere in Ireland's affairs.' After condemning 'Britain's rejection and continual usurpation of Irish sovereignty', the statement concluded by quoting Patrick Pearse: 'Ireland unfree shall never be at peace.'[115] The organisation was signalling its determination to prove the truth of Pearse's prophecy; action soon followed.

On 25 February 2000, a bomb partially exploded outside Shackleton barracks in Ballykelly, County Londonderry. A few days later, police recovered a rocket launcher, which was believed to be destined for an impending attack in the Dungannon area of County Tyrone. Further incidents followed: March brought the interception of 500lb of explosives at Hillsborough in County Down; April saw the bombing of another army barracks, this time Ebrington in Derry itself; and May saw both hoax device-induced chaos in Belfast and a failed mortar attack on an army observation post near Crossmaglen in south Armagh. Thereafter the focus switched to the British mainland. On 1 June 2000, a bomb exploded underneath Hammersmith Bridge on the Thames in London. No one was hurt and the structure did not collapse, but the damage was sufficient to cause serious disruption. More importantly, Britain's capital had been hit by a successful terrorist attack for the first time since the second IRA ceasefire of 1997. Furthermore, the message to be gleaned from this burst of activity was clear: the Real IRA was back in action and posed a potent threat. The anticipated decommissioning of Provisional IRA weaponry had not occurred, but McKevitt had clearly decided the moment to strike had arrived. The RIRA leader saw these early operations as his organisation getting its 'feet wet'. They were, he told Rupert, now definitely 'back to war', though as intended, they were eschewing claims of responsibility for the time being, until he felt they were ready to stand the 'heat'.[116]

There was still a strong expectation that PIRA decommissioning would follow at some point and this would work to the benefit of an already-operative Real IRA. Nevertheless, over time it became clear that the predicted rush of recruits would not materialise. Of the Provisionals' approach to decommissioning, McKevitt told Rupert that they were 'telling their people one thing and the politicians another … [but] in fact what they are telling the politicians is the truth'. In spite of that, however, he now acknowledged that they had skilfully created enough ambiguity to dilute the impact of the process.[117] That process had seen the creation, in May 2000, of an inspection regime of Provisional IRA arms dumps by international observers. According to Rupert, McKevitt did not expect this to yield a significant boost for his own organisation. The way it was handled, he felt, had averted a groundswell of opposition from the republican grassroots. There would, therefore, be no flood of converts and the RIRA was faced with a slower process of gaining support, spread out over years. To this end, the purpose of the first attacks of the campaign was merely to gain support: '… he knows it will take more and more daring attacks to actually cause the Brits to capitulate.'[118] It was about displaying a capacity to act and proving that they could move beyond

Omagh.[119] The strike against the British capital was an important part of this strategy; so too, the geographical spread of attacks in Northern Ireland, from the north-west to the south of the province.

Late June/early July 2000 brought a bomb attack on the Belfast–Dublin railway line at Meigh Bridge in south Armagh – an operation that McKevitt later described as essentially a training exercise, which also sought to test the response of the security services.[120] More serious was the detonation of a car bomb outside a police station in Stewartstown in County Tyrone, the first car bomb to be deployed by the Real IRA since Omagh. In the drive to 'take the war to England', meanwhile, it was clear that McKevitt was thinking big. Rupert had previously been informed that the group had a sleeper agent in Boston in the United States. This man, a South African former member of the Foreign Legion, was judged an expert assassin, who was to be called in 'at such time as they decided to do a hit on [prime minister] Blair or that level of target'.[121] Though not quite of that magnitude, 2000 brought further high-profile attacks on the British mainland. In July, for instance, a bomb was left at Ealing Broadway tube station in west London, while a suspect package was also uncovered at Whitehall, the heart of British government. Two months later, on 20 September 2000, the group made international headlines when one of its operatives launched a rocket-propelled grenade at the headquarters of the secret intelligence service, MI6. McKevitt subsequently lauded this attack as a 'real winner' and vastly preferable to such incidents as the Stewartstown car bomb, which ran the risk of ending in 'catastrophe'. In line with this, he spoke of his desire to carry out four MI6-style operations a year against what he considered 'prestige targets'. As to what this meant in practice, he gave as an example a possible attack on the British gun boat stationed in Carlingford Lough on the Irish border. This vessel had 'long been a target' and, apparently, McKevitt felt inspired by the al-Qaeda assault on the USS *Cole* in Yemen (in September 2000). This had suggested to him a way to carry out the assault, via a 'remote control device' that could steer a boat carrying explosives to the target – remote control making up for the absence of Irish suicide bombers.[122]

Alongside such vistas, the RIRA chief also wanted to deploy smaller devices and hoax alerts every three to four weeks, targeting the British railway system and other key infrastructure. There were, he claimed, several teams on the British mainland ready to act on a rotational basis, to cause maximum disruption. Naturally, London was identified as a particularly key target; indeed, it was central to the reformed Real IRA's strategic thinking. The hope was that ongoing attacks in Northern Ireland would show that, irrespective of arguments to the contrary, the conflict was not settled. Simultaneous strikes on London would then sway public opinion there, against a continued commitment to the province, as people became 'sick of the delays and gridlock and the insurance companies sick of the [damage] claims'. The result, it was imagined, would be a clamour calling on the government to withdraw from Northern Ireland.[123]

Though rudimentary, the approach did at least carry some logic – even if that logic itself rested on some highly questionable assumptions (as shown by the Provisional IRA's failure to secure victory when operating a similar strategy from a more advanced base). Irrespective of such problems, the Real IRA was determined to press ahead, fuelled by McKevitt's conviction, as relayed to Rupert, that this was 'the last chance for armed rebellion in Ireland'. To succeed, he was determined to 'mount a viable campaign'.[124]

The relatively efficient opening of that campaign doubtless encouraged McKevitt that things were running his way. From the United States, in the summer/autumn of 2000, Rupert could report that the surge in Real IRA activity had generated a 'lot of enthusiasm' and reinforced the readiness of many within the IFC to support McKevitt's organisation in preference to the CIRA, which was decried as a 'do nothing geriatric brigade'.[125]

Back in Ireland, meanwhile, the leadership of the RIRA-aligned 32 County Sovereignty Movement felt confident enough to issue a veiled challenge to the Provisionals within their west Belfast stronghold. In August 2000, a meeting was held by the organisation's prisoner support group, the IRPWA, at Brennan's Bar in that part of the city. Held under the banner '*Craic agus Ceol*', the official purpose of the event was to raise funds for dissident republican prisoners.[126] Based on his conversations with McKevitt, however, Rupert offered a different assessment of an event that was 'all to do with turf and nothing to do with fundraising'. It was about challenging the Provisional republican movement in its own heartland and testing the latter's willingness to respond.[127] Viewed from this perspective, the Brennan's Bar gathering seemed to indicate the mounting confidence of the RIRA–32CSM nexus and its members' growing sense of their own strength vis-à-vis the Provisionals. It also signalled the return of the 32CSM as a public force, actively making a case that could justify Real IRA attacks. The same month, members of the movement travelled to Geneva in Switzerland for the 'First International Conference on the Right to Self-Determination and the United Nations', organised by the somewhat eccentric 'International Human Rights Association of American Minorities', in the hope that they might establish a new set of relations with would-be foreign sponsors/supporters.[128]

After the short period in which McKevitt had looked to Republican Sinn Féin as possibly providing a public crutch to his covert, military outfit, he had fallen back upon the 32CSM. This was still not to be a 'political party' in the fullest sense and there was to be no question of the 32CSM enjoying a separate personality. Predominance continued to reside firmly with the 'military' entity and it was at no stage envisioned that the 32CSM would engage in constitutional or electoral activity. Still, the political wing was viewed as having a role to play. It was to prepare the ground ideologically for the Real IRA – to contextualise, explain and legitimise its activity.

In line with this, in January 2000, the 32CSM's 'new year' statement had described the Good Friday Agreement as offering nothing but the 'modernisation of the 1921 treaty'. The reality, it declared defiantly, was that 'the Republic cannot be suppressed or defeated.'[129] Sinn Féin, by dint of its support for the Agreement, was said to be 'giving international respectability to what is fundamentally an armed occupation of a small country by the British imperialist parliament'. On this view, the Agreement constituted 'the greatest danger ever to the restoration of national sovereignty to the Irish people …'.[130] This message was expanded upon in the group's Easter missive for 2000, which affirmed that even though 'recent years have seen dark days', now 'Republicanism is rebuilding.' The 32CSM described itself as 'the inheritors of the Republican creed so many, indeed too many, have had to die to uphold' and it offered a 'clear message to the British militarists':

> … as surely as you have been challenged by every other generation of Irish people you will be challenged by this one. The British state is making a very serious mistake if they take co-option of the Provisionals into the British system as the defeat of Irish Republicanism.[131]

The core impulse here was one of defiance, with the implicit threat of violence to come. Reference was made to the traditional republican narrative and the extent to which 'the Republic' and *true* Irish sovereignty remained fulfilled. The RIRA–32CSM nexus was laying claim to the banner of authentic republicanism – a banner allegedly set aside by the Provisionals on their acquiescence in the Good Friday Agreement. As Real IRA-affiliated prisoners declared in Easter 2000, 'We are not dissidents but the true standard-bearers of the Republican Movement.'[132]

In keeping with such a view, the 32CSM continued to draw attention to the perceived shortcomings of the Provisional movement, particularly when Sinn Féin was felt to have suffered a political reverse. Thus the suspension of the institutions in February 2000, after the Provisional IRA had declined to begin decommissioning, was said to prove that the 'Stormont Deal was a poor deal for Irish Republicans'. No-one, it was claimed, should have expected anything else. What was required, according to the 32CSM, was 'for all to return to a Republican strategy that will end British rule in Ireland and restore true democracy'.[133] In similar vein, the March/April 2000 edition of the group's bi-monthly newspaper *The Sovereign Nation* claimed that the suspension of the Agreement was a 'seminal moment', which underscored the fact that the peace process worked to 'a humiliation agenda'. The same edition quoted Francie Mackey as declaring, 'The reality the Provisionals have to face is that, having, as Brendan Hughes recently put it, "left the heart of Republicanism behind", they are powerless to oppose what is still quite clearly the political hegemony in the six counties, that is British state-backed Unionism.' The 32CSM argued that it was time for people to consider alternatives to the Provisionals: 'The luxury of wallowing in anger or despair at the direction in which the Stormont process sidetracked Republicanism has been well and truly cast aside.'[134] Instead, the moment for active opposition was said to have arrived.

Subsequently, when the spring 2000 crisis in the peace process was resolved by the deal which allowed for the inspection of Provisional IRA arms dumps, an article on the 32CSM website rebuked the 'embarrassing scale and speed of the U turn' performed by the Provisionals. They had, it was said, 'desecrated the memory of those Republicans, both from previous generations and those of the past three decades, who sacrificed their lives attempting to end British rule in Ireland'. For this reason, it pronounced that it was 'time for the Provisionals to take the honest decision and cease using the political label of Republican'.[135] Only the 32CSM, it was claimed, could genuinely lay claim to such a mantle.

Significantly, in a clear echo of McKevitt's approach to recruitment on the 'military' side, the lion's share of this criticism was aimed at the Provisional movement's leadership – with a view to persuading 'grass-roots' republicans of the 32CSM's case. *The Sovereign Nation* was clear that the peace process represented a 'leadership sell-out', which was likely to have caused 'consternation and disbelief' among lower-ranking Provisionals.[136] This line of argument was developed further in the years that followed. On one occasion, the 32CSM's close US-based ally Martin Galvin asked, 'How long will Sinn Féin remain party to a British Stormont administration which tries to criminalise Republican political prisoners? How long will the Republican grassroots, who understand, and feel this issue so deeply, allow them to do so?'[137] Elsewhere, as the Provisional IRA moved towards actual weapons decommissioning (first carried out in October 2001), the 32CSM again attacked what it described as the 'Machiavellian Provisional leadership' around Gerry Adams and Martin McGuinness; the destruction of weaponry was said to be merely the 'logical conclusion of their current political strategy'. The very readiness of the Provisionals to consider decommissioning was held to be just one symptom of 'the political cancer' that had 'infested that movement in recent years'. Again, the point was pressed that having apparently accepted the legitimacy of British rule in Ireland 'in perpetuity', the Provisionals had 'permanently removed themselves from the Republican family'.[138]

In a further reproach to the course taken by Sinn Féin, the senior 32CSM member Marian Price told the group's June 2000 annual general meeting that what she termed the 'Michael Collins "stepping stone" theory', as adhered to by the Adams–McGuinness leadership, had been a 'disaster', which carried 'dire' implications for 'Irish Republicanism as an ideology'. She invoked republican history to claim that the Provisionals were merely following in the footsteps of the Official IRA ('the Sticks'): 'what we are witnessing today in the present political process in the North is merely the implementation of the old Gardiner Place, Sticky adage of "using the system to overthrow the system".' This, she averred, was absurd and destined to fail, with those pursuing such a strategy merely becoming part of that system.[139]

The strength of this critique can be gauged if one considers the depth of hostility that had long existed between the Officials and the Provisionals. To take but one small example, Éamon Collins, in his account of life inside the republican movement during the 1980s, described an incident in which, during a heated exchange, he accused Gerry Adams of speaking like a 'Stick'. In Collins' words:

> [Adams] looked shocked. I had hit him with the accusation that his competitors within the Provisional republican movement had been levelling at him since he first became the movement's most charismatic figure since Pádraig Pearse and Michael Collins. There was no greater insult that one Provo could level at another than to accuse him of following in the footsteps of the Official IRA.[140]

Now, the 'Sticky accusation' was very much part of the armoury of the Provisionals' opponents. For Marian Price and others it stood as an absolute indictment of where their former comrades had ended up. To quote Price again, they had engaged in the 'blatant and disgraceful sell-out of every principle and belief which genuine Irish Republicans hold dearly'.[141]

It was for this reason that Price and her fellow members of the 32CSM felt compelled to articulate an alternative republican viewpoint. As she would put it on a separate occasion, 'We can't let it go down in history that this was what the war was fought for … We have to get it recorded in history that this is not what Republicanism is about.' To some extent, Price's position as a 'dissident' was driven by a self-legitimising imperative, based on her understanding of what drove 'republicanism' – both on an organisational and personal level. As she explained:

> I do not apologise for any actions taken by the Republican Movement, but I always believed that the justification for it was that we were fighting for a greater cause, and that in many ways, the end justifies the means. But now, we're being told that this is the end. But this end didn't justify any of the means that have been used. Sunningdale was actually better than what we have on offer today![142]

In her opinion, the Provisional leadership should have pursued a fundamentally different course from the one it embarked upon in the

1990s: 'if they had come to the conclusion that the war was going nowhere, that we couldn't win ... [they should have had] the moral courage to say "the war is over, and we didn't win."' Instead, what Price claimed to find most objectionable was the 'dishonesty around the whole so called negotiations'. And it was the gap between Provisional rhetoric and the reality of what the movement had achieved which fuelled her critique of the peace process and Agreement.[143]

Price was not alone in making this case. In March 2001, the 32CSM followed up its original submission to the UN with an 'addendum' which focused on the iniquities of an agreement that had 'not brought the peace and stability promised'. The Agreement was said to have singularly failed to deal with the root cause of the problems in Ireland (the 'British presence') and instead produced only 'a steady upsurge in violence'. To press their view, delegates from the 32CSM even attended a session of the UN's Human Rights Committee in 2001. Yet, in this sphere, as previously, they achieved little – other than serving notice that the organisation was once more active.

Elsewhere, however, the theme of an 'unchanged 6-County State' was one that the 32CSM repeatedly emphasised in this era. During the Holy Cross primary school dispute in north Belfast in 2001, for instance, it condemned the 'gauntlet of sectarian hatred' to which it claimed Catholic children were being subjected. The 'raw bigotry and naked sectarian hatred of the Loyalist protestors' was vehemently denounced; and the whole incident was said to have exposed the lie of 'the so-called benefits of the peace process'. The reality, for the 32CSM, was that 'very little tangible change has actually been delivered across the six-counties.'[144]

A range of other 'evidence' was cited to demonstrate this latter point. The Northern Irish criminal justice system and RUC thus remained a constant source of antagonism for the 32CSM. In January 2000, for instance, a press release condemned the decision of the director of public prosecutions not to prosecute police officers allegedly involved in making death threats against the lawyer, Rosemary Nelson (who was murdered by loyalists in a car bomb attack in March 1999). The episode was said to be 'another horrific chapter in the long sordid history of the RUC, a history that spans eight decades of murder, repression and human rights abuses'.[145] The possibility that such a police force could be reformed, as provided for under the Good Friday Agreement, was emphatically ruled out. Bernadette Sands-McKevitt rejected the 1999 Patten report on policing, which aimed to do just that, stating, 'They will remain the highly equipped paramilitary force they have always been.' In her view, 'the religious make up of any police force in the six counties is of no interest to republicans. While any force upholds British rule in Ireland, it will be rejected by Republicans.'[146] Naturally, the shift in Sinn Féin's position on policing across this period, from one of 'Disband the RUC' to a call for the government to 'implement the Patten report', was the subject of extensive negative comment from the 32CSM.[147] The Provisional movement's leadership was said to have been 'deceived by the imperial conjurer's sleight of hand' and accepted only 'cosmetic changes' to an unreconstructed force. The 32CSM, by contrast, remained opposed to the RUC, the 'primary bulwark of British rule in Ireland'.[148]

Beyond the deficiencies of the police, the subject of republican prisoners was one that dominated much of the activity of the 32CSM and its Irish Republican Prisoners Welfare Association (IRPWA) offshoot. It was for this reason that the 32CSM set up its first committee in England in April 2000. A central focus for this branch was to be a campaign for the 'repatriation' of republican prisoners incarcerated on the British mainland (specifically, Tony Hyland, Liam Grogan and Darren Mulholland – three students who had formed a Real IRA 'active service unit' that was arrested in London in July 1998).[149] To protest against their particular 'plight', supporters were urged to write to Jack Straw, then home secretary.[150] In November 2000, the 32CSM hosted an IRPWA function at 'The Cock Tavern' public house in north London to raise funds for these and other 'political prisoners'. Efforts were also made to raise funds via the internet, with the IRPWA website offering visitors the chance to buy 'hand-made craftwork [made] by Republican POWs', such as mirrors (£75), bodhráns (£70), belts (£20) and handkerchiefs (£15).[151]

Within Northern Ireland, meanwhile, attention was focused on the alleged plight of prisoners being held in the high-security prison at Maghaberry.[152] By late 2002, republican inmates there had launched a protest in which all forms of co-operation with the prison authorities were withdrawn – and they were being punished in return. As a result, according to the IRPWA, 'tensions between republican prisoners and the authorities in Maghaberry jail have reached boiling point.' What was required, it was maintained, was a shift in the authorities' policies, with the granting of four demands: the segregation of republican and loyalist prisoners; the separation of long-term from short-term prisoners; a 'recognition [of republicans] as a grouping and political status'; and an end to the 'harassment of prisoners' families and visitors'.[153] To this end, the IRPWA and 32CSM were prepared to work with others including the IRSP and even Republican Sinn Féin (for once, setting aside its prohibition on intra-republican co-operation). The groups set up a steering committee to campaign for segregation, 'as a first step on the path to the Restoration of Full Political Status'. This aimed to copy the model of the H-Block-inspired agitation of the late 1970s–early 1980s and was called the 'Republican Prisoners Action Committee'. Comprising thirteen people, RSF and the IRPWA each made £100 donations to set up the group.[154]

Here, significantly, the publicity drive of the 32CSM was backed up directly by threatening language from the Real IRA. In May 2001, for instance, the latter had issued a statement which claimed that 'presently, in Maghaberry Prison republican prisoners are being ill-treated and denied political treatment.' Prison wardens, it was said, would therefore be held 'personally responsible for ill-treatment of captured Irish insurgents or [for] being involved in any attempt to criminalise them'.[155] This was reiterated the following March when the RIRA declared, 'If I were a prison officer I would be watching my back … in the past those within their ranks have paid a hefty price for their failed attempt at criminalising republicans.'[156] Similarly, the 32CSM also drew attention to the situation in Portlaoise in the Irish Republic, where it claimed republican prisoners were enduring 'beating[s] and brutalisation'.[157] An IRPWA statement linked events north and south, declaring, 'this approach by the administration in Portlaoise and Maghaberry is part of a dual strategy by the British and Free State governments to crush all true republican opposition to these nefarious political and counter insurgency policies.'[158]

On a variety of issues, therefore, it became clear in the period after 1999 that the 32CSM and its affiliates were determined to make their voices heard. In June 2000, to mark its wider resurgence, the Sovereignty Movement adopted a new constitution. This asserted, in familiar fashion, that 'the sovereignty and unity of Ireland are inalienable and indefeasible [sic].' It looked back to 'the Declaration of Independence, in word, deed and spirit, as established in 1918 and ratified by Dáil Éireann on January 21st 1919' and declared resolutely that 'partition is illegal.' On such reasoning, the organisation avowed to 'reaffirm the right of the Irish people to use *all legitimate means necessary* [emphasis added] to restore National Sovereignty'. As to what this meant in practice, there was reference only to the effort to foster debate, the importance of seeking support for national unity and engagement in 'an educational programme, agitation and fund raising', alongside attempts to establish 'international links in support of our objectives'.[159] Herein, there was little or no hint of the group's reported relationship with the Real IRA; indeed, the 32CSM formally denied any substantive link with the RIRA.[160] Nonetheless, few in official circles were prepared to accept such assertions.

Later that same year, Adam Ingram, MP, the junior minister at the Northern Ireland Office, affirmed that, in the eyes of the government,

> With regard to the relationship between the 32 County Sovereignty Committee and the Real IRA, the Government believe that they are two sides of the same coin. The 32 County Sovereignty Committee is RIRA's political wing, and as such the two are inextricably linked.[161]

In response, Francie Mackey declared defiantly that 'The 32 County Sovereignty Movement refutes allegations made that our movement is "inextricably linked" with any military organisation.'[162] And this position was later finessed further when Mackey again repudiated 'the spurious claim from pro-establishment journalists' that the 32CSM was 'linked to any military organisation'. The group's true position, according to Mackey, was simply that:

> Through well researched fact, we recognise why Irish men and women have for generations become volunteers in the IRA to end foreign armed aggression against Irish citizens and to uphold the ideals of the 1916 Proclamation, ratified by the Irish people with the Declaration of Independence. It is that position that the volunteers of Óglaigh na hÉireann claim to uphold and they view themselves as the legitimate army protecting national sovereignty against the armed aggressor. This position is difficult to disagree with ...[163]

Clearly, this was a long way from being an unambiguous disavowal of physical-force republicanism. And indeed, both Mackey's comments and the use of the phrase 'all legitimate means necessary' in the constitution of the 32CSM were pregnant with an unspoken endorsement of political violence. At times, certain members of the group were ready to make this more explicit. In May 2000, for example, Peadar Ó hAnnain of the 32CSM had written to *The Irish World* newspaper to declare that the organisation 'reaffirms without reservation the right of the Irish people to armed struggle in pursuit of national sovereignty'.[164] Elsewhere, Marian Price was typically unapologetic in declaring that:

> Armed struggle does have a place in the present and the future. I would say it's something I would not rule out ... another generation is going to have to take up the torch of republicanism and fight on ... It [physical-force republicanism] will continue while there is a British presence in Ireland.[165]

In a similar vein was the address Price gave to a January 2001 discussion forum celebrating the legacy of the 1981 hunger strikes. There, she stated, 'we affirm the role of the physical-force Republican tradition and Movement in Irish society.' The hunger strikers, Price noted, had all been 'members of either the Provisional IRA or the INLA, two organisations with very specific and definite political objectives and which engaged in ruthless and widespread violence to achieve those political ends'. She then invoked republican history to argue that 'our Republican forefathers, whose noble path the hunger strikers trod, never relied upon a popular mandate to pursue their political aims and campaigns of violence.' From 1916 down to 1997, Price maintained, successive generations had pursued physical force, often in difficult circumstances, because they believed 'in the inalienable right of the Irish nation to self determination and sovereignty and the right of the people of Ireland to use violence if need be to achieve their political ends'.[166]

Taken as a whole, then, there was little doubt that the 32CSM had re-established itself as an active political force, prepared to occupy and espouse ideological positions analogous to those of the Real IRA. At the group's June 2000 AGM, Francie Mackey had used his speech as chairperson to declare defiantly:

> Let me say loud and clear, the 32 County Sovereignty Movement is here to stay. Our analysis is gaining increasing support. We are

the only credible alternative in upholding the Irish people's right to National self-determination. There can be no attempt to ride two horses. Either you are with us in challenging British rule in Ireland or you are a collaborator.[167]

At the same gathering, Martin Galvin declared, 'We will continue to challenge the British for as long as it takes to end their rule in Ireland for ever.'[168]

The fact that the 32CSM could still command a level of support vastly inferior to that enjoyed by the Provisionals was felt to be no impediment to their self-assigned mission. Indeed, as already indicated, the group seemed to relish their minority status; for this, with its resonance of 1916, appeared only to bear out the sense that they were, as they claimed to be, 'the true inheritors of the republican creed'. In the eyes of the 32CSM, the leaders of the 1916 Easter Rising, 'although small in numbers, [had] proven to be correct'.[169] To people like Sands-McKevitt, Price and Mackey, this confirmed the extent to which they were following in the proper footsteps of their republican forbears. It was possible to see, in their own numerical weakness, the strength of ideological purity; and from this the conviction that they were the elite, republican vanguard of the contemporary generation. As Mackey would himself put it, 'History has shown that when many lost their nerve and threw up their arms in surrender, there were always the few and the brave to keep the faith and carry on the torch of republicanism on behalf of our future generations.'[170] The 32CSM, together with the Real IRA, now felt themselves to embody the 'few and the brave' of contemporary Ireland.

By autumn 2000, there were various reasons why those at the head of these groups could believe that the future was promising. The 32CSM had been reconstructed and was displaying a new public vigour in pressing its case. Simultaneously, as has been described, the Real IRA had shown itself capable of mounting a serious, violent challenge. David Rupert's accounts of the period reflect the growing confidence of Michael McKevitt that his group was making advances and growing in strength.[171] In conversation, McKevitt talked of the importance of taking a long-term view, with a view to building things up over two or three years. The RIRA leader did acknowledge that there were still problems – not least in terms of finance, which remained a major issue.[172] To rectify this, what McKevitt most wanted was an 'affiliation with another government', though he did also continue to look to a range of non-state actors as well. The aforementioned conference in Switzerland (in 2000) was seen as presenting various opportunities in this regard, with McKevitt anxious to secure State sponsorship for his new IRA; but the attendees (from the 32CSM) had failed to make the requisite contacts – much to his annoyance. The only positive benefit to emerge from the excursion was the establishment of a relationship with a group of Native Americans who had offered help and attorneys in the US to combat visa denials.[173] And yet, despite the endurance of such concerns, McKevitt's outlook was clearly imbued with an optimism that things were moving ineluctably forward. As Rupert reported, for the RIRA chief, 'it is like a relay race and right now the baton has come to him. If he goes it will go on ... he will carry the torch and if it is not successful it will go on to others.'[174] Behind the scenes, as much as in public, therefore, there was clearly a sense within the RIRA/32CSM universe that they were, as Mackey had declared, 'here to stay'.[175]

RESPONSES

In the face of this Real IRA/32CSM resurgence, the Irish government again sought talks with the group in September 2000. The taoiseach, Bertie Ahern, had previously sanctioned meetings with McKevitt in the aftermath of the Omagh attack (though whether or not these occurred prior to, or after, the RIRA ceasefire was disputed).[176] Now the link to the Real IRA, via Martin Mansergh and Fr Alec Reid, was reactivated. The initiative proved unrewarding, though, with a self-assured McKevitt informing them that he was not interested in dialogue; the only actor he wished to speak with, he insisted, was the British state. The only subject he said he was prepared to discuss was the age-old republican demand of British withdrawal from Ireland.[177]

A more pugnacious response to the rejuvenation of McKevitt's organisation came from a new and unexpected source: the Omagh Support and Self-Help Group (OSSHG). Founded in the aftermath of the 1998 bombing of Omagh, the OSSHG existed to represent those injured or bereaved in the attack.[178] Together with Victor Barker, the OSSHG, under the leadership of Michael Gallagher, developed a determination to pursue and confront, wherever possible, the men they believed to be responsible.[179] They set about campaigning against the Real IRA and the 32 County Sovereignty Movement, urging the government to take action, but also stepping forward to challenge dissident republicanism directly themselves. The 32CSM–IRPWA meeting in west Belfast in August 2000 had thus been accompanied by a protest of OSSHG members outside Brennan's Bar. Typically, the 32CSM attempted to dismiss this protest as simply part of an 'an orchestrated campaign to halt the event'.[180] The group accused the chair of the OSSHG, Michael Gallagher, of 'entering into the political arena and infringing on the rights of groups and individuals'. And in his speech to the 32CSM gathering, Martin Galvin claimed that if the event had been cancelled the 'real victims' would have been 'the wives and children of Irish political prisoners, and the Republican prisoners themselves'.[181] Marian Price added that 'sinister British elements' lay behind the OSSHG campaign.[182]

Such insinuations, however, failed to deter the members of the OSSHG, who continued to target the 32CSM and its activities. A particular focus lay in efforts to disrupt websites that were felt to be of ideological, or financial, support to the Real IRA. It was for this reason, for instance, that they lobbied Amazon to exclude the 32CSM from its 'associate programme', which linked the Amazon website to other online sellers. Under this scheme, Amazon paid up to 15 per cent in referral fees (plus bonuses) on subsequent purchases made. A website generating one thousand new customers for Amazon could thereby expect to earn up to $5,000. The 32CSM had encouraged visitors to 'support our prisoners' by shopping via their link to Amazon. Yet, under pressure from the OSSHG and after taking advice from the US State Department, Amazon terminated the connection.[183]

More significant still, meanwhile, was the fact that some within the OSSHG announced, in October 2000, that they would seek to finance a civil action against the Real IRA members they believed to be responsible for the 1998 attack.[184] Less than a year later, a writ of summons had been issued at the High Court in Belfast, to the effect that proceedings were being taken against five men: Liam Campbell, Séamus Daly, Séamus McKenna, Michael McKevitt and Colm Murphy. Significantly, it was as part of the effort to distance these individuals from Omagh that in December 2001 the Real IRA issued a statement (in response to the Ombudsman's report into the bombing) which claimed that 'MI5 handled two agent provocateurs' who were actually part of another

organisation and had been 'instrumental in the planning and implementation of the bombing that occurred that day'. The RIRA admitted
to having co-operated in the attack, but denied being to blame for it –
a claim that flew in the face of their contemporaneous admission of
responsibility. To explain the latter, the organisation argued that,
'Because of this co-operation and their use of our code word for three
warnings, we felt a moral obligation to accept responsibility for the
bombing.' The reality, it was asserted, was that the organisation had
had only 'minimal involvement in this terrible tragedy'.[185] Such
attempts to put space between the Real IRA and Omagh, however,
proved less than successful. In July 2002, the individuals concerned
were finally served with the writs.[186]

In response, the 32CSM again alluded to the supposedly 'darker'
forces, underpinning the OSSHG. It was worth asking, it suggested,
'whose agenda' lay behind the lawsuit, which was described as part of a
'nationwide witch-hunt' and 'unprecedented campaign of personalised
demonisation'. The 'understandable' anger of the Omagh victims was
said to be subject to 'cynical exploitation by counter-revolutionary elements in the media and political elite'.[187] Such allegations, though, did
not discourage those pursuing the case. Instead, the OSSHG would
remain a constant presence in the years that followed, a serious impediment to McKevitt's professed desire that his group might put Omagh
'behind it'. Ultimately too, the civil action initiated by some of the families would end in (widely unexpected) triumph. In June 2009, Mr Justice Morgan delivered a verdict that found four of the five men –
McKevitt, Liam Campbell, Colm Murphy and Séamus Daly – together
with the Real IRA as an organisation, liable for the 1998 bombing
(McKenna was absolved of any liability). Damages of £1.6million were
to be awarded to the families who took the action.[188] At the time of
writing, an appeal is pending, but for now, the judgment stands.

The ongoing legacy of Omagh was far from being the only obstacle to
McKevitt's ambitions in this period. No doubt of more pressing concern
for him in 2000–1 was the fact that the British, Irish and American
governments also signalled a greater determination to interdict his
movement's evolution. On 24 November 2000, it was announced that
the Irish minister for justice, equality and law reform, John
O'Donoghue, and the British secretary of state for Northern Ireland,
Peter Mandelson, had jointly requested that the American authorities

initiate a process to have the Real IRA 'designated' as a terrorist entity in the United States. The move came in response to a report commissioned by both the Garda commissioner and the Chief Constable of the RUC, which had weighed the likely benefits/drawbacks of such a step and concluded in favour of the shift (though here too, the pressure for designation coming from the OSSHG was also important, particularly in bringing the Irish government to shift position). It was hoped, in particular, that this would seriously inhibit Real IRA fund-raising in the US, which, as noted, was a key concern for McKevitt.[189]

The criteria for designation required that the organisation in question 'must engage in terrorist activity, or terrorism, or retain the capability and intent to engage in terrorist activity or terrorism'. It was also necessary that the activity in question threaten the security of US nationals or the US state. In recommending the Real IRA for inclusion, therefore, the British and Irish governments hoped to have it explicitly and internationally identified as a terrorist entity, with a capacity to damage US national security. A key consequence of this would be that American citizens, or those subject to US jurisdiction, would henceforth be prohibited from 'knowingly' providing 'material support or resources' to the group. In addition, members of a designated 'Foreign Terrorist Organisation' (FTO) would not be permitted to enter the United States.[190]

On 16 May 2001, the State Department officially added the Real IRA to its FTO list, along with any organisation operating under the banner of the 32CSM, 32CSC, RIRA and IRPWA.[191] The move came as a bitter blow to McKevitt's hopes that Irish America could provide major sponsorship to his organisation. In response, the 32CSM and IRPWA appealed through the courts for a judicial review of the State Department's decision, arguing that they had been unfairly traduced. Martin Galvin stated, in a submission to that appeal, 'To the best of my knowledge, 32 County does not have any members in common with the Real IRA, is a legally separate and distinct organisation, and does not provide material support to that group.'[192] This claim was endorsed by the putative head of the IRPWA in the US, Ann Loughman, who claimed that 'the IRPWA does not have any members in common with the Real IRA.' Both testimonies, however, were countered by the Irish government's assessment of the groups, as provided to the US State Department, that 'the relationship which exists between the Real IRA

and the 32 County Sovereignty Movement is such that the two organisations are inextricably linked, with key personalities holding dual membership. The 32 County Sovereignty Movement plays a subordinate role
to the Real IRA.' Further, the Irish authorities were clear that 'All facets of
the activities of the 32 County Sovereignty Movement are directed and
controlled by selected personalities with dual roles in both organisations.'
The IRPWA was said to be a 'sub-committee' of the 32CSM, created in
1999 and itself 'inextricably linked with the 32 County Sovereignty
Movement and the Real IRA'. These conclusions were supported by an additional judgment supplied by the British government – and ultimately
accepted by both the US State Department and the District of Columbia
Appeals Court.[193] In June 2002, the judge hearing the case denied the ap-
pellants a petition for a judicial review of the State Department's ruling;
the RIRA–32CSM coalition remained on the American FTO list.[194]

Within Ireland itself, meanwhile, not everything was running to plan
for McKevitt. In October 2000, Liam Campbell was arrested by Irish
police on charges of Real IRA membership. Not only did this deprive
the organisation of one of its most senior members, but also intensified the pressure on McKevitt personally. In the judgment of David Rupert, McKevitt was now forced to take greater 'hands on' control of
RIRA operations. At the time, the Real IRA leader still believed himself
to be 'untouchable', with the authorities 'afraid to take him out'
because he had too much support; but it was clear that the greater
responsibility increased his potential level of personal exposure.[195] The
possible consequences of this were doubtless emphasised by other successes achieved by the Irish police in this period. In March 1999, Colm
Murphy had become the first man to be charged in connection with
the Omagh bombing. Almost three years later, in January 2002, he
would be found guilty and given fourteen years for conspiring to cause
an explosion. This verdict was overturned in January 2005 and at his
re-trial in February 2010 Murphy was found not guilty.[196]

Elsewhere, in spite of McKevitt's avowed desire to avoid a feud, it
was clear that the Provisional IRA was stirring and taking steps to block
a major Real IRA revival. In February 1999, it was reported that the
Tyrone-based dissident Paddy Fox had been kidnapped and held captive
for a period by known Provisionals.[197] Other incidents of allegedly overt
hostility followed. In March 2000, for instance, there were suggestions
that senior figures in the Provisional IRA in west Belfast had threatened

a member of the 32CSM for selling *The Sovereign Nation* in 'their' area.[198] Most seriously, on 13 October 2000, the man said to be the Real IRA's Belfast commander, Joseph O'Connor, was murdered outside his west Belfast home, with the Provisionals held to be responsible. O'Connor's mother, Margaret, subsequently said she had no doubt that the Provisionals were behind the killing. In response, the Provisional IRA itself denied involvement.[199] Sinn Féin responded through Gerry Kelly, who described the murder as 'tragic', but refused to condemn it.[200] Others were not so reticent. The staunch republican critics of Sinn Féin, Anthony McIntyre and Tommy Gorman, issued a joint statement in which they stated publicly their 'unshakeable belief that the Provisional IRA carried out this assassination'. McIntyre and Gorman did also stress their 'stringent opposition to the Real IRA' and declared 'Republicanism should never again use guns in pursuit of its ideals.' Nevertheless, they condemned an act, which, they claimed, was designed 'to kill off any semblance of alternative republicanism'. It was, they declared, another example of 'history repeating itself in the murder of Irishmen by Irishmen in accordance with the needs of the British'. With a reference to that history, McIntyre and Gorman asked pointedly, 'What difference is there between the Free State murder of Rory O'Connor in defence of the 1922 British treaty and the murder of Joseph O'Connor in defence of the 1998 British treaty?'[201]

In the wake of the murder, armed and masked members of the Real IRA made two 'shows of strength' in Belfast, one of which occurred over the body of O'Connor. At the funeral, a variety of dissident or 'dissenting' republicans were present – including Brendan Hughes who helped carry the coffin.[202] Standing alongside a 12-foot floral wreath in the name of 'Óglaigh na hÉireann', Marian Price delivered the funeral oration and declared that O'Connor had 'lost his life at the hands of pro-British elements'. She proclaimed to the assembled crowd, 'Let there be no doubt; contrary to the deliberate misinformation being peddled by the Provisional movement and aided by RUC sources, those responsible for this foul murder have been clearly identified. Shame! Shame on you!' For Price, it was clear that 'the Provisional leadership chose to sanction such a dastardly act.' The Provisionals, she declared, were 'now reduced to an armed militia of the British State' and she asked acerbically, 'Is the murder of Volunteer Joe O'Connor part of the stepping stone strategy to a United Ireland?'[203]

For his part, McKevitt would tell David Rupert that he had been surprised by the murder. He thought it might have been a result of 'infighting' in the PIRA and efforts by the leadership to prevent an outflow of members. Still, he did not rush a response, despite the fact that his own members were calling for a revenge strike. It had actually fallen to McKevitt himself to conduct the RIRA investigation into the episode, on account of the fact that Campbell (who would have handled it) was, by that stage, in detention. In McKevitt's mind, the first order of business was to stop a 'bloodbath'. Clearly, he still felt the Real IRA could not take on the Provisionals head-on.[204] With that said, McKevitt did claim to have identified those responsible for the murder and a 'death warrant' was allegedly issued, to be 'carried out at a proper time'. McKevitt also professed to have turned down talks with Gerry Adams, aimed at mediating any burgeoning conflict.[205] The position, therefore, was not one of supine acceptance of what had occurred, but rather a calibrated mixture of restraint and menace.

All of this, of course, raised the question of the exact character of the relationship between the Provisionals and dissident republicanism. At one level, this was quite obviously highly antagonistic. As has been described, McKevitt viewed his former associates as engaged in a 'sell-out' of everything he believed to be correct. By the same token, they saw in him and his ilk the personification of undiluted, narrow 'militarism'. In line with this, Sinn Féin developed various formulae with which to brand those engaging in dissident activity at this time. For instance, in the aftermath of the Meigh Bridge and Stewartstown attacks of June–July 2000, both Mitchel McLaughlin and Martin McGuinness described the perpetrators as 'enemies of the peace process'.[206] In March 2001, Gerry Kelly elaborated further on this theme when he said of the Real IRA: 'They are a micro group. They have a wreckers' charter. They are anti-peace process and they are trying to wreck the whole idea of moving out of conflict and sorting out the situation.'[207] A few months later, in the wake of a shooting incident linked to the RIRA, McGuinness would further emphasise the unrepresentative and unconstructive nature of the dissident phenomenon, labelling them 'micro organisations that don't have any support whatsoever within our community'.[208] While in March 2002, after a bomb in south Armagh that injured two teenagers, Conor Murphy would argue that 'These people have nothing to offer, they have no strategy, no policies and no support.'[209]

Herein, one could see the reality of two visions competing for the heart of the same constituency – the 'republican base' – and certainly the Provisionals were prepared, as the O'Connor murder underlined, to deploy violence and intimidation to secure their position. At the same time, it is also clear that there was something of an umbilical, dialectic relationship between the Provisional movement and its dissident offshoots. For one thing, this was because McKevitt believed the path chosen by Gerry Adams and Martin McGuinness would ultimately end in failure – and thus work to his eventual advantage. His calculations were therefore informed by the impulse that he just needed to wait, to give Adams 'sufficient time to tighten the noose around his neck'.[210] On the other side too, there was a degree to which the very existence of McKevitt and his organisation was not a wholly negative thing for Sinn Féin. As the memoirs of Jonathan Powell reveal, the presence and activity of the dissidents served as a useful negotiating device for Sinn Féin during the years of the peace process.[211] In a similar vein was the argument made publicly by Mitchel McLaughlin in April 2001 when he criticised British handling of the peace process. Judged to be unsatisfactory from a republican perspective, McLaughlin averred that this merely encouraged the dissidents, so that whereas 'after Omagh they couldn't walk down the street to buy a packet of cigarettes', now they could claim Sinn Féin had been 'suckered'.[212] The message was clear: the British needed to 'give' more to Sinn Féin at the negotiating table, in order to bolster the party vis-à-vis its dissident rivals.

Moreover, there was an obvious limit to how far the Provisionals could ideologically dismiss the dissident case. As the above-quoted sentiments of people like Martin McGuinness, Gerry Kelly and Conor Murphy reveal, they criticised the dissidents on the grounds that they were 'anti peace' or lacking in support or strategy. But the same accusations could have been levelled at the Provisionals some ten to fifteen years earlier. Absent was any sense of moral condemnation of the continued resort by some republicans to violent methods. In this context, it should be accepted that there was some logic to the kind of argument put forward by Rory Dougan, when he contended, 'Sinn Féin has changed. Our argument in the 32 Counties [32CSM] now was their argument before ... We get our mandate from the same historic background where Gerry Kelly got his when he went to London on bombing missions in the 1970s.'[213] There was more than an element of truth in the dissident

charge that it was the Provisionals who had reformed their republicanism – that it was actually the mainstream movement who comprised
the real 'dissidents'. The latter could plausibly claim, in the mould of
Pearse, that they, not the Provisionals, were the ones faithfully adhering
to the path 'of those who never compromise'.[214] It was for this reason
that Sinn Féin was vulnerable to aspects of the dissident critique. As
Anthony McIntyre would put it, republicans had 'elevated the physical-
force tradition to a sacred level' and for years argued that it was 'justified to fight and kill to get rid of the British'. Now, Sinn Féin might try
to argue that such an approach was no longer justified, but the fact was
that the British remained in Ireland and, as a result, the 'intellectual
fingerprints' of the Provisionals were 'all over organisations like the
Real IRA'.[215]

This ideological symmetry was exacerbated by the reticence periodically shown by members of the Provisional movement when it came to
challenging the dissident narrative. Indeed, some of the arguments put
forward in the context of this quarrel would occasionally evoke a kind
of one-upmanship with regard to the strengths of the respective armed
organisations. A clear example of this was provided by a Sinn Féin councillor for Cookstown, Michael McIvor, who would later contend that
the dissidents were not serious because they had 'never killed a member
of the Brit forces'; rather they had, in his view, been 'blown out of pro-
portion' by the media and police: 'They have no support on the ground.
If they are so strong, how come there is [*sic*] no dead enemies?'[216]

Nevertheless, whether responding vocally or through more physical
means, there was little doubt that by late 2000/early 2001 the Provisional
movement had, like the governments, come to view the Real
IRA–32CSM as a serious threat. For this reason, the confidence exhibited
by McKevitt in this period was unsurprising. In a little over two years, he
had rebuilt an organisation out of the post-Omagh wreckage that was
capable of both challenging mainstream republicans ideologically and
launching a violent campaign against the British state. The truth of the
latter was confirmed by a string of attacks. At the start of November
2000, a policeman in Castlewellan was seriously injured by a booby-trap
car bomb which cost him a finger and thumb and forced the amputation
of one leg.[217] Before the year was out, further bombings had been prevented in County Fermanagh and in Belfast, with the powerful commercial explosive Semtex used on more than one occasion. The following

year, 2001, began with renewed efforts to kill a police officer – in Cookstown, County Tyrone and Claudy, County Londonderry – while a huge 1,100-pound landmine was uncovered in County Armagh. Only a few days after that last incident, a 200-pound mortar bomb was actually fired at Ebrington army barracks in Derry. The device failed to explode, but the RUC Chief Constable, Ronnie Flanagan, described it as nothing less than 'attempted mass murder'.[218]

After this spike in activity in Northern Ireland, attention again seemed to switch to the British mainland. On 14 February 2001, Stephen Menary, a 14-year-old cadet, was maimed by an explosive device hidden in a torch on a London Territorial Army base. Less than a month later, on 4 March 2001, a large car bomb detonated in a taxi that had been left outside the BBC's Television Centre in west London – the Real IRA's response to John Ware's October 2000 *Panorama* exposé of the men behind Omagh.[219] Unsurprisingly, this run of attacks generated much speculation that Britain now faced a renewed and deadly terrorist threat, which could conceivably destroy the Northern Irish peace process.[220]

And yet, even at this moment of putative success, as has been suggested, cracks in the edifice were already showing. In retrospect, for instance, the arrest of Liam Campbell would appear to have been a key moment, which deprived the Real IRA of one of its most capable operators. Even more significant was the fact that McKevitt remained wholly unaware of David Rupert's true loyalties and the damage being done to his group's prospects by his relationship with the American. As such cracks widened in the months that followed, the ephemeral nature of McKevitt's accomplishments became clear.

CONCLUSION: FAILURE

On 29 March 2001, McKevitt's illusions as to his own invulnerability from arrest were shattered when both he and Bernadette Sands-McKevitt were detained by Gardaí. Though his wife was soon released, McKevitt was subsequently charged with membership of an illegal organisation, the Real IRA, and with directing its activities between August 1999 and October 2000. When it then emerged that McKevitt's detention was based, in large part, on the depositions of David Rupert, the RIRA leader must have realised how grave a situation he was in.

Certainly, the 32CSM appeared somewhat wrong-footed at the revelations, as it scrambled to cover up the damage it must have known had been inflicted. Joe Dillon, for example, claimed that the 32CSM knew 'nothing about this man', even though the group's website had been registered in Rupert's name.[221] McKevitt would later be found guilty at the Special Criminal Court in Dublin in 2003 and sentenced to twenty years in prison, a conviction that was upheld at both the Irish Court of Criminal Appeal and the Supreme Court.[222]

The loss of its founder and most senior leader was clearly a major blow to the Real IRA. At least initially, however, there was some evidence that the group might survive and its campaign endure. The start of April 2001 saw the police forced to respond to a series of hoax alerts that paralysed Northern Ireland's railway infrastructure, while a 60-pound bomb was defused in Derry. On 12 April, a 200-pound mortar bomb was uncovered by police at Galbally in County Tyrone; and this was followed by a Real IRA statement to the media in which it promised to continue until the British finally withdrew from Ireland.[223] Two days later, a small bomb exploded at a postal sorting office in Hendon, London – a symbolic attack timed to coincide with the republican celebration of the Easter Rising (launched from the General Post Office in Dublin in 1916).[224] Over the summer of 2001, further attacks followed, both on the British mainland and in Northern Ireland. Police stations and RUC officers in Derry, Belfast, Strabane, Castlewellan and Draperstown in County Londonderry were all targeted, as was Belfast International Airport. On the mainland, the postal office at Hendon was bombed for a second time in May and then, in early August, a 100-pound car bomb exploded at Ealing Broadway in west London, injuring seven people after only a short and vague telephone warning had been given.[225]

The violence on both sides of the Irish Sea did not end there. November and December 2001 saw, variously: the discovery of a fully-primed, large car bomb near Armagh; the partial detonation of an incendiary device in a shop in Newry, County Down; and the attempted bombing of both the Dublin–Belfast railway line and a Customs and Excise office in Fermanagh. In 2002, fresh RIRA attacks were launched in Ballymena, Portadown, Downpatrick and Belfast against the new Police Service of Northern Ireland (the PSNI, which was brought into being in November 2001, as the successor force to the Royal Ulster

Constabulary). In February 2002, the deadly potential of dissident republican violence was demonstrated when the RIRA was reported to be responsible for the murder of Matthew Burns in Castlewellan.[226] In April 2002, a large firebomb was abandoned in the centre of Belfast – signalling an apparent relaxation of the RIRA's previously self-professed curb on the use of car bombs in Northern Ireland. Once again, too, British military installations were targeted. In one incident, in February, a civilian security guard, Peter Mason, lost arms, hearing and sight when he picked up a booby-trapped flask near an army training centre in County Londonderry. Though such attacks often seemed barely to register on the mainstream political radar, the journalist Kevin Myers, writing in *The Irish Times*, captured something of the devastation they caused for the victims when he described the 'abominable fate' of Peter Mason: 'In his mid-forties, he has been banished to a world in which there is no light, no sound, no dignity, no independence … an exile to a silent, lightless, touchless hell, one made by the Real IRA.'[227]

In popular consciousness, the fate of Peter Mason was soon eclipsed by that of another civilian worker at a military base. On 1 August 2002, David Caldwell became the first man to be killed by the Real IRA since Omagh, when he picked up a booby-trapped lunchbox at a Territorial Army base in Derry. The inquest into his death would later record that he suffered a 'horrendous death', on account of multiple injuries caused by the detonation of the device.[228] In a subsequent statement to the media, the 'Derry brigade of Óglaigh na hÉireann' claimed responsibility for the 'execution' of Caldwell.[229]

As with Omagh, the murder drew down near-universal condemnation upon the RIRA. Leading members of the mainstream republican movement such as Martin McGuinness were among those who voiced strident criticism. For McGuinness, the killing of Caldwell was 'absolutely and totally wrong' and was to be 'condemned in the most forthright and unequivocal terms'.[230] In response, the 32CSM restricted its disapproval to the actions of the PSNI, as it investigated Caldwell's murder. The arrest of several men linked to the Sovereignty Movement and the IRPWA (all of whom were later released without charge) was described as nothing more than 'an attempt by the British and Irish governments and the pro-agreement parties to marginalise' their supporters.[231] Moreover, the Real IRA showed itself to be in no mood to heed calls for it to cease its campaign. On the contrary, contemporary reports appeared to show an organisation going from strength to strength, with it said that former senior Provisionals, in places such as north Armagh, south Derry and south Down, had united with the dissident group, which could now claim a sizable presence within Northern Ireland.[232] Caldwell's death was followed too by other attacks, both within Belfast and elsewhere in the province.[233]

Against this background, it was possible to believe that the Real IRA was now in a position to replicate, at least in part, the campaign waged by the Provisional IRA – and that a degree of momentum was now with it. Nevertheless, in 2001–2 it was also possible to discern a counter-vailing tendency, which spoke of a campaign that was, in key respects, faltering and would ultimately fail to take off. For one thing, the RIRA was hit by a series of major arrests which removed important operators from circulation. In June 2001, for example, Gardaí arrested the Dublin-born brothers Kenneth and Alan Patterson, for possession of explosives; they would later receive lengthy prison sentences.[234] The following month, a former Irish army soldier, Richard Whyte, was ar-rested along with John Maloney, in connection with a Real IRA train-ing camp (and both were subsequently found guilty by the Special Criminal Court of membership of an illegal organisation).[235] Most high profile of all, July 2001 saw Slovakian police arrest Michael McDon-ald, Fintan O'Farrell and Declan Rafferty after a British-led 'sting op-eration' which saw the men trying to buy weapons from secret service agents posing as Iraqi arms dealers. They would later be sentenced to thirty years each in prison for their efforts.[236] October 2001 then brought the conviction and sentencing of Liam Campbell, to five years in jail for membership of the Real IRA.[237] Finally, in November 2001, police in Britain made a series of arrests in Yorkshire, which captured several of those involved in the mainland bombing campaign.[238]

Thus, for all the pessimism that RIRA activity caused among those who wished to see the Northern Irish peace process succeed, what remained under-appreciated, at least initially, was the extent to which the Real IRA project had actually come adrift. In May 2002, there were reports that the RIRA had initiated low-level negotiations with the Irish government in an effort to win concessions for its prisoners, in return for a ceasefire.[239] By autumn 2002, many of the group's senior figures, including McKevitt and Campbell, and several of their most trusted aides, were facing lengthy prison sentences. Attacks there had been, but aside from the maiming of several men and the killing of David Caldwell, the Real IRA had failed to deliver on its sinister threats. In a world in which 'success' was measured by the coarse resort to a 'body count' of enemy numbers killed, the Real IRA could take small pride in its accomplishments. There was little on its balance sheet to counteract the accusation that it was merely a pale imitation of the Provisional IRA, unable to pose a serious threat to the British state. Such sentiments were articulated most pointedly by Anthony McIntyre in a piece soon after the Caldwell murder, in which he noted:

> The Real IRA's war against whatever enemy it perceives to be out there continues unabated. A casual look at the fatalities resulting from Real IRA activity would lead to a conclusion that topping the target list are civilians – Irish, Spanish and English. British soldiers, RUC and loyalists are seemingly safe from Real IRA activity. I have no problem with that, feeling that little would be served by killing any out of the last three categories. I merely wish that the organisation would extend its protection policy to civilians as well ... The killing of David Caldwell was a brutal and futile waste of life. He didn't die because he was standing in the way of the Irish people as they march towards unification. Nor did he die because his death would help further facilitate the wishes of those same Irish people. He died as a calculated snub to those wishes ...[240]

The conviction that the 'armed struggle' was not reaping the anticipated dividends – and should therefore be re-evaluated – gained surprising adherents at this time. Criticism of the Real IRA's campaign developed within the organisation itself, fuelled by the increasingly sharp divide in outlook between those incarcerated by the authorities and those still at liberty. As 2002 progressed, this division hardened, as members disagreed on the best way forward. Finally, in October 2002, it emerged that there had been a split in the ranks, when a group of RIRA prisoners, together with their supporters on the outside, issued a statement urging the Real IRA leadership to stand down 'with ignominy'. That leadership was said to have neglected the prisoners, fraternised with criminals and failed to develop a meaningful strategy for the future.[241] Those now calling for the abandonment of the military campaign were said to include all five RIRA prisoners then in England, together with thirty-six out of thirty-nine men imprisoned in Portlaoise in the Irish Republic.

Most striking of all, it was Michael McKevitt himself who was said to be leading that group, having broken with Liam Campbell and only two other prisoners (Kieran Doherty and Thomas Redmond) who remained loyal to the outside leadership.[242] Whatever the outlook of specific individuals such as Campbell and McKevitt, there was no doubting that a major rift had developed within the Real IRA – a rift that required the formal separation of the two groups within the prison amid reports of major tensions between them.[243]

Shortly after the release of their public critique of the leadership, the dissenters formally dissociated themselves from the Real IRA and proclaimed the existence of a new body, the 'New Republican Forum' (for more of which, see below, pages 166–73). In a later interview with the *Forum* magazine which they also established, a spokesperson for them explained their decision. Therein, it was claimed that a year-long inquiry had been carried out and this had revealed 'corruption within the higher levels of the RIRA', with the organisation 'transformed into a financial enterprise for the benefit of a select few'. Other problems identified at that time were: a 'reckless approach to recruitment', the leadership's 'fraternisation with criminal elements' and 'their failure and inability to formulate a coherent long-term military-politico strategy'. It was for these reasons that the prisoners had asked the leadership to stand down; when this had failed to materialise, they had withdrawn their allegiance from them, in what was said to be an 'irreversible' split.[244]

The dissenting prisoners claimed that the remaining RIRA leadership had 'no functional organisation beneath them' and they called on their fellow republicans to 'accept political reality'. In a remarkable *volte-face*, the truth of this was now held to be that

> ... there is no support for armed struggle in Ireland at this time. And without popular support any armed campaign against British rule is doomed to failure. We believe it is the moral responsibility of the republican leadership to terminate any campaign when it becomes obvious that its continuance is futile.[245]

This position was not said to include any 'ideological concessions', with the prisoners declaring themselves to be still 'steadfastly opposed to the Belfast Agreement'. They acknowledged, however, that their hitherto 'non-existent campaign' had been 'reduced to an attempted operation every couple of months', and that this was no way to proceed. Consequently, they argued that a cessation was the only legitimate option left available. In making this call for an end to violence, the precedents they drew on were those provided by the decisions of earlier IRA incarnations, in 1923 and 1962, to 'dump arms' and halt campaigns that were demonstrably failing to achieve their objectives. It was this example that they wished the Real IRA to now follow. And though they predicted that such a move would be painful, they also maintained that it would be better than allowing the alternative to endure: an alternative in which 'a discredited and strategically bankrupt leadership remains blindly wedded to a fundamentally flawed and futile strategy which has led Irish republicanism into a political cul-de-sac'.[246]

For the faction of dissident republicans now aligned to Michael McKevitt – and particularly for McKevitt himself – this was a remarkable change of heart. Those who had once been committed to the unending character of physical-force republicanism – determined to keep the torch burning, or the baton in motion – were now calling for its termination. In so doing, McKevitt and his associates were perhaps conceding the failure of their once-ambitious project. The period since the second IRA ceasefire had seen two efforts to re-invigorate the cause of violent Irish republicanism. The first was lost amid the wreckage of Omagh; the second had, in many ways, similarly failed to recover from those events of 15 August 1998. McKevitt had been obsessed with 'getting past' Omagh's legacy, yet it had remained a millstone around the necks of would-be physical-force republicans. Efforts to avoid a repeat had hampered their capacity to act – and this contributed to their failure to win a critical mass of support for a renewed campaign.

This is not to say, of course, that there had not been moments when it had looked likely that the Real IRA could establish itself as a serious force, able to challenge the peace process. By autumn 2000, it was certainly 'back in business', and thereafter it carried out a series of attacks which captured political and public attention. Though it never matched the lethality of its Provisional IRA predecessor, it did show itself capable of inflicting substantial destruction and more than one life was devastated by its efforts. For a period, setbacks were matched by intermittent episodes of 'mini-triumph', which at least seemed suggestive of further success in the future. With all that said, though, the reality for the Real IRA was that its level of activity remained low by historical standards.

As Jonathan Tonge has highlighted, when compared to earlier purveyors of physical-force republicanism, the Real IRA had actually launched very few successful attacks. It managed only seven completed bombings across 2000–1. By contrast, in its 1939 England campaign, the IRA had detonated 127 bombs; while during the 'border campaign' in Northern Ireland in 1956–62, the annual average was for 100 operations.[247]

Seen from this perspective, then, the Real IRA's 'campaign' barely demanded the title. That this should have been so was doubtless a function of efforts made by the security services on both sides of the border (though particularly in the South). What had not been known to such leaders as McKevitt was the extent to which their organisation had been infiltrated – most spectacularly in the case of McKevitt's own confidante, David Rupert. It was this infiltration, alongside various other methods of security service interdiction, which helped prevent the Real IRA from gaining any genuine momentum. 'Successful' operations remained episodic rather than recurrent – and were punctuated by critical reverses. And it was this, in turn, which helped prompt the reassessments of late 2002 that fractured the organisation.

By the end of 2002, therefore, the second phase of dissident republican militancy appeared to have drawn to a close. Even then, the flame of physical-force republicanism had not been doused. Those still adhering to the way of 'armed struggle' pressed on. Within days of the public confirmation of the October 2002 split, for instance, the external Real IRA leadership co-ordinated a series of hoax alerts in Belfast, Lurgan and at Belfast International Airport in County Antrim; a defiant riposte to their internal critics and one which was accompanied by a statement warning 'all civilians to stay away from military installations and from crown forces personnel'.[248] Nonetheless, there was no hiding from the fact that the Real IRA still in existence was now a shadow of itself: to its critics, a pale imitation of a pale imitation. The men who had created the organisation were largely either in prison or on the way to so being; and the movement had experienced a debilitating split. Altogether, with the CIRA having failed to establish itself as a meaningful threat to the peace process, the prospects for 'armed struggle' looked bleak. And it was in this context that the centre of gravity for dissident republicanism moved elsewhere.

NOTES

1. For an account of all this, see Moloney, *A Secret History of the IRA*, pp.473–9.
2. Mooney and O'Toole, *Black Operations*, pp.31–5.
3. During this chapter, material attributed to David Rupert has been collated from the following sources: Evidence of David Rupert to the Special Criminal Court, Dublin, in the trial of Michael McKevitt, 23 June–17 July 2003; Evidence of David Rupert put before the High Court in Northern Ireland in the civil case taken against the alleged perpetrators of the Omagh Bombing, 7 April 2008–8 June 2009 (*Breslin & Ors v. McKenna & Ors*); Judgment of the High Court of Justice in *Breslin*, 8 June 2009 and the extensive newspaper coverage of the respective trials. Hereafter, simplified to 'Evidence of David Rupert'.
4. For further discussion of this see T. Hennessey, *The Northern Ireland Peace Process: Ending the Troubles?* (Dublin: Gill & Macmillan, 2000), pp.109–10.
5. For an account of the early history of the INLA, down to the murder of Costello, see J. Holland and H. McDonald, *INLA: Deadly Divisions* (Dublin: Torc, 1994), pp.4–119.
6. Ibid., pp.136–40.
7. Ibid., pp.215–16.
8. Ibid., pp.282–5.
9. *An Historical Analysis of the IRSP; Its Past Role, Root Cause of its Problems and Proposals for the Future*, IRSP Information Sheet (n.d.).
10. E. Mallie and D. McKittrick, *Endgame in Ireland* (London: Hodder & Stoughton, 2001), pp.251–2.
11. Evidence of David Rupert.
12. Mooney and O'Toole, *Black Operations*, p.135.
13. Ibid., p.126.
14. '"We Have Now Established a Sort of Republican Veto": Michael Farrell Interviews Gerry Adams, MP, Vice-President of Sinn Féin', *Magill*, July 1983, p.17. For discussion of this, see Frampton, *The Long March*, pp.20–3.
15. K. Toolis, 'McKevitt's Inglorious Career', *Observer*, 10 August 2003. For a fuller account see K. Toolis, *Rebel Hearts: Journeys Within the IRA's Soul* (London: Picador, 1995), pp.395–413.
16. *The Ballad of Ronan MacLochlainn*, available at the website of the Fianna na hÉireann, available via web cache at http://webcache.googleusercontent.com/search?q=cache:UIsIYAxFggcJ:www.fianna.netfirms.com/code/statements.html+%22A+rebel+by+nature%22+%22Yet+gentle+and+caring%22&cd=1&hl=en&ct=clnk&gl=uk
17. '"Real IRA Members" Jailed', BBC News Online, 21 May 1999, available at http://news.bbc.co.uk/1/hi/uk/349554.stm; see also Mooney and O'Toole, *Black Operations*, pp.119–25.
18. 'About Us', 32 County Sovereignty Movement Tyrone, available at http://www.32csmtyrone.com/aboutus.htm
19. E. Moloney, *Sunday Tribune*, 19 April 1998.
20. 'An Interview with Bernadette Sands-McKevitt from Radio Free Éireann', 32 CSM, 30 December 1997.
21. Ibid.
22. 'The Background and History', 32 County Sovereignty Movement, available at http://www.32csm.netfirms.com/code/home.html; 'About Us', 32 County Sovereignty Movement Tyrone, available at http://www.32csmtyrone.com/aboutus.htm
23. Mooney and O'Toole, *Black Operations*, pp.44–6.
24. 'Hard-liners Who Live in the Shadows', *Irish Independent*, 29 August 1998.
25. D. MacDonald, 'Mackey is Now an Outcast in Omagh', *Ireland on Sunday*, 23 August 1998; 'Return to Work by Sovereignty Movement Head Said to Have Disturbed Staff', *Irish Times*, 17 November 1998.
26. R. Donnelly, 'Mackey Stands by Challenge to SF Leadership', *Ulster Herald*, 18 December 1997.
27. G. Harkin, 'Adams Urges Calm as D-Day for Talks Approaches', *Irish News*, 27 March 1998; J. Mullin, 'Ten Tales of a Fragile Peace', *Guardian*, 1 April 1999.

28. 'Tributes for Man Shot in Robbery Attempt', *Irish Times*, 8 May 1998.
29. 'Links with Terror Group Rejected', BBC News Online, 17 August 1998, available at http://news.bbc.co.uk/1/hi/events/northern_ireland/latest_news/152512.stm
30. S. Breen, 'Proud of Her Sacrifice: Interview with Marian Price', *Village*, 4–10 December 2004.
31. Ibid.
32. R. Cowan, '"I Have No Regrets": Interview with Marian Price', *Guardian*, 13 March 2003.
33. Evidence of David Rupert.
34. Ibid.
35. 'The Background and History', 32 County Sovereignty Movement, available at http://www.32csm.netfirms.com/code/home.html
36. Cited in English, *Armed Struggle*, p.317.
37. *United Nations Submission*, 32 County Sovereignty Movement (1998), also available at http://www.32csm.info/UNsubmission.html
38. Ibid.
39. 'The Background and History', 32 County Sovereignty Movement, available at http://www.32csm.netfirms.com/code/home.html
40. 'Mackey is Refused Visa to US', *Irish Times*, 25 April 1998.
41. M. Sands, 'The Framing of Michael McKevitt: Introduction', *The Blanket*, 22 June 2006.
42. For more on Reid, see Moloney, *A Secret History of the IRA*, pp.220–86.
43. Dudley Edwards, *Aftermath*, pp.38–40.
44. Mooney and O'Toole, *Black Operations*, pp.112–15.
45. Ibid., pp.142–3.
46. Ibid., p.144.
47. See Dudley Edwards, *Aftermath*, pp 1–42.
48. Evidence of David Rupert.
49. E. Keogh and B. Carroll, 'McKevitt Denies any Connection with Bomb', *Irish News*, 19 August 1998.
50. 'Links with Terror Group Rejected', BBC News Online, 17 August 1998, available at http://news.bbc.co.uk/1/hi/events/northern_ireland/latest_news/152512.stm
51. 'Press Release: Sovereignty Movement Reaction to Political Misrepresentation', 32CSM, 24 August 1998
52. See Dáil Éireann Parliamentary Debates, vol. 494, 2 September 1998, available at http://www.oireachtas-debates.gov.ie/D/0494/D.0494.199809020004.html
53. *Offences Against the State (Amendment) Act 1998*, available at http://www.irishstatutebook.ie/1998/en/act/pub/0039/index.html
54. *Criminal Justice (Terrorism and Conspiracy) Act 1998*, available at http://www.opsi.gov.uk/acts/acts1998/ukpga_19980040_en_1; For a discussion of these issues, see C. Walker, 'The Bombs in Omagh and their Aftermath: The Criminal Justice (Terrorism and Conspiracy) Act 1998', *The Modern Law Review*, 62, 6 (November 1999), pp.879–902.
55. 'Sands-McKevitt's US Visa Turned Down', *Irish Times*, 21 August 1998.
56. 'Sands "Using" Brother's Memory', *Irish News*, 20 August 1998.
57. 'Press Release: Retract or Apologise Call to Media by Sovereignty Movement', 32CSM, 26 August 1998
58. 'Press Release: All Ireland Repression Fruits of Stormont Deal', 32CSM, 26 August 1998.
59. Blair, cited in Hennessey, *The Northern Ireland Peace Process*, p.108.
60. 'Real IRA Apologises for Omagh Bomb', BBC News Online, 18 August 1998, available at http://news.bbc.co.uk/1/hi/events/northern_ireland/focus/153629.stm
61. 'Second Statement of Real IRA, 18 August 1998', available at CAIN, http://cain.ulst.ac.uk/events/peace/docs/rira18898b.htm
62. 'INLA Ceasefire Declaration', 22 August 1998, available at http://irsm.org/statements/inla/980822.html
63. Cited in English, *Armed Struggle*, p.318.
64. 'The Futile Path of Militarism', *An Phoblacht/Republican News*, 20 August 1998.

65. D. Godson, *Himself Alone: David Trimble and the Ordeal of Unionism* (London: HarperCollins, 2004), p.396; Powell, *Great Hatred, Little Room*, p.176. For a contemporary account of the PIRA's role in forcing a RIRA cessation see L. Walsh, 'The Real IRA: "We Will Not Disband"', *Magill*, October 1998, pp.30–1.
66. Powell, *Great Hatred, Little Room*, p.176.
67. 'Continuity IRA Pledges Attacks', *Irish Times*, 16 December 1998.
68. B. Anderson, 'Give Us Your Arms, CIRA Urges Provos', *Irish News*, 2 December 1999.
69. Evidence of David Rupert.
70. Dudley Edwards, *Aftermath*, p.112; Mooney and O'Toole, *Black Operations*, p.189.
71. Evidence of David Rupert.
72. Ibid.
73. Ibid.
74. Dudley Edwards, *Aftermath*, 267.
75. Evidence of David Rupert.
76. Ibid.
77. Ibid.
78. Ibid.
79. Ibid.
80. Ibid.
81. J. Burns, 'Dissidents Defying the US Ban', *Financial Times*, 4 June 2001.
82. Evidence of David Rupert.
83. J. Holland, *Irish Echo*, 18–24 April 2001. See also 'Who We Are' and 'Mission Statement', Irish Freedom Committee.
84. For an example of the IFC's work, see the letter written to several major US newspapers in April 2000 by members of the Pittsburgh chapter of the group: F. O'Sé and E. O'Sullivan, 'Letters to the Editor: What's Good for the Goose ...', Liam Lynch Chapter of the Irish Freedom Committee, 21 April 2000.
85. Evidence of David Rupert.
86. Ibid.
87. Ibid.
88. Ibid.
89. Ibid.
90. Ibid.
91. Ibid.
92. Ibid.
93. Ibid.
94. Ibid.
95. Ibid.
96. Ibid.
97. Ibid.
98. Ibid.
99. Ibid.
100. Ibid.
101. Ibid.
102. Ibid.
103. Ibid.
104. Ibid.
105. Ibid.
106. Ibid.
107. Ibid.
108. Ibid.
109. Ibid.
110. Ibid.

111. Ibid.
112. Ibid.
113. Ibid.
114. Ibid.
115. 'For Immediate Release: Statement by Óglaigh na hÉireann', 32CSM, January 2000.
116. Evidence of David Rupert.
117. Ibid.
118. Ibid.
119. Ibid.
120. Ibid.
121. Ibid.
122. Ibid.
123. Ibid.
124. Ibid.
125. Ibid.
126. Archive copy of 'Craic agus Ceol', 32CSM website, 16 August 2000.
127. Evidence of David Rupert.
128. For the statement issued at the conference, see 'First International Conference on the Right to Self-Determination and the United Nations', available at http://i-p-o.org/self-determination.htm; for more on the organisation behind the conference see the 'International Human Rights Association of American Minorities', available at http://ihraam.org/activities.html
129. 'New Year Statement', 32 CSM, January 2000.
130. 'Press Release', 32CSM, 10 May 2000.
131. 'Statement from the National Executive, 32 County Sovereignty Movement: Easter 2000', 32 County Sovereignty Movement [hereafter 32CSM], 6 May 2000.
132. 'Statement from Republican POWs Maghaberry Prison: Easter 2000', archived from the Irish Republican Prisoners' Welfare Association [hereafter IRPWA] website on 23 August 2000.
133. 'Press Release: Statement by Rory Dougan', 32CSM, 28 February 2000. See also 'Press Release: Statement by Bernadette McKevitt', 32CSM, 16 February 2000.
134. 'End British Rule Now!', *Sovereign Nation*, 2, 3 (March/April 2000).
135. 'Entering and Accepting British Political System', 32CSM, 21 April 2000; see also 'Provo Leadership Sell Out!', *Sovereign Nation*, 2, 4 (May/June 2000).
136. 'Provo Leadership Sell Out!', *Sovereign Nation*, 2, 4 (May/June 2000).
137. Ibid.
138. T. O'Hanlon, 'A Farewell to Arms: After Weston Park, Is Provo Decommissioning Imminent?', *Sovereign Nation*, 4, 3 (August 2001).
139. Marian Price, *Speech to 32CSM Árd Fheis 2000*, Carrickarnon, County Louth, 24 June 2000.
140. É. Collins, *Killing Rage* (London: Granta, 1997), pp.222–6.
141. Marian Price, *Speech to 32CSM Árd Fheis 2000*, Carrickarnon, County Louth, 24 June 2000.
142. C. Twomey, 'The Interview: Marian Price', *The Blanket*, 1, 1 (Winter 2002).
143. Ibid.
144. T. O'Hanlon, 'A Gauntlet of Sectarian Hate', *Sovereign Nation*, 4, 4 (September/October 2001).
145. 'Press Release', 32 CSM, 8 January 2000. See also 'Press Release: Nelson Family Denied Justice', 32CSM, 21 April 2000.
146. 'Press Release: Statement by Bernadette McKevitt', 32CSM, 19 January 2000.
147. 'Press Release: Statement by Rory Dougan', 32CSM, 28 February 2000; 'End British Rule Now!', *Sovereign Nation*, 2, 3 (March/April 2000). For more on the shift in Sinn Féin's policy, see below, pages 205–7.

148. D. McHugh, 'RUC Propaganda Offensive Launched', *Sovereign Nation*, 4, 4 (September/October 2001).
149. 'Press Release: London Meeting Elects First 32 County Sovereignty Movement Committee in England', 32CSM, 21 April 2000.
150. IRPWA, 'Support the Repatriation of Republican POWs', *News in Brief*, May 2000.
151. Archive screenshot of the website of the IRPWA, 7 November 2000.
152. 'Dissident Fears as Jail Tension Mounts', *Andersonstown News*, 7 March 2002.
153. 'Press Release: Protest at Maghaberry Prison (IRPWA Statement)', IRPWA, 16 August 2002.
154. 'Press Release: Republican Prisoners Action Committee', IRPWA, 27 August 2002.
155. 'Real IRA Threatens Prison Officers', *Irish Examiner*, 1 May 2001.
156. 'RIRA Issue Chilling Warning to Prison Officers', *Andersonstown News*, 30 March 2002.
157. 'Press Release: Protest the Brutalisation of POWs at Portlaoise', 32CSM, 26 November 2001.
158. 'Press Release: Call to Government to End Political Discrimination Policy – Statement by Marian Price, Chairperson of IRPWA', IRPWA, 24 November 2001.
159. *Constitution of the 32 County Sovereignty Movement*, as adopted at AGM, 24 June 2000.
160. P. Crossey, '32-Group Denies Real IRA Links', *Irish News*, 26 June 2000.
161. House of Commons Hansard Written Answers for 22 November 2000, available at House of Lords Hansard for 5 December 2001, available at http://www.publications.parliament.uk/pa/ ld200102/ldhansrd/vo011205/text/11205-02.htm
162. 'Press Release', 32CSM, 24 November 2000.
163. 'Press Release: Statement by Chairman Francie Mackey on Behalf of the National Executive, 32 County Sovereignty Movement', 32CSM, 11 November 2002.
164. Ó hAnnain, 'Armed Struggle "a National Right": Letter to the Editor', *The Irish World*, 12 May 2000.
165. H. McDonald, 'Republicans' Defiant Dame Warns of War', *Observer*, 4 February 2001.
166. Marian Price, *Voice of the Lark Speech: Legacy of the Hunger Strikes: Lessons Learned, Lessons Forgotten*, Conway Mill, Belfast 31 January 2001.
167. 'Press Release: Address by Francie Mackey, Chairperson of the 32 County Sovereignty Movement', 32CSM, 2000; E. Keogh, 'Sinn Féin Accused of Collaborating with British', *Sunday Tribune*, 25 June 2000.
168. S. Breen, 'IRA "Surrender" Condemned at 32-County Group's AGM', *Irish Times*, 26 June 2000.
169. F. McNally, 'Sovereignty Movement Marks Easter Rising', *Irish Times*, 16 April 2001.
170. 'Press Release: New Year's Statement from Francie Mackey, National Chairperson', 32CSM, January 2001.
171. Evidence of David Rupert.
172. Ibid.
173. Ibid.
174. Ibid.
175. 'Press Release: Address by Francie Mackey, Chairperson of the 32 County Sovereignty Movement', 32CSM, 24 June 2000.
176. B. O'Kelly and S. MacCarthaigh, 'Priest's Meetings with RIRA Prompted Ceasefire', *Sunday Business Post*, 10 November 2002; B. O'Kelly, 'Ahern's Denials Fail to Convince', *Sunday Business Post*, 10 November 2002; M. O'Regan, 'Ahern Says Mansergh Met McKevitt', *Irish Times*, 15 October 2003.
177. Dudley Edwards, *Aftermath*, p.176; Evidence of David Rupert.
178. 'Omagh Support and Self-Help Group, Omagh Bomb Digital Archive, available at http://hq-obda-01.welbni.org/Osshg.html
179. Both Victor Barker and Michael Gallagher had lost sons in the Omagh bombing of 1998. See Dudley Edwards, *Aftermath*, pp.1–42, 134–5, 142–3.
180. IRPWA, 'Belfast Success for Republican Prisoners', *News in Brief*, Spring/Summer 2000 (21 August 2000).

181. Martin Galvin, *Speech to IRPWA Meeting*, Belfast, 18 August 2000.
182. 'Press Release', IRPWA, 18 August 2000.
183. N. Webb, 'Billionaire Bans RIRA Political Wing from Web', *Sunday Independent*, 10 December 2000.
184. Dudley Edwards, *Aftermath*, p.176.
185. *Statement by the Leadership of the Real IRA*, 14 December 2001.
186. Dudley Edwards, *Aftermath*, pp.220, 250–1.
187. D. McHugh, 'Omagh Case – Whose Agenda?', *Sovereign Nation*, 4, 4 (September/October 2001).
188. Dudley Edwards, *Aftermath*, pp.321–3; 'Omagh Bombing Judgment: Relatives Win Landmark Civil Case', *Daily Telegraph*, 8 June 2009.
189. 'Press Release: Designation of "Real IRA" under United States Law', Department of Justice, Equality and Law Reform, 24 November 2000.
190. 'Fact Sheet: Foreign Terrorist Organisations', US Department of State, Washington DC, 15 August 2002.
191. 'Press Statement: Office of the Spokesman: Northern Ireland: Designation of the "Real IRA" as a Foreign Terrorist Organisation', US Department of State, 16 May 2001.
192. 'Declaration of Martin Galvin', in the *United States Court of Appeal for the District of Columbia Circuit: 32 County Sovereignty Committee et al. vs US Department of State*.
193. 'Brief for Respondents in Case: United States Department of State and Colin Powell, Secretary of State', in the *United States Court of Appeals for the District of Columbia Circuit No. 01-1270*, pp.16–20.
194. *32 County Sovereignty Committee v Department of State* 292 F.3d 797 (DC Cir. 2002).
195. Evidence of David Rupert.
196. R. Dudley Edwards, 'A Miserable Week for the Families of Omagh Victims', *Sunday Independent*, 28 February 2010.
197. 'My Kidnap Ordeal at Hands of the Provos', *Daily Record* (Scotland), 5 February 1999; 'IRA Man "Abducted", says MP', *Irish News*, 6 February 1999; H. McDonald, 'Peace Takes Another Beating', *Observer*, 7 February 1999.
198. 'Paper Seller "Under Threat"', *Irish News*, 17 March 2000.
199. S. Breen, 'Crowds Cheer Belfast Show of Strength by "Real IRA"', *Irish Times*, 18 October 2000.
200. S. Breen, 'SF Refuses to Condemn Killing of "Real IRA" Man', *Irish Times*, 17 October 2000.
201. 'Killing Republicans – That Was Not Our War', *Irish News*, 17 October 2000. As a coda to the O'Connor murder, it is worth noting that Joe's brother, Fred, was himself later shot in a paramilitary attack believed to be the work of the Provisional IRA in April 2004. See M. Coleman, 'Brother of Real IRA Man Shot in Ankles', *Belfast Telegraph*, 18 April 2004.
202. S. Breen, 'Shots Fired at Funeral of "Real IRA" Member in West Belfast', *Irish Times*, 19 October 2000.
203. Marian Price, *Funeral Oration for Joseph O'Connor*, Belfast, 18 October 2000. See also S. Breen, 'Shots Fired at Funeral of "Real IRA" Member in West Belfast', *Irish Times*, 19 October 2000.
204. Evidence of David Rupert.
205. Ibid.
206. D. Sharrock, 'Real IRA "Chief Suspect" after Ulster Rail Bomb', *Daily Telegraph*, 1 July 2000; M. Unsworth, 'Flanagan Says Tyrone Car Bomb Probably Planted by "Real IRA"', *Irish Times*, 10 July 2000.
207. R. Donnelly and S. Breen, 'Real IRA Set on Destruction – Kelly', *Irish Times*, 6 March 2001.
208. R. McGregor, 'Shooting Condemned', *Irish News*, 8 June 2001.
209. 'Bomb Attack was "Designed to Kill"', BBC News Online, 3 March 2002, available at http://news.bbc.co.uk/1/hi/northern_ireland/1851040.stm
210. Evidence of David Rupert.

211. Powell, *Great Hatred, Little Room*, pp.147–8, 216, 264, 274.
212. N. Watt, 'Bombers Widen the Republican Divide', *Guardian*, 16 April 2001.
213. W. Paul, 'Rebels on the March', *Scotland on Sunday*, 11 March 2001.
214. See above, page 39.
215. W. Paul, 'Rebels on the March', *Scotland on Sunday*, 11 March 2001.
216. W. Scholes, 'Dissidents "Not Serious" – SF Man', *Irish News*, 28 June 2006.
217. 'RUC Believe Dissident Republicans Responsible for Down Attack', RTÉ News, 1 November 2000, http://m.rte.ie/news/2000/1101/dissidents.html
218. G. Jackson, 'RUC Blames "Real IRA" for Mortar Bomb Attack', *Irish Times*, 24 January 2001.
219. S. Tendler, 'Attack was "Revenge for Naming Real IRA"', *The Times*, 5 March 2001. See also 'Panorama: Who Bombed Omagh?', BBC One, 9 October 2000.
220. D. Sharrock, 'Real IRA Scores Propaganda Coup with BBC Bomb', *Daily Telegraph*, 5 March 2001; N. Hopkins and R. Cowan, 'Bomb Threatens Peace Process: Real IRA Blast Rocks BBC Studios: Warning of More Attacks: Police Fear Two Terror Campaigns on Mainland', *Guardian*, 5 March 2001; P. Taylor, 'The Bombers have Blown a Hole in More than the BBC: The Blast is a Rallying Cry to all Those Disillusioned with the Peace Process', *Guardian*, 6 March 2001; J. Burns, B. Groom and J. Murray Brown, 'Bombs Warning Places City on High Alert: Call for Vigilance after Dissident Irish Republicans Attack BBC', *Financial Times*, 6 March 2001.
221. 'Mystery Figure Can Unmask Real IRA', *Belfast Telegraph*, 14 April 2001.
222. 'Court Convicts McKevitt on Both Charges', *Irish Times*, 8 August 2003; 'Court Rejects McKevitt Plea Against Terror Conviction', *Irish Times*, 31 July 2008.
223. S. Breen, '"Real IRA" Warns it Will Continue', *Irish Times*, 13 April 2001.
224. F. Millar, 'Blast at Post Office Depot Blamed on "Real IRA"', *Irish Times*, 16 April 2001.
225. C. Walker and S. Tendler, 'Post Office Bomb Raises Fear of Terrorist Campaign', *The Times*, 7 May 2001; A. Hibberd, S. Pook, D. Graves and D. Sharrock, 'Bomb Rocks London Street: Real IRA Blamed as Car Blast Injures Passers-By and Shatters Shop Windows Near Tube Station', *Daily Telegraph*, 3 August 2001; N. Hopkins, 'The Bomb That Could Have Been London's Omagh', *Guardian*, 4 August 2001.
226. 'Group Claims it Ordered Five Men to Leave NI', *Irish Times*, 5 March 2002; A. Wallace, 'Man Gunned Down in Car Ambush after Personal Feud', *Belfast Telegraph*, 1 November 2004.
227. K. Myers, 'An Irishman's Diary', *Irish Times*, 26 March 2002.
228. 'Horrific Last Moments of Real IRA Bomb Victim', *Londonderry Sentinel*, 6 March 2007.
229. 'Real IRA Admits Role in Army Base Murder', *Irish Independent*, 22 August 2002; G. Moriarty, '"Real IRA" Admits Murdering Civilian Worker in Explosion', *Irish Times*, 22 August 2002.
230. M. Unsworth, 'Killing of Civilian is Condemned by All Sides', *Irish Times*, 2 August 2002.
231. M. Canning, 'Strabane Man Arrested After Murder of Contractor', *Ulster Herald*, 8 August 2002.
232. L. Clarke, 'RIRA Threat "At Highest Since Omagh"', *Sunday Times*, 4 August 2002; 'Turf War Flares as Top Provo Defects', *Sunday Life*, 11 August 2002; 'RIRA Gains Provo Bomb Expert', *Sunday Life*, 18 August 2002; M. Sheehan and J. Lee, 'Ulster Base for Real IRA', *Sunday Times* (Ireland edition), 18 August 2002.
233. 'Bomb Alert After Van Hijacked', *Irish Times*, 31 August 2002; S. Breen, 'Dissident Republicans are Blamed for Attack on Police', *Irish Times*, 4 September 2002.
234. D. MacDermott, 'Three in Court After Garda Explosives Find', *Irish Independent*, 16 June 2001; 'Twins Jailed Over Bomb Factory', *Irish Times*, 12 December 2001.
235. T. Harding, 'Ex-Soldier Who Ran Sniper Camp Jailed', *Daily Telegraph*, 2 November 2002.
236. M. Sheehan and N. Rufford, 'MI5 Posed as Arabs in Terrorist Arms Sting', *Sunday Times* (Ireland), 15 July 2001; 'Dissident Republicans Get 30 Years', BBC News Online, 7 May 2002, available at http://news.bbc.co.uk/1/hi/northern_ireland/1971436.stm
237. 'Real IRA Man Jailed for Five Years', BBC News Online, 23 October 2001, available at http://news.bbc.co.uk/1/hi/northern_ireland/1615833.stm

238. 'Villagers in "Real IRA" Alert Allowed Home', *Yorkshire Post*, 16 November 2001; 'Real IRA Bombers Jailed', BBC News Online, 9 April 2003, available at http://news.bbc.co.uk/1/hi/uk/2930957.stm

239. 'RIRA Secretly Sues for Peace', *Ireland on Sunday*, 15 May 2002. See also M. Sheehan, 'Real IRA Barters for Peace', *Sunday Times* (Ireland), 9 June 2002; D. Lister, 'Real IRA Holds Secret Ceasefire Talks with Dublin', *The Times*, 2 July 2002.

240. A. McIntyre, 'Silent but Lethal', *The Blanket*, 11 August 2002.

241. 'Statement from Republican Prisoners', *Forum Magazine*, February 2003; T. Harding, 'Real IRA Men Tell "Corrupt" Leaders to Wind Up Group', *Daily Telegraph*, 21 October 2002; L. Walsh, 'Corruption Brings Down Terror Group', *Sunday Independent*, 20 October 2002.

242. B. O'Kelly, 'Portlaoise's RIRA Prisoners Say End Armed Campaign', *Sunday Business Post*, 13 October 2002.

243. L. Walsh, 'Bitter Split Between Real IRA Factions in Portloaise', *Sunday Independent*, 3 November 2002; V. Robinson, 'Real IRA Tensions Erupt in Jail Clash', *Irish News*, 7 January 2003.

244. 'Interview with Republican Prisoners', *Forum Magazine*, February 2003.

245. Ibid.

246. Ibid.

247. Tonge, '"They Haven't Gone Away, You Know"', p.685.

248. D. Keenan, '"Real IRA" Warns of More Attacks on Army Bases', *Irish Times*, 22 October 2002.

4

A Flickering Flame: The Nadir of Dissident Republicanism, 2002–6

From the moment that the Northern Irish peace process had begun to gather momentum, there had emerged a body of republicans who, though not part of any formal organisational framework, were deeply critical of Sinn Féin and the broader Provisional movement. Of particular importance here was the group of ex-prisoners who coalesced around what Richard English has termed a 'dissenting' movement.[1] Prominent members of this broad and loosely defined circle included Anthony McIntyre, Tommy Gorman, Tommy McKearney and (until his death in February 2008) Brendan Hughes. They claimed, for various reasons, to view continued armed struggle as pointless. McIntyre, for instance, noted that for him, 'Omagh was a defining moment. It convinced me to sever all moral support for the armed struggle to achieve a united Ireland ... A united Ireland is not worth the life of my daughter. It was not worth the lives of the two unborn children at Omagh, or any of the others.'[2] At the same time, McIntyre and his associates also rejected the peace strategy being pursued by Sinn Féin.

As far back as the mid-1990s, when still a member of the party, McIntyre had voiced concerns over the direction in which Sinn Féin was headed. It was, he told a 1995 internal party conference, likely to lead only to 'a partitionist fudge'. Interestingly, on that same occasion, he also felt it necessary to state, 'this leadership are the people responsible for rubbing the noses of the British state in their own dirt over the past twenty-five years ... This leadership is not going to sell us out. Any suggestion they will is ridiculous.'[3] Suffice to say this latter strand of his analysis did not survive. Over time, he and others like him would come to view the Adams-led republican movement as hungry only for power. The Provisionals were said to have abandoned their ideological credentials and embraced a process that brought only defeat, albeit a defeat that was subsequently portrayed as a victory.

To those so minded, the 'peace strategy' of the Provisional movement and especially the Good Friday Agreement were the targets of much criticism. The latter, it was averred, was not a republican settlement; nor did it contain the potential to so be. And as in the words of Marian Price noted earlier, it was not seen as an adequate return on the many years of violence and 'sacrifice'. Anthony McIntyre in particular captured this sentiment in his brutal assertion that the GFA was better understood as 'Got Fuck All'.[4] Elsewhere, McIntyre argued that the Agreement was of a type that had previously been rejected by republicans over the course of the conflict and questioned why it should now be deemed suitable:

> If it [the Agreement] is progress, then why could we not have had it in 1974? Why could we not have [avoided] the long war and [gone] for a strategy similar to this? Why did so many people have to die to bring us back round to accepting what we rejected in 1974, and called everybody else bastards for accepting?[5]

The shared analysis of such dissenters was that, viewed from the vantage point of the late 1990s, the Provisional IRA's 'means' did not justify the 'ends'; and Sinn Féin support for the Good Friday Agreement was akin to 'turkeys celebrating Christmas'. That this should have been so was because:

> The political objective of the Provisional IRA was to secure a British declaration of intent to withdraw. It failed. The objective of the British state was to force the Provisional IRA to accept – and subsequently respond with a new strategic logic – that it would not leave Ireland until a majority in the north consented to such a move. It succeeded.[6]

For McIntyre, as he argued in 2002, the reality was that Sinn Féin had 'conceded more than any other party' in the peace process:

> They have been defeated on every issue from the question of a British withdrawal, the consent principle, decommissioning, the total abolition of Stormont, and policing. Republicanism has been completely hollowed out to the point where its shell has been filled with core constitutional nationalist rather than republican

positions ... The three 'D's of Provisional republicanism – defence, defiance and dissent – now stand for defeat, decommissioning and dissolution.[7]

From a similar vantage point, the former Belfast Provisional IRA commander Brendan Hughes was another who spoke to the sense that republicans had been let down by the outworking of the peace process. On a personal level, he claimed that he did not 'feel any satisfaction whatsoever' with that process. Instead, Hughes judged people to be 'demoralised and disillusioned' by the 'futility of it all'. In his assessment:

> From a nationalist perspective alone what we have now we could have had at any time in the last twenty-five years ... And in the process we have lost much of our honesty, sincerity and comradeship ... The political process has created a class of professional liars and unfortunately it contains many republicans.[8]

Hughes' critique was extended further to include the accusation that many within the mainstream republican leadership had profited personally from the peace process, attaining 'comfortable positions', while many of their followers had been 'left behind'.[9]

This was a theme that Hughes returned to in an April 2000 interview with John McDonagh, of the American-based 'Radio Free Éireann' (a transcript of which was later reproduced by the 32 County Sovereignty Movement – an indication of the ideological cross-fertilisation among those opposed to the Provisionals' trajectory). During that discussion, he complained about the lack of change in social and economic conditions on the ground in west Belfast – and referred to his own experience of struggling for work: 'I see the working class being exploited again ... and ... Republicans allowing people to exploit the ordinary working man and woman.' This was set against a wider political context, which he claimed to have never visualised in his 'wildest dreams'. Sinn Féin, he maintained, had ended up 'playing the Brits' game'. Hughes averred that while he had hitherto remained quiet out of 'loyalty' to the republican movement, he now feared that there were many within that movement who had abandoned their principles and become 'careerists'. By contrast, he praised the example of Marian Price, by this stage aligned with the 32CSM, for having 'the guts to stand up ... and say something that she believes is wrong'. For Hughes, republicans needed to 'get back

to the principles of republicanism'. In making this case, he admitted
that he did not have a ready 'alternative' to Sinn Féin, but he called for
an 'open and honest debate' to discuss the future direction of Irish
republicanism.[10]

What such outbursts revealed was that it was not simply to the end
result of the peace process that people like Hughes and McIntyre
objected. Rather, it was the very character of that process, the manner
in which it was handled by the Sinn Féin leadership and the alleged
transformation in republicanism that it had induced. In line with this,
in 2001 McIntyre attacked what he called the 'constructive fudge' and
'creative ambiguity' which he felt had made the peace process 'the
intellectual farce that it is'. The trigger for that caustic assessment was
the arrest in Colombia of three men linked to the Provisional IRA and the
subsequent denials of the men issued by Sinn Féin. What this incident had
revealed, according to McIntyre, was that, for Sinn Féin, 'the right-
wing palate of corporate America must be assuaged even if it means
behaving as St Peter no matter how often the cock crows.' It was thus
another example of the bizarre reversals occasioned by the peace
process:

> Twenty years ago as prisoners died and people trudged the streets
> in a bid to save them, who would have thought that Sinn Féin,
> gorged on fudge and ambiguity, would dismiss Irish political pris-
> oners as a 'non-story'? Sinn Féin should have no reason to be em-
> barrassed over republican prisoners. But such prisoners may now
> have every reason to be embarrassed over Sinn Féin.[11]

In 2000, this strand of 'dissenting' republicanism came together to form
the Irish Republican Writers' Group (IRWG), 'an amalgamation of people inclined towards radical politics'.[12] From this came the magazine
Fourthwrite, intended as a medium through which disaffection might
be expressed. Over the next seven years, intermittent editions of the
publication gave space to a range of dissident republican voices (together with those of occasional non-republican contributors as well).
Despite (or perhaps because of) its eclectic character, however, *Fourthwrite* never really gained any serious traction in republican circles.

Far more significant was another venture to emerge from those
linked to the IRWG. In 2001, the online journal *The Blanket* was
launched as an electronic outlet for voices critical of the mainstream

republican project. Driven by the sharp and articulate McIntyre, this devoted much of its coverage to analysis of the Provisionals, particularly their alleged concessions, climb-downs and defeats. In 2003, for example, in the aftermath of a failed round of peace process negotiations, McIntyre predicted that Sinn Féin would eventually conclude a deal with unionists, of whatever stripe, because the party leadership 'craved institutional power'.[13] North and south of the border, far from being motivated by any coherently 'republican' ideology, the Provisional movement's leadership was said to be 'committed to power and power alone'.[14]

It was on this understanding that McIntyre had long predicted eventual disbandment of the Provisional IRA. By 2002, on his estimation, 'time ha[d] run out for an armed IRA.'[15] And in early 2004, he was clear that 'The IRA as we have come to know it will ultimately be dissolved when Sinn Féin decide that there is nothing else to do but go back into government in the North.'[16] It was for this reason that McIntyre viewed the peace process as representing a triumph for the British state: 'They more than anyone else have gained from the peace process, having obtained an end to the IRA campaign – the one consistent objective of British state strategy since 1970.'[17] Moreover, the abandonment of the IRA was, in McIntyre's view, always likely to be accompanied by an endorsement of the police from Sinn Féin. As one 2003 article noted, 'The decision to become part of the structure of the RUC was taken a long time ago.'[18]

In order to highlight the supposed reality of the situation, *The Blanket* seized on any issue that appeared to show the Adams–McGuinness leadership for what it was. It thus developed a scathing critique around the subject of weapons decommissioning by the Provisional IRA. By accepting it, so the argument ran, the Provisional leadership had served to 'delegitimise and criminalise the previous Republican resistance'.[19] Furthermore, McIntyre fiercely mocked the absurdity of those grassroots republicans who believed the purported claims of the leadership (around the time of the first and second acts of IRA decommissioning) that de Chastelain had been 'duped': 'an intellectually cauterised and strategically moribund body of people'.[20] 'It never happened – Again', wrote McIntyre, 'There are even some who will swear to having been there when decommissioning didn't happen – again.'[21]

There was a growing emphasis too on the revelations concerning informers acting within the Provisional republican movement. The claims levelled against men such as Freddie Scappaticci (albeit which he firmly denied) and Denis Donaldson in 2003–5 were repeatedly used to de-legitimise the leadership of that movement. With regard to Scappaticci, for instance, McIntyre noted that he had one thing in common with Gerry Adams: 'Both set out to destroy the IRA and both succeeded.'[22] This supposed affinity between British agents and the course set by the Provisional leadership developed into a familiar refrain: 'Martin McGuinness worked as a British minister; Denis Donaldson worked as a British agent. At the risk of oversimplifying, the minister's job is to shaft republicanism; that of the agent is to shaft Republicans … there is no clear blue ideological sea between minister and agent.'[23]

In developing his case, McIntyre was always careful to affirm his own opposition to any return to violence. In a March 2001 interview with *The Guardian*, for instance, he declared, 'Omagh should never have happened and when it did, those should have been the last deaths … republicans should have found out by now, armed strategy is the road to disaster.'[24] In line with this, as has been noted, his criticism of the Real IRA was often scathing.[25] After the murder of Belfast man Daniel McGurk (see below, page 177), McIntyre wrote, 'As a fighting force the Real is considered a very shabby pretender to the IRA throne. Stephen Hawkins [sic] would be hard pushed to come up with a reason for its existence … After almost a decade in the field it should accept that it is not fit for purpose.'[26]

Still, *The Blanket* was not averse to giving the 32 County Sovereignty Movement space to publish statements and press releases on its website.[27] Equally, significant sympathy was evinced for the imprisoned Real IRA leader, Michael McKevitt. The post-trial statement issued by McKevitt, for instance, in which he claimed to have been 'systematically denied the right to a fair trial' appeared on *The Blanket*.[28] McIntyre himself wrote a piece questioning the validity of the trial and argued that 'The grief-stricken victims of the Omagh bombing are being offered vengeance in place of justice.'[29] Thereafter, *The Blanket* also published excerpts from a pamphlet written by McKevitt's sister-in-law, Marcella Sands, entitled *The Framing of Michael McKevitt: Omagh, David Rupert, MI5 & FBI Collusion* as well as further articles and interviews that allowed McKevitt to put his message across.[30]

Moreover, it was clear that McIntyre felt significantly more respect for the 32CSM and its membership than he did for Sinn Féin. In a report on a 2004 Easter oration in Derry, addressed by Marian Price, McIntyre noted that those present were 'republicans that I at any rate did not agree with but republicans nonetheless'. Viewed from this perspective, the unreconstructed nature of Price's views was something to be cast in positive light, vis-à-vis the contemporary stance of the Provisionals:

> She maintained that her movement would never accept a partitionist assembly and that the Northern state was irreformable. She promised unremitting and ceaseless resistance ... A Chinese wall may separate her views from my own today but at least I knew I would not hear her tell us that she had starved for Stormont, had never been in the IRA, or that she had only gone to England for the Cheltenham Races and had inadvertently been caught up in a dastardly republican plot to bomb the British capital.[31]

There was, therefore, more than a little ambiguity in the attitude of McIntyre and *The Blanket* towards those still supportive of violent republicanism.

Alongside this, another central thesis for *The Blanket* centred on the social control that was allegedly exercised by the Adams–McGuinness leadership within republicanism: 'people are more afraid of being marginalised than of being wrong ... Ostracism is a powerful tool carefully honed to exert maximum pressure upon those who decline to conform.' The same piece referred to the leadership's 'thought police' and the way in which it was 'committed to zero tolerance of alternative viewpoints'. 'Dissent' was said to be treated as a 'contagious disease' within the ranks of the Provisionals, where a 'regime of truth' enforced a 'pervasive culture of conformity'.[32] In line with this, *The Blanket* gave a platform to those who left Sinn Féin and were prepared to criticise the internal culture of the party. The Kilkeel-based councillor Martin Cunningham, for example, was said to have been a 'casualty of the Sinn Féin leadership's "go-Stick strategy"', whose experience belied 'the pretence that Sinn Féin was somehow a democratic party'.[33] In an interview with McIntyre, Cunningham claimed that the atmosphere within the party was one of 'Dictatorship, just dictatorship. Total control. Total censorship ... Anybody who disagrees with the party is sent on their way.'[34]

Similarly elsewhere, it was asserted that there was an 'ongoing systematic campaign by the Provisional republican movement to suppress those other Republicans who are opposed to the Provisionals' political project'.[35] Much emphasis was placed on apparent attempts by Sinn Féin to control nationalist communities and IRA attacks aimed at those who were opposed to the Provisionals.[36] As has been described, this led McIntyre to publicly identify the Provisional IRA as responsible for the murder of Joseph O'Connor in October 2000. This action, moreover, appeared to generate a response from the Provisional movement. It was subsequently reported that McIntyre's house was picketed, and in February 2001 he claimed to have been assaulted in reprisal for speaking out.[37] This did little, however, to deter *The Blanket*; on the contrary, the intimidation was used as further evidence of Provisional efforts to hold unchallenged sway over certain communities.

To prove this point further, attention was drawn, *inter alia*, to the examples of Brendan Shannon, Brendan Rice and then especially the case of Robert McCartney in 2005. The latter was described as a symbol of how 'the IRA have lost their way'. The McCartney murder was portrayed as an attack on 'the hard-earned legitimacy and rich history of republicanism'; the 'vicious criminality' of the murderers was said to have placed 'clear blue water' between the current IRA and its antecedents. The Provisional IRA, it was argued, had simply become a 'militia' of 'Greenshirt Thugs', for a Sinn Féin that sought to 'violently impose the peace process'.[38]

Another individual whose treatment at the hands of the Provisional leadership was much publicised by *The Blanket* was Richard O'Rawe. In 2005, O'Rawe released a revisionist account of the 1981 hunger strike which claimed that the IRA leadership – and principally Gerry Adams – had rejected a deal that could have saved the lives of six of the hunger strikers.[39] O'Rawe also suggested that this was done in order to facilitate the electoral ambitions of Sinn Féin: 'six men were sacrificed to bring Sinn Féin onto the constitutional altar.' In a lengthy interview carried out by McIntyre, O'Rawe claimed that the IRA leadership had urged him to 'pull' the book prior to its publication. At the core of this, it was alleged, was a 'shameful cover-up to protect the leadership from acute questioning'.[40] Moreover, after the book's release, O'Rawe said that he had been 'demonised' by the leadership as a result – and made 'persona non grata [and] someone who was to be ostracised'.[41]

Taking forward this theme of the hunger strikes and their possible abuse by the Adams–McGuinness leadership, in August 2006 McIntyre gave the oration to the Annual H-Block Hunger Strike Commemoration in Bundoran, County Donegal. During this address, he attacked the Provisional movement's exploitation of the hunger strikes for political gain. He also lambasted their 'commercialisation' of the event and their attempts to turn it into a 'profit-making industry'. On this basis, McIntyre pointed to the 'ethical decay' that had beset republicanism during the 'corrupt peace process'. It had, he averred, in an echo of Marian Price, 'fallen prey to the Stick virus'.[42]

Time and again, a theme to which *The Blanket* returned was the alleged lies and falsifications of the Provisional movement's leadership. According to McIntyre, 'Truth is a concept alien to the Northern conflict … Today, Sinn Féin and truth do not form a brace of words that rest easily in each other's company. Sinn Féin despite pretending otherwise is a truth repellent outfit.' The party was said to be wedded to 'a practice of organised lying' for the sake of its political ambitions.[43] The strategy of the leadership, it was argued, was 'based on an utter falsehood' – the failure to admit that the IRA had been defeated. As McIntyre had written as early as 1999, 'the defeat of the Provisional IRA [had been] hushed up by all sides' and kept hidden by a 'policy of organised lying, methodical lying'.[44] Thereafter, in his opinion, a resort to untruths had become the preferred modus operandi of Sinn Féin.

For this reason, a signature moment for McIntyre and *The Blanket* came with the unveiling of a 'No More Lies' campaign in May 2004. This pulled together a petition demanding that the Provisional leadership 'tell the truth' with regard to the peace process. Republicans were urged to 'reclaim the honour and integrity' of their cause and speak out against their 'criminalisation'. The petition declared accusingly, 'Our beliefs were traded for the realities of the current process, a process that suits the interests of political parties and not the common people.' What was required, it said, was a congress of republicans that might 'stand against the tyranny in our midst'. Signatories to the document included RSF-linked people such as Mickey Donnelly from Derry, together with dissident republicans such as Paddy Fox and ex-Sinn Féin members such as Martin Cunningham and John Kelly. The latter figures were both men who had left mainstream republicanism and attacked the internal culture of the Provisionals as 'totalitarian' and over-centralised. Also featured were the *Fourthwrite/Blanket* stalwarts Tommy Gorman, Brendan Hughes, Tommy McKearney and Anthony McIntyre himself.[45]

Another signatory to the 'no more lies' campaign was Dolours Price, sister of Marian, who the following year added her own personal addendum, in the form of an open letter to Gerry Adams, which was also published in *The Blanket*. In it, she offered a bitter assessment of what the Provisionals had achieved: 'Not a lot to see so many people dead for, hardly a resounding victory, not even a resounding compromise. I'd say you were fairly whipped.' And from there, Price addressed Adams in a series of barbed questions:

> How were you lured down the path you conned others to tread behind you? Was it the interfering cleric or the flattery of the Americans; did it go to your head, did the ego soar and at last did you see the possibility that you might be somebody? ... I should wish you well, Gerry, but my heart is too heavy to feel it and I cannot be a hypocrite. I have no regrets. My trust was abused.[46]

Through such outpourings, combined with the regular online articles, *The Blanket* easily established itself as the foremost intellectual thorn in the side of the Adams–McGuinness leadership – at least within republican circles. And yet, there was a wider field of criticism developing in this period, which analysed the Provisionals from a traditional Irish republican perspective.

THE NEW REPUBLICAN FORUM

Similar in nature to *The Blanket* was the New Republican Forum (NRF), which was created in January 2003 by those prisoners who had disassociated themselves from the Real IRA leadership a few months previously (see above, pages 145–6).[47] The Forum declared itself to be 'a coalition of political and community activists founded to challenge the political status quo in Ireland by providing a radical republican alternative to the mainstream political establishment'.[48] Much of its focus was on the Good Friday Agreement and the involvement of Sinn Féin in that accord. Interestingly, it made a specific point of acknowledging the weakness, hitherto, of traditional republican challenges to the peace process and/or Agreement: 'For the past number of years, Irish republicanism has been in disarray: the movement is in a demoralised state and seemingly impotent in opposing the British occupation.' In this context, the purpose of the NRF was to bring together republicans, so

as to 'lay the foundations for a new and revitalised national movement';
to 'chart a course for the future republican struggle'.[49]

As with the 32 County Sovereignty Movement, the NRF avowed
that it was not a political party; nor was it to be seen as 'an adjunct to
any military organisation'.[50] Among its four aims were commitments
to: a re-evaluation of republican history in order to 'learn from our
past and to utilise it as a springboard to the future'; an effort to establish 'new republican and community-based organisations to campaign
on local, national and international issues of republican significance';
a liaison with 'other progressive forces, nationally and internationally,
to further the cause of anti-imperialism'; and an attempt to create a
'range of progressive media outlets in Ireland' on the basis that 'a com-
pliant media ... is the greatest weapon in our opponents' arsenal.'[51]
This last pledge was itself interesting in that it no doubt reflected the
dissidents' own sense of being marginalised from the dominant narrative of the time, which was centred on the peace process – and according to which they were an atavistic remnant of a past era.

The NRF manifesto, issued in early 2003, elaborated further on
these goals. It stated that the group stood for the 'reunification of Ireland' and was against 'all aspects of British interference in Irish affairs'.
To this end, it declared itself resolutely opposed to the Belfast Agreement, 'which subverts the Irish people's inalienable right to self-determination'. Other aspects of the NRF's ideology included the
'promotion and development of Irish culture' and hostility to 'the resurgence of imperialism as a political ideology led by the United States'.[52]

From February 2003 through to August/September 2006, the NRF
published *Forum Magazine*. During that time, it ran to twenty-nine
editions that covered a variety of issues. Unsurprisingly, the most consistent theme, similar to what was occurring in *The Blanket*, was the
alleged betrayal of republicanism by the Provisionals. But this was combined with pieces on recent republican history, such as the creation of
the Free State in 1921–3, or the 1981 hunger strikes.[53] There were also
tributes to dead republicans and coverage of the 'plight' of republican
prisoners. And alongside this were pieces of opposition to US 'imperialism' (as allegedly embodied by western foreign policy in places like
Iraq and Palestine). With regard to the latter, though, the NRF was no-
ticeably quick to affirm that it 'opposes the actions of al-Qaeda as much
as it opposes the actions of the US and British governments'.[54]

To return to the core focus of the NRF, the first edition of *Forum Magazine* contained an instructive piece, 'Republicanism: A Failed Ideology?' This identified the numerous problems faced by the creed, foremost of which was said to be the fact that 'many of its former proponents' had 'abandoned it'. The consequence of this, it was acknowledged starkly, was that 'Republicanism has reached its nadir.' What was required now, according to the NRF, was an examination of the reasons for that failure, with the aim of rebuilding the 'credibility' of republicanism as a 'viable alternative to the status quo'.[55]

Along similar lines, a series of articles carried in the magazine from December 2003 through to January/February 2004 debated the subject, 'Is there an alternative to the Good Friday Agreement?' In response, one contributor, Liam Ó Ruairc, counselled patience, calling on republicans to be 'realistic' and accept their current weakness, while also preparing politically for the future so that they might 'seize the moment' when it came.[56] Darren Mulholland, meanwhile, recognised the 'disunity' within the republican family and described this as their 'greatest weakness'. Interestingly, however, he also argued that efforts to achieve unity were not the way to proceed, for reasons of 'practicality and desirability'. According to Mulholland, such unity was unlikely to be achieved any time soon. Moreover, he argued that Irish republicanism had, for the time being, become a 'toxic brew', by which he meant that the military organisations were 'characterised by criminality and incompetence'. What was required, Mulholland argued, was for dissident republicans to set aside disagreements on methods and embrace their 'strength in diversity' – with a broad, 'common manifesto', based on a 'vision of an alternative Ireland which everyone accepts as an improvement on the status quo'.[57] This theme was also taken up by Sean Mulligan in his contribution to the debate. The best option, in his view, was for the building of 'some sort of common position' among those opposed to the Good Friday Agreement. Another article, from Gerry Ruddy of the IRSP *árd chomhairle*, claimed that for republicans, it was 'not enough ... to curse the dark'; instead, they needed to construct a positive, tangible message. Unusually for those of this political persuasion, Ruddy also argued that 'it does little good to question the sincerity or genuineness of the PRM [Provisional republican movement]'. To his mind, their concessions were simply a function of their decision to 'enter into negotiations to see if they could advance their cause by purely political means'.[58]

Elsewhere, the premise that dissidents needed to accept the scale of the disaster they faced was taken up in an entirely separate piece entitled 'Betraying the Cause', which maintained that the republican cause had suffered 'its severest setback in generations'. A crucial aspect of the argument that followed was the suggestion that this 'defeat was entirely self-inflicted'. It was said to be a function of the Provisional leadership's actions and its decision to go along with the peace process. The aim of this process was said to have been the very thing that the British government had tried and failed to achieve over the previous three decades: the defeat of the IRA. In line with this, the idea was promulgated that the 'IRA ... was being sabotaged from within'. The illusory nature of the Provisionals' rationale for entering the peace process – the supposed power of a 'pan-nationalist consensus' in negotiations – was highlighted. The reality, it was argued, was that this had been 'the primary source of the disaster'. What had ensued as a result, it was said, was that 'the Provisional leadership [had] succeeded in turning what was at worst a political and military stalemate into a catastrophic disaster ... One would have thought that the IRA was on the point of defeat rather than being the most formidable guerrilla army in Europe.'[59]

In a similar vein elsewhere, the NRF bitterly criticised the Provisional 'counter-revolutionary betrayal', which was said to have 'devastated what was a strong, coherent and vibrant revolutionary movement'.[60] Building on this latter point, it was argued in another article that

> ... there will be those, however small in number, who haven't forgotten that this struggle wasn't an armed civil rights campaign in pursuit of 'parity of esteem' and 'ministerial portfolios'; that it was a national liberation struggle in which many young men and women paid the ultimate sacrifice ... this huge sacrifice and memory has been besmirched by the Provisional leadership's acceptance of the Belfast Agreement.[61]

Sinn Féin was thus said to have abandoned an 'orthodox republican analysis' on the nature of the British role in Ireland and on the position of unionists. What the party had ignored was the fact that 'Britain has a strategic interest in Ireland.' Its claims to the contrary were said to be 'duplicitous and misleading' and the Provisionals' acceptance of them had been a 'profound error of judgement'.[62]

The Provisionals, it was repeatedly argued, were in the process of

being converted into a form of 'constitutional nationalism', as reflected
in its supposed obsession with electoral considerations, above all else.
The 'prospect of doing well at the polls', it was believed, had over-
ridden 'every other consideration including republican principles and
objectives'.[63] For this reason, it was said that 'Sinn Féin, formerly a
revolutionary republican political party, has become a constitutional
nationalist political party, on a par with the SDLP and Fianna Fáil.'[64] As
a consequence of all this, the party was judged to be 'on the road to
nowhere'. In the words of one contributor to *Forum Magazine*, Sinn
Féin's 'electoral mandate means absolutely nothing in republican terms.
No matter how many votes they get or seats they win, they will not
force a British withdrawal from the six-counties via electoral politics.'[65]

Furthermore, this transformation within Sinn Féin was said to have
been underwritten by an internal ethos which held that 'no lie was too
big and no action too despicable.' This attitude was held to have
received official endorsement from both the British and Irish governments. For instance, in the wake of the attempted abduction of the
Belfast dissident Bobby Tohill by the Provisional IRA in early 2004, an
article in *Forum Magazine* noted that 'Dublin has turned a blind eye to
quite a number of incidents involving Provisionals, both north and
south of the border.' The 'whole so-called "peace process"' was said to
be built on 'nothing but lies'. On this reading, 'The list of lies was
virtually endless … [and] they sold out the republican struggle with this
very tactic.'[66]

In all of this, it is possible to discern the same analytical framework as
that adhered to by other dissident groups – from Republican Sinn Féin,
to the 32 County Sovereignty Movement, to *The Blanket*. From this perspective, the settlement accepted by the Provisionals was judged to be a
poor return on the years of violent conflict; equally, its inability to deliver
a republican solution in Ireland was lamented. As to why the Agreement
should nonetheless have been accepted, an explanation was found in
the alleged weakness of Provisional leaders such as Gerry Adams and
Martin McGuinness. Whether through exhaustion, poor political
analysis, or as a result of more sinister machinations (particularly a yearn-
ing for power), they were held to have betrayed a once-strong republican
movement. The responsibility for Provisional defeat thus lay four-square
with them. Republicanism, as a whole, was judged to have been devastated
as a result. And on this reading, the once-mighty Provisional IRA had

been laid low, not by the security forces but by its own leadership, which had consciously sold the republican movement 'down the river'.

Unsurprisingly, then, great emphasis was placed in *Forum Magazine* on the notion that there would be further 'sell-outs' by the Provisional leadership. From 2003, it was said to be 'inevitable that they will accept the reformed PSNI/RUC and ultimately take their seats on policing boards'.[67] Thereafter, it was regularly suggested that Sinn Féin would accept a 'reformed RUC'.[68] By the same token, a further article pointed towards the 'all too inevitable act of PIRA disbandment'. And in this context, another staple of dissident republican discourse was deployed, with an effort made to compare Gerry Adams to Cathal Goulding (the Official IRA leader from whom the Provisionals had broken in 1969–70), the aim being to make explicit the parallels between the Sinn Féin leader and the hated 'Sticks': 'For over a decade many republican dissenters have predicted that the decommissioning of physical-force republicanism and the acceptance of [a] reformed British state in Ireland would be the culmination of the Adams–Goulding strategy.'[69] Furthermore, it was argued that the disbandment of the IRA was now an option, because 'no viable militant republican alternative is in existence' which could pull in disgruntled volunteers.[70]

The completion of the decommissioning process by the Provisional IRA in 2005 was described by *Forum Magazine* as marking 'the final PIRA humiliation'. The event was said to be a product of 'political surrender', with this having preceded the eventual 'military surrender':

> The PIRA has left the field without having attained any of its initial political objectives and without its arsenal intact. Revolution has been replaced with constitutionalism. The demand for British withdrawal has been replaced with a craven pursuit of political power in partitionist institutions in both parts of the island ... By any standards it is an ignominious end for what was once the world's most effective guerrilla army.[71]

In an article the following year, the founder of the Real IRA, Michael McKevitt, concurred. The British state had, he averred, through the political process, 'inflicted the political and military defeat upon the provisionals which it could not achieve in the field', with the result that the latter had engaged in 'a wholesale political and military capitulation'.[72]

In the face of such developments, the task of dissident republicans

was described as being to create 'an efficient and highly organised propaganda machine', which could confront the Provisionals and make the
case against the Agreement.[73] Or, in the view of one *Forum* contributor, it was for the building of a '"realistic" Republicanism' that could
'meet the demands of the twenty-first century'. The aim of such a
movement would be to challenge Sinn Féin – to deny it the 'open field'
it had enjoyed to that point. It would, it was contended, also prevent
republicanism from being captured by 'criminal elements' who were
allowing it to be 'dragged through the gutter'.[74]

The conclusions to be drawn from these different analyses, though,
were not so coherently laid out. Republicans, one author argued,
should not suggest that 'armed struggle is an end in itself'. On the contrary, 'republicans should not be angry with the Provisional leadership
because they abandoned the armed struggle, republicans should be
angry because they abandoned republicanism.'[75] Further elaborating on
this theme, another article was explicit in acknowledging the 'RIRA's
failure'. Criticism was also reserved for 'a faction of apolitical, mili-
taristic republicans who believe that to argue for a termination of armed
activity under any circumstances, one ceases to be a republican'. The
reality was said to be that armed struggle had never been 'a matter of
principle'; a fundamental prerequisite was alleged to be the existence
of 'mass support'. The absence of the latter in the present era was
judged to make 'the continuation of a low intensity campaign' 'futile'.
Indeed, it was described as 'immoral' to risk the loss of life in such
circumstances.[76]

In similar fashion, the prisoners, on whose initiative the *Forum
Magazine* had been launched, were adamant that they did not support
a renewed military campaign. During a 2005 interview with one of
their number, Declan Caroll, he reflected on the split within the Real
IRA of three years previously and asserted that the decision to
withdraw allegiance from the outside leadership had been the correct
one. He claimed that rational observers would agree with the views of
a fellow prisoner, Ciarán Mac Lochlainn, who had observed: 'there
exists at present "something between an illusion of war and an aspiration
to wage war, but there is no war".' The fact was, Caroll maintained,
that 'the current strategy of the main dissident groups is futile and is preventing the emergence of a genuine democratic republican alternative
to the provisional movement.' Nevertheless, he was not absolute in his

rejection of physical force; instead, it was a qualified dismissal of it as an option *at the present time*:

> ... armed struggle is not a viable option ... for the foreseeable future ... [but] one can predict no further than that – [today] armed struggle will not be a factor in Irish political life ... [but] we don't have the right nor are we entitled to speak for future generations ... if British government interference in Irish affairs remains undiminished, future generations may once again decide to take up arms in pursuit of national independence.[77]

The message, in other words, appeared to be that physical-force republicanism was temporarily gone, but not forgotten; the underlying impulse was that the 'pike might have to be put in the thatch' for the time being, but the torch would be passed on by those who remained defiantly set against the Provisionals' betrayal.

THE MILITARY OPTION ENDURES

Against this background, it was perhaps unsurprising that there were those not prepared to wait for 'future generations' to carry forth the war against British 'interference in Irish affairs'. In spite of the dismal state of the surviving republican paramilitary organisations in the wake of the Real IRA's 2002 split, military activity, of some sort, continued. As in 1999, when the RIRA had convulsed in the aftermath of Omagh, in 2002–3 it was those working under the banner of the Continuity IRA that led the way, engaging in irregular (and mostly unsuccessful) operations. In January 2003 this group said it was behind attempts to target premises in, first, Keady in south Armagh and then Dungannon, County Tyrone, with fire-bombs. The following month it claimed responsibility for a bomb that exploded at a Territorial Army base in Belfast, as well as a more serious device that damaged the police station in Enniskillen, County Fermanagh. And across 2003, the name of the CIRA continued to be linked with attempted or abandoned attacks, as well as periodic arms finds.

The INLA, for its part, continued to adhere to its 'military' ceasefire, and a 2003 statement made it clear that 'the INLA does not see a return to armed struggle as a viable alternative at this time.' The group's position remained one of opposition to the Good Friday Agreement ('a failed and flawed agreement') and Northern Ireland ('a failed political entity'); but it also acknowledged that the referenda which had approved the Agreement had shown 'the will of the Irish people'. For this reason, the INLA remained committed to its self-defined cessation. At the same time, it refused to follow the Provisional movement and engage in arms decommissioning as part of any 'squalid political deal'. Instead, the group said it would retain its weapons for self-defence, but maintain a 'no first-strike policy'.[78]

In addition to these organisations, the faction of the Real IRA that had rejected any ceasefire clearly remained committed to a violent campaign. In January 2003, Damien Okado-Gough of Derry's free 'Channel 9' TV News was given an interview by a RIRA army council member who declared that the organisation remained 'steadfast in our allegiance to the principles and ideology for which our comrades and predecessors sacrificed so much'. The October 2002 statement from Portlaoise was described as 'absolute treachery' and 'an attempt to force a ceasefire on this movement by two individuals'. The allegations made in that statement (presumably with regard to the descent into criminality and the absence of any leadership strategy) were said to be 'a complete red herring'. Moreover, the still-belligerent leadership claimed to have consulted prisoners elsewhere in Northern Ireland and in England and found that they were 'in total support of the leadership of Óglaigh na hÉireann'.[79] Asked if there was any possibility of a ceasefire, the answer was an unequivocal no: 'We cannot envisage a ceasefire in any circumstances other than in which a declaration of intent to withdraw from the occupied Six Counties is made by the British government.'[80] The RIRA representative also denied there had been any contacts with others regarding a possible ceasefire.

The interview offered an enlightening insight into the worldview of unreconstructed republican militants. They totally rejected any notion that the Agreement could serve as a stepping stone to Irish unity – as argued by the Provisionals – and instead described it as a 'negation of Irish democracy'. There was also the refutation of any suggestion that the Provisional IRA had somehow been motivated less by republican goals than by the injustices experienced by the Catholic/nationalist community within Northern Ireland (again, there were hints that Sinn Féin was attempting to revise history in this way): 'The Republican struggle was never about economic and social change within the

Six-County state – it was about destroying that very state and getting the British out of Ireland.'[81]

More generally, the RIRA spokesperson's words demonstrated a devotion to the time-honoured constructs of standard republican thinking. On the subject of unionism, for instance, there was little sympathy for the idea that those who wished Northern Ireland to remain British might be inspired by genuine ideological attachment. Rather, the Real IRA encouraged them 'to assert their position within the Irish nation' and accept that they too were the 'victims of British imperial and colonial history'. Curiously, the group's representative also felt able to assert that 'more people from a Unionist background are becoming disillusioned with their positions viz. a viz. [sic] the British Government, the United Kingdom in general and the subordinate and the subservient attitude to the British monarchy in particular.' The evidence for this shift in attitudes was left unstated.

The Provisionals, meanwhile, were said to now occupy the role of 'poacher turned gamekeeper'. Their leaders were judged to have 'followed the path of others in abandoning the Republic' and become 'integral components of partitionist political systems'. Consequently, members of that group were now 'no longer Republicans … They have gone from revolutionary Republicanism to constitutionalism Nationalism.'[82] By contrast, the Real IRA remained committed to an uncompromising view of the applicability of violent actions in the struggle for Irish freedom: 'Armed struggle has always been the right of every Irish person in asserting their independence from a foreign invader. The British continue to claim sovereignty over part of our country and while that is the case armed struggle will always be justified.'[83]

When asked about the extent of their own support base, the RIRA's representative claimed it was 'considerable, certainly sufficient, principled and politically aware'. Moreover, in response to the question of how an armed campaign could be justified, given that a majority of the Irish people had voted for the Good Friday Agreement, he responded by quoting de Valera's attitude to the 1921 Treaty: 'the Irish people did not have the right to vote for treachery.' In line with this, the contention was that by opposing the latest 'sell-out', the Real IRA was following in the footsteps of a 'long and noble tradition' that involved being in a minority and operating without electoral mandate. The assumption was that 'in the future, history will judge us to be correct in our political analysis.'[84]

This anticipated, retrospective endorsement was again entirely in keeping with the ethos of 'no compromise' physical-force republicanism as sculpted by Patrick Pearse. The RIRA narrative thus pointed backwards, drawing succour from the lineal succession that ran from Easter 1916 to the events of 1919–21 and down through the successor republican movements of the twentieth century; equally, it looked forwards to the future, in which their refusal to abandon the true path would be legitimated by subsequent generations.

Upon these theoretical foundations, those members of the Real IRA who were opposed to a cessation of violence continued to pursue the path of violence. As it pledged at that year's Easter commemoration, the group was committed to 'the long haul until ultimate victory is achieved'.[85] From April 2003, a group operating under the name of the RIRA reappeared, with a foiled attempt to detonate a bomb outside the Laganside courts complex in Belfast. A couple of months later it was announced that a major bomb, concealed within a van that was destined for Derry, had been intercepted. And in July 2003, the police revealed that they had broken up a 'spy ring', linked to the RIRA, which was operating out of the Royal Victoria Hospital in Belfast. Clearly, the group was far from inactive. In addition, there were some suggestions that the disparate military factions within dissident republicanism might be united into a single bloc. By August 2003, for example, Paddy Fox, a leading dissident from east Tyrone, was being heralded as the man who could possibly unite the various splinter groups.[86] Elsewhere, informed commentators noted that the Campbell faction of the Real IRA – which had rejected any possibility of a ceasefire – had displaced the McKevitt faction as the majority shareholder of the brand by the middle of 2004.[87]

From the autumn of 2003 still-violent republicans (whether operating under the flag of CIRA or RIRA) appeared to adopt a new tactic: the targeting of the new civilian infrastructure of the PSNI, as embodied by the new District Policing Partnerships (DPPs). There was doubtless an appreciation of the fact that these bodies – a key part of the post-Agreement 'settlement' on policing in Northern Ireland that had been envisaged by Patten – needed cross-community support if they were to succeed. For this reason, from a dissident perspective the intimidation of nationalist members of the DPPs made some sense; they could be viewed as a possible weak point through which the political process might be undermined. As a result, in various locations across the province, members of DPPs found themselves subject to both hoax warnings and actual attacks.[88]

From January 2004, the Independent Monitoring Commission (IMC) began to issue reports on the state of paramilitary organisations in Northern Ireland – offering a new insight into these groups, based on a mixture of public and security source information.[89] Its findings in 2004–5 seemed to confirm the languid and fissiporous nature of dissident republicanism. The IMC's first report in April 2004 thus claimed that the CIRA leadership had only 'tenuous' control over its units, with the latter acting 'in the main autonomously'. A similar situation was said to exist with regard to the Real IRA, which was judged to have little 'central strategy'. Moreover, from November 2004, the IMC formally acknowledged that there were 'two distinct factions' within the RIRA, confirming the reality of the 2002 split and its enduring legacy.[90]

In spite of this, the very fact of the organisations' existence was said to bear witness to the desire of a minority to continue 'the Republican struggle by physical violence'. Moreover, the Real IRA was itself described as being, in spite of its internal divisions, 'potentially a very dangerous terrorist group'. It was clear, in other words, that the flame of physical-force republicanism was still there – and though its light might have dwindled to unprecedentedly low levels, it continued to burn. Moreover, it could have occasionally lethal consequences, an example of which was provided by the August 2003 murder of Daniel McGurk in the lower Falls area of Belfast.

An image of 'sporadic' CIRA activity was conveyed in the IMC reports of November 2004 and May 2005; while in the October 2005 report, the CIRA was described as being only 'intermittently active'.[91] One of its more noteworthy actions had seen the organisation attempt to provoke violence during the Orange parades of 12 July 2005 in Belfast; the IMC held it responsible for the throwing of blast and petrol bombs against the security forces on that occasion.[92] The RIRA, meanwhile, was depicted as still being 'the most active' of the dissident republican groups and was said to pose a serious threat.[93] The efforts of both groups to target members of the police continued to be a consistent feature of their respective strategies, as evinced by the threats, hoax devices, incendiary attacks, postal bombs, shootings and violent assaults launched against PSNI members, police stations and DPP members.[94]

With regard to the latter, one of the most high-profile incidents was the brutal attack on the deputy chair of the Policing Board, Denis Bradley, in 2005 (not the first time he had been targeted).[95] Elsewhere, elements of the RIRA were also noted to have engaged in a spate of incendiary attacks against major shopping centres in March 2005; and later that year, the group was described as being 'violent, dangerous and determined'.[96]

Overall, however, the fortunes of both the RIRA and CIRA continued to decline in this period. The resumption of violence proved faltering, as indicated by the foiling of various attacks. The RIRA's efforts were characterised more by disappointment than success. By the same token, the CIRA, which had described its attempt to bomb a Belfast PSNI station in January 2005 as the 'start of things to come', failed to make a major breakthrough.[97] More broadly too, the two groups' efforts to recruit and train had proven faltering – despite the perceived opportunities provided by the formal standing down of the Provisional IRA in July 2005. Attempts to target disaffected Provisionals had, in the estimation of the IMC, met with only 'very limited success'.[98] Militarily inclined dissident republicans suffered significant reverses, with a string of activists arrested and imprisoned.[99] Prior to 2005, there had also continued to be a serious question mark over the space that would be afforded to the dissidents by the Provisionals. The murder of Joseph O'Connor in Belfast in 2000 has been discussed; so too, the dissenters' accusations of Provisional IRA intimidation and violence. Speculation as to the possible eruption of a deadly feud between mainstream and dissident republicanism was strengthened by the murder, in March 2003, of Keith Rogers, a Provisional IRA volunteer who was shot dead in Cullaville in south Armagh.[100] In May 2003, Gareth O'Connor, also from south Armagh, was believed to have been abducted and murdered by Provisional IRA members.[101] Alongside these were other reports of assaults and abductions of men alleged by the Provisionals to be dissidents, including George McCall, Stephen Moore, Kevin Perry, Brendan Rice, Brendan Shannon and Bobby Tohill.[102]

Moreover, following the McGurk murder in autumn 2003, Provisional rhetoric seemed to harden. Gerry Adams thus described it as a 'brutal and senseless' act, steeped in 'gangsterism'.[103] While in the wake of the killing, an editorial in the *Andersonstown News*, under the control of former Sinn Féin councillor Máirtín Ó Muilleoir, gave an unforgiving editorial assessment of the RIRA:

Derided and rejected by the vast majority of this community, these micro-groups continue blindly down the road to nowhere, ostensibly fighting a war against the British, but in reality doing nothing more than visiting grief and pain on this community. It is all too obvious that the vast bulk of the energy – physical and mental – of dissident republicans goes into attacking other republicans in the most hysterical fashion. Given such behaviour, it was only going to be a matter of time before guns were turned on those who, for whatever reason, place themselves outside the magic circle of 'republican purity'. If the Real IRA and its supporters represent republican purity, then this community wants nothing to do with it. What this community does want is for these people to go away and to go away now.[104]

Somewhat ominously, a further editorial stated that there were 'echoes of the infamous Irish People's Liberation Organisation (IPLO)' – a reference to the violent republican splinter group that had been forcibly suppressed by the Provisional IRA in October 1992.[105] The newspaper reported too that five Real IRA men had fled Belfast for fear of action and that 'The lower Falls is now bracing itself for an all out war on the RIRA – similar to action taken against the now disbanded IPLO in 1992.'[106]

In spite of such predictions, though, the Real IRA was not to be diverted. It would later announce that it had 'disciplined' some members who were involved in the McGurk killing and were judged to have acted for their own ends.[107] Later still, it would acknowledge that the murder was 'criminally wrong'.[108] But in neither instance was there any sense that McGurk would be the last to die at the hands of the organisation. Instead, the Real IRA proclaimed that its 'war' would continue.[109]

Nevertheless, perhaps because of the various problems they had experienced, there appeared to be a growing willingness on the part of violent dissidents to concentrate on 'soft targets' such as Protestant families or Orange halls. The IMC accused the RIRA of harassing the former in some rural areas of Northern Ireland; arson attacks on the latter were more generally attributed to the CIRA.[110] That the organisations should be willing to engage in such activity seemed only to confirm their relative impotence – and their inability to strike against higher-value targets such as the PSNI or British army.

More broadly, the sense of fragmentation and discord within dissident republican ranks only strengthened over this period. From October 2005, the IMC began routinely to include in its reports a section that described the actions of 'dissident republicans generally', listing incidents which could not be attributed with certainty to any particular group.[111] The eighth report of the IMC in early 2006 elaborated on this, describing the shifting allegiances that seemed to characterise the dissident republican world, with ties often being based on personality or family connection. Significantly, it was noted that this could lead to co-operation between CIRA and RIRA personnel at a local level – with the erosion of formal hierarchies of command and control.[112] At the same time, the inference appeared to be that such phenomena were a symptom of disarray within dissident circles.

This impression of disintegration was reinforced by the appearance of two new organisations, identified by the IMC in 2006: Saoirse na hÉireann (SNH) and Óglaigh na hÉireann (ONH). The former was said to comprise 'disaffected, and largely young, republicans, mainly from the Belfast area'. ONH, meanwhile, was described as having 'splintered' from the CIRA and to be based mainly in County Tyrone, around the town of Strabane.[113] June 2006 seemed to bring the emergence of yet another group with 'the appearance of a number of armed men at a graveside in the North West … calling themselves the Republican Defence Army (RDA)'.[114] The men in question had gathered at the graveside of a recently deceased republican, Séamus O'Kane from Castlefin near Strabane, and promised to take action against 'paedophiles, druggies, criminals and people who are working under the umbrella of British intelligence'.[115] Beyond their initial 'show of strength', however, nothing more was heard of the RDA. Finally, it was reported in May 2008 that an organisation calling itself the 'Irish Republican Liberation Army (IRLA)' had issued a declaration in late 2007 threatening members of Sinn Féin who were involved in District Policing Partnerships.[116] The IRLA was said elsewhere to be a splinter from the Belfast CIRA.[117] Like the RDA, though, the IRLA appeared little more than a passing entity. Either way, what all of this seemed to confirm was the late 2007 conclusion of the IMC that even though 'there was an attempt to achieve greater unity among dissident republicans … in practice the evidence is of more fragmentation.'[118]

In spite of these seemingly insuperable difficulties, again perhaps the most important (and surprising) feature of this often-confusing picture was the simple fact that violent dissident republicanism survived. As previously, the underlying belief behind such actions appeared to be the notion that the 'flame' had to be kept burning; the fight had to be kept going – even in the face of overwhelming odds. This sentiment was most clearly articulated by Ruairí Ó Brádaigh, speaking in February 2003 in the aftermath of the attack on a police station in Enniskillen that injured six police officers:

> These are indications that militant republicanism is not dead. Maybe you can say these things are only a token and instead of a flame they are only a spark, but so what, it is there. That is the lesson of history and none of us can change that. History didn't stop evolving when the Stormont agreement was signed.[119]

The RSF president's words reflected the importance attached to the violent act itself – which almost took on the role of a kind of militant, or deadly, 'street theatre'. Certainly, this ethos was indicative of the vanguard-ist and self-consciously elitist ethos which underpinned both CIRA and RIRA activity in this period. Isolated though they might be from wider public support, these dissidents ardently believed that the conduct of armed actions remained necessary to keep the republican cause alive. As the IMC concluded in 2006, the two groups remained, respectively, 'committed to terrorism' and 'active and dangerous'.[120] The reality was that the security services were never able to extinguish their brand of militancy. That this should have been so was in part due to the continued existence of an ideological framework that legitimated violence.

INCUBATION OF THE IDEOLOGY

The post-2002 existence of various republican groups which held to a line fervently critical of the Provisionals has already been noted. Initiatives such as the New Republican Forum, the Irish Republican Writers' Group and *The Blanket* all helped preserve more traditional modes of Irish republicanism. In addition, it is possible to make the case that by their very existence they helped, either implicitly or explicitly, lend succour to those still prepared to engage in violent actions. More directly still, there remained those organisations that were far less ambiguous in the support they gave to the actions of the paramilitaries.

In this period, the fortunes of those groups most closely linked to

armed republican groups tended to mirror those of their militant counterparts. As a result, the experience of groups such as the 32CSM and
RSF was likewise one of decline. To give but one example, the publicity organ of the 32CSM, *The Sovereign Nation*, disappeared in 2002
(having first been published in August 1998). It then re-appeared with
five editions in 2004, but came out only twice in 2005 and 2006.

With that said, though, it would be a mistake to see the 32CSM as
having been extinguished altogether. The group took any opportunity
it could to put across its well-established message. As Francie Mackey
declared in 2004:

> We must get our message, the republican message, out loud and
> clear without ambiguity that for as long as the British government
> maintain an illegal sovereign claim to part of our country there
> will be people to challenge them. We must never reach a point
> where our forefathers died in vain.[121]

To this end, the 32CSM published a series of leaflets in this era outlin-
ing its various positions. One declared that the suspension of Stormont
in 2002 should have left no-one in any doubt as to 'who exactly wields
power in the six counties'. The reality, it said, was that the peace
process and Agreement had merely given Sinn Féin a 'small share in
administering British rule'. Far from being in Stormont to 'wreck' it, the
Provisionals were said to be bound in to the structures of partition,
with no 'ace card' to play; decommissioning had gone and it was predicted that Sinn Féin would soon join the policing board.[122]

Another pamphlet rejected the notion that Northern Ireland could
be reformed and held the problems of the province to be a function of
the British presence: 'The conclusion reached by the Republican
Movement was that Sectarianism was a symptom, British rule the
cause.' On this interpretation (one previously held to by the Provisionals), sectarianism was used by the British to maintain their position in
Ireland. The peace process was said to have forced Sinn Féin 'to jettison its republicanism in favour of a nationalistic, territorial scramble
for more and more votes'. In this way it had entrenched sectarianism
and was incompatible with 'Real Republicanism' which 'is all-inclu-
sive and values all citizens equally'. The 32CSM then claimed that it
would not 'stoop to the anti protestant, "Celtic supporter" mentality
that seems to have become endemic in Catholic working-class areas in

recent years'. Instead, it promised to invoke the 'spirit' of 1916 in its politics.[123]

Taking forward the historical analogy, a further leaflet in the series celebrated the eightieth anniversary of the end of the Irish civil war by drawing a comparison between the Good Friday Agreement of 1998 and the 1921 Treaty. Both were said to be a violation of Irish sovereignty. Where Sinn Féin and the Provisionals had once 'heroically' defended the sovereignty principle, they were now deemed to have 'strayed from the path of true republicanism'.[124] This line of argument was also reiterated by Francie Mackey at the 2004 32CSM Easter oration. There, he referred to the Provisionals as 'revisionists' who were using the memory of 1916 to further their own political ambitions.[125]

Elsewhere, in his 2005 New Year statement, Mackey declared that the results of the peace process were clear to see: 'The Unionist veto has again been secured and implemented.' Equally, he contended that 'the PSNI/RUC have not changed ... they are a political armed entity imposing the will of the British Government.'[126] In an example of the synergy between the political and military arms of the movement, the parallel New Year statement from 'Óglaigh na hÉireann' (the Real IRA version) likewise condemned Britain's 'colonial police' and saw the group pledge to continue its struggle for 'a genuine and lasting democracy in Ireland'. It rejected calls from 'the hypocrites in the British, Dublin and Stormont administrations to become involved in the "democratic" process', because this was a 'twisted version of democracy', arising out of the denial of Irish sovereignty and partition.[127] As Francie Mackey put it on another occasion, on this view, the very meaning of 'democracy' could be contested:

> Mandates in Ireland mean different things to different people ... Our sovereignty mandates us to act in its defence. Its violation by the British government mandates us to seek its restoration. The 32CSM will not abandon our mandate.[128]

According to this analysis, no genuine republican could consciously be involved in such a process, the obvious implication again being that the Provisionals had placed themselves outside the republican family. The 'unprincipled leadership' of that movement was said to have 'abandoned the principles of the 1916 Proclamation'.[129] The attempt by Sinn Féin to claim the 'lineage' of the Proclamation was described as 'disgusting', given that 'their actions are alien to that great document of 1916.'[130] All of this was held to stand in stark contrast to the 32CSM, which would 'never besmirch the reason for which [the leaders of 1916] died by an acceptance of anything that falls short of their stated objective'. Mackey declared that his group would 'continue to uphold the principled stand they took on behalf of the Irish people'.[131]

In this way, it remained the case that the 32CSM preferred to attack the *leadership* of the Provisionals rather than the movement as a whole. Given the ongoing policy changes being embraced by that movement, there clearly remained an expectation that it was possible to win over sections of the Provisional rank and file. To this end, the 32CSM continued to anticipate the next Provisional 'sell-out'. As previously, much was made of what was assumed to be an imminent endorsement of the police: 'they are preparing to grasp the nettle of joining the PSNI/RUC … they will use British laws to attack republicans.' Here, the notion of historical inevitability in the evolution of the Provisionals was also highlighted – with these next steps portrayed as 'the natural progression of the process they signed into'.[132] This emphasis on a linear narrative was further underlined in the wake of the PIRA statement that formally ended the armed struggle in July 2005: 'This statement is merely the logical conclusion in a process signed up to by the Provisionals in April 1998.'[133] In this way, attention was drawn to the fact that the 32CSM *could* make a plausible case that it had been right all along; they *could* claim to have been proven correct by the passage of events.

Naturally, the 32CSM was quick to seize on episodes like the Denis Donaldson affair, which seemed to prove the cogency of their own 'leadership-focused' narrative of Provisional-decline – in this instance because a prominent member of the Provisional leadership had been shown to be actively working for the British state. *The Sovereign Nation* stressed that the 'outing of senior Sinn Féin strategist Denis Donaldson' came 'hot on the heels of the exposure of IRA internal security chief Fred Scapiticci [sic] as a British agent'. The revelations, it argued, had made it clear that 'two pivotal players in the leadership machine' were 'long term British agents working to deliver Britain's counter insurgency agenda'. With regard to the latter, it went on to note, 'The British "security agenda" has been fulfilled and delivered. It has been a total success for the British as a strategy to defeat republicanism … British strategy and the Sinn Féin leadership's strategy now overlap to a remarkable degree.' The supposed fusion of objectives between the British state and the Provisional leadership was a theme repeatedly pressed, with the reader invited to ponder the meaning of recent disclosures: 'At what stage does seemingly total incompetence by the Adams McGuinness leadership take on the form of strategic design?' The scarcely-concealed suggestion was that 'the Adams and McGuinness clique' was effectively complicit in 'Britain's counter insurgency strategy'. The article ended by insisting that 'Republicans must demand answers' from a leadership that has consistently refused to be 'clear and truthful with the republican base'.[134]

Similar in character was Mackey's 2006 indictment of Sinn Féin for having engaged in a 'fundamental misrepresentation of the basic republican position'. In that instance, he also specifically challenged the Provisional movement's attempt to assert control over legacy of the hunger strikers, given that Sinn Féin acceptance of the Agreement was said to have undermined 'the legitimacy of their struggle'.[135] The message was clear: through their participation in the peace process, the Provisionals were assumed to have forsaken the essence of true republicanism. As the 32CSM chairman put it in 2003, 'By signing the agreement they have signed away the Irish nation. They have criminalised what Pearse and Connolly stood for, and what republicans stand for today.'[136]

Against this ideological background, the 32CSM was determined to follow the clarion call of Mackey and make its voice heard. Inevitably, for example, the group was strident in its efforts to discredit the character of David Rupert as the trial of Michael McKevitt approached in 2003. In a piece that appeared on the group's website in February of that year, Rupert's background was said to be a 'murky story of embezzlement, corruption and ... contacts with many criminal elements in the US which included the mob and FRU [Force Research Unit]/MI5 in Ireland'. Again, there were suggestions that Rupert might have been partly responsible for the Omagh bombing; emphasis was also drawn to his relationship with MI5, 'the same organisation responsible for murder and strife in Ireland for the past 33 years'. Indeed, MI5 was said to be the one beneficiary of the trial. By comparison, the McKevitts were described as 'the most vilified family in the history of the Irish troubles'.[137]

Alongside such agitation in defence of the RIRA leader, the 32CSM continued to engage in various activities by which it could both proselytise the faith and challenge the dominance, in republican terms, of the

Provisional movement. In 2003, in the run-up to the Northern Ireland Assembly elections, the 32CSM initiated a 'boycott' campaign, issuing leaflets that urged people to 'Vote Nobody!' It claimed there had been '5 years of concessions with nothing to show' and urged republicans to abstain from involvement in the elections 'because only by voting for nobody can you show your contempt for British administration in Ireland'.[138] In the event, the campaign was a categorical failure. In that poll, Sinn Féin's dominance of the Catholic/nationalist community was confirmed; it became the second largest party overall in Northern Ireland, winning 162,758 votes (24 per cent of the total), compared to the SDLP's tally of 117, 547 (17 per cent). This marked an increase of some 20,000 votes as compared with the previous Assembly election in 1998 – a sure sign that the 32CSM's call for voter abstention had made little impact.[139]

In spite of such disappointments, the 32CSM did continue to seek expansion wherever possible in this period. In 2003 the group held its first Easter parade and commemoration in Belfast – for so long a purely Provisional stronghold.[140] Equally, with regard to Northern Ireland's 'second city', in April 2004 it was reported that the 32CSM was to open an advice centre, to be shared with the IRPWA, in the Bogside in Derry; that same month they had held an illegal rally to commemorate 1916 in the Creggan area of the city, where the guest speaker was Marian Price.[141]

On top of this, the group persisted with its UN initiative, regardless of the lack of traction this appeared to generate.[142] Within Ireland, meanwhile, in October 2005 the 32CSM launched a new document entitled *Irish Democracy: A Framework for Unity*. Submissions were sent to the British and Irish governments, Sinn Féin and the unionist parties, detailing the party's vision for 'Irish democracy and Irish sovereignty'.[143] At the launch of his group's initiative, Mackey emphasised the shortcomings of the Agreement, which had, in his opinion, failed to challenge British sovereignty. To expose the truth of this, a series of questions were posed to various actors. The British, for example, were asked, 'Does the British Government at some future date foresee the ending of the Union between the Six NE Counties of Ireland and the UK?' To the Irish government, questions turned on whether it viewed 'the GFA as a mechanism towards Irish unity' and how it proposed to win unionist consent. The 'broad Unionist community' itself was asked to consider whether the ending of the Union might be 'probable' or 'inevitable'. Finally, from Sinn Féin, the group demanded to know, 'What is the basis of incompatibility between membership of Sinn Féin and the 32CSM?' and whether the party was prepared to hold discussions with the 32CSM. Other questions focused on Sinn Féin's attitude to sovereignty, national self-determination, the Agreement and 'the use of armed force' to defend and restore Irish sovereignty.[144] In June 2006, Mackey reported to his associates that the only response to this 'strategic initiative' had been 'silence', thereby 'confirming our view that the current peace process is predicated on exclusion and is thus fatally flawed'.[145]

Elsewhere, the campaign for segregation in Maghaberry prison that the Sovereignty Movement had initiated in 2002 and continued thereafter saw the group operating on more comfortable, recognisably 'republican' terrain. The campaign itself had both a practical and ideological impulse. With regard to the former, it was said to be about the preservation of the republican prisoners' safety, as 'up until then [they] had to cope with a hostile and life threatening environment.' More important, however, was the fact that it was a bid for the 'de facto recognition of their political status'.[146] In this way, it tapped into a key 'republican' issue (the assertion of the politically inspired character of Irish republican violence), which, even for those unsupportive of the RIRA–32CSM, generated an automatically sympathetic response. In mid-2003, for example, over 100 people attended a support rally in the Provisional heartland of west Belfast.[147] That same month, an editorial in the generally pro-Sinn Féin-leaning local newspaper, the *Andersonstown News*, described the authorities' integration policy as 'a major error' and noted resonantly that

> ... the no-wash protest will also resonate with the broader republican community with its obvious echoes of the protests of the late 1970s and early 1980s ... This could provide a rallying point for the small and disparate republican groups on the outside, which do not currently enjoy a great measure of public support.[148]

Allegations of brutality towards prisoners, the paper claimed, would 'strike a chord' with republicans; and for this reason, it called on the British government to 'reverse this crazy prison policy'.[149]

The push for in-prison segregation saw protests at the headquarters of the Northern Ireland Prison Service by supporters on the outside, together with rooftop protests, mass cell-wrecking and then a dirty and no-wash protest.[150] The man claiming to be the 'OC' of up to twenty RIRA inmates, John Connolly (from Newtownbutler, County Fermanagh), also sent a statement to *The Observer* newspaper saying that they were 'prepared to do whatever it takes' to force a change of policy, with suggestions they were preparing for a full-blown hunger strike.[151] In the meantime, at the end of July 2003, a mix of RIRA, CIRA, INLA and non-aligned republican prisoners in Portlaoise announced that they would launch a seventy-two-hour fast in support of demands for segregation in Maghaberry; this was to be followed by subsequent, weekly forty-eight-hour protests.[152]

Eventually, the prison authorities felt compelled to concede the demands in all but name.[153] This success, though marginal, was subsequently heralded as a significant achievement. A statement issued by republican prisoners in 2004 claimed that, 'We, the Republican prisoners, have borne witness not to the defeat of Republicanism, but to the rise of a rejuvenated movement across the island of Ireland. We remain fully confident of our eventual victory.'[154] What is more, the realisation of segregation did not bring an end to the prison-related campaign; rather, that concession was effectively 'banked', with the 32CSM and its allies then moving on to what it deemed to be the next big issue. The IRPWA thus continued to claim that there were 'serious abuses' ongoing in Maghaberry, human rights infringed by the 'bully boy' attitude of prison staff.[155] By the end of May 2004, new rounds of protests had begun after former RIRA leader Michael McKevitt rejected terms for temporary release to attend his mother's funeral. In response, prisoners were punished with the loss of both a month's privileges and some remission.[156] At the same time, there were new threats (ultimately unrealised) of a hunger strike in protest at policy, especially the level of control exerted over prisoners and the practice of strip searching.[157]

On 1 April 2006, the IRPWA held a 'protest for political status' in Derry, both to commemorate the twenty-fifth anniversary of the 1981 hunger strikes and to oppose the fact that the British government, in its view, continued to treat 'captured Republican volunteers as criminals ... [and] portrayed their struggle as a criminal conspiracy rather than a legitimate resistance to colonial rule'.[158] Soon after, it was announced that Aiden Hulme, then in jail in England, was launching a hunger strike in pursuit of his 'repatriation' to Ireland.[159] In the event, that strike ended after just four days because of medical complications. Nevertheless, attention continued to be focused on Hulme's demands and the 32CSM–IRPWA was not alone in making the case. That same April, Paul Doyle of the New Republican Forum organised a protest at the Department of Justice in Dublin, demanding urgent action be taken to return Hulme to Ireland; and partly in response, a senior official in the Irish embassy in London agreed to meet Hulme in prison.[160] On 17 June 2006 another picket was organised by the NRF, this time outside the GPO in Dublin, to protest at Hulme's situation. According to a report published in *The Blanket*, some sixty to seventy people attended, drawn from a variety of republican organisations, including Sinn Féin. That party's general secretary, Mitchel McLaughlin, publicly called on the Irish government to intervene to secure Hulme's return.[161] In December 2006, Aiden and his brother Robert were both moved from the UK to Portlaoise.[162]

In pushing the prison issue, some of the arguments made by the 32CSM/IRPWA found echo in the commentary of Anthony McIntyre and *The Blanket*. There, the notion that incarcerated members of still-violent republican organisations should be classed as 'political prisoners' was accepted as self-evident; so too a narrative that held the authorities north and south as fundamentally responsible for any problems in the jail.[163] Such matters, it would seem, drew an instinctively sympathetic response from within the broader republican family. As McIntyre would later write, during a further round of prison-centred protest:

> The Maghaberry screws are at it again, beating and harassing republican prisoners. These days few things from the political past annoy me. I have grown accustomed to the failures and the futility, the lies and the let downs. Life goes on, it always finds a way. Prison related matters are different. They grip me like few other things. I witnessed so much violence by the screws in the H-Blocks of Long Kesh, on occasion being subject to it, that when I learn of it taking place again anger leeches through me.[164]

It was the ability of the prisons to induce such a response that made it strategically useful for groups like the 32CSM, expanding their potential base of support (this is not to say, of course, that the members of 32CSM did not themselves feel strongly about it).

Further testament to the unifying capacity of issues related to republican prisoners can be gleaned from the fact that the 32CSM was again joined in its activism by the otherwise alliance-shy Republican Sinn Féin, which, as been described, continued to articulate its own traditionalist message irrespective of the party's political marginalisation.[165] In June 2006, a new prison campaign was launched in Maghaberry, this time involving prisoners refusing to eat meals in their cells. This was backed up by weekly twenty-four-hour 'solidarity' fasts in Portlaoise prison in the Irish Republic. Publicity on the outside was in part co-ordinated by an organisation calling itself the Republican Prisoners Action Group (RPAG); in reality, this appeared to be an adjunct to RSF. The protests were intended to highlight opposition to the 'Controlled Movement' policy then in operation within the jail, by which not more than three prisoners were permitted to be out of their cells at any one time and which required a staff-to-prisoner ratio of 4:2 or 3:1. This arrangement was described by the RPAG/RSF as 'excessively restrictive'. The prisoners wanted it removed and, in a conscious echo of the 1981 hunger strikes, they called for the granting of 'five demands': free association; an end to Controlled Movement; the right to full-time education; the provision of a separate visiting facility; and the right for the prisoners to organise their own landings.[166]

Beyond the prisons, RSF, as might have been expected, remained devoted to a purist conception of Irish republicanism, which imagined 'history' to be the ultimate arbiter of authority and legitimacy. In April 2006, the party's newspaper, *Saoirse*, thus described the 1916 Proclamation as sitting 'easily with any of the great documents of human progress and emancipation'. The Easter Rising was likewise said to be 'a seminal moment, not only in Irish history but in the history of anti-colonialism internationally'. In purely Irish terms, that Rising had, it was argued, 'inspired a new generation to take up once more the age-old fight for Irish freedom' and paved the way for the events of 1918–21. In the event, however, the promise of 1916 remained unfulfilled: 'the Ireland of 2006 is the result of the defeat of the freedom struggle of 1916–21.' Nonetheless, RSF claimed a 'direct and unbroken continuity with the men and women of 1916' and contended that 'The lesson of Irish history is clear, whilst British rule remains in any part of Ireland there will be resistance to it.' In line with this, the party pointed to the message from 'the leadership of the Republican Movement', noting that, 'The Irish Republican Army has declared that it is still very much alive in the form of the Continuity Irish Republican Army which remains active and dedicated to the achievement of Irish independence for however long this may take.'[167]

Unsurprisingly, for RSF, the steps taken by the Provisionals in 2005 were described as 'the final act of treason by those who would have described themselves as Republicans'.[168] The Provisional movement, it was maintained, had abandoned the true path. As Packy Carty of RSF's east Tyrone branch declared: 'We stand here today labelled dissidents but we have never distanced ourselves from Republican principles. It is those in the Provisional leadership who are the dissidents and through their actions they have copper-fastened British rule in our country and must be condemned for doing so.'[169]

RSF's own, religiously-inspired, devotion to republican doctrine was made explicit in the Bodenstown oration given that same year by Sean Maguire (son of Tom), which quoted the 1913 words of Patrick Pearse: 'We have come to the holiest place in Ireland: holier to us than the place where [St] Patrick sleeps in Down. Patrick brought us life, but this man died for us.' Maguire then went on to quote Pearse's famous 1915 epithet to Jeremiah O'Donovan Rossa: 'Life springs from death and from the graves of patriot men and women spring living nations.' Only RSF, he said, could claim to possess the 'unbroken sequence of loyalty and faithfulness to Tone's teaching right down to the present day'; they were the 'faithful inheritors of a glorious past', who could 'pass on our inheritance clean and unsullied to our children and grand-children and generations yet to come. Let the generations be able to look back on us and say they were faithful and they left us a priceless legacy.'[170] The absolutist and eternal character of this vision was thereby made explicit; so too the extent to which it could never accommodate the concessions made by the Provisionals. Such concessions were judged immoral when set against historical legality:

> Sovereignty is unalienable and cannot be voted away no matter how great the majority. The referendum which purports to withdraw the claim to the Six Counties is invalid because the Six Counties are an integral part of the ancient Irish nation. The Six Counties are as much part of *Críoch Fodhla* [the territory of Ireland] as any other country.[171]

By the beginning of 2007, according to Ó Brádaigh, the 'net' had 'finally closed on the Provisionals', with that movement taking 'the final step on the road of compromise, betrayal and sell-out', a road that was said to have begun in 1986. What remained, he declared, was RSF, constituting the 'sole political alternative' and occupying the ground of 'solid and unequivocal Irish Republicanism'.[172]

In this way, RSF joined the 32 County Sovereignty Movement, as well as newer groups like the New Republican Forum and that connected with *The Blanket*, in offering critical analysis of the Provisionals, based on long-established republican positions. Consequently, even as the Northern Irish peace process edged forward in the years 2002–6, the ideology of Irish republicanism did not disappear.

CONCLUSION

The period after the Real IRA split in 2002 saw dissident republicanism reduced to its lowest ebb. The failure of that organisation's second attempted campaign led to further retreat and fragmentation. Prospects for violent republican 'armed struggle' against the British state had scarcely looked as bleak as they did in the years 2003–5. Intermittent actions conducted by the CIRA and RIRA indicated that the military torch had been preserved, but this was a flickering flame rather than a burning brush.

The irony was that this period also saw something of a hiatus in Northern Ireland's political process. After the October 2002 suspension of the institutions provided for by the Good Friday Agreement, it would be another five years before they were resurrected. Attempts to negotiate their return in 2003 and 2004 proved abortive. The Assembly elected in 2003 became (in)famous for the fact that it never actually sat; the body remained suspended for the duration of its lifespan. What this, in turn, reflects, is the extent to which much commentary over the years on how the dissident threat can best be tackled has been misplaced. So often, an implicit assumption within that commentary has been the notion that the Agreement and its institutions represent the best antidote to the challenge of dissident republicanism. Yet, in reality, the period in which the Agreement was almost wholly in abeyance also marked the nadir of violent dissident republicanism.

By contrast, Sinn Féin reached its political apex over the same timeframe. In 2001, in Northern Ireland, it had displaced the SDLP as the largest party within the Catholic/nationalist community – a longstanding goal of the Provisional leadership. At Assembly elections in 2003, European elections in 2004, and the British general election of 2005, this position was confirmed. In the process, Sinn Féin established itself as comfortably the second-largest party in the province as a whole (behind Ian Paisley's DUP).[173] South of the border, meanwhile, Sinn Féin had secured a major breakthrough at the 2002 Irish general election when it increased its representation from one to five seats. And in the 2004 European elections there, the party had secured over 10 per cent of the vote. From that position, many were anticipating a Sinn Féin return of over ten seats at the next parliamentary elections, with the possibility of the party becoming 'kingmakers' in the Dáil. Though neither scenario materialised, the period from 2002 down to at least 2005 appeared nothing short of triumphant for Sinn Féin. Certainly, the party seemed untroubled by the challenge it faced from dissident, or more traditionally minded, republicans.

Nevertheless, as electorally irrelevant as such groups as Republican Sinn Féin or the 32 County Sovereignty Movement were during this era, they stuck obdurately to their interpretation of the Irish republican creed. In so doing, they were joined by newer expressions of non-violent 'dissident republicanism' such as the New Republican Forum, the Irish Republican Writers' Group and *The Blanket*. Together, these served to incubate the ideology and fill the vacuum that was left by the failure of physical-force republicanism. They ensured that the central tenets of the faith were not lost, while they simultaneously developed a narrative that was deeply critical of the Provisionals. The alleged 'lies' and perfidy of the latter were castigated, as was the wider peace process. In the shared view of these otherwise disparate groups, Sinn Féin was judged, by its involvement in that process, to have abandoned the republican cause.

By 2007, this message had been refined and restated *ad nauseam*. Indeed, from this period, the sense appeared to gather in certain of these dissident circles that, the case having been made, there was nothing further that could be done. Moreover, there was a sense that the Provisionals were now lost for good. The de facto 'standing down' of the IRA in 2005 coupled with the political settlement of 2006–7 (more of which below) perhaps generated a sense that there was no longer any sense of debating the question of where Sinn Féin was headed and the rights or wrongs of this in republican terms. It was for this reason that in 2008, after seven vehement years, *The Blanket* was wound up. In a valedictory article, Anthony McIntyre described the online journal as having been 'an analytical tracking device which monitored and predicted changes within Provisional republicanism as a result of the peace process'. The reality of the situation, he claimed, was:

> We are now in a post-republican world where others, such as éirígí, have picked up the baton and hope to reverse the order of things ... [*The Blanket*'s] fate, just like its role, was inextricably bound to Provisional republicanism whose long slow strangulation it traced. When Provisionalism, as a republican project, reached the knacker's yard, from *The Blanket*'s perspective little remained to be said ... *The Blanket* was a chronicle of a death foretold. It diagnosed the virus that ravished and consumed the body of republicanism. The dissection of the corpse involves a different branch of pathology.[174]

It was for this reason that the enterprise was now brought to a conclusion.

In similar fashion, the website of the NRF was also closed down at the beginning of 2008 and the group itself seemed to stop functioning. By that point, it would seem there was a sense in which *The Blanket* and the NRF, as loci of debate and discussion, had served their purpose. Now it seemed time for more activist entities to take up the baton. There was a wider perception too that after four years of inertia, the dissident republican world was increasingly entering a state of flux; and it is this latest period of instability that the final chapter of this book will consider.

NOTES

1. English, *Armed Struggle*, pp.318–21.
2. W. Paul, 'Rebels on the March', *Scotland on Sunday*, 11 March 2001.
3. A. McIntyre, *Speech Made to Sinn Féin Internal Conference, the RDS, Dublin*, 30 September 1995.
4. J. Bew, 'Defeat, Decommissioning and Dissolution? An Interview with Anthony McIntyre', *The Cambridge Student*, 28 November 2002.
5. Cited in English, *Armed Struggle*, p.319.
6. 'We, the IRA, Have Failed', *Guardian*, 22 May 1998, also in A. McIntyre, *Good Friday: The Death of Irish Republicanism* (New York: Ausubo, 2008), pp.6–8.

7. A. McIntyre, 'Time Has Run Out for an Armed IRA', *Observer*, 20 October 2002.
8. A. McIntyre, 'A Dark View of the Process: Interview with Brendan Hughes', *Fourthwrite Magazine*, March 2000.
9. Ibid.
10. 'Radio Free Éireann Interview with Brendan Hughes', 32CSM, 22 April 2000.
11. A. McIntyre, 'An Ambiguity that Corrupts', *Observer*, 2 September 2001.
12. 'Editorial', *Fourthwrite*, no. 1 (March 2000).
13. A. McIntyre, 'Paying the Price', *The Blanket*, 29 November 2003.
14. A. McIntyre, 'The Right Road to Power', *The Blanket*, 12 December 2003.
15. A. McIntyre, 'Time Has Run Out for an Armed IRA', *Observer*, 20 October 2002.
16. A. McIntyre, 'A Subtle but Brilliant use of the IRA', *The Blanket*, 11 January 2004.
17. A. McIntyre, 'One More For the Road ... And Another. Come Back Tony & Bertie, The Crack's 90', *The Blanket*, 24 October 2003.
18. A. McIntyre, 'For Whom the Bell Tolls', *The Blanket*, 19 January 2003. See also A. McIntyre, 'The Police Process', *The Blanket*, 30 June 2004; A. McIntyre, 'The Paravisional Alliance', *The Blanket*, 18 July 2004.
19. 'Another Victory for Unionism', *Sunday Tribune*, 4 July 1999.
20. 'Sinn Feign', *Parliamentary Brief*, December 2001.
21. 'It Never Happened – Again', *The Blanket*, 9 April 2002.
22. 'More Spies May be Lurking in Sinn Féin's Cupboard', *Irish Times*, 20 December 2005.
23. 'Poison', *The Blanket*, 23 December 2005.
24. R. Cowan, 'Ex-Paramilitary Warns of Terrorism Deaths', *Guardian*, 6 March 2001.
25. See above, pages 137, 145. Other writers for *The Blanket* were also prepared to articulate strong criticism of still-violent republicanism. See, for example, P. Fitzsimmons, 'Dissident Republicans: Rebels Without a Plan', *The Blanket*, 17 April 2002; D. Carlin. '"Dissident Republicanism"', *The Blanket*, September 2003.
26. A. McIntyre, 'Mary McGurk – Giving Voice to the Abandoned', *The Blanket*, October 2005.
27. See, for example, J. Dillon, 'Death Threats and Harassment by the RUC/PSNI', *The Blanket*, 11 May 2003; 32 County Sovereignty Movement, 'Abduction of Republican', *The Blanket*, 12 October 2003; 32CSM Press Release, 'DPP Cover Up RUC/PSNI Malpractice Yet Again', *The Blanket*, 9 January 2005.
28. M. McKevitt, 'Statement of Michael McKevitt', *The Blanket*, 6 August 2003.
29. A. McIntyre, 'Revenge, Not Justice', *The Blanket*, 11 August 2003.
30. M. Sands, 'The Framing of Michael McKevitt: Omagh, David Rupert, MI5 and FBI Collusion', *The Blanket*, 22 June 2006; M. McKevitt, 'End Coalition with US', *The Blanket*, 2 February 2006; 'Interview with Michael McKevitt', *The Blanket*, April/May 2006.
31. A. McIntyre, 'The Laughter of Our Children', *The Blanket*, 18 April 2004.
32. 'It Never Happened – Again', *The Blanket*, 9 April 2002.
33. A. McIntyre, 'Sinn Féin and Democracy Be Damned: Martin Cunningham Interviewed (Part One)', *The Blanket*, 12 March 2004.
34. A. McIntyre, 'Sinn Féin A Dictatorship: Martin Cunningham Interviewed (Part Three), *The Blanket*, 21 March 2004. See also A. McIntyre, 'Sinn Féin – Sold a Pup: Martin Cunningham Interviewed (Part Four), *The Blanket*, 21 March 2004. For a further example, see *The Blanket*'s 2004 coverage of events in the Rathenraw estate in Antrim: A. McIntyre, 'Repression in Rathenraw', *The Blanket*, 16 August 2004; A. McIntyre, 'Rathenraw Threat', *The Blanket*, 19 August 2004.
35. 'The Rite of Passage', *The Blanket*, 3 October 2003.
36. 'Out of the Ashes of Armed Struggle ...', *The Blanket*, 5 September 2002; 'Hammering Dissent', *The Blanket*, 5 January 2003.
37. S. O'Neill, 'Groups Slam "McIntyre Witchhunt"', *Irish News*, 10 February 2001.
38. 'Quis Separabit? The Short Strand/Markets UDA', *The Blanket*, 29 May 2005 ; 'Time To Go', *The Blanket*, 21 February 2005.
39. R. O'Rawe, *Blanketmen: An Untold Story of the H-Block Hunger Strike* (Dublin: New Island Books, 2005).
40. A. McIntyre, 'The Blanket Meets Blanketmen', *The Blanket*, 16 May 2006.

41. R. O'Rawe, 'The Hunger Strike: Was There a Deal?', *Irish News*, 28 September 2009.
42. Provided in McIntyre, *Good Friday: The Death of Republicanism*, pp.111–17. For a further example of McIntyre's argument that the peace process induced a more general moral corruption, see A. McIntyre, 'Spot the Light', *The Blanket*, 21 December 2004.
43. McIntyre, 'The Battle Against Truth', *The Blanket*, 19 August 2007.
44. A. McIntyre, 'The Imperfect Peace: Terence O'Neill's Day Has Come', *Belfast Telegraph*, 18 August 2004.
45. 'No More Lies', *The Blanket*, 31 May 2004.
46. D. Price, 'An Open Letter to Gerry Adams', *The Blanket*, 31 July 2005.
47. B. O'Kelly, 'New Lobby Group Claims Mass Support of Veteran IRA Prisoners', *Sunday Business Post*, 26 January 2003.
48. 'An Introduction to the New Republican Forum', New Republican Forum [hereafter NRF] available at http://web.archive.org/web/20080119024934/www.newrepublicanforum.ie/About+the+NRF/aboutthenrf.htm
49. Ibid.
50. Ibid.
51. Ibid.
52. 'The New Republican Forum Manifesto', NRF, available at http://web.archive.org/web/20080119024934/www.newrepublicanforum.ie/About+the+NRF/aboutthenrf.htm.
53. S. Mulligan, 'An Unfinished Revolution', *Forum Magazine*, March 2004.
54. 'After Madrid', *Forum Magazine*, April 2004.
55. 'Republicanism: A Failed Ideology?', *Forum Magazine*, February 2003.
56. L. Ó Ruairc, 'Seize the Opportunity, Seize the Moment', *Forum Magazine*, December 2003.
57. D. Mulholland, 'Strength in Diversity', *Forum Magazine*, December 2003.
58. G. Ruddy, 'An IRSP Alternative', *Forum Magazine*, December 2003.
59. 'Betraying the Cause', *Forum Magazine*, April 2003.
60. 'Interview with Republican Prisoners', *Forum Magazine*, October 2003; for a similar line of argument see also P. Maguire, 'Does Britain Have a Strategic Interest in Ireland?', *Forum Magazine*, January/February 2004.
61. P. Maguire, 'End of the Line for the Provisionals?', *Forum Magazine*, August/September 2004.
62. P. Maguire, 'Does Britain Have a Strategic Interest in Ireland?', *Forum Magazine*, January/February 2004.
63. 'Peace and its Discontents', *Forum Magazine*, November 2003.
64. Ibid.
65. L. Sheridan, 'Sinn Féin: On the Road to Nowhere', *Forum Magazine*, August/September 2004.
66. J. Burke, 'Sinn Féin: Going for the Big Lie', *Forum Magazine*, April 2004.
67. 'Interview with Republican Prisoners', *Forum Magazine*, October 2003.
68. 'Interview with Michael McKevitt', *Forum Magazine*, April/May 2006.
69. P. Maguire, 'End of the Line for the Provisionals?', *Forum Magazine*, August/September 2004.
70. Ibid.
71. P. Maguire, 'The Final PIRA Humiliation', *Forum Magazine*, October 2005.
72. 'Interview with Michael McKevitt', *Forum Magazine*, April/May 2006.
73. 'Betraying the Cause', *Forum Magazine*, April 2003.
74. 'Criminality: The New Scourge of Republicanism', *Forum Magazine*, August/September 2003.
75. Ibid.
76. 'Post-Belfast Agreement: Is Armed Struggle a Viable Option?', *IRIB* [*Irish Republican Information Bureau*], August 2003. The material in this piece copied much from the Prisoners' Interview of earlier in the year.
77. 'Interview With Republican Prisoner', *Forum Magazine*, December 2005. Interestingly, much of Mac Lochlainn's article had also been published in the pro-Sinn Féin newspaper, *Daily Ireland*. In that version, though, he was more forthright in calling on dissidents to accept that the 'war' was over and stating that 'the decision to place the lives and liberty of young republicans at risk stops being merely wrong and becomes immoral'. See C. Mac Lochlainn, Letter to the editor, *Daily Ireland*, 15 October 2005.
78. 'INLA Statement on 5th Anniversary of INLA Ceasefire, 22 August 1998', Irish Republican Socialist Movement, available at http://irsm.org/statements/inla/030822.html

79. *Transcript of Interview Between Damien Okado-Gough and Member of RIRA Army Council*, January 2003 (available in Linenhall Library Northern Ireland Political Collection).
80. Ibid. See also 'Real IRA Will Keep Waging "War"', UTV, 31 January 2003.
81. *Transcript of Interview Between Damien Okado-Gough and Member of RIRA Army Council*, January 2003. For an example of Sinn Féin's reshaping of the Provisional IRA's struggle, see Gerry Adams' interview with *The Guardian* in 2007: N. Stadlen, 'Interview with Gerry Adams, Part I', *Guardian*, 12 September 2007.
82. *Transcript of Interview Between Damien Okado-Gough and Member of RIRA Army Council*, January 2003.
83. Ibid.
84. Ibid.
85. S. Breen, '"Real" IRA Pledges to Keep Up Campaign', *Irish Times*, 22 April 2003.
86. L. Clarke, 'Revealed: New Terrorist Mastermind', *Sunday Times*, 17 August 2003.
87. See, for example, H. McDonald, 'Most IRA Prisoners Held in Irish Jails', *Observer*, 29 August 2004.
88. 'Policing Board "Will Continue" Despite Threat', *Irish Times*, 11 September 2003; D. Keenan and A. Beesley, '"Real IRA" Threat to Policing Partnerships', *Irish Times*, 17 September 2003; S. McKay, 'Real IRA Steps Up Threats Campaign Over NI Policing', *Sunday Tribune*, 21 September 2003; B. Mullen, 'Serve the Police and We'll Bomb You', *Derry Journal*, 21 October 2003; P. Bradfield and A. Erwin, 'Attacks Won't Deter Me: O'Neill', *News Letter*, 1 October 2004; 'Police Probe Dissident Rooftop Protest', *Derry Journal*, 5 October 2004; 'Device Sent to Home of DPP Member', BBC News Online, 17 February 2005, available at http://news.bbc.co.uk/1/hi/northern_ireland/4272835.stm
89. 'About the IMC', the Independent Monitoring Commission, http://www.independentmonitoringcommission.org/index.cfm; 'How We Do It', the Independent Monitoring Commission, available at http://www.independentmonitoringcommission.org/doit.cfm
90. *First Report of the Independent Monitoring Commission* (London: Stationery Office, April 2004); *Third Report of the Independent Monitoring Commission* (London: Stationery Office, November 2004). The continued existence of this division was also evident in reports of physical in-fighting between the two sides in prison. See, for instance, T. Brady, 'Seven Hurt in Prison Brawl Between Real IRA Factions', *Irish Independent*, 18 January 2005.
91. *Third Report of the Independent Monitoring Commission*; *Fifth Report of the Independent Monitoring Commission* (London: Stationery Office, May 2005); *Seventh Report of the Independent Monitoring Commission* (London: Stationery Office, October 2005).
92. *Seventh Report of the Independent Monitoring Commission*.
93. *Fifth Report of the Independent Monitoring Commission*; *Seventh Report of the Independent Monitoring Commission*.
94. *Third Report of the Independent Monitoring Commission*; *Fifth Report of the Independent Monitoring Commission*; *Seventh Report of the Independent Monitoring Commission*.
95. *Seventh Report of the Independent Monitoring Commission*. Bradley's home had previously been targeted with petrol bombs in February 2004. See 'Petrol Attack on Vice-Chairman', BBC News Online, 13 February 2004, available at http://news.bbc.co.uk/1/hi/northern_ireland/3484295.stm
96. *Seventh Report of the Independent Monitoring Commission*.
97. *Fifth Report of the Independent Monitoring Commission*.
98. *Seventh Report of the Independent Monitoring Commission*.
99. S. Breen, 'Renegade Real IRA Thugs Smashed', *Sunday Life*, 20 July 2003; 'Man Jailed for Storage of Bomb Parts in his Garage', *Belfast Telegraph*, 6 December 2003; 'French Court Sentences 3 in Real IRA Trial', *Reuters*, 11 December 2006; J. Mooney, 'France to Seek Extradition of Real IRA Arms Suspect', *Sunday Times* (Ireland), 24 December 2006.
100. L. Walsh, 'They Still Haven't Gone Away You Know', *Irish Independent*, 9 August 2003.
101. M. Coleman, 'Father Lashes Out at IRA Lies', *Belfast Telegraph*, 1 September 2003.
102. A. McIntyre, 'Hammering Dissent', *The Blanket*, 5 January 2003; A. McIntyre, 'Crippling Critique', *The Blanket*, 25 June 2003; A. McIntyre, 'In the Shadow of Fear', *The Blanket*, 15 September 2003; A. McIntyre, 'The Rite of Passage', *The Blanket*, 3 October 2003; A.

McIntyre, 'Kidnapped', *The Blanket*, 2 November 2003; A. Martin, '32CSM Condemns PIRA Shooting of Republican Activist', *The Blanket*, 19 January 2004; A. McIntyre, 'Kelly's Cellars', *The Blanket*, 25 February 2004; A. McIntyre, 'The Enforcers', *The Blanket*, 1 March 2004. See also H. McGee, '"I Thought I Was Going to Get Killed. I said to Myself, I'm Going to Get Stiffed"', *Sunday Tribune*, 17 March 2002; 'IRA Targets Dissidents', *Sunday Times* (Ireland), 21 September 2003; M. Fitzgerald, 'Provos Accused Over "Kidnap"', *Belfast Telegraph*, 3 October 2003; S. Breen, 'Provos Planned to Make Tohill "Disappear"', *Sunday Life*, 22 February 2004.

103. S. Breen, 'How do Gerry and the Boys Keep a Straight Face?', *News Letter*, 21 August 2003.
104. Editorial, 'RIRA Murder: It Was Just a Matter of Time', *Andersonstown News*, 18 August 2003.
105. Editorial, 'Echoes of the Past in RIRA Behaviour', *Andersonstown News*, 25 August 2003.
106. A. Morris, 'Attacks Follow Funeral', *Andersonstown News*, 25 August 2003. For a similar analysis, see P. Colgan, 'Fears of Inter-IRA Feud Grow', *Sunday Business Post*, 31 August 2003.
107. 'Real IRA Men "Disciplined"', *Irish Independent*, 13 January 2004.
108. M. McCrory, 'Real IRA Admits McGurk Murder', Irish News, 13 June 2007.
109. 'Still at War', front page, *Sunday World*, 2 November 2003.
110. *Seventh Report of the Independent Monitoring Commission; Eighth Report of the Independent Monitoring Commission* (London: Stationery Office, February 2006).
111. *Seventh Report of the Independent Monitoring Commission.*
112. *Eighth Report of the Independent Monitoring Commission.*
113. *Eighth Report of the Independent Monitoring Commission; Tenth Report of the Independent Monitoring Commission* (London: Stationery Office, April 2006).
114. *Twelfth Report of the Independent Monitoring Commission* (London: Stationery Office, October 2006).
115. '"We Promise You a Bloodbath"', *Sunday World*, 25 June 2006.
116. *Eighteenth Report of the Independent Monitoring Commission* (London: Stationery Office, May 2008).
117. S. Breen, 'Republicans Face Death Threats as Tensions Grow', *Sunday Tribune*, 25 March 2007.
118. *Seventeenth Report of the Independent Monitoring Commission* (London: Stationery Office, November 2007).
119. D. Lister, 'Republican Diehard Awaits New Militancy', *The Times*, 13 February 2003.
120. *Twelfth Report of the Independent Monitoring Commission.*
121. F. Mackey, 'Easter 2004, Arbour Hill, Dublin: Oration Given on Easter Sunday at the Graveside of the 1916 Leaders', *The Blanket*, 11 April 2004.
122. *Suspension of Stormont: Suspension of Democracy?* (32CSM Educational Department, n.d.).
123. *Sovereignty and Sectarianism* (32CSM Educational Department, n.d.).
124. *80 Years Under Attack: Who Still Stands by the Republic?* (32 CSM Educational Department, 2003).
125. F. Mackey, 'Easter 2004, Arbour Hill, Dublin: Oration Given on Easter Sunday at the Graveside of the 1916 Leaders', *The Blanket*, 11 April 2004.
126. F. Mackey, '2005: New Year's Statement from the 32 County Sovereignty Movement', *The Blanket*, January 2005. For a similar set of arguments, see also F. Mackey, 'Can Republicans Succeed Without Upholding National Sovereignty?', *The Blanket*, 6 February 2005.
127. 'Óglaigh na hÉireann New Year Statement, 2005', *The Blanket*, January 2005.
128. F. Mackey, 'Misrepresentation of Republican Position Must be Addressed', *The Blanket*, 2 March 2006.
129. 32 County Sovereignty Movement, 'Easter Oration 2005', *The Blanket*, Easter 2005.
130. Press Release: 'Francie Mackey Easter Statement', 32CSM, 2006.
131. 32 County Sovereignty Movement, 'Easter Oration 2005', *The Blanket*, Easter 2005.
132. Ibid.
133. 32 County Sovereignty Movement, 'PIRA Statement "Neither Surprising Nor Historic"', *The Blanket*, 28 July 2005.
134. '"A Man With Whom We Can Do Business" – Brigadier General Sir Michael Glover: An Analysis of the Denis Donaldson Affair', *Sovereign Nation*, February/March 2006. This was

a theme to which Mackey would return in his 2006 Easter statement. See 'Press Release: Francie Mackey Easter Statement', 32CSM, 2006.
135. F. Mackey, 'Misrepresentation of Republican Position Must be Addressed', *The Blanket*, 2 March 2006.
136. S. Breen, '"Real" IRA Pledges to Keep Up Campaign', *Irish Times*, 22 April 2003.
137. R. Kelly, 'Press Release: MI5 Dirty Tricks in Ireland Continue', 32CSM, 17 February 2003.
138. *Vote Nobody!* 32CSM leaflet, 2003.
139. Figures taken from the Northern Ireland Elections website, available at http://www.ark.ac.uk/elections
140. S. Breen, '"Real" IRA Pledges to Keep Up Campaign', *Irish Times*, 22 April 2003.
141. 'Group With Real IRA Links to Open Centre', *News Letter*, 19 April 2004.
142. F. Mackey, 'Easter 2004, Arbour Hill, Dublin: Oration Given on Easter Sunday at the Graveside of the 1916 Leaders', *The Blanket*, 11 April 2004.
143. S. O'Neill, '"Political Terrorists" to Hold Conference', *Irish News*, 26 October 2005.
144. 'Feature: A Framework for Unity', *Irish Republican News*, 8–11 November 2005.
145. F. Mackey, 'Irish Democracy, A Framework for Unity', *The Blanket*, 27 June 2006.
146. M. Price, '"A Means to Fight Back": An Extract from a Speech Given to the International Symposium on Isolation, in Florence, Italy, 19–21 December', *The Blanket*, December 2003.
147. 'Rally Over Dissident Jail Protest', BBC News Online, 19 July 2003, available at http://news.bbc.co.uk/1/hi/northern_ireland/3080433.stm
148. Editorial, 'Prison Issue Must Be Resolved', *Andersonstown News*, 12 July 2003.
149. Ibid.
150. See, for example, 'Minister Denies Prisoners Assaulted', *Irish Times*, 10 July 2003.
151. H. McDonald, 'Hunger Strike Threat by Real IRA', *Observer*, 6 July 2003. See also S. Breen, 'Dissidents Pull a Fast One', *Sunday Life*, 31 August 2003.
152. S. Breen, 'Portlaoise Prisoners to Fast for 72 Hours', *Irish Times*, 26 July 2003.
153. L. Clarke, 'Maghaberry Segregation Recommended', *Sunday Times* (Ireland), 31 August 2003; B. Rowan, 'Jail Report Opts for "Separation"', BBC News Online, 5 September 2003, available at http://news.bbc.co.uk/1/hi/northern_ireland/3084492.stm
154. 'POW Easter Message 2004: Easter Message from the Irish Republican Political Prisoners in Maghaberry Gaol, County Antrim', 32CSM, April 2004.
155. M. Mulholland, 'Further Serious Abuses of Republican POWs', *The Blanket*, 13 May 2004.
156. T. Brady, 'Real IRA's "Dirty" Protest in Prison is Sweet and Neat', *Irish Independent*, 31 May 2004.
157. 'Real IRA Dishes Out Hunger-Strike Threat', *Sunday Life*, 30 May 2004; T. Brady, 'Real IRA Prisoners Call Off Their Rubbish Protest', *Irish Independent*, 18 June 2004.
158. 'Press Release: 25 Years On – Political Status Still Denied', IRPWA, 24 March 2006. See also M. Hall, 'Republican on Fourth Day of Hunger Strike', *Daily Ireland*, 10 April 2006.
159. M. Hall, 'Republican on Fourth Day of Hunger Strike', *Daily Ireland*, 10 April 2006.
160. C. Young, 'Embassy Man to Visit Hunger Striker', *Daily Ireland*, 19 April 2006.
161. P. Doyle, 'Aiden Hulme Repatriation Picket', *The Blanket*, 19 June 2006.
162. 'Repatriate Aiden Hulme Campaign', éirígí, available at http://www.eirigi.org/campaigns/aidenhulme2.html
163. A. McIntyre, 'Portlaoise Prison and Compassionate Parole', *The Blanket*, 20 May 2004. See also A. McIntyre, 'Hope Against Hopelessness', *Fourthwrite*, no. 4 (2000); A. McIntyre, 'Protest at Dundonald House', *The Blanket*, 3 July 2003.
164. A. McIntyre, 'Maghaberry and its Violence', *The Pensive Quill*, 9 May 2010, available at http://thepensivequill.am/2010/05/maghaberry-and-its-violence.html
165. 'Prison Protest Escalates', *Irish Republican News*, 23–27 June 2006, available at http://republican-news.org
166. Republican Prisoners Action Group, 'Protest Continues in Maghaberry', *The Blanket*, 26 June 2006.
167. 'The Struggle Goes On', *Saoirse*, April 2006.
168. 'Statement From the Leadership of the Republican Movement', *Saoirse*, April 2006.
169. 'Na Fianna Members Commemorated in Co. Tyrone', *Saoirse*, April 2006.

170. '"Bobby Sands and His Comrades Died on Hunger Strike Rather Than Wear a Prison Uniform"', *Saoirse*, July 2006.
171. Ibid.
172. 'RSF: Leading the Struggle', *Saoirse*, January 2007.
173. Figures taken from the Northern Ireland Elections website, available at http://www.ark.ac.uk/elections
174. A. McIntyre, 'The Blanket, One Last Time', *The Blanket*, 18 May 2008.

5

The Flame Reignites: Resurgence, 2006–10

SPACE TO OPERATE

In May 2006, it was revealed that MI5 still devoted over a fifth of its budget to combating the various branches of the Real IRA and Continuity IRA.[1] Eight years after the Good Friday Agreement, which was meant to have ended the conflict in Northern Ireland – and just ten months after the 7/7 attacks on London – it was a remarkable admission. At a time when the security services might have been expected to be totally preoccupied with the threat emanating from radical Islamist terrorists, a significant portion of their attention was directed towards violent Irish republicanism. In spite of the fallow years after 2002, it was clear that that phenomenon had survived. What is more, as has been described, the ideology had been kept alive in that 'wilderness' period by non-violent groups such as the New Republican Forum and *The Blanket*, which had preserved a more traditional brand of republicanism, in the face of Sinn Féin's relentless pragmatism. The latter had been the subject of a constant and often searing critique, which emphasised the alleged abandonment of principle in pursuit of power. With each new deviation from the conventional path of Irish republicanism, the gap between the Provisional movement and its republican critics grew ever more obvious.

The 28 July 2005 statement from the Provisional IRA, which announced an official end to that organisation's 'armed struggle', offered the clearest evidence to that effect. After almost a decade of prevarication and hints that their peace strategy might be reversible, the Provisionals were publicly saying that there was no going back. The formal standing down of the group – followed by the completion of the weapons decommissioning process in September 2005 – left little room for doubt. After two and a half decades of commitment (admittedly, nominal at times) to the 'Armalite and ballot box' strategy, the

Provisionals had now embraced something approaching a 'ballot box alone' approach. Unsurprisingly, groups such as the Real IRA decried the Provisionals as having 'reached a new low with their public and humiliating surrender of weapons'. To this was added the defiant assertion that 'the provo leadership did not begin resistance to British occupation in Ireland nor can they end it.'[2] The RIRA-aligned 32 County Sovereignty Movement was also quick to claim that this was 'the final act of a surrender that started many years ago'.[3]

Similarly, for Ruairí Ó Brádaigh, 2005 confirmed the accuracy of his earlier predictions. Though it had taken some time, Adams and McGuinness, just as Cathal Goulding and the 'Stickies' before them, were judged to have fulfilled the path set for them from 1986:

> Yes, the people who head up the Provisional movement at the present time did learn from the Sticky experience and rather than having an *árd fheis* where they said 'we should go into Westminster, Stormont and Leinster House', they engaged in the inevitability of gradualness ... So they say, 'we'll go into Leinster House and the war will go on, in fact it will strengthen the war' ... But in fact, all experience shows that oil and water don't mix.[4]

The truth of his analysis, Ó Brádaigh averred, had now been proven. The Provisionals had, as the Continuity IRA put it, engaged in 'the final act of treason by those who would have described themselves as "Republicans"'.[5]

Such criticism was far from unexpected. Yet, for all their disparagement, it seems likely that the dissidents, of whatever hue, may well have welcomed the move by the Provisional IRA; for what it did do was present them with very real opportunities. On the one hand, the Provisionals' actions could be portrayed, as they were, as the fulfilment of long-made prophecies by the dissidents. At the same time, the official exit from the stage of the Provisional IRA opened up space – both practical and political – into which the dissidents could potentially move.

Crucial, here, was the wider political context. The Provisionals had been forced into acting as they did by the political damage inflicted on Sinn Féin in the wake of the Northern Bank robbery of December 2004 and the murder of a Belfast man, Robert McCartney, in January 2005.[6] Against the background of a new focus on IRA 'criminality', the Provisional leadership had sought to rehabilitate the image of Sinn Féin by removing the paramilitary millstone from around its neck. Election results north and south of the Irish border in 2005 had suggested a stalling of the party's previously dynamic expansion. To recover this momentum, it was hoped that the formal conclusion of the Provisional IRA's campaign might re-energise the peace process, bring renewed respectability to Sinn Féin and provide a platform for a deal in Northern Ireland that would see the party re-enter government. The institutions of the province (as provided for under the Good Friday Agreement) had been in abeyance since 2002 – precisely because of concerns over Provisional IRA activity. In 2004, negotiations between Sinn Féin and Ian Paisley's Democratic Unionist Party, aimed at achieving a new, 'comprehensive agreement', had come close to success, but foundered because of persistent doubts over IRA intentions. The subsequent bank robbery and McCartney murder had merely convinced many within the DUP (and the broader unionist community) that they were entirely right to be sceptical of republican *bona fides*. Thus, if Sinn Féin hoped that the events of July and September 2005 would truly re-animate the peace process, it seemed clear that the Provisional IRA would have to move genuinely into a 'new mode'; all of which made it likely that there would be physical space available for dissident modes of republicanism.[7]

Prior to this point, the active existence of the Provisional IRA had stood as a key obstacle to dissident growth. The ambiguity over that organisation's dedication to peace, for instance, had helped reconcile those who would otherwise have been attracted by the message of alternative groups. More significant still was the fact that the Provisionals, as described, had repeatedly acted to impede the development of such alternatives. Anthony McIntyre has referred to the 'levels of intimidation and ostracism' that would often be directed at those expressing views critical of the Provisional leadership.[8] As a tool of social control, this ostracism was all the more powerful for being backed by a threat of force. At various points, the existence of this 'iron fist', underpinning Provisional domination of the republican 'community', was made only too apparent. Numerous dissident figures complained of harassment, including physical abuse, from the Provisional IRA. At its most extreme, it was this phenomenon that brought the murder of alleged Real IRA organiser Joseph O'Connor in Belfast in October 2000. By killing him, the Provisionals had made it clear that they would not tolerate any challenge to their control of the republican areas in Northern Ireland's capital. Moreover, they had done it without any serious political repercussions.

Post-2005, however, it appeared unlikely that such 'internal house-keeping' could be cost-free for the Provisionals. Already, the furore generated by the attempted kidnapping of a Belfast dissident, Bobby Tohill, in February 2004 had demonstrated the likely damage that such actions could incur. Tohill was rescued by police from a van in which he appeared to have been kidnapped by four known members of the Provisional movement. The PSNI Chief Constable, Hugh Orde, had identified the IRA as responsible and the resulting controversy had helped scupper the ongoing 'review' of the Agreement. A year on, in the aftermath of the Northern Bank robbery and McCartney murder, Sinn Féin could not afford for the Provisional IRA to be caught *in flagrante* again. If the party wished for a return of devolved government to Northern Ireland – which it seemed increasingly evident that it did – then it needed the Provisional IRA to receive a clean bill of health from the Independent Monitoring Commission, which had been created to monitor paramilitary activity. This was judged a prerequisite if the DUP were to be inveigled into making an agreement to share power with republicans. Such a positive assessment, though, precluded the resort to intimidation and violence against rival republicans as practised by the Provisionals over previous years. Those rivals could now operate in a more favourable environment in which the costs of their activities were likely to be far lower.

At the same time, it is clear that the course pursued by Sinn Féin in its attempts to secure a settlement with the DUP opened up further political space within the republican sub-culture that the dissidents could realistically hope to occupy. The very fact that it was the party of Ian Paisley with which republicans were seeking to do business was itself likely to be a source of disquiet. Paisley, after all, was a man who had been the *bête noir* for many Catholics/nationalists – and especially republicans – throughout Northern Ireland's 'Troubles'. As recently as 2003, Sinn Féin's newspaper, *An Phoblacht*, had written of the DUP leader and his party:

> Paisley incites the mob but never stays long enough to witness the lynching … if mob violence has been the hallmark of Paisley's political rhetoric, unionist paramilitary violence has also been its bedrock. An astute politician, there have been few times when

Paisley has been prepared to publicly endorse unionist paramilitary violence but scratch the surface of the DUP and it's never far beneath.[9]

A year later, in the same publication, Danny Morrison had asked of Paisley, 'Why should this man's rantings be acceptable? Surely his sectarian comments disqualify him from having any say in our future, given his opposition to civil rights from 1968 and his subsequent record of activities?'[10] And yet, this was the man with whom Sinn Féin sought, from 2005 onwards, to reconstruct the devolved government of Northern Ireland.

Scarce wonder that republican critics of Sinn Féin were quick to deride the proposed link-up with the DUP. In late 2004, for example, Anthony McIntyre produced a piece which concluded in incredulous fashion:

> No amount of nonsense about the greatest leadership ever and the undefeated army can explain how a combination of both, in return for our toil and the ultimate sacrifice of our comrades, brought us to a point where, in the words of Gerry Adams, 'Sinn Féin will be putting Ian Paisley into power.'

McIntyre was far from alone in expressing such disbelief. And Sinn Féin's unambiguous embrace, post-2005, of a position where it did indeed seek to put Ian Paisley into power (and the realisation of that goal in May 2007) can only have raised further questions as to the direction of the party's policy.

CONCERNED REPUBLICANS

Reservations as to the course being pursued by Sinn Féin were doubtless strengthened by the growing focus in this period on the issue that emerged as the *sine qua non* of any Sinn Féin agreement with the DUP: republican endorsement of policing. In the months prior to what became known as the St Andrews Agreement (of October 2006), it had become clear that any settlement would require Sinn Féin to give its full support to the PSNI. Paragraphs five and six of the eventual Agreement made these demands explicit and brought Sinn Féin to a position it had long sought to avoid, or at least postpone to an indeterminate future point. That this should have been so was unsurprising given the sensitivity of the policing issue, in ideological terms, for many involved in the Northern Irish conflict. As the former deputy first minister of Northern Ireland, Séamus Mallon, once remarked, 'policing is key in this whole equation.'[11] For those of a republican persuasion this was particularly the case. Their 'traditional' position had long held that support for any police force in Northern Ireland would be unacceptable, as it amounted to the ultimate recognition of the British state's right to exert a monopoly of force within the province. Endorsement of the police was held to represent a final acceptance of Northern Ireland's right to exist. For this reason, the evolution of Sinn Féin's policy on the issue had been a slow and halting affair. And there were certainly grounds to believe that the party's leadership sought to defer, perhaps indefinitely, an answer to the question of whether it would support the police.[12]

Eclipsed by the focus on decommissioning in the peace process, Sinn Féin's refusal to support the police had scarcely been viewed as an impediment to the party's participation in government. Consequently, failed bouts of peace process negotiation in 2003 and 2004 (between Sinn Féin and first David Trimble's UUP and then Paisley's DUP) both envisaged republican endorsement of the PSNI, but only *after* Northern Ireland's institutions had been restored. Dean Godson has persuasively demonstrated that republicans initially sought to get into government without weapons decommissioning; their belief being that, once there, the institutions would not be collapsed even if no actual decommissioning followed. It seems only too plausible that the Sinn Féin leadership took a similar approach to the policing issue. By placing it on the back burner, Gerry Adams and his colleagues sought to sidestep the difficult questions it created for republicans, even as their party took its place in a revived Northern Irish Executive.

By 2005–6, however, the scope for further Sinn Féin prevarication had been dramatically reduced. The twin crises of the Northern Bank and the McCartney murder had ensured that far greater clarity would be expected of the party on the critical issue of law and order. Interestingly, the American government proved itself firmer on this point than either the British or the Irish. For one thing, republican fundraising visas to the United States were effectively suspended from early 2005 onwards, until such time as Sinn Féin committed itself to supporting the PSNI – a move that exerted important financial pressure on republicans.

Simultaneously, the US president's special envoy to Northern Ireland, Mitchell Reiss, was explicit in demanding that republicans give their backing to the police. As far back as March 2004, Reiss had been openly critical of Sinn Féin for purveying what he labelled 'massive untruths' about the Northern Irish police and called on the party to 'reconsider' its position. In similar vein, in late 2005 he had written that 'Sinn Féin has a responsibility to tell its constituents they should co-operate with the police – without fear of retribution.' On that latter occasion, Reiss's comments initiated a public row with Gerry Adams, which would continue into the middle of 2006.

One reading of the 2006 St Andrews negotiations, therefore, would be that they saw the British and Irish governments adopt a stance akin to that of the Americans – perhaps in recognition that formal republican endorsement of the police now stood as the DUP's central precondition for entry into government with Sinn Féin. In the words of the then deputy DUP leader, Peter Robinson, 'Before devolution can be restored, republicans must deliver an end to all paramilitary and criminal activity and signal, in both word and deed, support for the rule of law.'[13] Faced with a new consensus on this matter, encompassing all three governments and the principal representatives of unionism, Sinn Féin was at last forced to shift position.

On 19 October 2006, Sinn Féin announced that it would begin a consultation process lasting several weeks with its members over the St Andrews proposals. This was then followed by a 'special *árd fheis*' in January 2007, at which the party leadership secured 90 per cent support for a motion that effectively authorised endorsement of the PSNI.[14] In the intervening period the timetable provided for, under the terms of the St Andrews accord, had been allowed to lapse – a delay that was covered up by some 'creative accounting' on the part of the Northern Irish secretary of state, Peter Hain. In the end, however, Sinn Féin had delivered on its end of the bargain for the restoration of Northern Ireland's institutions. At first glance, it had apparently done so with little hint of dissent from within the Provisional movement – as evinced by the 90 per cent support for the leadership's position at the critical party conference.

And yet, there was more to it than that. One major explanation for the unhurried character of Sinn Féin's deliberations in 2006–7 lies with the sustained republican critique of the party that emerged in this period.

As the Provisionals proceeded towards acceptance of policing, a series of set-piece debates were organised across Northern Ireland, by self-proclaimed 'Concerned Republicans', under the banner 'Policing: A Bridge Too Far?' These meetings afforded those opposed to the move the opportunity to make clear their feelings. Moreover, the character and composition of the events were suggestive of a new impulse towards unity within the disparate ranks of republicanism. Among those who spoke at the debates – held at Conway Mill in Belfast, the Elk Hotel in Toome and the Tower Hotel in Derry – were well-known republicans such as Dominic McGlinchey Jnr, Gerry McGeough and Peggy O'Hara; and they were joined by delegates from a variety of organisations.[15] At these gatherings, the position adopted by critics of Sinn Féin was one based on traditional republican logic. This held that support for any police force within Northern Ireland was unacceptable. Endorsement of the police was seen as the ultimate acknowledgement of the British state's right to exert a monopoly of legitimate force within the province – to finally accept the right of Northern Ireland to exist – and something to be rejected at all costs.

Not only did each event draw a sizeable crowd and receive significant coverage in *The Blanket*, but also, interestingly for an ostensibly dissident-organised initiative, some were attended by representatives from Sinn Féin. Clearly, the party was concerned enough that it felt it had to respond to the phenomenon. At the Toome debate, for instance, Sinn Féin sent Declan Kearney to press its case. Others on the platform on that occasion included Francie Mackey from the 32 County Sovereignty Movement, Paul Little of the Irish Republican Socialist Party and Laurence O'Neill, a Belfast republican who had recently resigned from Sinn Féin. Perhaps unsurprisingly, *The Blanket*'s account of the gathering displayed little sympathy for Kearney's endeavours, which were described as 'weary'. At the same time, though, the journal was not uncritical in its response to the other speakers. Hence, Mackey's address was described as 'Jesuitical' in its exclusive focus on 'the question of national sovereignty'. And the overall assessment was that, while there was little to fault from a 'Republican traditionalist perspective', hearing Mackey was like 'listening to the Mass in Latin ... fine for the small number of traditionalists but little that would be understood by those large swathes not imbibed on traditionalist assumptions'.[16]

Similar in tone and outlook was the report of the Derry debate, which was chaired by John Kelly (formerly of Sinn Féin) and featured Gerry McGeough (ex-IRA), Tony Catney (another former Sinn Féin member from Belfast), Tony McPhilips (of Republican Sinn Féin), Francie Mackey (of the 32CSM) and Eddie McGarrigle (of the IRSP). According to Anthony McIntyre, what the meeting reflected was the fact that 'the numbers of angry people are growing steadily.' The focus of that anger was said to be the Sinn Féin 'sell out' and 'betrayal'. McIntyre, though, again noted the shortcomings of the dissident case:

> What I did not learn from the meeting was any outline for a way forward. True, Sinn Féin has no alternative to the administration of British rule and has accepted the British state's alternative to republicanism. Yet, republicans gathered in Derry showed little sign of developing the republican strategy they profess to hold. This gives Sinn Féin the advantage.[17]

Furthermore, he observed that Sinn Féin had 'shaped the meeting without even having to turn up'. That they did so was because

> ... the crowd was fixated with the party and expended its intellectual energy in highlighting its shortcomings. This may be an exercise that writers and critics can afford to pursue but for people ostensibly seeking to politically advance the republican project as a viable alternative to Sinn Féin, it was the 'opportunity to miss an opportunity'.[18]

Despite such limitations, the 'Concerned Republicans' movement did seem ready to pose a direct challenge to the political hegemony of the Provisionals. The tangible expression of this came in the Northern Irish Assembly elections that were held in March 2007. On that occasion, Sinn Féin was challenged in three constituencies by candidates standing on the 'Concerned Republicans' platform. Paul McGlinchey, the brother of the former INLA chief of staff, Dominic McGlinchey, stood in North Antrim, having resigned from Sinn Féin in December 2006 in protest at the shift towards giving support to the PSNI. In Fermanagh/South Tyrone the candidate was Gerry McGeough, a staunchly conservative, former IRA man who was arrested on the continent in the late 1980s for his part in attacks on British military bases. McGeough had left Sinn Féin in 2001 in protest at what he judged to be its liberal social agenda.[19] The 'Concerned Republicans' ticket was completed by

Peggy O'Hara, the mother of the dead 1981 hunger striker Patsy O'Hara, who stood in Foyle. With such a distinguished panel, in terms of republican credentials, many predicted that the result could be a splitting of the republican vote and a shortfall in support for Sinn Féin.

Expectations were raised further with the release of an open letter, just prior to the elections, which called for support for the 'Concerned Republican' candidates on the grounds that they were best placed 'to represent the concerns of grassroots Republicans'. Written in the name of 'Republican activists who served the Republican and Republican Socialist Movements in the armed struggle' and published in *The Blanket*, the letter was signed by over 300 prominent republicans from across Ireland. Their shared position was that the 'struggle' remained 'unfinished' and they firmly rejected 'the logic of the proposition that the interests of peace can be in any way served by our young people signing up to join the British Crown forces such as the RUC/PSNI'.[20] In this way, it appeared to be a major endorsement, from within republican circles, for those leading the electoral challenge to Sinn Féin.

In the event, however, the 'Concerned Republicans' failed to inflict any significant damage on their mainstream rivals (see table below).[21] Overall, the result of the election confirmed the electoral hegemony of Sinn Féin within nationalist Northern Ireland and gave the party the right to nominate Martin McGuinness to the post of deputy first minister in the new Northern Irish Executive.

Table 5.1
Performance of 'Concerned Republican' Candidates in Northern Ireland Assembly Elections, 2007

Constituency	C/R Candidate	Total First Pref Votes for C/R	% of Vote Won by C/R	Total First Pref Votes for S/F	% of Vote Won by S/F
Fermanagh/ South Tyrone	GerryMcGeough	814	1.8	16,833	36.2
Foyle	Peggy O'Hara	1,789	4.4	12, 649	30.8
North Antrim	Paul McGlinchey	383	0.9	7,065	15.9

Nevertheless, although it had proved a failure in an immediate sense, the 'Concerned Republicans' experiment did generate a more lasting legacy. In the first instance, this was because it had confirmed the existence within republicanism of a constituency that was less than satisfied with the trajectory of the Provisionals. Ultimately, in the context of an election – and in light of the vastly superior political prospects of Sinn Féin – many within this constituency had still felt willing to support the party, particularly as a way of striking at the DUP. Anthony McIntyre has offered anecdotal testimony to support such a conclusion:

> There was one man who did nothing but back-stab Sinn Féin each time I saw him – and would never ostracize me when others would. But then I actually saw him come down the street on the day [of the election] trying to get the vote out. A lot of people would come out to hobble the DUP. One of their biggest arguments in the assembly election was along the lines that you weren't going to allow [the DUP's] Diane Dodds to get a seat [in West Belfast].[22]

In this respect, Sinn Féin had once again proven highly adept at positioning itself as the voice of communal nationalism within Northern Ireland, with the result that even the party's critics were willing to lend it support in the context of the province's political 'ethnic one-upmanship'.[23] Even so, the creation of the 'Concerned Republicans' group had suggested a new readiness, within the extended and disjointed ranks of dissident republicanism, to mobilise and co-operate in efforts to contest the intra-republican supremacy of the Provisionals.

THE RETURN OF THE 32 COUNTY SOVEREIGNTY MOVEMENT

Elsewhere, the involvement of Francie Mackey in the various platforms and initiatives of late 2006–7 was indicative of the new level of energy emanating from the 32 County Sovereignty Movement (32CSM) at this time. The group declared itself to be 'coming out of a period of relative inactivity' following a period of re-assessment dating back to 2001–2; and while it had restated that it had no interest in becoming a political party, it spoke of its desire to serve as a 'credible Republican alternative'.[24] To this end, it did appear to have adopted a more activist ethos – and attained a new, far more elegant website. As far back as July 2002, the constitution of the 32CSM had been altered in order to broaden the horizons of the organisation, moving it beyond its obsession with the single issue of Irish sovereignty. Its aim since that time had been to 'promote the revolutionary ideals of Republicanism and to this end involve itself in resisting all forms of colonialism and imperialism'. As a leading member of the 32CSM, Marian Price, declared, the organisation stood firmly against 'multi national capitalist and imperialist aggression', wherever it occurred in the 'new world order' being constructed by the US and Britain.[25]

This desire for a broader perspective saw 32CSM members participate in protests against the arms company Raytheon in Derry in August 2006. Raytheon's crime was said to be that it was aiding the 'slaughter of civilians in Lebanon [by] their continuing supply of weaponry to the Israeli military'. The 32CSM declared its full support for 'the Lebanese and Palestinian people's struggle against Israeli aggression'.[26] In line with this worldview, the group also appeared to signal its endorsement of Hamas over what it termed the 'compromised Fatah organization' in 2007. By seizing power in the Gaza Strip, Hamas was said to have 'finally acted decisively against the Fatah threat' and disregarded an international community that had displayed 'an absolute contempt for the Palestinians and the democratic right for them to choose their own leaders'. The 'ordinary people of Gaza' had shown that 'it's a lot better to die on your feet than to live on your knees.'[27] Confirmation as to where the sympathies of the 32CSM lay was provided by its December 2007 AGM, which featured a motion sending 'solidarity greetings to anti-imperialist and resistance movements internationally such as Hamas, Hezbollah, etc'.[28]

Within the purely Irish context, meanwhile, the group declared its goal as being 'to identify and confront the infringements on our Sovereignty which although less blatant, could prove to be just as dangerous to Irish Freedom as British troops on our streets'. As to what this meant in practice, the 32CSM website cited the US military's use of Shannon airport, as well as multinational economic investment.[29] Political activity was to be guided by an effort to highlight the iniquities stemming from such violations of Irish sovereignty. Any and every opportunity was to be taken to press the 32CSM case. The 32CSM thus opposed the Lisbon Treaty (in both 2008 and 2009) – and in so doing attempted to make the link between it and what it felt were the deeper problems of Ireland. In the wake of the 2008 referendum defeat for Lisbon, the 32CSM declared, 'all arguments emanating from this protest concerning a democratic deficit inherent in the Lisbon Project must also be applied to British Parliamentary activity in Ireland ... We reject both.'[30]

The making of such 'parallel arguments' was said to be a key reason for the 32CSM's participation in the Lisbon debate – with that treaty seen as 'a vehicle to pursue our ends'.[31]

In line with this broader and more vigorous outlook, *The Sovereign Nation* (the newspaper of the 32CSM) now re-emerged, after a period of near catatonia, in more substantial form. To take but one example, an examination of the May/June 2008 edition is instructive as to the range of issues then being covered by the organisation. The stories featured there included:

- Calls to 'End Internment by Remand' in response to the arrest of the so-called 'Derry 4' in County Donegal, and their charging with being members of an illegal organisation;[32]
- Opposition to 'drug dealers' in the Shantallow area of Derry;
- Support for residents' unity against 'criminal gangs' in south Down;
- Criticism of the 'PSNI/RUC' and Sinn Féin's failures to hold the police to account;
- Complaints about the harassment of 32CSM members by the security services north and south of the Irish border;
- Objections to the British government's alleged 'criminalisation' strategy in Maghaberry prison and encouragement for the labours of the Irish Republican Prisoners Welfare Association;
- The disparagement of the retiring Irish prime minister, Bertie Ahern ('Good riddance to Bertie') who was said to have 'presided over massive inequality in the state', 'ruthlessly used internment against republicans opposing British rule' and overseen the 'faithful endorsement of the British demand that article 2&3 of the Irish constitution be deleted' so that 'Irish national sovereignty and national democracy' could be 'subverted';
- The assertion that the Good Friday Agreement had 'failed Republicans' and merely offered 'partition updated for the 21st century';
- The effort to publicise defections from Sinn Féin, such as that of Séamus Breslin in Derry who, in a letter to the editor, accused the Provisionals of having 'strayed away from the core objective of upholding the Republic as outlined in the 1916 proclamation';[33]

- Hostility to loyalism, which was said to inhabit a similar ideological world to fascism;
- The commemoration of the 1916 Easter Rising (in conjunction with other groups such as the IRSP) at various locations across Ireland;
- Remembrance of other important moments from Irish republican history, such as the 'Catalpa and the Fremantle escape', which helped prove 'the enduring potency of the Fenian legacy';
- An interview with a member of the 'Iraqi resistance', who explained how the violence there was a popular response to the 'provocations of US neo-colonialism'; Al Qaeda was said to have 'argued in a very principled way that only protracted armed struggle will advance their cause and reality confirmed their way of thinking' and was described as 'the first organisation of the resistance'.[34]

Alongside this revived *Sovereign Nation*, the public resurgence of the 32CSM was accompanied by a sense of its development as a more broad-based entity, with branches established in various locations across Ireland (each of these now possessing an internet presence). In February 2007, the group opened new offices, to be shared with the IRPWA and the 1916 Commemoration Committee, in Dublin.[35] Elsewhere, the 32CSM could now point to the existence of a Derry 32CSM, where none had previously existed – represented by both the Liam Lynch/ Patsy Duffy *cumann* and the Phil O'Donnell *cumann*.[36] In addition to this, there was a Cork 32CSM (the Finbarr Walsh *cumann*), a Dublin branch, as well as an outlet in Belfast.[37] In the autumn of 2008, the Charlie Kerins *cumann* was created in Kerry.[38] Other branches could be found in Monaghan, south Armagh, south Down and, most incongruously, Napoli.[39] Each local sub-division shared the same format and carried the same stories on its website, allowing for the cross-promotion of their various activities. There was also an embrace of new communications technology, with the respective blogs inviting their readers to visit the 32CSM on 'YouTube' as well as support pages on the social networking site 'bebo'.[40]

Each city branch of the 32CSM produced its own version of the organisation's newsletter, entitled *Beir Bua*. A quick glance at this in, for example, Derry shows it focusing on local issues such as the perceived problems of drugs ('Derry Cocaine Epidemic') or underage drinking and anti-social behaviour ('Derry 32CSM Launch Anti-Underage Drinking Campaign').[41] The message appeared to be designed to show the 32CSM as an activist organisation, engaged in the problems of the community – even as those same problems could also be described as in part emanating from loyalists or British government policy. In other words, the attempt was to draw attention to the 'national' question through a focus on 'social' and 'economic' issues – in much the same way as Sinn Féin had gone about building itself as a political party during the early 1980s.[42] Added to such pieces, though, was a recurring message that alluded to the perceived betrayals of the Provisionals. In Derry, for example, the local 32CSM asked, 'What ever happened to Martin McGuinness?' In the short piece that followed, the former words of McGuinness from the 1980s, when he had railed against 'quislings' and 'collaborators', were quoted back against him to suggest he had become one of the 'cheerleaders for British occupation'.[43]

Elsewhere, the political agenda of the 32CSM included: protests against the 'normalisation' of British–Irish and Northern Irish relations – as manifested in the visits of Ian Paisley and Sir Hugh Orde to the Irish Republic and the proposed future visit by the British queen to Ireland; support for the 'Shell to Sea' protestors in the Irish Republic; and criticism of the Celtic Tiger.[44] The group were also highly critical of efforts to resolve the Drumcree dispute, dismissing talks aimed at resolving the decade-long standoff as merely an effort to force a 'sectarian Orange march' down the Garvaghy Road in Portadown.[45]

As in previous years, much emphasis was placed on the 'principled' character of the 32CSM, in contrast with the leadership of the Provisionals who were judged to have 'abandoned the principles of the 1916 proclamation'.[46] Sinn Féin's leaders were regularly said to be nothing more than 'quislings', who were no more republican than members of the 'Dublin government'. The reality, according to Francie Mackey, was that the Provisionals had become 'Home Rulers' whose actions were 'alien to that great document of 1916'.[47]

In the autumn of 2006, the 32CSM launched a leaflet and poster campaign under the banner 'Disband the RUC/PSNI', which was timed to coincide with Sinn Féin's internal debate on policing. The Sovereignty Movement both highlighted the Provisionals' 'dramatic about-face' and declared that 'No matter how many cosmetic changes are made or how many Catholics join them, [the PSNI] is an institution that will remain solidly "100% Unionist".'[48] This issue was explored further in 2007 when the 32CSM published an article which argued that 'Accepting policing is the logical consequence of accepting the legitimacy of British Parliamentary activity in Ireland.' Any republican endorsement of policing was held to represent de facto approval for the 'political power which enacts it' and also 'the judiciary and penal systems which operate in tandem with it'. The conclusion to be drawn from this, according to the 32CSM, was clear:

> Partition remains the principle obstacle to the formation of accountable policing on the island of Ireland ... British policing in Ireland is beyond reform either from within or without ... The 32 County Sovereignty Movement submit that British policing in Ireland is unacceptable in any guise because its fundamental purpose is to secure British interests here.[49]

In line with this, Mackey published a separate statement in which he called on Gerry Adams and Sinn Féin to break with the Good Friday Agreement and all that flowed from it.[50] And in February 2007, he announced his support for the 'Anti British Policing' candidates (of the Concerned Republicans) in the upcoming assembly elections.[51]

Inevitably too, given the proclivities of republican culture, the 32CSM engaged in the usual commemorative events that punctuated their calendar. One such event, for instance, was held in July 2008 for Denis Spriggs, a member of the 'Old IRA' who died in 1921.[52] There, Francie Mackey made a determined effort to link the IRA of previous eras to today's circumstances:

> The same injustice ... the same British rule updated with special powers to discriminate against Nationalists and republicans ... Today murder is replaced with corrupt laws, intimidation and harassment by British police in Ireland and upheld by establishment parties in Stormont.

Those parties were held to be 'the modern day equivalent of the Home Rulers'; the corollary of this being that those who opposed the peace process and Good Friday Agreement were the true inheritors of the mantle of what the Sinn Féin publicist Danny Morrison once called 'the Good Old IRA'. In line with this, Mackey described those who had fought for 'Irish freedom' in years gone in reverent tones: 'The role to uphold and protect the sovereignty of the Irish nation was a noble cause throughout our history and continues to be so today.'[53] As a eulogy to the cause of physical-force republicanism – and an effective 'call to arms' – Mackey's message seemed clear.

Herein lay one of the enduring central, yet often unspoken, core purposes of the 32CSM: to build ideological support for the still-violent republicanism of the Real IRA. The revived *Sovereign Nation* continued to publicise actions by 'Óglaigh na hÉireann', such as their August 2006 'attacks on targets of an economic, political and military nature in the south Down area'.[54] Elsewhere, Gary Donnelly of the 32CSM's Derry branch was comfortable referring to the Real IRA as simply 'the IRA' in late 2007; and in an interview with *The Sunday Times*, he confirmed that he viewed 'armed opposition' to British rule in Ireland as 'legitimate'.[55] Significantly, in July 2008, the new Shantallow *cumann* of the 32CSM was reported to have predicted that the 'struggle' would 're-start in Derry' because there, the conditions for armed struggle would return.[56]

Overall, then, from 2007 onwards, the 32CSM exuded a new, more confident ethos than it had in previous years. As the front cover of *The Sovereign Nation* for August/September 2008 declared, 'We're here to stay!' The article was a response to calls in Derry for 'Anti Agreement Republican Separatists' to disappear after the murder of a pizza delivery man, Emmett Shiels. He had been shot dead after apparently intervening in a feud between dissident republicans and another man. In the face of the hostile criticism the killing had generated, the 32CSM was defiant: 'The Irish Resistance Movement will not be forced to disband.'[57]

In the autumn of 2008, the 32CSM outlined its position on talks – in response to a suggestion from Denis Bradley that the movement might be engaged in dialogue. Talks, it declared, could not be conducted on the same basis as the existing political process. That process was judged to have created an Agreement that was inimical to republicanism. The 32CSM view of the settlement in Northern Ireland was that 'the entry fee into the talks which created it was that republicans had to accept the legitimacy of partition as a predetermined outcome.'[58] Elsewhere, the group emphasised that it would 'talk to anyone on the issue of our national sovereignty and national self-determination', but 'anyone wishing to discuss issues with us must first go through our National Executive.'[59]

Such arguments reached to the heart of why the 32CSM had been created and why it continued to exist: the opposition of its members to the parameters upon which the peace process was based, which prioritised unionist consent. Sinn Féin, by participating in that process, was alleged to have become part of the political establishment – north and south.[60] Furthermore, the weight attached to the need for any discussions to be 'open' and unambiguous was a function of another key element of the dissident narrative. This held that the leadership of mainstream republicanism had, in large part, deceived their supporters and engaged in a morally compromised process.

THE REPUBLICAN NETWORK FOR UNITY

If the growing vigour exhibited by the 32CSM in this period represented the revival of a near-dormant entity, there were also signs that new manifestations of Irish republicanism were being generated. Thus, the 'Concerned Republicans' movement that had emerged towards the end of 2006 did not disappear in the aftermath of the 2007 elections. Instead, the leading figures behind that initiative signalled their intention to continue to contest the allegiance of the republican constituency. The result was the formation of the Republican Network for Unity (RNU), which, according to its website, is the successor to the group formerly known as 'Ex-POW's and Concerned Republicans against RUC/PSNI'.[61] In keeping with its origins, much of the new group's energy was devoted to criticism of what it insisted on terming the 'RUC/PSNI'. The RNU website, set up in 2007, declared that the organisation's purpose was to offer 'principled opposition to Republican endorsement of British policing in Ireland'; this, though, was also to be used as a vehicle for a broader critique of the Provisional republican leadership. As the organisation's mission statement declared:

> ... the lack of true accountability in policing highlights deeper failings in Sinn Féin's current strategy and the political settlement the leadership endorsed. While nationalists may be permitted to sit on the Policing Board they will in essence be unable to hold the PSNI to account or to deliver meaningful change. Furthermore, in a broader context they can be in government but will be unable to make a decision without having the support of unionism. The veto remains.[62]

In line with this, the RNU was quick to seize on any issue that seemed to confirm the validity of its analysis. It highlighted, for example, the building of a vast new MI5 headquarters in Belfast, which was said to be indicative of the British desire to remain in Ireland for the long haul.[63] Taken as a whole, it articulated a familiar form of republicanism, with a focus on certain conventional themes: the fundamental malignancy of the British state, the irreformability of Northern Ireland and the alleged plight of republican prisoners.

A key figure in the process that led to the creation of the RNU was the Belfast republican Tony 'TC' Catney, who had resigned from Sinn Féin in late 2006. A former Sinn Féin *árd chomairle* member and director of elections, Catney had also served sixteen years in prison for an IRA murder; his brother-in-law is the senior Sinn Féin figure, Gerry Kelly.[64] Soon after his departure from Sinn Féin, Catney went public with criticisms of the Provisional leadership. The latter, he claimed, was attempting to smear him by the accusation that he was a member 'of an armed organisation' – a charge that he 'categorically' denied.[65] When later asked about his view of ongoing republican violence, Catney claimed that actions like the Real IRA's murder of two soldiers in 2009 were 'not imbued with a progressive, revolutionary ethos'. The truth was, he said:

> In twenty-three years, the military input of the dissidents in terms of fatalities of occupation forces was zero, until [the Real IRA attack on] Massereene. The point is, no way am I a pacifist and in no way do I feel the need to hang my head in shame because of past deeds carried out for the IRA. But I believe that armed struggle is dictated not by anybody's blood lust, but by the social and practical circumstances on the ground at any given moment in time. It is obvious, at this moment in time, that it is the political landscape that needs to be addressed and not the military landscape.[66]

At the time of his exit from Sinn Féin, Catney described himself as simply an 'Irish republican' who had resigned from the party, because of 'the lack of internal debate on matters of policy and strategy and the manner in which membership were expected to blindly follow a leadership-led policy without question or dissent'.[67] In 2009, speaking in the small garden shed at his home in west Belfast, the 51-year-old Catney maintained that he had had doubts over the direction of that 'leadership-led policy' since 31 August 1994, the date of the first Provisional IRA ceasefire. Even then, on his recollection, the move felt like 'capitulation' and seemed to have been 'born out of leadership fatigue and frustration'.[68] Thereafter, Catney felt that the Provisionals had made a series of 'tactical and strategic mistakes': the Good Friday Agreement, the loss of articles 2 and 3 (from the Irish constitution) and acceptance of the Mitchell Principles, which he described as a 'disgrace'. At each stage he argued that the leadership had pursued 'Machiavellian politics' in order to hide their failures. For him, personally, the endorsement of policing in Northern Ireland was the final straw. Republicans should have held out, he argued, for a 'proper policing service rather than accepting a police force'. It was the failure of Sinn Féin, in his eyes, to do this which led to his resignation.[69]

On top of this, Catney also had reservations stemming from what he believed was the 'very one-sided implementation of the Agreement'. In particular, he was vehement in his opposition to the passage of Orange Order parades through Catholic areas of Northern Ireland. Such incidents were described as an 'obscenity', exercises in 'coat-trailing and ... oppression', which demanded republican opposition. The fact that Sinn Féin had failed to prevent them, he maintained, was a product of the party's wider willingness to 'roll over to the DUP'. In this respect, Catney's critique is representative of the unease with which many republicans viewed the deal that had been made with the party of Ian Paisley. For Catney, it proved that Sinn Féin 'are not revolutionary, they are not radical and in many instances their policies do not reflect a republican agenda'. What was required, in his view, was a 'new political vehicle' that could 'challenge the partitionist status quo' and engage in real 'oppositional politics'.[70]

To this end, the RNU was envisaged as a focal-point for those interested in 'oppositional politics'. In Catney's assessment, 'the alternative republican landscape is all over the place ... the process of shedding activists since 1994 has been diverse and varied ... there needed to be some way of people coming together to articulate joint positions.'[71] As its name suggested, therefore, a key goal for the RNU was to serve as a node or hub into which different forms of dissident republicanism could connect. To this end, the RNU's website claimed to 'salute all other like minded groups' (however this was to be defined). And the organisation's online 'photo gallery' gave graphic illustration of how this affinity for fellow republicans was expressed in practice. Visible there were various examples of the RNU's co-operation with others. In September 2008, for instance, it was involved in anti-internment protests in Derry, alongside the 32CSM.[72] Likewise, in November 2008, around thirty members of the 32CSM and the RNU combined forces in the Markets region of Belfast to protest against the 'homecoming' parade of the Royal Irish Regiment. By the same token, the group's 'links' section – which lists those groups with whom the RNU declares solidarity – includes the 32CSM, Saor Éire, *The Starry Plough* (the publication of the IRSP–INLA), the Coalition of Irish Republican Women, the Irish Freedom Committee, Anthony McIntyre's personal website ('The Pensive Quill') and *The Blanket*.[73]

There were limits to how far the possibilities for co-operation extended. Catney, for one, was highly critical of Republican Sinn Féin and their self-declared position, as he saw it, of 'having occupied the holy grail'. He had, he asserted, 'absolutely no time or respect for their political view or philosophy'. Catney was also critical of the new republican group éirígí (see below), which he saw as lacking substance. Beyond that, however, he was a firm advocate of the proposition that republicans needed to come together to debate publicly their 'points of difference and commonality and build around the latter'.[74]

This focus on efforts to bring together a range of republican critics of Sinn Féin had been underscored by the wider circumstances in which the RNU publicly announced its arrival on the scene in 2007. On 17 January 2007, a meeting had been held at the Tower Hotel in Derry, chaired by John Kelly and featuring members of both the 32CSM and IRSP, together with some independents. Those present had debated the question of policing and expressed opposition towards Sinn Féin, the Good Friday Agreement and the PSNI.[75] Subsequently, a further meeting was organised in Derry by Danny McBrearty, this time in May, at the Ancient Order of Hibernians hall. It discussed the building of a 'common platform' among those opposed to the Provisionals and featured members of the RIRA and CIRA, together with representatives of the 32CSM and IRSP, and ex-IRA and INLA prisoners.[76] At that year's Easter commemorations too, Joe Dillon of the 32CSM had saluted the 'co-operation among various republican organizations which [had] yielded obvious dividends' in the campaign against the PSNI. On this basis, he urged yet greater levels of 'unity'.[77] This message was echoed in the Easter statement issued by the Real IRA, which declared, 'diversity is a strength, not a weakness. Republican diversity and Republican unity can co-exist.'[78]

All of this was then followed by a joint Bodenstown commemoration in which the 32CSM, the IRSP and members of the 'Concerned Republicans' movement took part, in the context of a 'Republican Unity initiative' aimed at 'the development of a radical Republican alternative to the failed politics of partition and the Good Friday Agreement'. The participants there pledged to 'work on areas of agreement' on the understanding that 'far more unites us than divides us'.[79] On this basis, the establishment of the Republican Network for Unity was formally announced. Brian McFadden of Derry, delivering an address for the RNU, stated, 'The theme of today's commemoration is unity among Republicans. The fact that this gathering has been jointly agreed among a range of groups and individuals is a small but positive step in the right direction.'[80] Significantly, McFadden went on to state that:

> In the interests of building Republican unity, we should be careful not to fall into the trap of vilifying Sinn Féin supporters. For the most part, it is the leadership who are the villains. It is our job to win back the ordinary Republican people and we are confident of doing this by winning the argument and by making our agenda relevant to our communities, the working class Irish Republican Community.[81]

An olive branch was effectively being held out to potentially disaffected members of the Provisional movement. It was the leadership of that movement, rather than the rank and file, which was to be held culpable for the state of contemporary republicanism. The message was that grassroots republicans could join the ranks of Sinn Féin's critics, safe in the knowledge that they would not be impugned for their previous loyalty to Sinn Féin. As Francie Mackey said in his speech to the event, it was believed that there were 'serious reservations' within the Provisionals about the 'direction in which they are being led by the Provisional leadership'. As a result, the 32CSM and RNU wished to invite all republicans, 'to bring to fruition the Republican project'.[82] The 32CSM's commitment to republican unity was confirmed at the group's AGM later that year, as well as in its 2008 'New Year Statement'.[83]

Since the 2007 gathering, Bodenstown has served as the venue for annual 'Unity Commemorations', involving the 32CSM, the IRSP and the RNU. In 2008, Marian Price delivered an oration there in which she talked of the development of the 'Republican Unity initiative' and the way in which it had 'moved beyond its birth phase of joint commemorations and onto the streets as real political activism addressing the core issues that Irish republicanism needs to address'. In a pointed section of her address, Price declared, 'The debate as to where former republicans have travelled to is over.' The Provisional leadership, it was said, were now entirely part of the establishment. It thus fell to others, such as those gathered there at Bodenstown, to move forward, while attempting to draw in all republicans unhappy with the trajectory of Sinn Féin.[84]

The appeal made by Marian Price on that occasion appeared to be heeded, at least in some quarters. In early 2008, the RNU organised a 'Truth and Lies' discussion event at the Gasyard in Derry, which featured contributions from Éamonn McCann of the Socialist Environmental Alliance (SEA), Francie Mackey of the 32CSM and Tony Catney. Participants debated the use of 'armed struggle', the Good Friday Agreement, the rights and wrongs of taking seats in Stormont and the question of support for the PSNI. Interestingly, on that occasion, a Sinn Féin representative, Gary Fleming, did attend in an effort to articulate the party's position – though the impulse for the meeting came from those opposed to the Provisionals' approach.[85]

Similarly, on 7 November 2008 the RNU jointly hosted a meeting at the Tower Hotel in Derry under the banner 'The Good Friday Agreement: 10 Years On'. The purpose of this gathering was to call for coordination between the various republican groups. What emerged was an additional 'new umbrella group', the Republican Forum for Unity (RFU), which would seek 'to unite the 32 County Sovereignty Movement, the Irish Republican Socialist Party, the Republican Network for Unity, and a number of independent republicans who are opposed to the strategy of Sinn Féin'.[86] The 32CSM contribution to the event offered an unambiguous vision of the RFU's purpose:

> For us the Forum is a mechanism to political action. It is not a talking shop. It is a body of persons listening and collating republican and socialist viewpoints with the intention of translating those views into agreed political action ... The GFA has failed. The 32CSM has no intention in [*sic*]wasting any more time re-

stating this. With the assistance of the Unity Forum ... we are going to try and build a political alternative to Partition itself. We are not hung up on the past. We are not hung up on former comrades. We are not hung up on holy grails. We are content with the legitimacy of our position and see no reason to constantly dwell on it.[87]

Once more, the point was being pressed that the time for debating the course taken by the Provisionals was over. This is not to say that the dissidents were calling for an end to criticism of that movement; manifestly they were not and their public contributions would continue to highlight what they believed to be the inadequacies and contradictions of mainstream republicanism. Yet, at the same time, a clear line was being drawn, ideologically, under the debates of the previous decade. The 32CSM and others were saying that the time for ruminating over the events of the past was now gone. Instead, the impulse was to look to the future, to build something new. Moreover, the hope was that a degree of co-operation might be established between all of those opposed to the status quo in Ireland, including many who had hitherto remained within the Provisionals, simply for the want of any meaningful alternative. Through a new spirit of co-operation, the hope was that a serious challenge could be posed to Provisional hegemony over the republican sub-culture.

THE COLLAPSE OF THE SINN FÉIN PROJECT?

That the mainstream republican movement might be vulnerable to such a challenge became increasingly clear in the years after 2005. Already, there was little question that it was on dubious ground, in terms of traditional republican ideology, in the path it had pursued since the 1990s. To a significant extent, though, the departures from established belief had been justified on the twin grounds that there was little alternative and, more particularly, that they appeared to deliver results. From 1994 to 2004, Sinn Féin's vote increased, at every election in which it stood, north and south of the border. It was a remarkable run of success. The party was transformed in Northern Ireland from being a minor player, with no MPs at the time of the first IRA ceasefire, to enjoying a position of electoral hegemony over the Catholic/nationalist population. In the Irish Republic over the same period, Sinn Féin moved from near extinction (it won less than 1 per cent of the vote at local elections in 1991) to emerge as a national party with over 10 per cent of the vote and five TDs in the Dáil.[88] On the basis of this shift, many predicted that Sinn Féin representation would be in double figures and the party would control the 'balance of power' after the next Irish general election, enabling it to strike a political deal and enter coalition government. When placed alongside the party's mandatory position in the Northern Ireland Executive, there thus emerged the possibility of Sinn Féin ministers in power on either side of the border. The triumph in their respective jurisdictions of Mary Lou McDonald (Dublin) and Bairbre de Brún (Northern Ireland) in the 2004 European elections had appeared to herald just such a development. Furthermore, the presence of the party in government, north and south, was expected to provide a tangible symbol of Sinn Féin's successful pursuit of its 'United Ireland' agenda.

Such positive vistas, though, were not to materialise. Again, the impact of the Provisional IRA's 2004–5 transgressions proved decisive. In the British general elections of May 2005 Sinn Féin confirmed its dominance of the northern nationalist community, but failed to destroy the SDLP altogether (as many had anticipated).[89] The suspicion to emerge from this – acknowledged even by some senior republicans – was that the party might have reached a ceiling, beyond which further gains in Northern Ireland would be marginal at best. Without question, it had established itself as the hegemonic electoral force for nationalists; the 2007 Northern Irish Assembly elections certainly confirmed this.[90] And yet it was far from clear where else the party could go. In this context, attention focused particularly keenly on the progress of Sinn Féin south of the border. It was there, however, that it was to experience its biggest disappointments.

At the May 2007 Irish general elections, the party singularly failed to achieve the 'big leap forward', for which it had hoped. Far from increasing its representation in the Dáil, the party's number of TDs fell from five to four. Prior to the poll, Martin McGuinness had predicted that Sinn Féin would be the 'story of the election'; he was right, but not for the reasons he had hoped.[91] As the inquest into the party's modest performance began, much attention focused on the position of Gerry Adams. In RTÉ's pre-election 'Prime Time' leaders' debate, Adams was judged by many to have displayed his incomprehension of the finer detail of southern political life – and particularly the Irish economy.[92] Several commentators subsequently deemed this to have been a key moment in the campaign and asked whether he should now stand down as party leader. More generally, others began to speak of Sinn Féin as a party in decline.[93]

In August 2007 it was reported that one of the party's councillors from Galway city, Daniel Callanan, had left the party.[94] His departure was followed, in October, by the resignation of prominent Dublin councillor Nicky Kehoe. Kehoe had previously been a Sinn Féin candidate during the 2002 Irish general election and come within a few hundred votes of winning a seat for Dublin.[95] His decision to step down was in turn followed by that of fellow Dublin councillor Felix Gallagher.[96] And in November 2007, Thomas Pringle, another locally elected member of the party (this time in Donegal) also quit, complaining of Sinn Féin's 'top down approach to decision making'.[97]

Neither were the defections limited to south of the border. Sinn Féin suffered a series of prominent defections in Northern Ireland in late 2006–early 2007 by members expressing both opposition to endorsement of the PSNI and concerns over the party's wider trajectory. In September 2006, for example, two councillors from Magherafelt District Council, Oliver Hughes (brother of the 1981 hunger striker, Francis) and Patsy Groogan, resigned.[98] The Fermanagh region, meanwhile, seems to have been particularly badly hit. In October 2007, Bernice Swift, a local councillor from the area, was suspended from Sinn Féin, having criticised the District Policing Partnerships (DPPs), which the party was set to join, as 'meaningless talking shops'. She subsequently resigned altogether.[99] Earlier in the year, another Fermanagh councillor for Erne West, Poilín Uí Cathain, had quit her seat in protest at the party's decision to support the PSNI.[100] And most high profile of all, Gerry McHugh, a Sinn Féin MLA for Fermanagh/South Tyrone, left the party in December 2007, claiming that the 'direction Sinn Féin is taking is more about appeasement of the British government and administering British rule in Ireland rather than working towards the end of British occupation'.[101]

Such anxiety over the direction of the party was scarcely assuaged by the party's performance in the 2009 local elections in the Irish Republic. There, the party's vote proved stable and it retained the same number of seats (330) overall.[102] It again failed, though, to *increase* its share of the vote – strengthening the view that the growth spurt of the previous decade had been brought to an end. Target seats were missed and, most worrying of all for its leaders, the Sinn Féin vote in Dublin collapsed, with the party losing half of the seats it had won on the city council there four years earlier. In a by-election the same day, Sinn Féin's veteran candidate Christy Burke missed out on a Dáil seat in Dublin Central.

In the aftermath of these results came renewed speculation as to a 'crisis' within Sinn Féin.[103] Those making the case for the existence of internal dissension could point to the remarkably frank article that was published in Sinn Féin's *An Phoblacht* newspaper in July 2009. Written by Toireasa Ferris, daughter of senior Kerry republican (and Sinn Féin TD) Martin Ferris, this condemned the party's failures in the South and asked pointedly, 'As a party, what are we at and where are we going?' Ferris's critique was galvanised by the sense of failure in an election that 'should have been our[s] … but … wasn't'. In seeking to understand why this was the case, she offered a stark assessment:

> If we are honest with ourselves we will admit that the majority of those who we need to put a 1 or a 2 after our logo on a ballot paper unfortunately see us as a Northern-based party, irrelevant to the everyday concerns of people in the 26 Counties. Voters are unclear about what we stand for, which is not surprising as I'm sure many of us are starting to wonder about this also. We have been trying to appeal to too broad a spectrum of people and as a result have lost touch with our base. For this reason, among others, we were seen as neither a credible alternative to the Government nor a party of protest. After more than a decade working for the party down this end of the country, it hurts to say it but the fact is – Sinn Féin simply means nothing to the bulk of people in the South … The party is suffering an identity crisis – what are we trying to achieve in the 26 and what do we stand for besides a united Ireland? We can't afford to wait any longer to answer these questions.[104]

In what appeared an implicit rebuke of the Adams–McGuinness leadership and its preference for grandiose rhetoric and a broad-brush strategy, Ferris claimed that Sinn Féin should 'Forget the notion of trying to be a catch-all party that appeals to everyone' and abandon the 'constant "rights talk" by our national spokespeople'.[105] That Toireasa Ferris should have been the one to deliver such a message seemed to confirm the presence of serious unrest inside Sinn Féin.

This was accompanied by a further spate of resignations that suggested a fraying of party unity. The most prominent of these saw the departure of the aforementioned Christy Burke – a Sinn Féin activist since the 1970s.[106] Also to resign at this time was John Dwyer, a Sinn Féin councillor in Wexford, who had once seemed set to claim a seat for the party in the Dáil. Dwyer suggested that Sinn Féin had made 'a fundamental mistake by failing to realise that the south is not comparable with the six counties where Sinn Féin knows what its support base is.'[107] In July, a Dublin councillor, Louise Minihan, became the third southern member to abandon the party in quick succession. In her resignation statement she claimed that:

> Sinn Féin has, over the course of the last twelve years, moved steadily away from the core values of Irish socialist republicanism and is no longer willing, or able, to challenge the British occupation of the Six Counties or the rotten capitalist system which is causing so much hardship to working families across Ireland today.

For this reason, Minihan had concluded, 'the battle for the heart of Sinn Féin is lost.'[108] Clearly, she was not alone in this assessment. As previously, defections were a cross-border phenomenon. The same month as Minihan's departure, Gerard Foley, a local councillor in Strabane (who had once served as council chair) quit the party. He had previously refused to sit on the local DPP, in violation of the party's post-2006 policy.

January 2010 then brought two further attacks on the character of Sinn Féin from those with an insider view. The first came with the resignation of yet another Dublin councillor, Killian Forde, who accused the party of being suffused with 'sycophantism' and over-valuing 'loyalty and obedience'.[109] Elsewhere, in an echo of Toireasa Ferris's concerns, a Sinn Féin councillor from Tipperary, Séamus Morris, publicly complained that the party leadership had not 'come to grips with the fact that we are becoming totally irrelevant in Irish politics'. The party was said to be haemorrhaging votes and people south of the border and Morris called on Gerry Adams to step down as party leader.[110] The previous autumn, Adams had summarily dismissed any notion that he might resign from the position he had held for twenty-six years, asserting, 'It isn't an issue at this time. I'm the party president and *sin é* [that's it].'[111]

Still, what Morris's comments appeared to confirm was that not everyone within Sinn Féin remained convinced their leader was the best man for the job. Where once Adams had been seen as their greatest electoral asset (with polls consistently showing him to be one of the most popular party leaders south of the border in the period 2002–4), now there were signs that the lustre had gone. Old accusations returned to haunt him in 2010, with the publication of Brendan Hughes' posthumous account of life in the IRA. Therein, Adams was said to have directly ordered the murder of Jean McConville, a Belfast mother of ten who was 'disappeared' by the IRA in 1972.[112] Such allegations had been made before, denied and the Sinn Féin leader had weathered them with little difficulty.[113] Now, though, in a context in which his party appeared to be stagnating politically, this perhaps added to the sense that Adams simply came with too much 'baggage' to be genuinely successful with the wider electorate. If some within the Provisional movement were beginning to reach this conclusion, their concerns can scarcely have been eased by the altogether new scandal that engulfed Adams from late 2009. Just prior to Christmas that year, a niece of the Sinn Féin leader, Áine Tyrell, publicly claimed that Liam Adams, brother of Gerry, had sexually abused her when she was a child. In the weeks that followed it emerged that Gerry had known about the allegation since at least 1987 – and there were forceful suggestions, again denied, that he had been involved in a cover-up.[114] The damage done to the Adams 'brand' by all of this remains to be seen, but the episode seemed to serve as an additional symptom of the deficiencies now being seen in a leadership that had been *in situ* for the best part of three decades.

In this sequence of events, it was possible to see the embryo for a serious internal critique of the point Sinn Féin had arrived at by 2009–10 – and of the leadership that had led them there. Republicans had been persuaded by the Adams–McGuinness leadership to acquiesce in a swathe of ideological sacrifices. First, the decommissioning of IRA weapons and then, in particular, an endorsement of policing in Northern Ireland had been bitter pills to swallow. For the most part these had been accepted, on the premise that these were integral components of what was, however painful, a successful strategy – a strategy that was slowly, but surely, delivering Irish unity. Shorn of that success, though, all that remained were the compromises. It was this that pushed those that did leave the party in this era to act as they did. As the senior RNU figure Tony Catney put it:

> The thing that was called a process [towards Irish unity] has no movement in it at all. It is completely static and, by definition, it is not a process. It is now an institution. And it is an institution that is firmly based on the premise that the 'Six Counties' really is 'Northern Ireland', and really is part of the United Kingdom.[115]

Catney was far from alone in his sense that 'the project', for republicans, was not running according to plan; and indeed, in this context, a further unravelling of the Provisional movement's internal cohesiveness may prove inevitable in the future.

ÉIRÍGÍ

The failures of Sinn Féin south of the border in this period helped stir another new form of Irish republicanism into existence: éirígí. Created in Dublin in April 2006, this group took its name from the Irish for 'rise up'. It was founded by a group of former Sinn Féin activists who had become disillusioned about the direction of the mainstream republican movement. Its chairperson, Brian Leeson, is an articulate, former Sinn Féin *árd chomhairle* member and national organiser. In his mid-thirties, Leeson had been involved with the Provisionals from 1989 until 2006, when he left over both their 'gradual abandonment of the core national position on the national question' and their 'gradual movement away from the correct left, socialist position'.[116] As with people like Tony Catney, Leeson's view was that Sinn Féin had fared poorly during the peace process:

> The IRA was fought to a standstill on the battlefield – or certainly the leadership believed it was fought to a standstill – and they moved the battlefield into the negotiating arena. There they were defeated. And off the back of that defeat you are now in a period of post-defeat – a historic defeat I would say, with parallels to the post-1921 period. And if you study what happened from 1921 to 1931, republicanism went through the same somersaults, demoralisation, fragmentation, splintering, ever-decreasing circles of frustration ...[117]

Again here, it was possible to see a narrative centred on the inadequacies of the Provisional movement's leadership. In making such a case, Leeson was prepared to turn the rhetoric of people such as Gerry Adams back against them:

> Some people such as Adams would have said that the Provisionals were on a journey ... Gerry was driving and Cork was the final destination – victory. Others might have argued it was Limerick we were going to, with Limerick being defeat. Now, the road separates at Portlaoise ... So you have a journey from Dublin to Portlaoise, where you're on the same road to Cork or Limerick and then it splits at Portlaoise ... Now I think there's an argument to be made that from 1998 through to 2004, possibly that five, six, seven-year period, you hadn't got to Portlaoise. But now you have, and the destination for that movement is clearly Limerick ... The trajectory it is on cannot be changed.[118]

It was this realisation, according to Leeson, which pushed him and others to leave Dublin Sinn Féin and consider alternative ways forward. A particular gripe for them was the shortcomings of the Provisional movement in the Irish Republic. According to Leeson, this was only too apparent, even before Sinn Féin's failures in the 2007 general election – and it was this that helped precipitate his resignation: '[Within the Provisionals] there was little knowledge and less interest in the South ... when you went south of a line from Dundalk to Sligo, ignorance and lack of interest were close bed-fellows.'[119] In the face of this, Leeson felt a new group, capable of 'strategic thinking' across the island from a republican perspective, was required. It was never his intention, he contends, 'to go home' after leaving Sinn Féin; rather, he wished to build a 'vanguard party or organisation to carry the revolution' – and the result was éirígí.[120]

Alongside Leeson, other early éirígí activists included Daithí Mac an Mháistir, Donal O'Driscoll, Geraldine Dougan (a former Sinn Féin MLA who left the party in 2007 in opposition to its endorsement of the PSNI) and Joanne McDonald, the sister of former Sinn Féin MEP Mary Lou McDonald.[121] In 2009, Louise Minihan, the Dublin Sinn Féin councillor who had quit the party in protest at its shortcomings, joined éirígí.

Éirígí first came to attention with its 'Reclaim the Republic' campaign, which saw it distribute full-colour copies of the 1916 Proclamation across the Irish capital. The group claimed to have delivered some 45,000 prints across Dublin by the end of October 2006, with it aiming to have dispensed a further 15,000 by the end of the year – statistics that appeared to suggest an organisation possessing not insignificant financial resources and energy (though Leeson would dispute the former). From October 2006, éirígí launched a further project centred on the notion, 'what the proclamation means to me'. This aimed to pull together the writings of various contributors to offer their reflections on the Proclamation. Among the contributors invited to participate were Francie Mackey of the 32CSM, Tommy McKearney (formerly involved with the *Fourthwrite* and *The Blanket* circles), Gerry Ruddy of the IRSP and various individuals drawn from other 'left-wing' groups such as Roger Cole of the Peace and Neutrality Alliance, Eugene McCartan of the Communist Party of Ireland and Ciarán Ó Brolcháin of the James Connolly Debating Society.

In the first instance, then, the aim of éirígí appeared to be the promulgation of a traditional republican narrative, centred around such key ideological pillars as the 1916 Proclamation – the archetypal expression of romantic Irish nationalism. Its earliest activity seemed to suggest it was more of a cultural/intellectual lobby group than anything else. However, it was also prepared to involve itself in the prison protests described in previous chapters. It was thus an active voice calling for the 'repatriation' of Aiden Hulme from England.[122]

More significantly, in May 2007, éirígí held its inaugural *árd fheis* in Dublin, and there the decision was taken to move from being a 'campaigns group' to being a 'political party ... a truly revolutionary political party'. To this end, the group now 'adopted a written constitution' that reflected a 'socialist republican philosophy'. Further, éirígí committed itself to an effort to 'effect a British withdrawal from the occupied six counties' and establish 'a thirty-two county Irish Socialist Republic based upon the principles of sovereignty, democracy, liberty, justice, equality, community and international solidarity'.[123]

In the wake of this new overtly political orientation, June 2007 brought the launch of a polished newsletter, to be published online every month by éirígí. The first edition announced the evolution of the group into a political party and also claimed that it had expanded to include members from across the country; it was no longer, it claimed, a purely Dublin entity. This growth included the development of the organisation north of the border. In March 2007, it took its 'Reclaim the Republic' campaign into Northern Ireland, with 'the first distribution of éirígí material in the occupied six counties'.[124] The newsletter also pointed to the range of activities with which éirígí was involved. This included traditional republican pursuits such as commemorative events for past republican 'struggles'. In 2007, for instance, it held two ceremonies to celebrate the anniversary of 1916.[125] Significantly too, on 22 September 2007, Bernard Fox, a prominent former Provisional republican from Belfast, delivered the oration at éirígí's Thomas Ashe commemoration – an event which also marked the start of the organisation's campaign for British withdrawal from Northern Ireland.[126] A year later and Fox was again involved with the group – this time participating in a series of Hunger-Strike themed meetings, in Dublin, north Armagh, Belfast, south Derry and Fermanagh, to mark the launch of the film *Hunger* (directed by Steve McQueen). Others involved included Jake Jackson (the former cell-mate of Bobby Sands) and Tommy McKearney.

Elsewhere, much of éirígí's energy was devoted to a self-avowedly radical social and economic agenda. It therefore initiated a campaign to 'defend Ireland's natural resources', which involved protest action against the Shell gas pipeline and terminal at Corrib in County Mayo. The group emphasised how, in its view, 'billions of euros worth of Irish gas have been literally given away to the private energy companies.'[127] Interestingly, it also pointed to the work of the Centre for Public Inquiry – a controversial non-governmental organisation in the Irish Republic, which had produced reports into what it labelled 'The Great Corrib Gas Controversy'.[128] Éirígí called for the nationalisation of Ireland's natural resources. Under the banner of 'We only want the earth!', its members were involved in a campaign that called for 'the public ownership of all natural resources'. The campaign took as its focus two specific areas: 'namely that of the giveaway of Ireland's oil and gas reserves and the attempts to introduce water charges in both the Six and Twenty-Six County states'.[129] In the context of the protests against Shell in County Mayo, éirígí publicly advocated the adoption of 'the long-established tactic of civil disobedience' – which entailed sit-downs and the occupation of Shell's gas refinery. Such 'peaceful protests', the organisation claimed, had been met with 'state violence' by the Gardaí.[130] In October 2007, in the wake of one protest at the

Shell refinery at Ballinaboy, Brian Leeson claimed that the police were 'protecting one of the world's most destructive and ruthless corporations'; they had been ordered by their 'political masters in Leinster House', he claimed, to 'ensure that Shell's rape and plunder be allowed to continue apace without disruption'.[131]

Éirígí's involvement in this kind of campaign was scarcely surprising. As has been noted, protests against Shell have been a feature of the broader republican milieu. Republican Sinn Féin have endorsed the umbrella group 'Shell to Sea', as indeed have the mainstream Sinn Féin party. It does, though, raise the question of éirígí's attitude towards possible co-operation with other 'republican' groups. Here it is worth remembering Tony Catney's professed scepticism of éirígí; for, suffice to say, the sentiment is reciprocated. When asked about the potential for republican unity, Leeson was brusque in his assertion that

> ... many initiatives appear to us to be not much more than sloganeering ... on paper, the idea of unity, or strength through unity, sounds very, very good, but when you sit in a room and one group is pursuing its own strategy, which is based upon an analysis very different to our own, the possibility of any unified front lasting any length of time is very limited. One could share a platform with an organisation on a given issue, but if that [group], or one of its affiliates goes off and kills twenty civilians then you have real problems for the organisation unaware of its plans to do that ... The basis for all unity must be both ideological and tactical. So if you're pursuing different tactics, how can different groups work together?[132]

For this reason, Leeson and éirígí preferred to confine the sphere of co-operation to single-issue campaigns, such as those opposing Shell or the Lisbon Treaty.

Whatever the focus of its activities, éirígí does appear to have generated a certain level of dynamism. In part this has been achieved by its skilful use of the new media. Of all the dissident republican organisations surveyed here, éirígí has shown itself adept at exploiting an online presence. Brian Leeson has referred to the 'empowering character of the internet' and the extent to which this has afforded his group 'a platform that allows us to get our voice and message out there in a way that you just can't do in a newspaper'. In his estimation, the relatively low cost of a website and the ability to disseminate widely images and sound have provided éirígí 'with an opportunity that people ten years ago didn't have'.[133] Driven by such insights, éirígí has established itself as a frontrunner, where other expressions of militant Irish republicanism have been rather slow to embrace the potential of the internet.[134]

In May 2009, éirígí held its third *árd fheis*, an event attended by several external guests, including Maura Harrington of the 'Shell to Sea' campaign and Bernice Swift, the independent republican councilor from Fermanagh in Northern Ireland, who had resigned from Sinn Féin in 2007 in protest at the party's move towards an endorsement of the PSNI. At that *árd fheis*, a new policy paper was adopted, entitled 'Elections, Elected Institutions and Ireland's Revolutionary Struggle'.[135] This confirmed – after what was heralded as a four-month-long internal debate – the intention of éirígí to contest future elections 'on a tactical basis'.[136] The sole determining factor was to be whether or not 'the contesting of those elections will advance éirígí's revolutionary objectives'. In addition to this, the party also stated that if it won seats in the Irish parliament or at local council level it would 'participate in those elected institutions on a tactical basis'. The same, though, was not to apply to either Stormont or Westminster, which would be approached on an abstentionist basis only, as they were 'British institutions'.[137] In adopting this position, one senior éirígí member has spoken of the group's desire to avoid 'going down the constitutional path'. They would, it was claimed, 'learn the lessons of the past' and not recognise the 'legitimacy of any of these institutions'; rather, such participation as did occur was about acting 'as some people said they were going to do some twenty years ago ... we're going to wreck [those institutions] from the inside and the outside.'[138]

Alongside the debate over electoralism, the 2009 *árd fheis* also saw éirígí pledge to 'actively oppose' any council events in Northern Ireland that were to be held to mark 'Armed Forces Day' at the end of June. This was said to be part of its agenda to challenge 'every aspect of the British occupation of the six counties' and build 'popular resistance to British rule'.[139] In line with this, éirígí held a protest against the event in Belfast city centre and produced a promotional 'YouTube' video of its efforts (replete with a soundtrack that somewhat bizarrely mixed Rage against the Machine with Enya).[140]

In August 2009, the party gained a further boost when it was announced that a former Sinn Féin councillor in Northern Ireland, Barry Monteith, had joined éirígí, effectively becoming its first elected member in the province.[141] That same month, éirígí confirmed that it did indeed intend to stand candidates in the next local government elections scheduled for Northern Ireland in 2011.[142]

By the middle of 2009, then, éirígí had clearly grown in stature and emerged as a hub for republicans disaffected with mainstream republicanism, on both sides of the border. Brian Leeson could point to an éirígí membership of some 150–200 people, drawn via a 'stringent recruitment policy' that focused more on 'quality and ability to influence' others than numbers.[143] A reflection of this could be seen from the fact that the group had enjoyed some success in attracting prominent former members of the Provisional movement into its ranks. The decision of Bernard Fox to speak at an éirígí commemoration has already been mentioned. Others drawn to the group included the Craigavon republican Colin Duffy and Breandán Mac Cionnaith, a former Provisional IRA member (jailed in 1981 for his part in bombing a Royal British Legion hall) and the leading figure in the Garvaghy Road Residents Coalition that had played a central part in the protests at Drumcree during the 1990s[144] In 2008, Mac Cionnaith became éirígí's general secretary.[145] Also present alongside these two men at the group's 2009 protest against Israeli actions in Gaza was Gerard Rice.[146] It remains unclear whether Rice has formally joined éirígí, though he has been involved in other protests organised by the group; if confirmed, it would mean that in Rice and Mac Cionnaith éirígí had won over two of the three men who played a key role in directing Sinn Féin's anti-Orange parade agitation during the 1990s (the third being Donncha Mac Niallais).[147] It is perhaps against this background that the group's pledge to 'stand with communities that want to resist Orange parades' should be seen.[148]

Mac Cionnaith, meanwhile, was another who, like Leeson, had left Sinn Féin in late 2006, because of its perceived weakness on both national and social issues. With regard to the former, he had come to feel that they were 'bedding down partition and bedding down the system in the north'. Equally, on social issues he felt Sinn Féin was engaging in a 'fairly dramatic shift towards the centre'. As a result, he had resigned and later looked to éirígí as offering 'a whole new departure from what has been established republican thinking'.[149] At the core of this, ironically, was to be a *reassertion* of what Mac Cionnaith called the 'politics of 1916', albeit with a premium placed on the thinking of James Connolly. It was for this reason that éirígí's main annual com-memoration was held in honour of Connolly at Arbour Hill cemetery in Dublin.[150] In June 2009, at his neat home in Portadown in the 'British-occupied North', Mac Cionnaith explained the significance of the event:

> I would say Connolly actually produced the political message when he turned around and said the cause of Ireland was the cause of Labour and the cause of Labour was the cause of Ireland. They can't be severed. And I think an organisation like ourselves needs to ensure that a balance is struck and maintained between those two elements – the national question and the social and economic question.[151]

In seeking to carry forth such a message, éirígí wished to move away from the 'elitism that you had within Sinn Féin' and, according to Mac Cionnaith, eschewed the 'traditional republican model' by which there was a political party on one hand and an armed wing on the other.[152] Éirígí's aim, in Mac Cionnaith's eyes, was that it would put

> ... clear blue water between ourselves and the Shinners, but also clear blue water between ourselves and those other groups ... on the one hand you have groups that are ready and willing to get into the armed struggle again without even having a credible di-rection behind it; on the other hand, you have Sinn Féin, who have essentially become a constitutionalist party here in that they're willing to accept partition, accept the state here in the North. And it's almost as if we're trying to develop – and I hate to use the term – a third way that is neither acceptance of the state and partition and doesn't mean that we're going to send young lads to jail for nineteen, twenty years ... and it'll take time for peo-ple to see that we are serious about that.[153]

In the context of éirígí's desire to distinguish itself from Sinn Féin, November 2008 had seen the group effectively flex its political 'muscles' in Northern Ireland for the first time when it organised a protest against the 'homecoming' parade of the Royal Irish Regiment (RIR) in Belfast. The banner under which it held the event was 'Britain's Murder

Machine out of Ireland'. And this move represented a direct challenge to Sinn Féin, which up until the moment éirígí announced its demonstration had been ignoring the issue. Éirígí's action appeared to force Sinn Féin to hold a similar protest against the RIR parade. Ultimately, Sinn Féin's protest proved to be a bigger draw in terms of numbers, attracting an estimated 1,500 people, as compared to the éirígí protest, which set off from Divis Tower at the bottom of the Falls Road and involved around 200–300 participants. Nevertheless, what this episode seemed to indicate was the developing ability of éirígí to define the political agenda. As Mac Cionnaith observed, 'we forced the Shinners on to our ground'; and by this he meant physically as well as metaphorically:

> If you look at every march towards the city centre that's ever been organised by Sinn Féin over the years they've gone along the Falls Road up Divis Street, Castle Street and in to the city centre ... But now when they had their march it was Falls Road, Grosvenor Road ... They actually had to move away from their standard set-piece march.[154]

More broadly, meanwhile, Mac Cionnaith saw the significance of the November 2008 march as 'the first protest in Sinn Féin's own heartland of west Belfast that has not been Sinn Féin organised', which 'sent a message out to the Shinners and to many other people'.[155] Sinn Féin had felt pressured to respond to éirígí's initiative in order to preserve its republican credentials – a fact that cannot have gone unnoticed in dissident republican circles.

What is more, those in attendance at the éirígí protest (which was prevented from marching into Belfast city centre by the PSNI) included notable republican luminaries such as Brenda Downes (whose husband Sean had been killed by a rubber bullet at a Sinn Féin rally in 1984) and Alex McCrory (a former H-Block republican political prisoner and 'blanketman').[156] Of equal significance was the address given to éirígí supporters on the day by the group's chairperson, Brian Leeson. During his remarks, Leeson said that the protest represented a display of 'disciplined republicans' who were intent on showing the British that

> ... we can march on our streets without their permission and that we can do so on our terms. The day will come when we will fight them, but today is not that day. Today we make our protest. We show them that republicanism has awoken.

Going on, Leeson spoke of a 'difficult decade' for Irish republicanism in which many had become disillusioned and disappointed, while 'many of the mistakes of history' had been repeated. At the same time, he claimed that history also demonstrated the capacity of republicanism for regeneration: 'What we are witnessing now here today is the rebirth of a militant Irish republicanism.' It was not, he said, going to be a quick or easy effort to bring an end to British rule, so 'as we rebuild a new generation of resistance, let patience and discipline be our watchwords.' However, the reality was that 'Nothing will distract us over these coming years as we rebuild a militant, radical, socialist republicanism from Belfast to Cork, from Dublin to Derry.'

Leeson then concluded his speech by directly addressing 'Britain's paramilitary police', of whom he asked that they take a message 'back to their masters in Downing Street':

> I want them to tell their masters that 'you saw republicans again on the streets of west Belfast today' … And tell them finally that you looked into the eyes of a risen people … the risen people were not afraid. You tell your masters that! … We have defied the British parades commission and we have defied their paramilitary police … We are rebuilding republican resistance across this island.[157]

Against the background of such militant rhetoric, several commentators had already begun to question exactly where éirígí stood on the use of violence. In late 2008 Leeson gave an interview to *The Spark*, the online magazine of the Workers Party of New Zealand, in which he was asked for his views on 'armed republican activity'. He replied as follows:

> Any population that has the misfortune to find itself under foreign occupation has the right to use armed force to remove that occupation. Whether it was the French resisting the Nazi occupation or the Vietnamese resisting Franco-American aggression, the principle is the same. And that principle also extends to the Irish context.[158]

The significance of these remarks can be judged from the fact that when asked for his assessment of the situation in Ireland, Leeson argued that 'The British occupation of the north of Ireland is as real today as it ever was.' Viewed from that perspective, the comments clearly amounted to an endorsement of the legitimacy of violent republican activity. The only caveats to this position were practical in nature. To quote Leeson,

> ... while any people may have a principled right to use armed struggle, it may not always be tactically or strategically the correct option. We believe that there are other, more effective ways to challenge and defeat British rule in Ireland today.[159]

This less-than-forthright rejection of violence has meant that doubts have continued to be raised as to the gap between éirígí and more militant forms of dissident republicanism.

The propensity of the group's members to get themselves arrested has done little to ease such doubts. In this regard, éirígí was subjected to particular pressure, in the aftermath of the March 2009 murders, to clarify its position on the use of violence. Breandán Mac Cionnaith, in an interview with the *Irish News*, gave the following (again, somewhat ambiguous) response:

> Éirígí is an open, independent, democratic political party which is not aligned to, or supportive of, any armed organisation. While supporting the right of any people to defend themselves from imperial aggression, éirígí does not believe that the conditions exist at this time for a successful armed struggle against the British occupation. As can be seen from the recent attacks on Britain's armed forces it is clear that not all republicans agree on how the British occupation should be resisted at this time. Those who carried out those attacks are best placed to explain their own rationale.[160]

After Colin Duffy, who had previously been involved with éirígí, was arrested (and subsequently charged) in connection with the killings, the group seemed keen to distance itself from him, claiming that he had left their organisation three weeks earlier.[161] This was a line of argument subsequently repeated by Brian Leeson when another éirígí activist, Dominic McGlinchey Jr, was questioned about the incident as well (though it should be noted that McGlinchey was released without charge).[162] Remarkably, a third former member of éirígí, Brian Shivers, was later charged with murder in relation to the Massereene attack.[163] (At the time of writing, the trials of Duffy and Shivers are still pending.) Still, Leeson stood by his assertion that 'no members of éirígí have been arrested in recent days – a fact that could have been easily established by contacting éirígí.'[164] Leeson also condemned the 'despicable trial by media' that he felt was taking place; and took the opportunity to reiterate, almost word for word, Mac Cionnaith's position with regard to éirígí's views on violence.[165] Again, this hardly represented a decisive turn away from the 'politics of the gun'. At most, éirígí's position on the use of violence appeared to be one of 'not right now'. As one spokesman for the group, Éamann MacManais, put it, 'Certainly a lot of members involved [in éirígí] come from a military background and make no apology for that. But there is no appetite for going back to armed struggle at the moment.'[166]

At his Portadown home in June 2009, against the incongruous backdrop of an effervescent fish tank, Mac Cionnaith was adamant that on the subject of 'armed struggle', éirígí 'don't need to have a position on it'. The group, he avowed, did not have 'any armed movement and is not allied to, or supportive of, any of the armed groupings out there'. And yet, when asked as to the possibility that there might be a role for violence in the future, his answer was more circumlocutory:

> I don't know … but if you take a scenario that was to arise where, just like 1969, you actually have the state suppressing popular movements, you know these movements are going to have to defend themselves in some shape or form … how are they going to address that? I don't know … At the same time, if armed actions were going to free the country, it should have been free ten years ago.[167]

Others within éirígí seemed even less willing to present a moderate face to the world. On 13 March 2009, the same day that the murdered policeman Stephen Carroll was buried in Craigavon, éirígí held its first official function in west Belfast. The keynote speech there was delivered by the organisation's chairperson in the city, Rab Jackson. During the course of that address, Jackson declared that in Northern Ireland 'there is no constitutional power in this country with either the power or the will to change [current conditions]. No government, parliament, nor assembly. We must do it ourselves.' From there he offered an encomium to the efforts of various groups such as the United Irishmen, the Young Irelanders, the Fenians and the Irish Citizens' Army – all armed groups that had engaged in violent campaigns – before adding, 'Those who relied solely on constitutional politics within the British framework ninety years ago were doomed to failure. The same is true today.' At the core of Jackson's speech was an obdurate message:

> We in éirígí believe that small groups of committed people can help
> create change ... No one can predict how the State – north or south
> – may react to this. Nor can we say never when talking about
> tactics for revolution. But one thing is certain: like never before
> we have to build as a people ... we are dedicated to seeing the
> ideals of ninety years ago become a reality ...We are a new political
> party, we're fresh. But we inherit the collective experience of years
> of struggle. Militant social republicanism is here to stay.[168]

On offer here was a clear vision of militant Irish republicanism, which
would not confine itself to the purely constitutional realm. The veneration attached to the example of 'ninety years ago', when Sinn Féin
had stood alongside an active IRA that had fought and killed British
forces, made plain that violent methods were not to be irrevocably ex-
cluded. The fact that he specifically referred to various other armed organisations simply drove home the point; so too, his explicit refusal to
rule out a resort to violence.

It is a stance with which Brian Leeson seems to agree. When pressed
on the matter in June 2009, the éirígí chairperson also sought to situ-
ate himself historically:

> It would be hypocritical of us to adopt a position that armed strug-
> gle in the context of national liberation is wrong under all condi-
> tions. That would just be rank hypocrisy. We come from the
> revolutionary, conspiratorial, insurrectionary republican trend. As
> a party we've taken a view that, as things stand today, the condi-
> tions for a successful armed struggle do not exist ... I think the
> position of it being a tactic, at a theoretical level, is probably a fair
> enough analysis of where most people in éirígí would be coming
> from. They wouldn't have a principled objection to the concept.
> I mean if they did, they'd have a principled objection to 1916,
> 1798, 1803, 1848, 1867, the border campaign, the insurrection
> that began in '69–'70 ... it would fly in the face of all our history
> to say there is a principled objection.[169]

Thus, for all the talk of Connolly, it is clear that éirígí has in no
way relinquished affection for Pearse and his nationalist liturgy. The
socialist intent of the former continues to be balanced by the romantic
insurrectionism of the latter, a fact demonstrated by the choice of the
1916 Proclamation as the means by which éirígí effectively announced

its existence to the world. In this regard, it might be said that Jackson, Leeson and éirígí as a whole continue to create and sustain an ideological hinterland into which those prepared to engage in republican 'armed struggle' can move. Furthermore, the period of 2006–9 saw the emergence of a new stratum of republicans of whom this could be said; for alongside the flowering of dissident republican *political* activity there was a simultaneous evolution in the paramilitary world.

THE RETURN OF THE MILITANTS

The Continuity IRA had previously survived as an active organisation throughout the peace process – albeit one operating at a relatively low level. This existence was maintained in the years after 2005. It periodically laid claim to various attacks on security service personnel and installations, loyalist bonfires and Orange halls. The CIRA took responsibility for a number of hoaxes as well, some of which caused serious disruption, such as one targeted at Down Royal Race Course in November 2005. In October 2006, the Independent Monitoring Commission (IMC) – the organisation set up in 2004 to monitor paramilitary activity – noted that the organisation was determined to launch a campaign of violence. It did also conclude, however, that CIRA 'capabilities do not generally match its aspirations and the police North and South have had a number of welcome successes against it'.[170] As an example of the latter, attention was drawn to the fact that an allegedly senior member of the CIRA had received a substantial prison sentence in Dublin, in July 2006.

Such problems notwithstanding, though, the CIRA was still believed to be responsible for both a range of paramilitary 'punishment' shootings and the firebombing of a series of retail outlets in north Antrim and Belfast in October 2006 – the latter attacks being justified on the basis that B&Q, the chain store in question, was a 'legitimate target' because it supplied the British army.[171] Less quixotic incidents followed. In November 2006, the CIRA was thought to be behind a shooting incident which targeted a police station in Keady in County Armagh.[172] This was followed a month later by a failed pipe bomb attack on Lurgan's PSNI station and the abandonment of a landmine near Rosslea in County Fermanagh.[173] Other attempts to strike at the security services followed, with the group particularly active in Belfast and in counties

Armagh, Fermanagh and Down.[174] The CIRA's continuing focus into 2007–8, according to the IMC, was to 'carry out attacks in order to disrupt the political process in Northern Ireland'.[175] To this end, it remained 'active, dangerous and determined'.[176]

The localised nature of the CIRA threat – limited as it largely was to specific regions – was a reflection of an earlier IMC conclusion: that the group's leadership exercised only 'tenuous' control over its units, which acted 'in the main autonomously'.[177] For this reason, the vigour of the CIRA in any given area was determined by the character of its membership in that locale. Furthermore, this potentially fissiparous aspect of the organisation's make-up contributed to a lethal split in the CIRA in late 2006–7. In its February 2006 report, the IMC had referred to the emergence of the new splinter group, 'Óglaigh na hÉireann' in the Strabane area.[178] Initial assessments questioned the long-term viability of this new entity, yet by January 2007 it was being reported that ONH had become 'more dangerously active' and was engaged in the targeting of PSNI officers[179] Further attacks followed, with the targeting of DPP members and a PSNI officer in the vicinity of Strabane in April 2007; the organisation was also blamed for pipe bombs that were thrown at that town's PSNI station in July and December 2007.[180] In February 2008, the first murder attributed to ONH was believed to have occurred with the killing of a former Real IRA member, Andrew Burns, in County Donegal.[181]

Throughout this time, the most active – and notorious – group within that world continued to be the Real IRA itself. Established back in 1997 as the most potent republican challenge to the Provisional IRA, the RIRA – or at least, a body claiming to inherit the title deeds of that organisation – had thereafter appeared in various forms. In October 2002, as has been described, after the imprisonment of its founder member, Michael McKevitt, together with other leading figures (such as Liam Campbell and Séamus McGrane), the RIRA had experienced a debilitating split. The legacy of this was such that, six years later, the IMC could still identify two distinct factions operating under the Real IRA banner.[182] In spite of these problems, which meant that the group often lacked a formal structure or hierarchy, the RIRA continued to be identified as 'potentially a very dangerous terrorist group' and 'the most active of the dissident republican groups'.[183] Confusingly, in the period that followed, one RIRA faction would increasingly lay claim to the banner of ONH – and would actually displace the original Strabane-based ONH as the group most associated with the term.[184]

In October 2006, the IMC reported that there had been an 'escalation' in RIRA activity earlier that year, focused on the Ballymena area, with attacks on a police vehicle, an Orange hall and two schools.[185] This 'mini-surge' was maintained down to December, with the planting of further incendiary devices in six DIY stores and two other shops across Northern Ireland – a tactic that was subsequently estimated to have caused well over £10 million worth of damage.[186] In the same period, a PSNI station in Craigavon was the subject of a failed mortar attack and the Real IRA was said to have reached its 'highest level of sustained paramilitary activity' since late 2004–5.[187]

No sooner had such a conclusion been arrived at than the Real IRA's impetus appeared to stall somewhat: in April 2007, the IMC noted that the organisation had been 'less active in the three months under review than it was in the preceding three months'.[188] However, a second, more enduring, and ultimately more dangerous, escalation in RIRA activity appeared to follow from late that year, continuing into 2008. This brought the attempted murder of two off-duty Catholic police officers in November 2007: one in Derry and the other in Dungannon.[189] In the former incident, Constable Jim Doherty was targeted as he sat in traffic after he had dropped his son off at school.[190] The same *modus operandi* was deployed in the attack on Constable Paul Musgrave in Dungannon, which was timed to coincide with the gathering of the local DPP, at which Sinn Féin was due to take its seats for the first time. That meeting was duly postponed.[191] More seriously still, the fact that no-one was killed in either incident seemed more down to luck than any active interdiction on the part of the security forces; the victims were badly injured in the assaults. In the wake of the attacks, the Real IRA promised to 'continue to target Crown forces at a time and place of our choosing'.[192] A 'new year statement' also pledged that attacks on the 'British police in Ireland' would go on, with 'repercussions' threatened against anyone helping the police.[193]

This was followed in February 2008 by a high-profile interview given by a member of the organisation to the *Sunday Tribune*, in which the Real IRA declared a resumption of violence after a three-year period of 'reorganising'. A 'renewed offensive' was to be undertaken, it was said, against those 'who promote and protect the illegal occupation

Legion of the Rearguard

of the six counties – British soldiers, RUC/PSNI members and British government ministers'. Simultaneously, Francie Mackey of the 32CSM condemned the leadership of the Provisionals for having 'failed the republican base' and called on them to relinquish the name of Sinn Féin. They were, he averred, 'not espousing republicanism any more and they are following in the steps of de Valera after 1922'.[194] For Mackey and the 32CSM, as much as the RIRA, the mantle of true republicanism lay elsewhere, with those still committed to 'armed struggle'.

That this uncompromising message could not be ignored was confirmed within a couple of months by another near-lethal attack on a police officer. In May 2008, a Catholic member of the PSNI, Ryan Crozier, was seriously injured by an under-car bomb in Spamount, near Castlederg in County Tyrone.[195] And by the end of the year, the Chief Constable of the PSNI, Sir Hugh Orde, was describing the threat from the dissidents as being at its highest level for six years. In evidence to the House of Commons Northern Ireland Affairs Committee, he affirmed, 'Without question, the intensity has increased. The determination of the main groups, Continuity IRA and Real IRA (RIRA), is clear by the evidence of the level of attacks and variety of attacks.'[196]

The difficulties faced by Orde and his men, as they attempted to frustrate the ambitions of the militants, were doubtless increased by the amorphous nature of the enemy they faced. It was possible, as has been described, to discern the broad outlines of groups acting under the various banners of 'Continuity IRA', 'Real IRA' and 'Óglaigh na hÉireann'. And yet the boundaries across these entities often appeared fluid: it was not always easy to tell where one ended and another began. The problems of identification were further compounded by the readiness of the groups to utilise names of convenience for 'false flag' operations. The IMC and newspaper reports referred to the appearance (and, often, rapid disappearance) of several 'groups' of varying substance: Saoirse na hÉireann in Belfast, the Republican Defence Army in Strabane, the Irish Republican Liberation Army in Belfast and Republican Action Against Drugs (RAAD) in Derry.[197] In the face of this confusing array, the IMC itself acknowledged that it was often impossible to attribute an action to one specific group. This difficulty was exacerbated still further, it asserted, because 'one feature of dissident republican groups is a tendency for things sometimes to be personality-driven or dependent on family or local allegiances, rather than on ideology.'[198]

The consequences of this phenomenon were at first sight somewhat contradictory: a tendency towards both ever 'more fragmentation' and, at the same time, a greater capacity for co-operation and group-over-lap at the local level.[199]

The corollary of this, in turn, was that it became increasingly diffi-cult for those standing outside the closed, conspiratorial world of Irish republicanism to determine, with total confidence, who exactly was doing what. Instead, it was possible merely to stand back and assess the bigger picture. The contours of that picture, though, were unmistak-able; for what it showed was an upsurge in violent dissident activity.

Moreover, it was clear that certain areas had emerged as the repeated foci of that activity. Thus, the May 2008 attack in Castlederg was followed by further attempts to kill PSNI officers in Rosslea (June) and Lisnaskea (August). Both towns in south Fermanagh had seen repeated attacks on the police over previous years. The same could be said of Craigavon, which in late 2008 witnessed serious rioting in the republican-dominated Tullygally and Drumbeg estates. It was subse-quently reported that 'veterans of the Provisional IRA's North Armagh brigade', who had now departed that organisation, were responsible for orchestrating the violence there.[200] Not only did the disturbances in-clude the throwing of stones and petrol bombs, but also shots were fired at a police patrol – a sequence that directly prefigured the incident that would bring the murder of Stephen Carroll in the same location seven months later. Back in 2007 too, police officers recovering 400 pounds of explosives in the town had come under sustained attack from coordinated rioters; and prior to that there had been a failed mortar attack on the PSNI there in December 2006.[201] Craigavon, then, appeared to have become something of a 'hot-bed' of dissident activity – long before the death of Constable Carroll exposed this to a wider audience.

Indeed, the whole north Armagh region emerged as an area of real concern to the security services at this time. Lurgan, for example, just a couple of miles from Craigavon, was another place to experience a series of dissident-related incidents.[202] There, the Kilwilkie estate served as the effective hub of militancy. As far back as 1999, this area had witnessed serious rioting with vehicles hijacked, placed on the railway line and burnt in an effort to lure the police into the estate.[203] Similarly, in 2005, police responding to a bomb placed inside a hijacked car in Lurgan had been targeted by a crowd from Kilwilkie throwing missiles and incendiary devices, leaving seven officers hurt.[204] Further unrest was recorded in spring 2007, with rioters again bombarding the police with stones and petrol bombs; in that instance, there were also reports of prominent pro-CIRA graffiti in the estate.[205] In some ways, Lurgan's enduring belligerence was unsurprising. It was there that the last RUC men to die at the hands of the Provisional IRA were murdered in July 1997, in an attack claimed by the 'North Armagh Brigade Óglaigh na hÉireann'.[206] Moreover there were indications that a strong traditional republican nucleus had endured in the area. Republican Sinn Féin's publicity director, Richard Walsh, has specifically cited 'places like north Armagh, around Lurgan and then Craigavon' as areas of some growth for the party.[207] According to Martin Duffy, a press officer for RSF, fourteen out of twenty-four CIRA prisoners in Maghaberry prison in early 2010 were from Lurgan and its environs. Duffy also claimed that his party could sell up to 600 copies of their monthly newspaper, *Saoirse*, in and around the town.[208] Significantly, during RSF's Easter commemorations the previous year, party president Ruairí Ó Brádaigh had opted to deliver his oration at the Lurgan commemoration, the parade for which began in the Kilwilkie estate.[209]

Elsewhere, there were reports, by the end of 2008, that a 'revived IRA' had come into existence in Dungannon in County Tyrone and was taking action against suspected drug dealers. With other dissident activity registered in Coalisland and Cookstown, there were suggestions that republican east Tyrone was moving, en masse, into the dissident camp. Again, to some extent, given the well-known strength of republican convictions in the area, this seemed far from surprising. More unlikely was the relatively strong dissident presence that appeared to be established in the Fisherwick estate of Ballymena in County Antrim. There, in early 2005, a police operation had uncovered several firebombs.[210] Later that same year, a controversial republican parade was organised within the estate by the 'Friends of William Orr Republican Flute Band', despite the opposition of the unionist parties, the SDLP and Sinn Féin. Another march a year later served as a platform for speeches by the 32CSM and the IRSP.[211] More worrying still, it was reported by July 2006 that there was a 'threat against police officers' in Ballymena, with young people in the Fisherwick estate thought susceptible to dissident recruitment.[212]

It was, therefore, against this background of growing dissident potency that Northern Ireland approached the start of 2009. September 2008 had brought the discovery of a 220-pound explosive device in a hedge in Jonesborough in the hitherto largely quiet area of south Armagh – a worrying indicator to the security services that that leviathan of republican devotion might also now be stirring. A month later, the discovery of a major bomb in the Newtownbutler area of south Fermanagh foiled what seemed set to be a major attack; and in January 2009, a 300-pound car bomb was found abandoned in the Castlewellan area of County Down.

On 7 March 2009, the day before the attacks at Massereene barracks in County Antrim, PSNI Chief Constable Sir Hugh Orde said that the threat posed by dissident republicans was at a 'critical' level. It was for this reason that he requested the Special Reconnaissance Regiment (SRR) be deployed to Fermanagh to help gather intelligence on the dissidents.[213] One security source was quoted as saying, 'The RIRA and CIRA are no longer obsessed with the notion of mounting a "spectacular" bomb attack on a high-profile target ... It is just as likely that, sooner or later, a PSNI officer on the beat will be shot dead by a stranger who simply walks up to them and produces a gun.'[214] Within days, those words would come to look all-too prescient, as the attack on Massereene barracks, which claimed the lives of two soldiers, was followed by the murder of Constable Stephen Carroll in Craigavon.

TIPPING POINT?

Sinn Féin's halting response to the March 2009 attacks was clear. The party had been caught off balance, in part because of its criticism, immediately prior to the murders, of Hugh Orde's decision to call in the SRR. Adams had said that the move risked opening up 'the old agenda' and was 'not the way forward'; rather, it was a 'retrograde decision'.[215] Such words seemed highly inauspicious when placed in the context of lethal dissident attacks.

The party then failed to react for some fourteen hours after the army base killings in Massareene. When it finally did issue a statement, Gerry Adams' words were less than categorical. The attacks, he said, were an 'attack on the peace process' and had been 'wrong and counter-productive'. He also went on to say that 'Those responsible have no support, no strategy to achieve a united Ireland. Their intention is to bring British soldiers back onto the streets.'[216] What did not feature in Adams' words was a moral condemnation of the attacks as absolutely wrong. Moreover, Sinn Féin's critique of the dissidents that they had 'no strategy' to achieve Irish unity, raised the question of exactly how the Provisionals proposed this could be achieved.

After the death of Constable Carroll on 9 March 2009, Sinn Féin's Martin McGuinness famously appeared to harden his party's position, declaring: 'These people are traitors to the island of Ireland, they have betrayed the political desires, hopes and aspirations of all of the people who live on this island ... They don't deserve to be supported by anyone.'[217] McGuinness's words offered a marked clarity – and a welcome acceptance by Sinn Féin that the dissident threat was both real and one that needed to be rejected in uncompromising terms. In this respect, it was a clear shift in McGuinness's own position. Back in late 2007, he had played down the actual threat from dissidents and claimed that many of their attacks were actually being directed by British intelligence services who were waging a 'dirty peace'.[218]

Even so, it was noticeable that this undeniably strong denunciation was applied to the death of the Catholic PSNI officer rather than the deaths of the two British army soldiers. Moreover, there are grounds for suggesting that McGuinness had perhaps gone further than he intended, or certainly than his party felt comfortable with. It is striking that coverage of the attacks in Sinn Féin's *An Phoblacht* newspaper tacked much more closely to the line taken by Adams; McGuinness's 'traitors' comment – lauded extensively elsewhere – did not feature at all.[219]

In addition to this, Sinn Féin appeared less than wholehearted in its support for the police investigation into the murders. When the PSNI moved to extend the detention period of several men being held in connection with the Massareene attack, Sinn Féin MLA Alex Maskey stated his opposition to anyone being held for longer than seven days. Further protests were registered against people being kept in custody. Gerry Adams too stated that while it was important not to 'minimise' what had happened, neither should people 'exaggerate what occurred'. He also continued to criticise Hugh Orde's decision to summon the SRR, saying that it marked a 'return to the bad practices of the past'.[220]

In articulating such positions, though, Sinn Féin adopted a position not all that far removed from the dissidents themselves. After several men had been arrested for alleged involvement in the Massereene attack, a protest against 'internment by another name' was held outside the Antrim Serious Crime Suite. Those present included members of the 32CSM, the RNU and the IRSP.[221] By opposing the detentions, Sinn Féin – in spite of its professed support for the PSNI – appeared to be acquiescing in a de facto convergence between dissident and mainstream republican narratives – albeit around a political agenda that was fundamentally being shaped by the dissidents. That this should have been so was a function of the enormous difficulties that attacks on members of the British security services created for the Provisional movement – a difficulty stemming from that movement's heritage.

The reluctance of the Provisionals to sever links with the ideological past had already been evident in their responses to previous incidences of dissident violence. After the Real IRA's attempted murder of two PSNI officers in November 2007, for instance, the leading Derry Sinn Féin member Raymond McCartney wrote in the *Derry Journal* that the dissidents had 'nothing to offer strategically, tactically or politically in ending British rule in Ireland'. But what he did not say was that still-violent republicans were wrong, or that such attacks should be condemned. His inability to make such a case stemmed from the Provisionals' own understanding of the conflict in Northern Ireland, which itself required the legitimisation of a resort to violence. As McCartney asserted:

> Let no-one be in any doubt that history will record that the IRA was in the vanguard of shifting British policy in Ireland. It was successful for a variety of factors but fundamental to this was its ability to justify and sustain itself in political and strategic terms and, in so doing, ensure popular support.[222]

In other words, what separated the Provisionals from the dissidents, according to McCartney, were their effectiveness and their popular support.[223] As a defence against the dissident narrative, however, such arguments were on far from rock-solid ground. McCartney might deride the notion that those still pursuing violence were trapped in a 'comfort zone of believing that they require no mandate except that of the British presence in Ireland', and yet, this was precisely the belief system upon which the Provisionals' own campaign had been fought.[224] Moreover, with Sinn Féin rarely gaining more than 10 per cent of the vote in Northern Ireland throughout the years of the 'Troubles', the question of how much support the Provisional IRA enjoyed from the public was open to serious question. As Anthony McIntyre observed, 'The difference lies in the size of the minorities willing to lend support to their campaigns against both British state and the democratically expressed will of the Irish people.'[225]

For Sinn Féin, the campaign waged by the Provisional IRA is still held, at a fundamental level, to be entirely legitimate. To give but one example, in February 2010, Ógra Shinn Féin (the youth wing of the party) held a commemoration for three IRA volunteers who died during the conflict. The event was addressed by Martin McGuinness who spoke of his memory of the deaths of volunteers and their selfless heroism.[226] Gerry Adams, meanwhile, has repeatedly refused to question the validity of the IRA's campaign. The commentator Malachi O'Doherty has been most forceful in noting that 'Adams' continuing pretence that the IRA had a good war does nothing to discourage the new generation of republicans.'[227]

In other respects, too, there were serious grounds, even now, to question the extent of the Provisional movement's commitment to democratic process and, particularly, the legal order. In late 2007, a south Armagh man, Paul Quinn, was beaten to death with iron bars near Cullyhanna.[228] The Provisional IRA was widely suspected of involvement and the IMC reported that, though the leadership of that organisation had not authorised it, local IRA members had been involved.[229] Sinn Féin's response, however, was one of denial. Conor Murphy, the local MP and minister in the Stormont Executive, said that he had spoken to the IRA and claimed to be 'satisfied with the assurances' that they had given him.[230] In the wake of the murder, no members of the Provisional movement came forward to give information to the police.

Elsewhere, raids on senior south Armagh Republican Thomas 'Slab' Murphy, led to him and his brothers reportedly agreeing to hand over a £1million criminal assets portfolio to revenue officers in Britain and the Republic of Ireland, following an investigation into illegal smuggling on both sides of the border. In the aftermath of these raids, Gerry Adams described him as 'not a criminal. He is a good republican.'[231] Conor Murphy made a similar assessment of Sean Hughes, also of south Armagh, when Hughes' assets were frozen by the Serious and Organised Crime Agency (SOCA) in November 2009. Murphy described Hughes as a 'sound republican' and someone who had spent 'his entire adult life engaged in the struggle for Irish unity and independence'; the police raids were described as 'unacceptable' and without 'justification'.[232] In all of this there were echoes of Gerry Adams' comments in 2005, in the wake of the Northern Bank robbery and McCartney murder, in which he had said, 'We know what a crime is both in the moral and legal sense, and our view is the same as the majority of people. We know that breaking the law is a crime. *But we refuse to criminalise those who break the law in pursuit of legitimate political objectives* [emphasis added.]' Left open here was the question of exactly what did fall within the classification of 'legitimate political objectives'. And through such ambiguities there remains a suspicion that for Sinn Féin, crime, if committed in the name of republicanism, occupies a different category.

Against this background, there was the obvious dissonance from a traditionalist republican perspective of seeing someone like Martin McGuinness speaking strongly against those who had carried out the 2009 attacks in Massereene and Craigavon. Unsurprisingly, the 32CSM dismissed his words as 'an act of desperation' from someone who 'still claims to be a republican but who is clearly on the side of the British'; indeed, McGuinness was labelled a 'Crown minister'.[233] The former Sinn Féin councillor for south Armagh, Jim McAllister, responded to McGuinness by noting, 'Even the SDLP, or Fine Gael or Fianna Fáil, never called the IRA traitors. They called them fools, madmen, wrong, murderers, but never traitors. I think McGuinness made a serious mistake.'[234]

Anthony McIntyre could not but resist asking, 'who is McGuinness to talk of treachery?' And he described his former comrade as a 'British micro minister', before adding, 'Like a chastened moral dwarf in the land of the giants, there he was screaming "midget" at everybody else.' McIntyre did add that he had 'never felt the slightest inclination' to join the Real IRA, an organisation he dubbed the 'Make Believe IRA' on the basis that he felt it was unlikely to succeed, given it possessed 'a much less robust militarily efficient organisation than the Provisional IRA'. For this reason, he claimed there was 'no reason for me to change my mind'. Still, he concluded that for McGuinness to condemn such groups as traitors, given that 'the logic we preached in the Provisional IRA is their logic', was actually 'treachery against truth'.[235]

When seen in this light, it is clear that the March 2009 murders – and their aftermath – gave an insight into the upheavals then under way within the Irish republican world. They testified both to the survival of militant dissident republicanism and to the growing capacity of this phenomenon.

In the wake of those attacks, the attention of the British media – and that of the wider world – flitted back, briefly, to Northern Ireland. For the most part, however, the approach of many within the media was to treat the events of March 2009 as the atavistic eruption of some otherwise-distant past. The dominant rhetorical response – that there should be 'no return to the Troubles' – glossed over the extent to which the March murders were part of a broader spectrum of dissident activity. That activity, as has been shown, stretched back to the Agreement and beyond. Though occasionally at a low ebb, it had never disappeared – and since 2006–7 its trajectory had been slowly, but steadily, upwards. In this regard, the post-Massereene comment from the PSNI Chief Constable Sir Hugh Orde that dissident republicanism, though 'very dangerous', was 'in its death throes', seemed misplaced.[236]

Moreover, as the broader public sphere has again turned away from the 'dreary steeples of Fermanagh and Tyrone', the resurgence of dissident Irish republican activity has appeared to proceed regardless. In April 2009, the Real IRA issued a statement on Easter Sunday in Derry and gave an interview to the *Sunday Tribune* newspaper in which it threatened members of the PSNI and ex-IRA informers, and also pledged to carry out attacks in Britain. The group described itself as ready to 'engage in [the] tactical use of armed struggle'.[237] Post-Massereene, the Real IRA felt that the 'idea of an unarmed civilian police force' had been exposed, thereby preventing a key part of the 'normalisation' agenda from moving forwards in Northern Ireland.[238] With regard to McGuinness's comments, the group offered the following veiled threat:

> A former comrade [Martin McGuinness] has come full circle and, with a knight of the British realm at his shoulder, he has labelled our gallant volunteers as traitors to justify his Redmondite stance and home rule politics. Let us remind our former comrade of the nature and the actions of a traitor. Treachery is collaborating with the enemy, treachery is betraying your country. Let us give our one-time comrade an example. Denis Donaldson was a traitor and

the leadership of the Provisional movement, under guidance from the British government, made provision for Donaldson to escape republican justice in the same manner as Freddie Scappaticci. It fell to the volunteers of Óglaigh na hÉireann to carry out the sentence and punishment demanded in our Army Orders and by the wider republican family. No traitor will escape justice regardless of time, rank or past actions.[239]

The Continuity IRA also used its Easter commemoration that year to warn of further attacks: 'As long as British occupation forces remain in Ireland, that will be the inevitable result of their presence here. The lessons of history are working out again in our time.'[240] From his cramped office in Dublin, Ruairí Ó Brádaigh declared himself 'surprised in a way that it didn't happen earlier … this has been and will be part of the situation.'[241]

Subsequently, bombs were left at police stations in Derry and New-townbutler. Further attacks followed, targeting Orange halls in south Armagh and County Antrim, while threats were made against DPP members and meetings. In August 2009, in a fresh sign that the relative quiet of south Armagh, in dissident terms, might be coming to an end, masked armed men staged a roadblock outside the village of Meigh. The protagonists distributed leaflets warning motorists not to co-operate with either the police or, significantly, Sinn Féin. Equally portentous was the fact that a police patrol, which had observed the roadblock, withdrew for fear of an armed confrontation.[242] The following month, a 600-pound roadside bomb was discovered near Forkhill, again in south Armagh. The device, which had a command wire running across the border into the Irish Republic, was attributed to a faction of the Real IRA that, as has been mentioned, increasingly preferred to go simply by the banner Óglaigh na hÉireann (ONH).[243] September also brought a new bout of serious rioting in the Kilwilkie estate in Lurgan, where a lorry and van were hijacked and placed on the Belfast–Dublin railway line (closing it for thirty-eight hours).[244]

In October there were two further major attacks by the Real IRA/ONH. The first saw a bomb explode under the car of a woman in east Belfast, less than a mile from Police HQ. The device was intended for her partner, a PSNI dog handler, to whom she often gave a lift to work; it was placed under the passenger seat and detonated by a mercury tilt-switch device, a marked increase in sophistication.[245] Less than a week later, another explosion occurred inside a Territorial Army base in north Belfast, though no-one was hurt.[246]

Towards the end of the year, the pace of dissident activity seemed only to mount. In November 2009, bomb-making equipment was found during a four-day search of Maghaberry prison and the governor of the complex quit after his personal details were found in a cell holding a dissident republican prisoner.[247] Elsewhere, it was reported that twenty-four-hour security had been restored to dozens of judges in Northern Ireland, due to the threat posed by RIRA.[248] The range of targets vulnerable to potential attack appeared to be increasing rapidly.

Simultaneously, there were suggestions that the security services seemed to be struggling to keep pace. In late 2008, the chief constable Sir Hugh Orde had admitted that, despite the fact the dissidents were 'well infiltrated both north and south', the police did not have a 'full intelligence picture' of the threat they faced.[249] A year later, the chairman of the Police Federation, Terry Spence, contended that the police were 'dangerously under-resourced' to tackle dissident republicans and he was fiercely critical of the decision to jettison the 500-strong full-time police reserve. By that stage, according to Spence, the police had dealt with some 420 'viable devices' in 750 security alerts in Northern Ireland over the previous two years.[250] Several months later, the PSNI area commander for Londonderry, Chris Yates, would admit that:

> Quite a sizeable majority of my officers at Strand Road are only PSNI officers. A lot of the experience we would have had from the previous terror campaign have left the organisation, and undoubtedly left skills gaps ... These are not skills that you simply expect people to pick up off the shelf and do. These are all skills – including counter terrorism – that we are having to learn all over again.[251]

Though Yates was quick to affirm that the process of re-training was, by that stage, complete, he also acknowledged that the shooting of Jim Doherty back in 2007 had come like a 'bolt out of the blue'.[252] He thus appeared to admit that the upsurge in dissident activity from that point had caught the police off guard.

Furthermore, there were indications that, irrespective of Yates' assurances, for much of 2009 the police were less than confident in dealing with the dissident threat. In May 2009, for instance, it was being suggested that parts of south Fermanagh, particularly Rosslea, Lisnaskea,

Newtownbutler and Donagh, had effectively become 'no-go areas' for PSNI patrols because of CIRA activity.[253] Elsewhere, there were reports that concerns over police officers being lured into dissident-laid 'traps' were seriously impeding the PSNI's ability to respond to incidents. After a robbery in July in which a cash machine was removed from a wall in south Armagh, for example, the police apparently took over twelve hours to respond.[254] In October 2009, residents in the village of Clady in County Tyrone had to seal off a road themselves after the police did not turn up to the scene of a suspect van. Interestingly, in the aftermath of that incident, Sinn Féin Policing Board member Daithi McKay censured the slow nature of the police response and the danger this had caused to people's lives, noting, 'If the PSNI is unable to adequately respond to these incidents, then it is worth considering looking at a specific unit or specially trained officers to deal with such issues.'[255] Those capable of some level of retrospection noted the irony of Sinn Féin's criticism, which effectively called for the creation of a 'special branch' of the police to respond to terrorism.[256]

More disconcerting for the authorities, though, was the fact that dissident attacks continued. On 18 November 2009, the British army recovered a 'horizontal mortar' device in Armagh, which was primed for use against police officers. Four days later, two near simultaneous attacks saw the partial explosion of a 400-pound car bomb outside the Policing Board's headquarters in Belfast and a foiled attempt on the life of a police officer in Garrison, County Fermanagh.[257] In the latter incident, four men were arrested by undercover police acting on information supplied by the Special Reconnaissance Regiment.[258] Still, this setback did not deter those determined to re-invigorate a violent republican campaign. Between December 2009 and March 2010 there was a succession of shooting incidents, or bomb attacks outside police stations in south Armagh (Crossmaglen, Keady, Bessbrook), Belfast and Derry. In February, a 250-pound car bomb detonated in Newry outside the town court house, seventeen minutes into a half-hour warning, as police were still evacuating the area. Remarkably, no-one was hurt, but the attack generated international headlines. Locally, much disquiet was voiced, not merely over the attack but also over the fact that a vehicle, believed to have been used as the getaway car, lay abandoned in Drumintee in south Armagh for two days before going missing, despite it having been reported to the police.[259]

More serious still, in terms of human cost, was the attack the previous month on the car of a Catholic police officer, Peadar Heffron, from Randalstown, County Antrim. Heffron, an Irish-language specialist for the PSNI and captain of the police GAA team, was also the cousin of Sinn Féin national chairperson, Declan Kearney. As a result of the attack, claimed by the ONH branch of the Real IRA, Heffron would later have his leg amputated and bowel removed.[260]

In November 2009, the IMC had judged that the 'seriousness, range and tempo' of violent republican activities had 'changed for the worse' over the previous six months. The threat level was described as 'very serious' and higher than at any time since the formation of the IMC in 2003.[261] This assessment was confirmed by the organisation's twenty-third report in May 2010.[262] Earlier that year, it had been reported that MI5 was actually tracking more 'threat to life' plots from dissident republicans than from Islamist extremists – a stark statistic given general public perceptions as to where the terrorist threat lay.[263] Equally arresting was the verdict of Dermot Ahern, the Irish justice minister, who said in February that the danger posed by the various arms of violent dissident republicanism was now as great as that associated with the Provisional IRA during the 'Troubles'.[264]

What the foregoing demonstrates, therefore, is the extent to which, by the opening months of 2010, violent dissident republicanism had both generated a steady rhythm of attacks and impacted on official consciousness. The one major counterpoint to the trend of escalation was the decision of the INLA to formally announce, on 11 October 2009, that its armed struggle was over. The group had previously stated that 'armed struggle at this present time is futile' and would only result in 'young working-class people going to jail'.[265] Its decision to officially renounce violence (and later decommission its weaponry) was thus welcomed. Nevertheless, while capable of serious and deadly violence, the INLA had already been on official ceasefire since 1998 and, at the organisational level, it had abandoned any notion that it might prosecute a war against the British state.[266] That mantle had long since passed to those in the dissident IRAs. And the latter seemed to have demonstrated that Massereene and Craigavon were not isolated episodes, but part of a continuous drum-beat of incidents.

Furthermore, of equal concern to their opponents was the extent to

which such dissident groups appeared to be strengthening and extend-
ing their control over key republican districts; within that sub-
culture, the power of the Provisionals seemed to be waning. Hitherto,
attempts to challenge the hegemony of mainstream republicanism had
been met with decisive, often violent, riposte. Now, there were clear
signs that a power shift had been affected. The removal of the Provisional IRA as an active force appeared to create something of a vacuum
in republican 'heartland' areas, into which dissidents could move.

One additional consequence of this, which doubtless helped stir support for the dissidents, was the fact that former Provisionals now found
themselves vulnerable to harassment from hostile groups within communities that they had once dominated. Deprived of access to the violence
that had guaranteed their social control, the Provisionals faced, in parts,
something of a 'backlash'. This manifested itself in at least two fatal assaults that were carried out in Belfast and Dungannon during 2008. In
the former case, the victim was Frank 'Bap' McGreevy, a well-known republican (and former IRA prisoner who had served a life sentence) from
the Falls Road area of the city, who was brutally beaten to death in his
home.[267] In Dungannon, Éamon Hughes, a former republican, was
stabbed to death in September 2008, having been assailed by an armed
gang. Subsequent reports claimed that, in the aftermath of the Hughes
murder, local Provisionals had regrouped and moved to expel a series of
individuals from Dungannon; and in so doing had disregarded orders
from the Provisional IRA's command structures in Belfast.[268] They had,
in other words, de facto, 'gone dissident'.

Beyond these two incidents, it was possible to identify other indica-
tors which suggested the collapse of Provisional control across Northern Ireland. In various locales, the structures of the movement, in what
were once 'heartland' communities, became increasingly difficult to
identify in this period. In south Derry, Derry itself, east Tyrone, north
Armagh and parts of south Armagh, there were signs that the Provisionals had, in terms of the republican sub-culture, conceded ever
greater swathes of the province to the dissidents.

Soon after the announcement that the first 32CSM 'advice centre'
was being opened in Derry, for example (see above, page 186), reports
began to emerge that the Real IRA was taking a more active role in policing 'crimes against the community' in the city, expelling those accused of
anti-social behaviour or drug dealing.[269] By 2009, there was a noticeable

surge in paramilitary attacks in republican areas of Derry.[270] Many of these were claimed by the aforementioned RAAD, which was said to include former PIRA members in its ranks and be an organisation determined to 'remove the scourge of drug dealing from within the local community'.[271]

In November 2009, RAAD issued a threat, saying it was prepared to take 'immediate and direct action' against drug dealers in Derry. The onus was said to be on dealers to 'come forward' and admit their involvement in 'this death trade' if they wished to avoid being targeted.[272] Later that month the group paraded two 'cocaine mules' before selected media representatives. The men were forced to apologise, but were told that, having admitted their wrongs, they could get on with their lives.[273] During 2009 as a whole there were reported to have been seventeen shooting incidents in Derry, of which eleven were perpetrated by RAAD, and four by the INLA. The police also said they believed there to be dual membership between those two groups.[274]

In February 2010, the Real IRA in Derry claimed responsibility for killing one of its own members (and former prisoner), Kieran Doherty. The group claimed that Doherty had admitted his involvement in the drugs trade and had been court-martialled (and killed) as a result.[275] In this way, the RIRA hoped to burnish its anti-drugs persona and confirm an image of itself as protector (and controller) of the nationalist community in Derry. Such endeavours were not new (the Provisional IRA had long advertised its efforts against drugs); neither were they confined to Northern Ireland. South of the border too, the dissidents appeared eager to exploit involvement in drugs-related vigilantism to establish their community credentials. There were suspicions that this impulse may have led the Real IRA in Dublin to carry out the murder of 21-year-old Darren Guerrine in early 2008.[276] Meanwhile, in September 2009, the 32CSM issued a warning to drug dealers in Cork that they would be killed if they did not stop their activities. The 'Cork brigade of Óglaigh na hÉireann' promised that it would no longer allow 'our children [to] be destroyed by drugs in our communities'. On that occasion, the Real IRA also claimed the shooting of a man in October 2008, which had left him paralysed from the waist down: 'a heroin dealer was identified and tracked to the northside of the city where action was taken against him.'[277] At the time, many saw the threats more as bluster than genuinely dangerous; but in January 2010,

Gerard 'Topper' Staunton was murdered in Cork and the Real IRA admitted responsibility.[278]

Through such actions, the RIRA and its allies hoped to confirm their control of certain 'republican' communities on either side of the Irish border. Vigilante violence against 'anti-social' activity was a means by which they could assert their authority and enforce their will on a given locality. In Derry the 32CSM sought to capitalise on this in early 2010 by launching a campaign against the PSNI, warning shops and businesses not to serve members of the police: those that failed to heed the advice were then to be picketed.[279] Though the Sovereignty Movement denied there was any violent intent, clearly such an initiative relied on the exertion of social pressure and intimidation. The aim was to isolate and hamstring the PSNI within Derry. In the process, the 32CSM and its allies were de facto usurping the function of the state and affirming the legitimacy of their own existence. At the same time, within internal republican circles they were positing a direct challenge to the Provisionals.

The success of this challenge can be gleaned from the concurrent evidence that the Provisionals' own support network was in retreat. In May 2006, for instance, there were reports that Sinn Féin had closed its last office in the Bogside area of Derry – a one-time bastion of support for the party and the home area of Martin McGuinness. On that occasion, too, a prominent former republican prisoner, Brian McFadden, criticised the party for having 'forgotten about the people' and abandoned its principles.[280] The significance of those words lay in the fact that Brian was the son of Barney McFadden, a well-known Sinn Féin member from Derry who had died four years earlier. Then, Sinn Féin's *An Phoblacht* newspaper had described Barney McFaddden as the 'father of Derry republicanism'; while during his funeral oration, Martin McGuinness had labelled him a 'colossus of the struggle in Ireland' and said 'Barney was intent that republicans would represent the people. He had an absolute desire to see Sinn Féin as a party of the people.'[281] Against such a background, the critique of the son was a fierce indictment of the extent to which the party was alleged to have failed to fulfil his father's aspirations.

Elsewhere, there were growing numbers of reports testifying to burgeoning levels of dissent within, and defections from, the Provisional IRA.[282] In November 2009, the IMC had noted a surge in the number of recruits for both the CIRA and RIRA. While the majority of these were said to be 'inexperienced young males', there was also evidence that 'former republican terrorists [had] as individuals provided services in some instances to dissident republican groups.'[283] According to the well-informed journalist Suzanne Breen, the dissident groups enjoyed regionally fluctuating levels of support. The CIRA was said to enjoy pockets of support in north Armagh, Fermanagh and Belfast. By comparison, one faction of the Real IRA was judged to be strongest in County Londonderry, south Down, east Tyrone and Fermanagh; while those more associated with the ONH banner had a foothold in Belfast and south Armagh.[284]

By early 2009, newspapers were reporting that the Real IRA-aligned ONH had claimed responsibility for several paramilitary-style shootings in west Belfast – employing the violent methods of social control that were previously the near-exclusive preserve, in that area, of the Provisional IRA.[285] This group would grow in prominence over the course of that year. In April 2009, the BBC noted that there had been some twenty 'punishment attacks' over the preceding twelve-month period (as compared to just seven in the previous year), the vast majority in republican areas and fifteen of them claimed by ONH.[286] Across the board, statistics collated by the PSNI revealed a reversal of the previous pattern, whereby such 'punishment attacks' had been growing less frequent. Between 2001 and 2007, there had (with the exception of 2003) been a steady fall in the numbers of these occurring each year. In 2007, only twelve shootings and assaults had been attributed to republican paramilitaries (as compared to the post-1998 'peak' of 199, which was recorded in 2001). The equivalent figure for 2009 was fifty-six – an almost five-fold increase. Early indications were that 2010 was likely to replicate this – suggesting that the events of 2009 were no anomaly.[287]

This renewed willingness to engage in vigilantism in republican areas of Belfast also seemed to be reflected in the emergence of the community organisation Concerned Families Against Drugs (CFAD). Based in north Belfast, CFAD was labelled as 'vigilante' by the IMC in its 2009 report; however, leading members such as Paul Carson and Martin Óg Meehan have rejected this allegation as 'scurrilous' and insisted that it is purely a 'campaigning group'.[288] Irrespective of whether CFAD is indeed just a 'community group', what its creation does demonstrate is the extent to which a growing number of republicans are now seeking to organise in local communities, outside the purview of the Provisional movement. Both Carson and Meehan were well-known republicans, the latter the son of the late Martin Meehan, arguably the most respected IRA man to come out of Ardoyne during the 'Troubles'. Their very presence in CFAD was thus as noteworthy as the actual activities of the organisation.

In May 2009, it was reported that the car of Bobby Storey – a well-known Provisional republican – had been burnt out in west Belfast. In itself, it was a minor incident and it was far from clear whether it was inspired by any political motive. Nevertheless, the fact that it could have occurred at all – when set against the backdrop of the McGreevy murder the previous year, the rise of ONH and the creation of CFAD – was a sign of how far the authority of the Provisionals had slipped.

The reality of this was confirmed in July 2009 when the Ardoyne area of north Belfast was convulsed by three nights of serious rioting. On the first night of trouble, shots were fired at police; the RIRA/ONH later claimed responsibility for the attack.[289] Attempts to calm tensions, led by leading Provisionals such as Storey and Gerry Kelly, proved futile. Significantly, among those who criticised their actions was Martin Óg Meehan.[290] It subsequently emerged that éirígí activists had been involved in organising protests against an Orange march through the area (though the chairperson of éirígí, Brian Leeson, maintained that theirs had been a purely peaceful protest and no members of the group had been involved in the rioting that followed).[291] The RNU was also linked to the unrest. It too denied orchestrating the disturbances, though a spokesperson for the group, Ronan Moyne, said the rioters were 'right to resist' the presence of the police and Orange Order 'in their community'.[292]

In the weeks that followed the Ardoyne rioting, the Sinn Féin president, Gerry Adams, felt it necessary to attack publicly the dissidents of various hues, accusing them of being wedded to 'old-fashioned physical forcism' that amounted to little more than 'vanity'.[293] He also criticised the political organisations for failing to explain themselves, specifically citing éirígí and claiming that they were disingenuous about their true position:

> Say what you want about Sinn Féin. When we thought that the IRA was entitled to use armed actions we went out and defended that. They can't have it both ways. Two British soldiers are killed.

What for? Just to prove that they could be killed? A police officer was killed. What for? All of these people ran for cover.[294]

It was increasingly clear, however, that a growing cadre of republicans were no longer willing to listen to the words of Adams.

The readiness of some hitherto acquiescent members of the Provisional movement to ask questions may well have been reinforced by what might be termed 'the dynamics of death' in this period. In 2008 the death occurred of two towering figures, whose passing seems likely to have increased the potential for a haemorrhaging of support from the Provisionals. The first of these was that of Brendan Hughes in February 2008. An iconic member of the republican movement from Belfast, 'The Dark', as he was affectionately known, had in his later years become a serious critic of the Adams–McGuinness leadership. Moreover, his death was greeted by the dissident organisations as a key, watershed moment. Hughes' unswerving devotion to the cause – and life lived in poverty – was contrasted with the allegedly ostentatious, but less substantial, republicanism of contemporary Sinn Féin. The 32 County Sovereignty Movement described him as 'an uncompromising and uncompromised Republican', 'a soldier's soldier', who had 'never wavered in his dedication to the establishment of a Thirty Two County Socialist Republic'. Hughes' tragedy, it was said, was to have been 'betrayed and sold-out by those he would call comrades'. In the end, he was alleged to have been 'appalled at the path Gerry Adams took the Movement' and disillusioned about the end results. Hughes' ultimate assessment was said to have been that 'We were conned big time.'[295] Such sentiments were echoed by the RNU, for whom the death of Hughes also appeared to take on major significance. A substantial section of the group's original website was thus set aside to the memorialisation of the man whom it described as 'one of Ireland's true heroes'.[296] Similarly, the final edition of *The Blanket* was largely devoted to Hughes and coverage of his funeral. Anthony McIntyre noted that he had 'carried a charisma which won him the respect of opponents as well as the admiration of friends'. Furthermore, Hughes' funeral was said to be a 'grim reminder' for 'those who wish to protect his memory and defend the socialist republican values he espoused': 'we may weep but we dare not sleep.'[297]

Obviously, it is hard to measure the impact of such things, but it would seem that, for those already involved in the various strands of dissident republicanism – and others – the passing of Brendan Hughes induced a yet-greater willingness to liberate themselves from the shadow of the Provisionals.

The same can surely be said of another death in this period – that of Brian Keenan in May 2008. Keenan had long been regarded as one of the most militant members of the Provisional leadership, a 'natural soldier' whose commitment to republicanism was beyond reproach. Even those critical of Sinn Féin did not question Keenan's enduring revolutionary credentials. Thus, Anthony McIntyre wrote of what he termed the 'enigma of Brian Keenan':

> In the early days of the peace process when activists were suspicious on hearing Gerry Adams talk of alternatives to armed struggle, Martin McGuinness was held up as the immovable rock against which would flounder any attempt to dilute the core tenets of republicanism. When he took on the persona of the suit, activists looked to Gerry Kelly. As he quickly morphed into a pebble Brian Keenan with his granite-like reputation came to be relied upon. On one of Martin Meehan's early paroles I expressed reservations about the path we were pursuing. Meehan's response was that he had spoken to Keenan and that there was no way Keenan would support a peace process unless it delivered a victory. Therefore, if Keenan supported the ceasefire it looked a safe bet. Meehan was not alone in viewing matters through this prism ... Unlike many of his colleagues Brian Keenan escaped the charge from republican opponents that he was tailoring himself in order to better embrace the establishment. He was not a suit. Any time I saw him he always seemed as poor as a church mouse. He preferred Rock Bar pints to junket wine. While some stingy comments have been made that he benefited from the Provisional movement having paid for his cancer treatment, if true, it was one of the better things it did with its money.[298]

For McIntyre, then, Keenan remained an incorruptible bastion of republicanism, even within an otherwise corrupted movement. Again, it is a difficult thing to verify, but it seems probable that many within that movement took a similar view, encouraged by Keenan's well-advertised, hardline convictions. The ex-IRA informer, Sean O'Callaghan, has said of Keenan:

> He would have been the one who could have overthrown the

republican leadership if he saw fit. If Brian had felt that Adams and McGuinness were leading the movement down a blind alley he would have been prepared to effect some kind of coup. The danger was always that, stuck in a corner, he would have been quite ready to start shooting people. And everyone knew that.[299]

Given Keenan's reputation within the closed world of Irish republicanism, this reputation was doubtless shared by others. There were, it seems likely, many who felt that for as long as Keenan was there, there was some hope. And by the same token, many who probably took the view that if it was 'good enough for Brian', it was good enough for them.

Seen from this perspective, the extent to which the death of Keenan may have dealt a serious blow to the integrity of the Provisional movement becomes clear. Those for whom Keenan had served as an intellectual bulwark against doubt and recrimination were now left exposed to their reservations. With his passing, mainstream republicanism lost a critical sheet anchor – and it seems likely that this gravely reduced its capacity to fend off the dissident challenge.

CONCLUSION

It would seem, therefore, that the period 2006–10 saw the confluence of various events and factors that brought the situation to a potential 'tipping point' in the history of dissident republicanism. The direction taken by the Provisionals, in terms of their support for a DUP-led power-sharing Executive in Northern Ireland, coupled with their endorsement of the PSNI, had generated serious anxiety in republican circles. At the same time, the apparent failure of the party's 'southern project' caused new questions to be asked of the extent to which the ideological prices being paid were actually a worthwhile investment. All of this opened up space, ideologically, into which would-be dissidents might move. And as the possibilities open to dissident republicanism expanded, so too did the range of its manifestations. Older groups such as the 32 County Sovereignty Movement and Republican Sinn Féin were joined by new formations such as the Republican Network for Unity and éirígí.

It is important, here, to recognise the autonomous dynamic at play in such developments. There is a part of the collective republican psyche which holds that, regardless of circumstance or present adversity, the movement will always return and, ultimately, triumph. It was this ethos that helped nourish dissident republicanism through the fallow years of 2002–6. It was precisely that same ethos which ensured that, as conditions changed, republican organisations of one hue or another would seek to exploit them, as they did after 2006.

That they were afforded the opportunity to do so was in part a function of the departure from the scene of the Provisional IRA. By September 2008, the British secretary of state for Northern Ireland, Shaun Woodward, had confirmed that the organisation had 'met its commitment' and effectively gone out of existence.[300] Prior to that point, and especially in the years before 2005, the PIRA had served as a tool of social control, helping to inhibit the growth of dissident republicanism. Its absence created the physical space in which the new groups could preach their message with ever greater confidence.

Finally, the ability of the mainstream movement to deflect that message has been further eroded by a series of deaths, which, for different reasons, have impacted on the dissident–Provisional rivalry in a major way: those of Brendan Hughes, Brian Keenan, Éamon Hughes and Frank McGreevy.

As to how this will play out in the future, it is possible only to guess. There are still other factors, not discussed at length here, which may decisively influence the course of events. The ongoing controversy surrounding the 1981 hunger strike, for instance, may yet inflict a fatal blow on the credibility of the Provisional movement's leadership. (The publication of Richard O'Rawe's 2005 book *Blanketmen* did, as he had hoped, generate a debate over whether the IRA leadership outside the prison might have prolonged the hunger strike for political benefit.)[301] The same may also apply if there are further revelations as to the existence of British spies and agents within the upper echelons of that leadership. For a movement not fully recovered from the fallout from the Scappaticci and Donaldson allegations, it is far from clear how resilient the Adams–McGuinness nexus would be in that eventuality.[302]

For now, though, what can be said with certainty is that militant Irish republicanism, in both political and violent form, has returned to the landscape of these islands and will remain there for some time to come.

NOTES

1. M. Evans, 'Stretched MI5 Told to Redouble Efforts Against Real IRA', *The Times*, 22 May 2006. Three years later and the picture was little different. See H. McDonald, 'MI5 Spends £40m Tracking IRA Dissidents and al-Qaida', *Observer*, 24 May 2009.
2. 'RIRA Plans New Offensive', *Derry News*, 4 August 2005.
3. 32 County Sovereignty Movement, 'PIRA Statement "Neither Surprising Nor Historic"', *The Blanket*, 28 July 2005.
4. Ruairí Ó Brádaigh, interview with the author, Dublin, 24 June 2009.
5. 'Statement From the Leadership of the Republican Movement', *Saoirse*, April 2006.
6. For further detail on these events, see L. Clarke, 'Bank Raid "Was Work of the IRA"', *Sunday Times*, 26 December 2004; 'Police Say IRA Behind Bank Raid', BBC News Online, 7 January 2005, available at http://news.bbc.co.uk/1/hi/northern_ireland/4154657.stm; H. McDonald, 'Grieving Sisters Square Up to IRA', *Observer*, 13 February 2005.
7. For more in-depth discussion of all of this, see Frampton, *The Long March*, pp.158–70.
8. A. McIntyre, 'A Blanketman Still Fighting to be Heard', *The Blanket*, 4 March 2005. See above, pages 163–4.
9. L. Friel, 'The DUP Exposed', *An Phoblacht*, 18 December 2003.
10. D. Morrison, 'The Paisley Problem', *An Phoblacht*, 9 September 2004.
11. Mallon cited in 'On the Record', BBC One, 21 January 2001.
12. For more on the question of Sinn Féin's approach to policing, see Frampton, *The Long March*, pp.174–5.
13. Robinson, cited in S. Dempster, 'SF "Must Back Police Before Sharing Power"', *News Letter*, 20 October 2006.
14. 'Extraordinary Árd Fheis – Political Pressure Falls on Paisley: Adams Hails "Truly Historic Decision"', *An Phoblacht*, 1 February 2007. C. Ní Dhonnabhain, 'Extraordinary Árd Fheis – Afternoon Session 2: Motion Passed by Huge Majority', *An Phoblacht*, 1 February 2007.
15. A. McIntyre, 'Conway Mill Debate', *The Blanket*, 29 November 2006; 'Toome Debate', *The Blanket*, 21 December 2006; 'Derry Debate', *The Blanket*, 21 January 2007.
16. 'Toome Debate', *The Blanket*, 21 December 2006. See also M. Galvin, 'Telling Moment at Toome', *The Blanket*, 20 December 2006.
17. 'Derry Debate', *The Blanket*, 21 January 2007.
18. Ibid.
19. 'Gerry McGeough Biography', Gerry McGeough Blog, available at http://gerrymcgeough.blogspot.com/2007/02/gerry-mcgeough-biography.html
20. 'Irish Republican Ex-POWs Against the RUC/PSNI and MI5', *The Blanket*, 6 March 2007.
21. Data compiled from the BBC's coverage of the Northern Irish Assembly elections: http://news.bbc.co.uk/1/shared/vote2007/nielection/html/main.stm
22. Anthony McIntyre, interview with the author, 30 October 2009.
23. This argument has been developed particularly by Henry Patterson, as in his unpublished seminar paper to the Cambridge University Irish Studies Group, 'Sinn Féin and the Peace Process: The End of the Republican Project?' See also Frampton, *The Long March*, pp.126–8.
24. 'About Us', 32 County Sovereignty Movement Tyrone, available at http://www.32csmtyrone.com/aboutus.htm
25. M. Price, 'The Spectre of Imprisonment: IRPWA Speech, Third International Conference Against Isolation, Berlin', *The Blanket*, 15 December 2004.
26. 'Rage Against Raytheon!', *Sovereign Nation*, October/November 2006.
27. 'Hamas Secure Victory in Gaza: Discredited Fatah are Driven Out as Israel and US Side with Abbas', *Sovereign Nation*, July/August 2007.
28. Motions 15 and 17 in 'Motions for 2007 AGM', 32 CSM, 1 December 2007.
29. About Us', 32CSM, available at http://www.32csm.info/aboutus.html
30. 'Editorial: No to Lisbon! No to London!', *Sovereign Nation*, August/September 2008.
31. 'The Lisbon Treaty: An Outline of the 32CSM Campaign', *Sovereign Nation*, August/September 2008.
32. 'End Internment by Remand', *Sovereign Nation*, May/June 2008.

33. For more on Breslin, see 'Former Prominent Member of Derry Sinn Féin Joins 32CSM', Derry 32 County Sovereignty movement, 3 April 2008, available at http://www.derry32csm. com/2008/04/former-prominent-member-of-derry-sinn.html

34. The readiness of dissidents to place their 'struggle' in Ireland in a broader global context was also in evidence in a 2004 speech given by Marian Price in which she spoke out against 'multi national capitalist and imperialist aggression' and the 'new world order' allegedly being constructed by the US and Britain. In her view, 'Long Kesh and the H-Blocks rank as a testament to Britain's failure to control Ireland just as Abu Ghraib will become in Iraq'. See M. Price, 'The Spectre of Imprisonment: IRPWA Speech, Third International Conference Against Isolation, Berlin', *The Blanket*, 15 December 2004.

35. 'Dublin Office of 32CSM/IRPWA Opens', 32CSM Message board, posted 10 February 2007, 23.40, available at http://admin2.7.forumer.com/a/posts.php?topic=7145&start=

36. 'Lynch/Duffy Cumann 32CSM Derry City', 32CSM, available at http://www.freewebs. com/*cumann*/; 'Derry 32CSM Launch New Cumann', 32CSM, available at http://www. derry32csm.com/2008/04/derry-32csm-launch-new-*cumann*.html

37. 'Cork 32 County Sovereignty Movement', available at http://www.cork32.blogspot.com/; 'Belfast 32 County Sovereignty Movement', available at http://belfast32.blogspot.com/

38. 'Kerry 32CSM *cumann* Launched', *Sovereign Nation*, August/September 2008.

39. '32 County Sovereignty Movement', available at http://32csm.info/index.html

40. For more on this issue, see H. McDonald, 'MP Calls on YouTube to Remove Real IRA Propaganda Videos', *Observer*, 2 August 2009. See below, footnote 134.

41. Liam Lynch/Patsy Duffy Cumann, 32 County Sovereignty Movement, Derry City, *Beir Bua: The Honest Voice of Republicanism*, 6, 1 (May/June 2008).

42. See Frampton, *The Long March*, pp.26–32.

43. Liam Lynch/Patsy Duffy Cumann, 32 County Sovereignty Movement, *Beir Bua*, 6, 1 (May/June 2008).

44. 'Shell 2 Sea Protestors Arrested', *Sovereign Nation*, August/September 2008.

45. 'Dissidents in Bid to Disrupt Parade Talks', *News Letter*, 14 June 2008.

46. F. Mackey, 'Can Republicans Succeed Without Upholding National Sovereignty?', *The Blanket*, 6 February 2005.

47. 'Press Release: Francie Mackey Easter Statement', 32CSM, 2006.

48. '"Disband the RUC/PSNI": Launch of New 32CSM Leaflet and Poster Campaign', *Sovereign Nation*, October/November 2006.

49. 32 County Sovereignty Movement, 'No Other Law: The Politics of Policing in Occupied Ireland', *The Blanket*, 15 January 2007.

50. F. Mackey, 'The Issues That Need Debated', *The Blanket*, 16 January 2007.

51. F. Mackey, 'British Policing Must Never Be Acceptable in Ireland', *The Blanket*, 20 February 2007.

52. 'Commemoration on Sunday 6th July 2008 to Remember Volunteer Denis Spriggs. Murdered by British Forces', *Sovereign Nation*, August/September 2008.

53. Ibid.

54. 'Óglaigh na hÉireann Attack Economic, Political and Military Targets', *Sovereign Nation*, October/November 2006.

55. S. McKinney, '"No Evidence RIRA Attacking Solely Catholics"', *Irish News*, 20 December 2007; D. Young, 'Unity Call for Dissidents to Take on British', *Belfast Telegraph*, 28 January 2008.

56. 'Struggle Will Re-Ignite in Derry – 32CSM', *Irish Republican News*, 17–23 July 2008.

57. '"We're Here To Stay!"', *Sovereign Nation*, August/September 2008.

58. 'Dialogue with Republicans – Setting the Record Straight', *Sovereign Nation*, August/September 2008.

59. 'Talks Must be Transparent', *Sovereign Nation*, August/September 2008.

60. 'Editorial: No to Lisbon! No to London!' *Sovereign Nation*, August/September 2008.

61. 'About Us', Republican Network for Unity, available at http://www. republicannetwork.ie/aboutUs.aspx

62. Archive copy of original RNU website, at http://www.freewebs.com/concernedrepublicans/

63. Ibid.

64. C. Barnes, 'Killer: I'm No Terror Boss', *Sunday Life*, 19 July 2009.
65. T. Catney, 'Always Tell the Truth: Letter to the *Irish News*', *Irish News*, 2 December 2006.
66. Tony Catney, interview with the author, Belfast, 22 June 2009.
67. T. Catney, 'Always Tell the Truth: Letter to the *Irish News*', *Irish News*, 2 December 2006.
68. Tony Catney, interview with the author, Belfast, 22 June 2009.
69. Ibid.
70. Ibid.
71. Ibid.
72. Archive copy of original RNU webpage, at http://www.freewebs.com/concernedrepublicans/apps/photos/photo.jsp?photoID=12780764
73. Archive copy of 'Links' on original RNU website, at http://www.freewebs.com/ concerne-drepublicans/
74. Tony Catney, interview with the author, Belfast, 22 June 2009.
75. S. Brett, 'Return to Violence Not Ruled Out', *Belfast Telegraph*, 18 January 2007.
76. 'Ex-SF Man Denies Dissident Move Reports', *Irish News*, 21 May 2007.
77. 'Easter Commemorations, 2007: Republicans Across the Country Reaffirm their Commitments and Ideals', *Sovereign Nation*, July/August 2007.
78. 'Óglaigh na hÉireann Easter Statement', *Sovereign Nation*, July/August 2007.
79. 'Editorial: Republican Unity Bodenstown Commemoration – Small but Significant Steps Taken', *Sovereign Nation*, July/August 2007
80. 'Bodenstown Orations 2007', 32CSM, available at http://32csm.info/orats.html#ir
81. Ibid.
82. '32CSM Statement: Republican Unity Bodenstown Commemoration – Small but Significant Steps Taken', *Sovereign Nation*, July/August 2007.
83. *New Year Statement by the 32 County Sovereignty Movement*, 2008.
84. 'Republican Strength is Growing Daily: Bodenstown 2008', *Sovereign Nation*, August/September 2008
85. *Bloody Sunday 2008: Truth and Lies* (pamphlet available at http://www.serve.com/pfc/cases/bs/bs2008.pdf); 'Republicans Agree to Differ at Bloody Sunday Event', *Derry Journal*, 1 February 2008. See also Francie Mackey, *32CSM Address to RNU Meeting*, Derry, January 2008; Tony Catney, *RNU Address to Meeting*, Derry, January 2008.
86. 'Hardline Republicans Meet in Derry', *Derry Journal*, 7 November 2008; 'Irish Republican Forum for Unity', available at http://republicanunity.blogspot.com/
87. '32CSM Address to Republican Forum for Unity', Derry 32CSM, 7 November 2008, available at http://www.derry32csm.com/2008/11/32csm-address-to-republican-forum-for.html
88. See Frampton, *The Long March*, pp.131–56.
89. 'The 2005 Westminster Elections in Northern Ireland', ARK Northern Ireland Elections website, available at http://www.ark.ac.uk/elections/fw05.htm
90. 'Northern Ireland Assembly Elections 2007', ARK Northern Ireland Elections website, available at http://www.ark.ac.uk/elections/fa07.htm
91. E. Moloney, 'SF Leaders Too Slick for the Party's Own Good', *Irish Times*, 31 May 2007.
92. RTE, 'Prime Time Leaders' Debate', 16 May 2007. For a discussion of the debate see 'Prime Time Election Debate: The Wee Four …', Slugger O'Toole, 16 May 2007, available at http://sluggerotoole.com/2007/05/16/prime-time-election-debate-the-wee-four/
93. H. McDonald, 'Goodbye Mary Lou as Adams Fails', *Observer*, 27 May 2009; L. Clarke, 'Sinn Féin Loses its Appeal', *Sunday Times*, 27 May 2009; J. Cusack, 'Result Shows Adams Out of Touch in South', *Sunday Independent*, 27 May 2009; C. Thornton, 'Has an Overconfident Adams Lost the South?', *Belfast Telegraph*, 29 May 2007; T. Peterkin, 'Adams Suffers Poll Backlash', *Daily Telegraph*, 29 May 2007.
94. 'Callanan May Quit Politics', *Galway City Tribune*, 31 August 2007.
95. Kehoe came within a few hundred votes of becoming a TD. See 'Dublin Central: General Election 17 May 2002', Elections Ireland, available at http://electionsireland.org/counts.cfm?election=2002&cons=85. For his resignation see F. Sheahan, 'SF Deny Claims They "Gagged" Kehoe', *Irish Independent*, 6 November 2007.
96. 'Sinn Féin Councillor Resigns', *Evening Echo*, 21 October 2007.

97. For discussion of the Pringle resignation see 'Donegal Sinn Féin Councillor Resigns from Party', Slugger O'Toole, 7 November 2007, available at http://sluggerotoole.com/2007/11/07/donegal-sinn-fein-councillor-resigns-from-party

98. L. Clarke, 'Key Members Quit Sinn Féin Over Controls', *Sunday Times*, 24 September 2006.

99. 'Sinn Féin Split Over Joining Policing Body', *Impartial Reporter*, 5 October 2007; 'Councillor Resigns from Sinn Féin', BBC News Online, 2 July 2008, available at http://news.bbc.co.uk/1/hi/northern_ireland/7485593.stm

100. 'Parties Hit by More Resignations', BBC News Online, 1 March 2007, available at http://news.bbc.co.uk/1/hi/northern_ireland/6406185.stm

101. *Irish News*, 3 December 2007.

102. '2009 Local Elections', ElectionsIreland.org, available at http://electionsireland.org/results/local/2009local.cfm

103. J. McCarthy, 'The Partitioning of Sinn Féin', *Sunday Tribune*, 14 June 2009; L. Clarke, 'Adams is Hastening Death of Sinn Féin', *Sunday Times*, 26 July 2009.

104. T. Ferris, 'Where's Sinn Féin At? Where Are We Going?', *An Phoblacht*, 9 July 2009.

105. Ibid.

106. P. Logue, 'Burke Quits Sinn Féin', *Irish Times*, 9 June 2009.

107. V. Robinson, 'SF's Identity Crisis Must Be Tackled to Win Seats in the South', *Irish News*, 1 August 2009.

108. A. Morris, 'Éirígí Recruits its First Elected Sinn Féin Politician in North', *Irish News*, 1 August 2009.

109. C. McMorrow, 'SF Councillor Resigns With Stinging Attack on Party Chiefs', *Sunday Tribune*, 10 January 2010; H. McGee, 'Defecting Councillor Says SF has Become Directionless in South', *Irish Times*, 12 January 2010.

110. 'Morris Threatens to Quit Sinn Féin', *Nenagh Guardian*, 30 January 2010; 'Call for Adams to Quit Sinn Féin', *News Letter*, 28 January 2010.

111. 'Bullish Gerry Adams Insists: I'm Not Stepping Down', *Belfast Telegraph*, 7 August 2009.

112. E. Moloney, *Voices from the Grave* (London: Faber & Faber, 2010), pp.124–32.

113. The accusation had, for instance, been made in Ed Moloney's 2002 book, *A Secret History of the IRA*. On that occasion, too, Adams had issued a firm denial. See 'Adams Denies IRA Book Allegations', BBC News Online, 30 September 2002, available at http://news.bbc.co.uk/1/hi/northern_ireland/2288775.stm

114. S. Breen, 'How the Media's Failings Allow Gerry Adams to Rewrite History', *Belfast Telegraph*, 5 January 2010.

115. Tony Catney, interview with the author, Belfast, 22 June 2009.

116. Brian Leeson, interview with the author, Dublin, 24 June 2009.

117. Ibid.

118. Ibid.

119. Ibid.

120. Ibid.

121. N. Donald, 'SF Sisters Split Row', *Sunday Mirror*, 2 July 2006.

122. 'Repatriate Aiden Hulme Campaign', *éirígí*, http://www.eirigi.org/campaigns/aidennhulme2.html

123. 'Éirígí Becomes a Political Party', *éirígí Newsletter*, June 2007, available at http://www.eirigi.org/latest/newsletter/june.pdf

124. 'Éirígí Organise in Derry', *éirígí Newsletter*, June 2007.

125. 'Éirígí Commemorate 1916', *éirígí Newsletter*, June 2007.

126. 'Remembering Thomas Ashe', *éirígí Newsletter*, September 2007, available at http://www.eirigi.org/latest/newsletter/September_newsletter.pdf

127. 'The Battle for Control of Ireland's Natural Resources Heats Up', *éirígí Newsletter*, June 2007.

128. In 2006, the éirígí website linked to the CPI report, *The Great Corrib Gas Controversy*: http://www.publicinquiry.ie/pdf/Fiosru_2_LOW_RES_Final.pdf; for the links on éirígí's website, see http://www.eirigi.org/links/index.htm. For more on the CPI, see C. Murphy, 'Independent Newspapers and the Centre for Public Inquiry', *Village Magazine*, 15 December 2005.

129. 'Campaigns: We Only Want the Earth!', éirígí, available at http://www.eirigi.org/campaigns naturalresources/we_only_want_the_earth.htm.
130. Ibid.
131. 'Shell's Fences Taken Down and Returned to Sender!', éirígí, 13 October 2007, available at http://www.eirigi.org/latest/latest131007.html
132. Brian Leeson, interview with the author, Dublin, 24 June 2009.
133. Ibid.
134. In an era in which much concern has been expressed over the potential for online radicalisation, it is striking how little attention has been devoted to this subject in relation to Irish republicanism. The recent article by Lorraine Bowman-Grieve ('Irish Republicanism and the Internet: Support for the New Wave of Dissidents', *Perspectives on Terrorism*, 4, 2 (May 2010)) is a notable exception to this, although she focused primarily on the relatively marginal digital community linked with Republican Sinn Féin. The online presence associated with éirígí, the RNU and the regenerated sites of the 32CSM and its affiliates remains an area worth further study.
135. 'Éirígí's Successful Third Árd Fheis', éirígí, 18 May 2009, available at http://www.eirigi. org/latest/latest180509_2.html
136. 'Éirígí Takes Another Step Towards Elections', éirígí, 19 May 2009, available at http://www.eirigi.org/latest/latest190509_2.html
137. Ibid.
138. Breandán Mac Cionnaith, interview with the author, Portadown, 22 June 2009.
139. A. McDonald, 'Éirígí Will "Actively Oppose" Armed Forces Day Events', *Irish News*, 18 May 2009.
140. 'Éirígí Protest Against "Armed Forces Day"', YouTube, 30 June 2009, available at http://www.youtube.com/watch?v=sY5pciaZgOM.
141. A. Morris, 'Éirígí Recruits its First Elected Sinn Féin Politician in North', *Irish News*, 1 August 2009.
142. N. McAdam, 'Republican Splinter Group Targets Council Elections', *Belfast Telegraph*, 4 August 2009.
143. Brian Leeson, interview with the author, Dublin, 24 June 2009.
144. For an example of Duffy's involvement in éirígí events, see 'Parade and Protest', Slugger O'Toole, 2 November 2008, available at http://sluggerotoole.com/index.php/weblog/com ments/parade-and-protest/. In late 2008, in the wake of dissident republican attacks on the PSNI, Duffy gave media interviews in which he was described as a 'leading figure in éirígí' ('Ex-Senior IRA Man Condones Dissident Shootings at Police', *Irish News*, 28 August 2008). The group's own website also featured reports that referred to him as an 'éirígí activist' ('"This is the New PSNI – Just the Same as the RUC"', éirígí, 27 August 2008, available at http://www.eirigi.org/latest/latest270808.html). For Mac Cionnaith's background, see T. Harnden, 'Orangemen Dig in For Long Campaign', *Daily Telegraph*, 6 July 1998.
145. 'Éirígí's Successful Third árd Fheis', éirígí, 18 May 2009, available at http://www.eirigi. org/latest/latest180509_2.html
146. See the videos at 'Good God, Gaza and Gonzo', Slugger O'Toole, 11 January 2009, available at http://sluggerotoole.com/index.php/weblog/comments/good-god-gaza-and-gonzo
147. Rice was also present at éirígí's 'Shell2Sea' activism. See 'Shell and their Cops are Losing Ground', éirígí, 10 November 2007, available at http://www.eirigi.org/latest/latest101107 _2.html. For more on the issue of Sinn Féin's anti-Orange parade agitation, see R. Dudley Edwards, *The Faithful Tribe: An Intimate Portrait of the Loyal Institutions* (London: HarperCollins, 2000), pp.350–65. Breandán Mac Cionnaith was the leader of the Garvaghy Road Residents' Coalition, Gerard Rice head of the Lower Ormeau Concerned Community and Donncha MacNiallis chairman of the Bogside Residents' Group.
148. Brian Leeson, interview with the author, Dublin, 24 June 2009.
149. Breandán Mac Cionnaith, interview with the author, Portadown, 22 June 2009.
150. See, for example, the 2009 commemoration, where Mac Cionnaith gave the main oration. The report of the event on the éirígí website noted that Connolly 'provided the basis for socialist republican thought in Ireland and plenty of examples for action'. See 'Connolly Remembered

at Arbour Hill', éirígí, 21 May 2009, available at http://www.eirigi.org/latest/ latest210509.html

151. Breandán Mac Cionnaith, interview with the author, Portadown, 22 June 2009.
152. Ibid.
153. Ibid.
154. Ibid.
155. Ibid.
156. 'Take the Message Back to Your Masters in Downing Street', éirígí, 2 November 2008, available at http://www.eirigi.org/latest/latest021108.html
157. 'Éirígí Oppose RIR Parade' (videos 2/3 and 3/3, available on YouTube at http://www. youtube.com/watch?v=L7gT1bnB-ZQ and http://www.youtube. com/watch?v=agoHKrdp 5P8&feature=related). See also 'Take the Message Back to Your Masters in Downing Street', éirígí, 2 November 2008, http://www. eirigi.org/latest/latest021108.html
158. 'Building an Alternative Movement in Ireland', *The Spark*, December 2008/January 2009, available at http://workersparty.org.nz/2008/12/07/building-an-alternative-movement-in-ireland
159. Ibid.
160. 'Éirígí is Not Aligned to Or Supportive of Any Armed Organisation, Spokesman Says', *Irish News*, 13 March 2009. See also 'Éirígí Response to Recent Events', éirígí, 10 March 2009, available at http://www.eirigi.org/latest/latest100309_2.html
161. D. Rusk and A. Morris, 'Arrested Republican "No Longer Member of éirígí"', *Irish News*, 16 March 2009.
162. 'Éirígí Condemns Trial by Media', éirígí, 16 March 2009, available at http://www.eirigi.org/latest/latest160309.html
163. B. McCaffrey, 'Barracks Murders Accused is Ex-éirígí', Irish News, 24 July 2009.
164. 'Éirígí Condemns Trial by Media', éirígí, 16 March 2009, available at http://www.eirigi. org/latest/latest160309.html
165. Ibid; A. Morris, 'Éirígí Slams Trial By Media', *Irish News*, 17 March 2009.
166. N. McAdam, 'Republican Splinter Group Targets Council Elections', *Belfast Telegraph*, 4 August 2009.
167. Breandán Mac Cionnaith, interview with the author, Portadown, 22 June 2009.
168. 'Éirígí's Rab Jackson Addresses Belfast Supporters', YouTube, available at http://www. youtube.com/watch?v=qU5RdCSmUlg
169. Brian Leeson, interview with the author, Dublin, 24 June 2009.
170. *Twelfth Report of the Independent Monitoring Commission.*
171. Four men were targeted in paramilitary shootings in Belfast in October 2006. See A. Morris, 'CIRA Claims Paramilitary-Style Attacks', *Irish News*, 17 October 2006; A. Morris, 'Man Shot in Fourth Continuity IRA Attack', *Irish News*, 20 October 2006. On the retail attacks, see A. Morris, 'CIRA Bid to Justify Firebombs Rubbished', *Irish News*, 24 October 2006.
172. *Thirteenth Report of the Independent Monitoring Commission* (London: Stationery Office, January 2007).
173. *Fifteenth Report of the Independent Monitoring Commission* (London: Stationery Office, April 2007).
174. *Seventeenth Report of the Independent Monitoring Commission* (London: Stationery Office, April 2007); *Eighteenth Report of the Independent Monitoring Commission* (London: Stationery Office, April 2007).
175. *Seventeenth Report of the Independent Monitoring Commission.*
176. *Eighteenth Report of the Independent Monitoring Commission.*
177. *First Report of the Independent Monitoring Commission.*
178. *Eighth Report of the Independent Monitoring Commission.*
179. *Thirteenth Report of the Independent Monitoring Commission.*
180. *Seventeenth Report of the Independent Monitoring Commission; Eighteenth Report of the Independent Monitoring Commission.*
181. *Eighteenth Report of the Independent Monitoring Commission.* See also S. Breen, 'Small, Splinter Dissident Group Behind Murder', *Sunday Tribune*, 17 February 2008.

182. See, for example, *Eighteenth Report of the Independent Monitoring Commission*.
183. *First Report of the Independent Monitoring Commission; Fifth Report of the Independent Monitoring Commission*.
184. For an explanation of this see *Twenty-First Report of the Independent Monitoring Commission* (London: The Stationery Office, May 2009). By the time of the IMC's twenty-second report in November 2009, the group declared that it 'had no further matters to report in respect of the Strabane group styling itself Óglaigh na hÉireann (ONH)'. From that time, when it referred to ONH, it was principally describing a faction of the Real IRA. See *Twenty-Second Report of the Independent Monitoring Commission* (London: The Stationery Office, November 2009).
185. *Twelfth Report of the Independent Monitoring Commission*.
186. *Thirteenth Report of the Independent Monitoring Commission*. See also 'The Afterlife of the IRA: The Dissident Groups Bent on Shattering the Peace in Northern Ireland', *Independent*, 8 November 2008.
187. *Thirteenth Report of the Independent Monitoring Commission*.
188. *Fifteenth Report of the Independent Monitoring Commission*.
189. *Eighteenth Report of the Independent Monitoring Commission*.
190. 'The Afterlife of the IRA: The Dissident Groups Bent on Shattering the Peace in Northern Ireland', *Independent*, 8 November 2008.
191. M. McCreary, 'Shooting of Off-Duty Officer Condemned', *Belfast Telegraph*, 13 November 2007.
192. '"Real IRA" Issues Threat to North Police', *Irish Times*, 28 November 2007.
193. '"Attacks on Police Will Go on in New Year" – Real IRA', *Derry Journal*, 8 January 2008.
194. S. Breen, 'War Back On– Real IRA', *Sunday Tribune*, 3 February 2008; A. Mullan, 'Mackey Slams Provos as RIRA Vows Resumption of Violence', *Ulster Herald*, 7 February 2008.
195. D. Rusk, 'Dissident Violence Has to Stop: A Wave of Near Misses for PSNI', *Irish News*, 17 November 2008.
196. Minutes of Oral Evidence Given to Northern Ireland House of Commons Select Committee, 5 November 2008 (HC 1174-i) , available at http://www.publications.parliament.uk/pa/cm200708/cmselect/cmniaf/c1174-i/c117402.htm
197. *Eighth Report of the Independent Monitoring Commission; Twelfth Report of the Independent Monitoring Commission*. See also 'Ex-Provos Swell RAAD Ranks', *Derry Journal*, 18 August 2009
198, *Eighth Report of the Independent Monitoring Commission*.
199. See, for example, *Seventeenth Report of the Independent Monitoring Commission*.
200. H. McDonald, 'Provisional IRA Defectors Behind New Ulster Violence', *Guardian*, 1 September 2008.
201. D. McAleese, 'Dissidents "Behind" Recovered Explosives', *Belfast Telegraph*, 8 August 2007.
202. S. O'Neill, 'RIRA Gunmen "Fired Shots During Riot"', *Irish News*, 26 April 2001.
203. 'Gangs Seize Vehicles on Nationalist Estate', BBC News Online, 20 March 1999, available at http://news.bbc.co.uk/1/hi/uk/300179.stm
204. 'Dissident Republicans Blamed for Hijacked Car Bomb', Breaking News.ie, 10 August 2005, available at http://breaking.tcm.ie/2005/08/10/story215484.html; B. Fatogun, 'Community Relations "Ruined" After Dissident Bomb Attack', *Irish News*, 11 August 2005.
205. C. Morrison, 'Dissident Republicans Keep Town in the Past', *Irish News*, 26 April 2007.
206. 'IRA Claims Lurgan Attack', *An Phoblacht*, 19 June 1997.
207. Richard Walsh, interview with the author, Belfast, 23 June 2009.
208. H. McDonald, 'Special Forces Intimidating Republicans in Northern Ireland, Say Dissidents', *Observer*, 21 February 2010.
209. '1916 Easter Commemorations 2009', *Saoirse*, April 2009.
210. 'Five in Court on Real IRA Charge', BBC News Online, 8 February 2005, available at http://news.bbc.co.uk/1/hi/northern_ireland/4245011.stm
211. C. Young, 'March Goes On, Say Organisers', *Daily Ireland*, 9 August 2006.
212. M. Connolly, 'Community Tries to Pull Young Back From the Brink', *Irish News*, 4 July 2006.
213. J. Mooney, '"Critical Threat" to Troops in North', *The Times*, 7 March 2009.

214. Ibid.
215. 'Orde Risks "Republican Support"', BBC News Online, 7 March 2009, available at http://news.bbc.co.uk/1/hi/northern_ireland/7930308.stm
216. L. Friel, 'Peace Process Under Attack', *An Phoblacht*, 12 March 2009.
217. 'Continuity IRA Shot Dead Officer', BBC News Online, 10 March 2009, available at http://news.bbc.co.uk/1/hi/northern_ireland/7934426.stm
218. 'British "Lead" Dissident Attacks – McGuinness', *Derry Journal*, 21 December 2007.
219. See *An Phoblacht*, 12 March 2009. The words of McGuinness quoted there raised far fewer issues from a republican perspective: 'I was a member of the IRA but that war is over now. The people responsible for Saturday night's incident are clearly signalling that they want to restart that war. They do not have the right to do that.' See L. Friel, 'Peace Process Under Attack', *An Phoblacht*, 12 March 2009.
220. N. Firth, 'Obama Backs Peace in Northern Ireland as Gerry Adams Says IRA Killings "Should Not Be Exaggerated"', *Daily Mail*, 17 March 2009; 'Rallies Against Attacks on Peace Process', *An Phoblacht*, 19 March 2009.
221. D. Rusk, 'Dissident Arrests: Charge or Free Those Held for 7 Days, Says Sinn Féin', *Irish News*, 20 March 2009.
222. R. McCartney, 'Real IRA on Road to Nowhere', *Derry Journal*, 23 November 2007.
223. Ibid.
224. Ibid.
225. A. McIntyre, 'Be Honest, Mr Adams: You No Longer Have a Strategy for a United Ireland', *Parliamentary Brief*, April 2009.
226. 'Great Turnout for 25th Anniversary of Charlie, David and Michael, Ógra Shinn Féin, 24 February 2010', available at http://ograshinnfein.blogspot.com/2010/02/great-turnout-for-25th-anniversary-of.html
227. M. O'Doherty, 'Dissidents Must Hear True Voices of the Past', *Belfast Telegraph*, 26 February 2010.
228. For an account of the brutal murder, see the testimony of Lord Laird, in the House of Lords: Lords Hansard Text for 12 November 2007, Columns 308–10, available at http://www.publications.parliament.uk/pa/ld200708/ldhansrd/text/71112-0010.htm
229. *Eighteenth Report of the Independent Monitoring Commission.*
230. L. MacKean, 'Murder Behind a Wall of Silence', 'Newsnight', BBC Two, 28 November 2007, available at http://news.bbc.co.uk/1/hi/programmes/newsnight/7113964.stm
231. D. Sharrock, 'Thomas "Slab" Murphy – Farmer or IRA Chief?', *The Times*, 8 November 2007; D. Sharrock, 'Ex-IRA Chief Thomas "Slab" Murphy to Hand Over £1m Criminal Assets', *The Times*, 17 October 2008; D. Rusk, 'Alleged Top Provo Also Pursued Over Finances: Republican's Assets Frozen', *Irish News*, 11 November 2009.
232. D. Rusk, 'Minister Says Raids Are Not Acceptable: Republican's Assets Frozen', *Irish News*, 11 November 2009.
233. 'Dissidents Reject "Traitor" Claim', *Derry Journal*, 13 March 2009.
234. D. Keenan, 'Lethal Remnants of an Old Order', *Irish Times*, 14 March 2009.
235. A. McIntyre, 'Who is McGuinness to Talk of Treachery?', *Independent on Sunday*, 15 March 2009.
236. Cited in 'Northern Ireland Terrorists are Like a "Cornered Animal", claims Sir Hugh Orde', *Sunday Times*, 15 March 2009. See also H. Orde, 'Evil of a Wicked Minority', *News of the World*, 15 March 2009.
237. S. Breen, 'Exclusive – Real IRA: We Will Take Campaign to Britain', *Sunday Tribune*, 12 April 2009; S. Breen, 'Massereene Murders Sets North Back Years', *Sunday Tribune*, 12 April 2009; 'Statement From the Real IRA to be Read Out at the 32 County Sovereignty Movement Commemoration in Derry Tomorrow', *Sunday Tribune*, 12 April 2009; S. Breen, 'How Real IRA Killed Denis Donaldson', *Sunday Tribune*, 12 April 2009.
238. S. Breen, 'Massereene Murders Sets North Back Years', *Sunday Tribune*, 12 April 2009.
239. 'Statement From the Real IRA to be Read Out at the 32 County Sovereignty Movement Commemoration in Derry Tomorrow', *Sunday Tribune*, 12 April 2009.
240. H. McDonald, 'Continuity IRA Issues Warning of More Attacks Against Police', *Observer*, 12 April 2009.

241. Ruairí Ó Brádaigh, interview with the author, Dublin, 24 June 2009.
242. 'No Support for Illegal Roadblock', BBC News Online, 24 August 2009, available at http://news.bbc.co.uk/1/hi/northern_ireland/8219182.stm
243. '"Splinter Group" Behind Road Bomb', BBC News Online, 9 September 2009, available at http://news.bbc.co.uk/1/hi/northern_ireland/8245581.stm
244. H. McDonald, 'Northern Ireland: Trouble Flares After Republican Dissidents Jailed', *Guardian*, 17 September 2009.
245. G. Moriarty, 'PSNI Partner Was Target of Dissident Republicans – Police', *Irish Times*, 17 October 2009; A. Morris, 'We Planted Car Bomb: ONH', *Irish News*, 17 October 2009.
246. http://news.bbc.co.uk/1/hi/northern_ireland/8320144.stm
247. H. McDonald, 'Northern Ireland Prison Boss Quits Over "Dissident Threats"', *Guardian*, 7 December 2009.
248. D. Sharrock, 'Judges' Families Under 24-Hour Security as Real IRA Increases Threat', *The Times*, 9 November 2009. See also H. McDonald, 'Judge Forced to Leave Belfast Home Amid Dissident Terror Threat', *Guardian*, 14 December 2009. For an overview of dissident activity, see 'Timeline of Dissident Activity', BBC News Online, 23 April 2010, available at http://news.bbc.co.uk/1/hi/northern_ireland/8340619.stm
249. D. McKittrick, 'The Afterlife of the IRA: The Dissident Groups Bent on Shattering the Peace in Northern Ireland,' *Independent*, 8 November 2008.
250. 'Police Cuts "Hit Dissident Fight"', BBC News Online, 24 September 2009, available at http://news.bbc.co.uk/1/hi/northern_ireland/8272855.stm
251. E. Sweeney, 'Yates Gives Views on Dissidents', *Londonderry Sentinel*, 3 March 2010.
252. Ibid.
253. J. Mooney, 'Gardaí "Know Identity" of Dissident Terrorists', *Sunday Times*, 24 May 2009.
254. D. McAleese, 'How the Terror Threat is Affecting Policing in Northern Ireland', *Belfast Telegraph*, 2 December 2009.
255. *Belfast Telegraph*, 10 March 2010.
256. Throughout the 'Troubles' RUC 'Special Branch' had been the greatest foe of republicans; during the peace process one of their uppermost demands was the disbandment of this 'force within a force'.
257. D. Sharrock, 'Dissident Republicans Blamed for 400lb Bomb after Christmas "Spectacular" Threat', *The Times*, 23 November 2009.
258. '400lb Bomb Left at Policing Board', BBC News Online, 22 November 2009, available at http://news.bbc.co.uk/1/hi/northern_ireland/8372713.stm
259. 'Police Under Fire as Bomb Car Mystery Deepens', *Newry Democrat*, March 2010.
260. 'Officer Critically Ill After Bomb', BBC News Online, 8 January 2010, available at http://news.bbc.co.uk/1/hi/northern_ireland/8447829.stm; H. McDonald, 'Northern Ireland Dissidents Use Remote Control Bomb in Attack on PSNI Officer', *Observer*, 17 January 2010.
261. *Twenty-Second Report of the Independent Monitoring Commission* (London: The Stationery Office, May 2010).
262. *Twenty-Third Report of the Independent Monitoring Commission* (London: The Stationery Office, May 2010).
263. J. Kirkup, 'MI5: More Terrorist Plots from Irish Republicans Than Islamic Extremists', *Daily Telegraph*, 1 January 2010.
264. 'Ahern in Warning Over Dissident Threat', RTÉ News, 28 February 2010.
265. 'INLA: We Have No Link to Killings', *Irish News*, 23 March 2009.
266. The INLA had previously been blamed for the murder of alleged drug dealers in Belfast and Derry, Kevin McAlorum (2004), Bryan McGlynn (2007), Emmett Shiels (2008) and Jim McConnell (2009). See A. Morris, 'INLA Arms Issue is Still to be Resolved', *Irish News*, 1 June 2009; E. Sweeney, 'Family Blames INLA for Shiels Murder', *Londonderry Sentinel*, 24 June 2009.
267. 'Thousands Mourn for Republican McGreevy', Belfast Telegraph, 22 March 2008.
268. J. Cusack, 'Revived IRA "Was Behind Expulsion of Drug Dealers"', *Sunday Independent*, 28 September 2008; Jim Cusack, 'Garda Chiefs Simply Don't Have the Will to Tackle Gangsters', *Sunday Independent*, 16 November 2008.

269. 'Real IRA Condemned', *Belfast Telegraph* (north-west edition), 18 May 2004; E. Houston, 'Real IRA in Cartel Claim', *Daily Ireland*, 20 May 2005.
270. See, for instance, 'Derry on Brink of "IPLO Style" Feud', *Derry Journal*, 22 April 2009.
271. 'Ex-Provos Swell RAAD Ranks', *Derry Journal*, 18 August 2009.
272. 'RAAD Issue New Threat to Drug Dealers: "Come Forward or Else"', *Derry Journal*, 10 November 2009.
273. 'Exclusive: RAAD Parade Cocaine "Mules"', *Derry Journal*, 27 November 2009.
274. 'Three in Court on Terrorist-Related Charges', BBC News Online, 21 December 2009, available at http://news.bbc.co.uk/1/hi/northern_ireland/foyle_and_west/8423114.stm
275. For more on the entire Doherty case, see: 'Derry Man Claims MI5 Tried to Recruit Him', *Derry Journal*, 3 November 2009; 'Real IRA: Kieran Doherty Admitted Drugs Link', *Belfast Telegraph*, 2 March 2010; T. Brady, 'Real IRA Man "Executed" for Informing About Drugs', *Irish Independent*, 26 February 2010; S. Breen, 'Brutal Murder of "One of Their Own" Shows Utter Lack of Mercy in Real IRA', *Sunday Tribune*, 4 April 2010.
276. J. Cusack, 'Dissident Republicans in Bomb Trade With Gangs', *Irish Independent*, 19 April 2009; 'RIRA Link to Murder After Drug Warning', *Belfast Telegraph*, 20 April 2010.
277. B. Roche, 'Real IRA Threatens to Kill Cork Drug Dealers', *Irish Times*, 17 September 2009.
278. 'Claim: Real IRA Killed Corkman', *Evening Echo* (Cork), 27 January 2010.
279. '32CSM Warn Shops on Police', *Derry Journal*, 12 February 2010; '32CSM Reject Calls to Drop PSNI Campaign', *Derry Journal*, 19 February 2010.
280. S. McKinney, 'SF Out of Touch With Grassroots – Ex-Prisoner', *Irish News*, 23 May 2006.
281. 'Barney McFadden – Father of Derry Republicanism Laid to Rest', *An Phoblacht*, 10 January 2002.
282. See, for instance, S. Breen, 'South Derry IRA Breaks Away from Leadership', *Sunday Tribune*, 23 July 2006; L. Clarke and J. Mooney, 'Why the Killers are Back', *Sunday Times*, 15 March 2009; J. Mooney, 'Terror Groups Unite in "New IRA"', *The Times*, 13 December 2009; J. Mooney, 'IRA "Master Terrorist" Defects to Dissidents', *Sunday Times*, 4 April 2010.
283. *Twenty-Second Report of the Independent Monitoring Commission.*
284. S. Breen, 'Unshakable Believers in the Power of the Bullet', *Sunday Tribune*, 15 March 2009.
285. M.L. McCrory, 'Paramilitary Style Attack Was Work of Dissidents', *Irish News*, 7 March 2009.
286. '"Surge" in Paramilitary Shootings', BBC News Online, 9 April 2009, available at http://news.bbc.co.uk/1/hi/northern_ireland/7989754.stm
287. Statistics taken from the Police Service of Northern Ireland website, available at http://www.psni.police.uk/ps_attacks_cy.pdf
288. *Twenty-Second Report of the Independent Monitoring Commission*; '"Vigilante" group meets IMC', BBC News Online, 9 December 2009, available at http://news.bbc.co.uk/1/hi/northern_ireland/8403069.stm.
289. A. Morris, 'Police Search at Dissident's Home', *Irish News*, 19 August 2009.
290. M. Óg Meehan, 'Aggressive Attitude of PSNI Triggered Violent Reaction', *Irish News*, 15 July 2009. See also S. Breen, 'The Fresh Face of Rioting is Nothing New in Ardoyne', *Sunday Tribune*, 19 July 2009.
291. D. Keenan, 'Radical Group Seek Republican Ground Lost by Sinn Féin', *Irish Times*, 27 July 2009.
292. D. McAleese, 'Little-Known Republican Group Warns of More Violence', *Belfast Telegraph*, 16 July 2009.
293. G. Moriarty, 'Dissidents Motivated by Vanity, Says Adams', *Irish Times*, 10 August 2009.
294. B. McCaffrey, 'Adams in Attack on Dissident Behaviour', *Irish News*, 8 August 2009.
295. 'Obituary: Brendan Hughes: Republican, Socialist, Volunteer', *Sovereign Nation*, May/June 2008.
296. Archive of original RNU website. It is also worth examining the independent, dedicated site to Hughes' memory, 'Brendan "Darkie" Hughes 1948–2008 RIP', available at http://dorcha.webs.com/. This features articles about and interviews with Hughes from various republican sources.
297. A. McIntyre, 'Weep, But Do Not Sleep', *The Blanket*, 24 February 2008.
298. A. McIntyre, 'The Enigma of Brian Keenan', The Pensive Quill, 25 May 2008, available at http://thepensivequill.am/2008/05/enigma-of-brian-keenan.html

299. Sean O'Callaghan, interview with the author, London, 12 December 2009.
300. 'Army Council is Redundant – Woodward', Northern Ireland Office, 3 September 2008, available at http://www.nio.gov.uk/army-council-is-redundant-woodward/media-detail.htm? newsID=15408
301. O'Rawe, *Blanketmen*. For further discussion of the debate around the Hunger Strike a useful, if partisan, resource is the website 'Uncovering the Truth About the 1981 Hunger Strike', available at http://www.longkesh.info/
302. In February 2008, Roy McShane, a long-time IRA man and chauffeur for Gerry Adams, was revealed as an MI5 agent. See 'Roy the Rat – Driver for Gerry Adams, Spy for MI5', *The Times*, 9 February 2008. Many continue to believe that there are other British spies within the senior ranks of the Provisional movement.

Conclusion

On a windy, but sun-kissed hill-side in Derry, in April 2010, Marian Price delivered an Easter Oration for the 32 County Sovereignty Movement. Against a backdrop of masked men in camouflage uniforms, she declared fervently,

> The root cause of the conflict has not been addressed in the so called peace process. Home Rule is not the issue that needs to be resolved. Pearse told us this in 1916. Devolution of limited powers to micro ministers is not the answer either. The 32 County Sovereignty Movement tells us this today. We do well to avoid clichés but the parallels of then and now are as stark as ever.... History is only in the past when history is resolved. We salute those who fought the British Empire in 1916. We salute those who fight that empire today... 1916 is unfinished business.[1]

A day later and some sixty miles away, in Belfast's Milltown cemetery, Pádraic Mac Coitir of éirígí gave his organisation's Easter address. Just as Price had done, he sought to emphasise the historical setting in which contemporary dissident republicans operated:

> We struggle because we are right in our pursuit of a Democratic Socialist Republic. We will continue that struggle no matter what our enemies may say. How many times have we heard in the past that we have no strategy and no mandate?... People like Thomas Clarke, Seán Mac Diarmada, James Connolly, Liam Mellows, Tom Williams, Brendan O'Boyle and every Volunteer buried in this cemetery who were labelled because they 'dissented' from this state and went out to fight for what was right. As Mac Piarais [Pearse] said, 'they think they have purchased half of us and intimidated the other half; they are wrong'. Given that is the case I am

proud to say that I too 'dissent' from the current state today. However the one thing I am not is a 'traitor', as I assume none of you here today are.[2]

The pointed reference to Martin McGuinness's 2009 post-Massereene 'traitors' comment, which drew cheers and loud applause, was not lost on any of those in attendance.[3] For the words of Mac Coitir and Price reflected their rejection of McGuinness and the Provisional republican movement.

More broadly, their respective groups, the 32 County Sovereignty Movement and éirígí, are part of a wider milieu of 'dissenting', or 'dissident' republicanism, which rejects the status quo in Ireland and believes history has not ended. In making this case, they are able to draw on a traditionalist form of Irish republicanism, which can plausibly assert lineage from 1916 and beyond. The central tenets of this dogma were articulated by Pearse and, to a lesser extent, Connolly. From there, the line of inheritance can be traced down through the different twentieth-century incarnations of republicanism, to the various dissident branches of the present day. This shared heritage – laid claim to by Republican Sinn Féin, the 32CSM, éirígí, the RNU, as well as the various armed branches of IRA or 'Óglaigh na hÉireann' now in existence – helps to generate shared strands of analysis. Contemporary dissident republicanism, though characterised by organisational diversity, exhibits a certain level of ideological homogeny.

For all the groups surveyed here, the problems that afflict Irish society, north and south of the border, can be traced back to partition. The division of the island is held to be a product of British imperial design, with Northern Ireland reduced to the status of colony: 'the British occupied north'. What is required, it is argued, is the completion of Irish 'national liberation', so as to achieve a united, independent Ireland, often envisaged as a restoration of the Republic that was 'lost' in 1916. To this end, the different organisations swear their commitment to some kind of 'revolution' in Ireland; albeit a revolution that, paradoxically, seeks not to overthrow, but to complete the unfinished legacy of their forefathers.

It is this outlook which inspires the 'oppositional' character of dissident republicanism. In its most extreme form, Republican Sinn Féin refuses to countenance any participation with existing institutions, which are judged to be a violation of national sovereignty. Since its creation in 1986, the party has clung to a rigid policy of parliamentary abstentionism; instead it calls for a totally fresh start in a 'New Ireland' (*Eire Nua*). Other groups, whilst perhaps ready to participate in the political status quo, at some level, profess themselves to be no less 'revolutionary' in intent.

Dissident republicans of all hues reject the logic of those who argue that they lack support, or have no mandate. For them, this is to miss the point; namely, that where questions of inalienable right and national sovereignty are concerned, such matters are irrelevant. Their collective view is that being popular is of no consequence, as compared to the virtue of being correct. Indeed, it might be said that many of the organisations examined here glory in their minority status. Certainly there is more than a hint of this in the ranks of Republican Sinn Féin, with its religious-like devotion to an unchanging republican dogma. The party faithful revel in their self-ascribed status as members of the initiated few. They see themselves as the guardians of the flame, whose contribution has been, in the words of Ruairí Ó Brádaigh, to 'keep the ideology intact'. The same is equally true of the 32 County Sovereignty Movement, whose members likewise claim the mantle of being 'the true inheritors of the republican creed'. Through its dedication to 'principled' Irish republicanism, the 32CSM is pledged to defend the 'sovereignty and unity of Ireland', both of which are held to be inviolable and indivisible.

For both groups, history offers the ultimate validation – and the guarantee of future success. The culture of the dissidents is steeped in commemoration and reverence for republican ancestry. Whether by reference to Charlie Kerins, the republicans of the 1940s, or Sean South of Garryowen, devotees see themselves as following in the footsteps of those who have gone before. At the apex of this historical edifice is 1916: the Easter Rising has bequeathed a legacy that demands fulfilment, as well as a paradigm that inspires future conduct. At the heart of this is the perception that an armed minority *can* act in pursuit of the 'national demand' and history will, in the end, vindicate them. In the view of Francie Mackey, the leaders of the 1916 rebellion, 'although small in numbers, [had] proven to be correct'. It is this belief that nourishes the violent campaigns of the Continuity IRA and the Real IRA, the two armed organisations with which RSF and the 32CSM are aligned.

Though they may claim to dispute the contemporary applicability of 'armed struggle', this is also a vision with which newer republican groups such as éirígí or the Republican Network for Unity cannot disagree; their subscription to the doctrine of 1916 and the nationalist gospel that flows from the Rising guarantees it. It is for this reason that senior figures in both organisations argue there can be no principled objection to violence, only a 'tactical' rejection of its use in the here-and-now. To do otherwise, as Brian Leeson noted, would be to 'fly in the face of all our history'. And in this regard, the emergence and growth of éirígí and the RNU is part of the broader ideological hinterland that helps sustain still-violent republicanism.

In all of this, of course, there is much that the dissidents share with the Provisionals (and even elements of mainstream Irish political culture). The ground on which they stand today is that which was occupied by Sinn Féin and the Provisional IRA from 1969 down to 1997. As Anthony McIntyre observed of the CIRA and RIRA in the wake of Massereene,

> both groups were earlier nurtured on the ideology of physical force by the leadership of Gerry Adams and Martin McGuinness. Both men insisted that armed struggle, which involved the killing of policemen and British soldiers, was a necessary and morally correct form of resistance. This logic continues to govern the Continuity and Real IRAs' actions to this day.[4]

Furthermore, as has been described, the refusal of the Provisionals to renounce the legitimacy of their own 'armed struggle' only strengthens the parallels that can be drawn. Today's dissidents are quick to emphasise the hypocrisy that infuses Sinn Féin's criticism of those still committed to violent republicanism; there is more truth to the charge than many Provisionals would care to admit.

To those of a dissident persuasion it is the Provisional movement that has shifted position. In the words of one disaffected republican, 'People could turn around and say that the real dissidents are Sinn Féin, because they moved away from their original opinion... [They] call other people dissidents but they didn't change their view... Sinn Féin changed their opinion and other people didn't.'[5] On this view, the Provisionals are judged to have 'sold out' and abandoned the cause. From whichever point of departure – be it abstentionism, the IRA ceasefires, acceptance of the Mitchell Principles, the Good Friday Agreement, weapons decommissioning or the endorsement of the PSNI – the collective view of the dissidents is that the Provisionals have lost sight of republican objectives and been absorbed into the system. Sinn Féin is described as having become part of the establishment, north and south of the border.

As to why this situation came about, there is widespread accord that the fault lies with the leadership of the Provisional movement, particularly Gerry Adams and Martin McGuinness. In the eyes of Ruairí Ó Brádaigh, they failed to learn the 'lessons' of history and simply followed the path trodden previously by others, such as de Valera. Others ascribe more base motives, with Anthony McIntyre and many in the dissenting republican movement seeing Adams and McGuinness 'craving institutional power'. Whatever the explanation, those opposed to the Provisionals are unified by the belief that the Adams–McGuinness leadership made fatal errors during the peaceprocess (some seeing the very decision to engage in that process, as mistaken). In the view of Brian Leeson, Sinn Féin, having opted to move 'the battlefield into the negotiating arena' had been defeated. Michael McKevitt concurs, noting that the peace process 'inflicted the political and military defeat upon the Provisionals which [the British] could not achieve in the field'. The end result was deemed to be the betrayal of republican principles and Sinn Féin's transformation from 'revolutionary' into 'constitutional' party.

Again here, the Provisionals, in their attempts to refute such accusations, were not helped by their own narrative of the recent conflict. This characterised the IRA as an 'undefeated army', or even contended, as did Joe Cahill at Sinn Féin's 2003 *ard fheis*, 'we've won the war, now let's win the peace'. Yet increasingly this stance raised rather difficult questions for Sinn Féin. To paraphrase McIntyre again, it could be asked, 'how was it that the undefeated army, could have ended up settling for a situation in which republicans appeared to be locked into the institutions in Northern Ireland, with Irish unity far from imminent?' At one stage, it seems clear, an answer to this question would have invoked Sinn Féin's electoral growth in the South and the prospect that the party might enter government on both sides of the border. That being the case, though, the apparent failure of Sinn Féin's 'southern project' in the 2006–7 period looms all the more significant. With that political postern closed off, attention focused back on the Provisional leadership and the place to which it had led the republican movement.

In this context, the criticism being advanced of the Sinn Féin leadership appeared to take on ever-more persuasive logic. Within the Provisionals at that time, there appeared to be a growing perception that the ideological compromises demanded of republicans were being made for nought. It is this that perhaps explains the sense that the dissident cause gathered considerable momentum from 2006 onwards. For instance, several of the key figures within today's dissident world abandoned Sinn Féin in that era – Brian Leeson, Breandán Mac-Cionnaith, Tony Catney and other, less well-known, but no less influential, republicans. Such figures have talked of their assessment, at that time, that the peace process was not delivering for republicans; to quote Leeson, 'the thing that was called a process had no movement in it'.

Anxiety on this issue can scarcely have been assuaged by the kind of rhetoric that emerged in the wake of the global 'credit crisis'. In June 2009, Martin Mansergh observed that the financial problems facing the Irish Republic meant there was zero appetite for any new campaign against partition. It was he said, 'hardly the moment to press claims to the North which we have renounced'. The prospect of a bid to unify Ireland was described as being 'a lot less compelling today than... two or three years ago'.[6] That it was Mansergh that offered this assessment was highly noteworthy; a historian, intellectual and Fianna Fáil TD, he is perhaps the leading exponent of a brand of constitutional nationalism that accepts many of the central constructs of Irish republican history and ideology, down to the moment when de Valera admitted defeat in 1923. Mansergh's comments led many to the conclusion that Irish unity was now truly off the agenda for the foreseeable future.

What the foregoing demonstrates, then, is the extent to which the internal dynamics of dissident republicanism are, in key respects, unrelated to the stability of the institutions in Northern Ireland. As discussed in chapter three of this study, the most fallow period from the dissident perspective was that of 2003–5. Yet crucially, this was also the period when the institutions of the Agreement were totally in abeyance. Indeed, some commentators spoke then of the Agreement as having been put into 'cold storage' for the indefinite future. Ironically, it is the period since the restoration of the Northern Ireland Assembly and Executive that has seen a surge in dissident activity – both politically and militarily.

What this highlights is the extent to which responses to the dissidents have in part rested on a false premise. For a long time, the logic has been that articulated by then Secretary of State, John Reid, in the aftermath of the March 2001 attack on the BBC's London headquarters; namely, that the key was to prove 'politics works', as a way of marginalising the forces of dissident republicanism. Others have spoken of the dangerous 'vacuum' that would result from any failure to entrench the Agreement. Conventional wisdom has posited that political instability in Northern Ireland would work to the benefit of those opposed to the peace process. To give but one example, it was none other than the PSNI Chief Constable, Sir Hugh Orde, who claimed in late 2008 that a 'vacuum' in politics would be 'exploited' by dissident republicans and would fuel their rise.[7] In reality, the opposite has been the case: it is against a backdrop of functioning political institutions that support for the dissidents has swelled.

All of which is not to say, of course, that political developments have no impact on dissident republicanism; manifestly, they do. But the nature of this impact needs to be more clearly understood. At the risk of repetition, it is worth re-stating what is meant here.

During the years 2003–5, RSF and the 32CSM were all-but obsolete, in terms of their ability to affect the political agenda. At the same time, the Real IRA and the Continuity IRA alike suffered reverses that severely diminished their operational capacity. The former even split, with what was initially the majority faction calling for a ceasefire. Simultaneously, Sinn Féin might be said to have been 'riding the crest of a wave'. Between 1994 and 2004 it enjoyed a decade of unbroken political growth. By 2003, it had vanquished the SDLP in Northern Ireland and appeared poised for major breakthroughs in the Irish Republic. On the basis of the old adage that 'success breeds success', the party seemed little troubled by dissident republican activity. In contrast to Sinn Féin's electoral rise, the dissidents appeared able to offer only a failing military strategy – and one decidedly inferior to that which the Provisional IRA had set aside in the 1990s. Politics, in other words, appeared to be being made to work to a republican agenda; that this would be so was the basis upon which the Provisional leadership had persuaded their movement to engage with the peace process in the first place.

Eventually, however, this state of affairs proved untenable. Given the basis upon which the peace process had been constructed (with unionist consent 'hard-wired' into the political framework) and given the divided nature of politics in Northern Ireland, there was always likely to be a ceiling to how far Sinn Féin could advance their republican agenda. The party leadership had reckoned that a place in government on both sides of the border and the slow detachment of Northern Ireland from the authority of Westminster would suffice as an adequate return on the years of conflict. The dissipation of core aspects of this vista appeared to weaken it substantially.

The result was the post-2006 shift in fortunes for dissident republicanism. Even during the lean years, traditional forms of the ideology had been kept alive in various ways. Obviously, RSF and the 32CSM had survived and by their very existence proved the staying-power of an intransigent mode of republicanism. Of greater import though were the less-structured modes of dissenting republicanism that came to the fore in the years after 2002. Groups like the New Republican Forum and *The Blanket* advanced a cogent and relentless critique of the Provisionals, which in its own way helped to 'keep the flame alive'.

As a consequence, as the Sinn Féin project began to run into problems, there was a ready-made discourse, based on the long-established tenets of historic Irish republicanism, for those dissatisfied with the status quo. Subsequently, the dissidents increasingly moved out of their long period of introspection, in which their focus had been almost entirely on the Provisionals. A fresh confidence developed and the dissident republican case was put with renewed vigour – in part because, as Marian Price had declared, 'the debate as to where former republicans have travelled to is over.'

The vitality of dissident republicanism has, therefore, not been determined by the waxing and waning of the institutions in Northern Ireland, so much as it has been circumscribed by an intra-republican dynamic. The reality is that there is no Republic; the dream of 1916 remains, in a self-evident way, unrealised. While that remains the case, it should be no surprise that there are those prepared to challenge the status quo – or that there are those prepared to make that challenge by violent means. Indeed, when set against the *longue durée* of Irish republican history there is something inevitable about it.

This after all, is how those supportive of continuing 'armed struggle' see it themselves. In late 2007, Gary Donnelly of the 32CSM told the *Irish News*, 'I believe whilst there's a British presence in Ireland there will be people who will resent it... In the words of Patrick Pearse "Ireland unfree will never be at peace." I think there's never been a truer statement.'[8] Soon after, Donnelly underscored this point, declaring, 'History has taught us that there always will be an IRA. Its evolution may ebb and flow but it will always be there as long as the border between north and south exists.'[9] On this issue, Ruairí Ó Brádaigh, though he continues to have his disagreements with the 32 County Sovereignty Movement, is in full agreement. In his view, 'If you read your history you will see that everything comes in cycles.'[10]

For Donnelly, Ó Brádaigh and indeed, the wider dissident republican world, the lessons of history are only too clear: they will perdure and ultimately, prevail. In this regard, the insight of Garda Commissioner Pat Byrne offers a fitting, if troubling conclusion; for Byrne spoke not as an apologist for physical force republicanism, but simply as someone offering an honest opinion when he declared: 'unfortunately you will always have some type of "IRA" while you have a British presence in Northern Ireland.'[11]

NOTES

1. Marian Price, *32CSM Easter Oration*, Derry, 4 April 2010, available at Derry 32 County Sovereignty movement, http://www.derry32csm.com/2010/04/32csm-easter-commemoration-2010-derry.html.
2. Pádraic Mac Coitir, *1916 Commemoration Speech*, Belfast, 5 April 2010, available at, éirígí, http://www.eirigi.org/latest/latest070410speech.html.
3. 'Éirígí Belfast Easter 2010 – Main Oration – 3/4', Youtube, 6 April 2010, available at, http://www.youtube.com/watch?v=Zmpi6eN-GL0.
4. A. McIntyre, 'Be Honest, Mr. Adams: You no longer have a strategy for a United Ireland', *Parliamentary Brief*, April 2009.
5. Lorna Brady, sister of deceased Real IRA member John Brady, speaking on 'Files reveal growing NI threat', Report for BBC Newsnight, 29 October 2009, available at, http://news.bbc.co.uk/1/hi/programmes/newsnight/8331976.stm.
6. F. Gartland, 'United Ireland less compelling now, says Mansergh', *Irish Times*, 10 June 2009.
7. Orde made the comments on the BBC's *Hardtalk* programme. Cited in, 'Political vacuum "being exploited by dissidents"', *News Letter*, 17 November 2008.
8. S. McKinney, '"No evidence RIRA attacking solely Catholics"', *Irish News*, 20 December 2007.
9. D. Young, 'Unity call for dissidents to take on British', *Belfast Telegraph*, 28 January 2008.
10. A. Morris, 'Veteran republican has no misgivings over IRA past: Ruairí Ó Brádaigh interview', *Irish News*, 17 October 2009.
11. M. O'Toole, 'Omagh's bombers may never be caught', *Irish News*, 13 March 2000.

Timeline of Violent Dissident Republican Activity

*W*hat *follows is an account of the activities of violent dissident republicans from 1986 to the present day. It was compiled using media and security reports; it aims for comprehensiveness, though doubtless there are still omissions. The central purpose of this chronology is to reassert the narrative of dissident republican activity and prove the lie of the notion that after 1998, Northern Ireland was a country 'at peace'.*

For the most part this timeline gives only the actions of dissident republicans; only occasionally does it reference the wider political context. Where possible reference has been made to the specific group involved, yet this was not always possible. Sometimes no specific organisation took responsibility; at other times members of one organisation claimed an attack in the name of another.

Places: NI (Northern Ireland); RoI (Republic of Ireland); US (United States)

Parties/Groups: CFAD (Concerned Families Against Drugs); DUP (Democratic Unionist Party); PUP (Progressive Unionist Party); RSF (Republican Sinn Féin); SDLP (Social and Democratic Labour Party); SF (Sinn Féin); UUP (Ulster Unionist Party); 32CSM (32 County Sovereignty Movement); RNU (Republican Network for Unity)

Paramilitaries: CIRA (Continuity IRA); INLA (Irish National Liberation Army); IRLA (Irish Republican Liberation Army); LVF (Loyalist Volunteer Force); ONH (Óglaigh na hÉireann); PIRA (Provisional IRA); RAAD (Republican Action Against Drugs); RDA (Republican Defence Army); RIRA (Real IRA); SNH (Saoirse na hÉireann)

Titles: FM (First Minister); DFM (Deputy First Minister); IICD (Independent International Commission on Decommissioning); IMC (Independent Monitoring Commission); MLA (Member of the Legislative Assembly); MP (Member of Parliament); PM (Prime Minister)

1986	Formation of the Continuity Army Council (CAC) – forerunner of CIRA

1994

5 January	CIRA fire shots over the grave of Tom Maguire in County Mayo, the first public action of the group; read the 1987 statement of Maguire confirming the legitimacy of the CIRA
31 August	PIRA declare 'a cessation of military operations'

1995

10 November	Gardaí intercept 1,500-pound homemade explosive near Carrickmacross, County Monaghan; say they believe they have prevented a major bomb attack in NI

1996

13 January	CIRA issue statement claiming to be the 'true Irish Republican Army'; pledge 'unremitting hostility to the British forces of occupation in Ireland'
9 February	PIRA, alleging bad faith from British government and unionists, end their 'cessation' and explode a bomb in London Docklands, killing two, injuring forty and causing £150 million worth of damage
13 July	1,200-pound dissident car bomb in Killyhevlin Hotel, Enniskillen, injures seventeen
29 September	250-pound dissident car bomb abandoned in Belfast; army carry out controlled explosion
21 November	600-pound dissident bomb fails to explode in Derry

1997

16 June	Two policemen shot dead in Lurgan, County Armagh by the PIRA – the last RUC officers to die at the hands of PIRA
19 July	PIRA call cessation
31 July	500-pound RIRA bomb near Lisbellaw, County Fermanagh defused by army
9 August	Hoax van bomb planted on Craigavon Bridge, Derry, prior to Apprentice Boys parade
3 September	CIRA issue a statement pledging to 'step up' their campaign; talk of a possible renewal of a bombing campaign on the British mainland
9 September	SF pledges to abide by the Mitchell Principles
11 September	PIRA say they would have problems with some of Mitchell Principles but that what SF do is up to them
15 September	SF joins talks
16 September	400-pound CIRA bomb causes extensive damage in Markethill, County Armagh
10 October	Michael McKevitt and eight supporters walk out of PIRA convention in Falcarragh, County Donegal
30 October	Holdall bomb left in Derry government building fails to detonate
20 November	Small bomb at Belfast City Hall, claimed by the Continuity IRA. The device, believed to be aimed at PUP offices, is defused
27 December	INLA kill Billy Wright, leader of LVF, in Maze Prison

1998

7 January	300-pound RIRA car bomb in Banbridge, County Down, defused
24 January	Car bomb explodes in Enniskillen – night club badly damaged; hoax bomb alert in Newtownbutler, County Fermanagh
20 February	RIRA car bomb injures eleven in Moira, County Down
23 February	Massive RIRA car bomb in Portadown, County Armagh – extensive damage

24 February	250-pound bomb found in field in County Cavan, RoI
3 March	Car bomb found on farmland in County Louth, RoI
10 March	Mortar attack on RUC base in Newry Road, Armagh
20 March	5-pound bomb thrown into bank in Derry fails to explode; claimed by CIRA
29 March	Incendiary devices destroy a carpet factory in Belfast; CIRA subsequently claims responsibility
3 April	Police intercept 1,000-pound car bomb at Dun Laoghaire, RoI, believed to be destined for central London
6 April	Police discover 3,000 pounds of fertiliser in north Belfast
10 April	Belfast Agreement reached and includes the provisions: NI's constitutional future should be determined by majority vote; all parties will use exclusively peaceful and democratic means; an NI Assembly with devolved powers be set up along with a power-sharing Executive; a British–Irish Council and a British–Irish Inter-Governmental Conference be established; release within two years of paramilitary prisoners of organisations on ceasefire; there to be a two-year target for decommissioning of paramilitary weapons; RoI to abolish its constitutional claim to NI; provision for new legislation on policing, human rights and equality
12 April	RSF call for No vote in planned referendum
21 April	32CSM reject Agreement as 'fundamentally undemocratic, anti-Republican and unacceptable'
30 April	Army defuses 600-pound bomb in Lisburn, County Antrim
1 May	RIRA member Ronan MacLochlainn shot dead by Gardaí during attempted robbery of a security van in County Wicklow
9 May	Two mortar tubes found in car park of hotel in Belleek, County Fermanagh; RIRA claims responsibility, formally announcing its existence
15 May	Car and trailer bomb abandoned in Kinawley, County Fermanagh
16 May	Army defuses bomb near Armagh RUC base
22 May	Yes to agreement in referendums in NI (71%) and RoI (94%)

24 May	Mortar attack on Forkhill RUC station in south Armagh
22 June	Landmine detonates near Drumintee in south Armagh
24 June	200-pound RIRA car bomb causes two injuries and £3 million of damage in Newtownhamilton, County Armagh
10 July	Three men with explosives arrested in London, believed to have reconnoitred shops in Fulham as possible targets. Jailed for twenty-two to twenty-five years each
13 July	1,400-pound bomb found abandoned between Moy and Black-watertown in County Armagh
1 August	500-pound RIRA car bomb in Banbridge, County Down; two police, thirty-three civilians injured; £4 million estimated damage
15 August	RIRA carry out bombing of Omagh, County Tyrone, kill twenty-nine and unborn twins and devastate town
18 August	RIRA announce 'suspension' of operations
19 August	Bertie Ahern promises introduction of 'draconian' anti-terrorist measures against dissident republicans
22 August	INLA announce ceasefire
26 August	Blair visits Omagh and promises draconian legislation to deal with paramilitaries not on ceasefire
1 September	Gerry Adams, SF president, says the war is over
2 September	Reports that PIRA have threatened RIRA and the 32CSM
4 September	Gun attack on RUC Landrover near Portadown, County Armagh
8 September	RIRA announces 'complete cessation of violence'

1999

14 January	Gun attack on west Belfast RUC station
4 May	Gun attack on Lisnaskea RUC station, County Fermanagh
20 October	Weapons shipment seized, ten arrested and underground firing-range uncovered in County Dublin

25 October	Rocket launcher and Semtex found in County Meath, RoI
27 November	UUP agrees to go into power-sharing Executive with Sinn Féin on understanding that PIRA will then decommission. Executive finally formed on 1 December
27 December	Kempton Park racecourse evacuated after hoax

2000

21 January	RIRA statement denounces NI Executive and those giving allegiance to 'corrupt, treacherous administration'; pledges to 'struggle' (though does not officially end cessation)
24 January	Significant arms cache uncovered in Limerick; arrests
6 February	CIRA bomb damages hotel in Irvinestown, County Fermanagh
11 February	Failure of PIRA to decommission causes Peter Mandelson to suspend the Assembly
February	Wave of hijackings and hoax bombs in Lurgan, County Armagh, in the Kilwilkie estate; it is reported that the PIRA's North Armagh brigade has defected to the dissident cause
25 February	RIRA bomb outside Ballykelly barracks, County Londonderry, fails to detonate fully
29 February	Rocket launcher and warhead recovered from near army base in Dungannon, County Tyrone
16 March	500 pounds of explosives captured at Hillsborough, County Down
6 April	RIRA bomb attack on Ebrington barracks, Derry
12 April	Failed CIRA mortar attack on RUC station in Rosslea, County Fermanagh
6 May	PIRA promise to begin decommissioning if Assembly and Executive restored
10 May	CIRA statement calls on PIRA to disband and give its arms to those 'prepared to defend the Republic'
19 May	Bomb alerts cause widespread disruption in Belfast

24 May   Failed RIRA mortar attack on army observation post near Cross-
              maglen, County Armagh

26 May   Gardaí seize bomb-making equipment at what is believed to be a
              RIRA bomb factory in Ballyfermot in west Dublin

30 May   Devolution restored

1 June   RIRA bomb damages Hammersmith Bridge, London

20 June   Partially exploded bomb found in grounds of Hillsborough resi-
              dence of secretary of state

24 June   32CSM conference attacks PIRA's 'first stop in a decommissioning
              surrender process'

26 June   Having visited PIRA arms dumps, two international arms inspec-
              tors report arms could not be used without being detected

30 June   Bomb explodes on Belfast–Dublin railway line in south Armagh

9 July   Car bomb explodes outside RUC station, Stewartstown, County
              Tyrone; attributed to RIRA – believed to be first car bomb since
              Omagh

19 July   Controlled explosion of RIRA bomb near Ealing Broadway tube
              station in London and suspect package in Whitehall

28 July   Report from Croatia on 13 July of three arrests and confiscations of
              substantial weaponry thought to be bound for RIRA

11 August   500 pounds of explosives apparently destined for Apprentice
              Boys' Derry march following day recovered by RUC

12 September 80-pound bomb partially explodes at army base at Magilligan,
              Derry; soldier treated for shock

13 September RIRA mortar attack on RUC station in Armagh city

20 September RIRA rocket-propelled grenade attack on MI6 HQ in London

25 September Train services from Belfast disrupted when 50-pound RIRA bomb
              partially explodes

9 October   BBC 'Panorama' programme accuses four men of involvement in
              Omagh bomb

13 October	PIRA murder RIRA's Joseph O'Connor
24 October	600-pound partially-constructed bomb seized in west Belfast; subsequently alleged to be bound for London
1 November	Booby-trap bomb in Castlewellan, County Down, seriously injures RUC officer, Reserve Constable David Fegan
11 November	Three men arrested after 200-pound mortar bomb found by RUC in van near Derrylin, County Fermanagh
27 November	Booby-trap bomb left under a car at Drumshane, near Lisnarrick in County Fermanagh, containing 2 pounds of commercial explosive, believed to be Semtex.
5 December	Protestant taxi driver, Trevor Kell, shot dead in north Belfast. RUC Chief Constable Ronnie Flanagan blames dissident republican paramilitaries; David Trimble later identified the RIRA as responsible.
14 December	Police in Belfast intercept primed bomb containing 1½ pounds of Semtex and arrest two men. Believed to be linked to RIRA
20 December	Gardaí seize seventy to eighty sticks of Frangex commercial explosives at a farm in County Kilkenny; police blame it on a CIRA grouping that was also close to the RIRA

2001

14 January	Police car damaged by RIRA bomb in Cookstown, County Tyrone
16 January	Police defuse 1,100-pound RIRA bomb near Armagh; 100-pound booby-trap bomb damages RUC station in Claudy, County Londonderry
23 January	RIRA mortar bomb, packed with 200 pounds of homemade explosives, fired at Ebrington barracks, Derry fails to explode. Flanagan describes it as 'attempted mass murder' by the use of a 'barrack-buster'
12 February	Gardaí discover Mark XV mortar device in woodland near Newtowncunningham in County Donegal in the Republic of Ireland (believed to be linked to the RIRA)
17 February	It is reported that explosions forced the closure of Belfast–Dublin railway line over the previous six days

21 February   Stephen Menary, a 14-year-old cadet, maimed by bomb attack on west London Territorial Army base

4 March   Substantial damage to BBC TV centre in west London; one injury

29 March   Michael McKevitt arrested by Gardaí and later charged with membership of an illegal organisation and directing terrorism

1 April   A series of hoax alerts on Northern Ireland's railway lines bring the total number of such alerts that year alone to thirty-three

3 April   RUC defuse 60-pound bomb in Derry

12 April   Fully-primed 200-pound mortar bomb found in Galbally, County Tyrone; defused

13 April   RIRA statement

14 April   Small RIRA bomb causes minor damage at a postal sorting office in Hendon, London (coincides with Easter Rising celebrations at the General Post Office in Dublin)

21 April   Grenade attack on a Derry RUC station

23–5 April   A series of hoax devices force the closure of the Belfast–Dublin railway line on the outskirts of Belfast and at Lurgan; it is also reported that two RIRA gunmen fired on police during rioting in the Kilwilkie estate in Lurgan, as army officers explored a suspect device on the nearby railway line; eleven RUC officers hurt in the disturbances

4 May   Blast bomb attack on Glen Road RUC station in Andersonstown, west Belfast

6 May   Small RIRA bomb in Hendon, London, injures one

14 May   Suspected attack on Bessbrook Mill barracks in south Armagh

16 May   RIRA designated by US government as foreign terrorist organisation, along with 32CSM

26 May   Rocket attack on Strabane RUC station – unexploded, improvised grenade uncovered

7 June   British general election; gun attack on polling station in Draperstown sees two RUC officers and a 21-year-old woman shot.

	McGuinness labels it an 'attack on the peace process' and blames 'micro organisations that don't have any support whatsoever in our community'
6 July	Three men arrested in Slovakia accused of trying to procure arms for RIRA; discovery of three arms dumps and training camp in County Kildare
19 July	Bomb thrown at Castlewellan RUC station, County Down
1 August	Controlled explosions of 40-pound primed RIRA bomb at Belfast International Airport
3 August	100-pound RIRA bomb at Ealing Broadway, west London, injures seven
17 October	Primed 350-pound bomb found near Sixmilecross, County Tyrone
23 October	PIRA says it has begun process of putting arms beyond use; some arms decommissioned
23 October	Liam Campbell jailed for five years for membership of the RIRA
29 October	Charles Folliard, a former loyalist prisoner, is shot dead in Strabane; dissident republicans are blamed
30 October	11-pound bomb detonated on bus outside west Belfast police station
3 November	RIRA bomb in Birmingham causes minor injuries to police
4 November	Royal Irish Constabulary becomes Police Service of NI
7 November	Twenty million contraband cigarettes seized in Dundalk believed to have come from Estonia. Linked to RIRA
9 November	Forty million cigarettes found in Warrenpoint, County Down, on cargo ship from Latvia. Linked to RIRA
15 November	Police in Yorkshire, England arrest men believed to be responsible for the RIRA mainland campaign. Five are later convicted for their part in the attacks, including the brothers Robert and Aiden Hulme
19 November	Weapons seized in Lurgan, County Armagh
20 November	Fully-primed large car bomb found near Armagh

21 November	Incendiary device partially explodes in shop in Newry, County Down
5 December	Army defuses 80-pound bomb under railway line between Newry and Dundalk
16 December	Bomb attack damages Fermanagh Customs and Excise office

2002

3 January	Pipe bomb attack on policeman's home in County Down
6 January	Seven men arrested in Dundalk linked to RIRA activity
8 February	Civilian security guard Peter Mason loses arms, hearing and sight after picking up a booby-trapped flask near an army training centre, County Londonderry
18 February	Police seize anti-tank RPG22 and other equipment from a housing estate in Coalisland, County Tyrone; four men arrested
3 March	Small bomb slightly injures two boys in County Armagh
29 March	Booby-trap bomb found under car in County Tyrone
8 April	PIRA says it has put more weapons 'beyond use'
12 April	Two bomb attacks on County Down police stations
16 April	Bomb attack on Garnerville police training college in Belfast; claimed by the CIRA
26 April	Large firebomb abandoned near Belfast city centre
28 April	150-pound bomb attack on Maghaberry Prison, County Antrim
7 May	Three men from County Louth jailed for thirty years each for seeking arms for RIRA in Slovakia from MI5 operatives pretending to be Iraqi agents (Operation Samnite)
7 May	Dublin man Robert Brennan convicted on membership charge and unlawful possession of a stun gun by Special Criminal Court. During his trial, a senior special branch officer told the court that the RIRA had carried out eighty terrorist attacks since October 1999
5 June	The Real IRA is linked to the kidnapping of a 16-year-old in County Down

5 June	Booby-trap bomb attack on Catholic police recruit in Antrim
2 July	Commons NI Affairs Committee report on financing of terrorism estimates that RIRA annually has 'running costs' of £500,000 but makes £1.5 million from criminality
3 July	News that leading NI politicians have been warned that dissidents are planning assassinations
17 July	Bomb thrown at police car near Downpatrick, County Down; claimed by the Real IRA. Sinn Féin MLA Mick Murphy says, 'The people who carried out this attack are opposed to the peace process and opposed to the Good Friday Agreement. They have little or no support and operate without either a mandate or indeed a strategy to achieve political change.'
23 July	'Barrack buster' mortar bomb used to attack on Ebrington barracks, Derry; no injuries
24 July	Bomb explodes on estate of unionist peer Lord Brookeborough, a member of the policing board
1 August	Builder David Caldwell killed by booby-trapped lunchbox at Territorial Army base in Derry
30 August	Hijacked bread van in Belfast is loaded with petrol before being abandoned; army carries out a controlled explosion
3 September	Gun attack on the PSNI in Downpatrick
18 September	Two bombs seized from car near Newry, County Down
21 September	Trimble says UUP will leave Executive on 18 January if PIRA does not show they have permanently abandoned violence
4 October	Police investigation produces evidence of PIRA spy ring at Stormont
15 October	Devolution replaced by direct rule from London
20 October	It becomes public that the RIRA faction around Michael McKevitt has accused the RIRA leadership of corruption and demanded it 'stand down with ignominy'; police defuse bomb at Castlederg station, claimed by Real IRA
21 October	Hoax bomb alerts in Belfast, Lurgan and at the international airport at Aldergrove in County Antrim – believed to be a response from the RIRA to the prisoners' statement calling for the leadership

to stand down. Real IRA in north-west issues statement warning 'all civilians to stay away from military installations and from crown forces personnel'

25 October	Controlled explosion of van bomb in Belfast city centre
6 November	Arrests and weapons seizure in Limerick
9 November	A series of hoax alerts in Belfast city centre cause traffic chaos

2003

8 January	Large firebomb defused at waterworks in Keady, County Armagh, claimed by the CIRA
13 January	Firebomb defused in Dungannon, County Tyrone, claimed by the CIRA
23 January	Bomb discovered at PSNI headquarters at Dundonald House on Stormont estate in east Belfast; caller to a newsroom claims it for the RIRA and links it to campaign for prisoner segregation in Maghaberry
2 February	Bomb explodes at Territorial Army base in Belfast. Sinn Féin lord mayor of Belfast, Alex Maskey, calls on 'these micro-groups to desist from this sort of activity and disband'
7 February	Controlled explosion of bomb in stolen car in Belfast
10 February	Six police injured in bomb in Enniskillen, County Fermanagh, claimed by the CIRA
18 February	One of two nail bombs thrown over fence of Belfast police station explodes
20 February	Weapons seized and arrest made in Donagh, County Fermanagh
12 March	Huge firebomb outside Laganside Belfast courts defused; claimed by RIRA
12 March	Keith Rodgers, a PIRA man from County Louth, is shot dead in south Armagh; suggestions of possible feud with RIRA members
9 April	Five men jailed for between sixteen and twenty-two years for orchestrating bombing campaign in England
16 April	Bomb outside offices of DUP politician defused; CIRA claims responsibility

1 May	Blair postpones assembly elections until the autumn, accusing the PIRA of refusing fully to abjure paramilitarism; governments propose blueprint for breaking impasse
5 May	Bomb found outside Belfast government building on day of Belfast City May Bank Holiday Marathon
6 May	Bomb found in Merrion Square, Dublin, linked to dissidents
7 May	Bomb thrown at police car in Armagh defused
12 May	Parcel bomb sent to Ulster Unionist Party headquarters in east Belfast partially explodes, no-one hurt
13 June	Gardaí find significant haul of explosives near Hackballscross, County Louth; six men arrested, of whom four charged
15 June	PSNI intercept 1,200-pound vehicle bomb in Derry
19 June	Garda seizure of 500-pound van bomb of CIRA at Inniskeen, County Monaghan
23 June	Beginning of trial of McKevitt for directing terrorism and membership of an illegal organisation
2 July	Police claim to have smashed a RIRA 'spy ring' operating at the Royal Victoria Hospital in Belfast
16 July	Arrests in Dundalk and Netherlands; 5.5 million cigarettes found in County Monaghan
19 July	Masked gunmen place an incendiary device on a hijacked bus in west Belfast and force the driver to drive it to Woodbourne PSNI station
30 July	Series of bomb hoaxes cause morning commuter chaos in Belfast, with hijacked and stolen vehicles left at various targets
3 August	Training camp uncovered near Clonmel in County Tipperary; nine men later jailed
6 August	McKevitt found guilty; subsequently sentenced to twenty years in prison
11 August	Arrests and weapons seizures in England (in Morecambe, Lancashire); elsewhere, bullets were sent to Denis Bradley, vice-chairman of the NI Policing Board, and an independent member of the DPP in Derry, Marian Quinn

17 August	Daniel McGurk murdered in west Belfast; RIRA blamed
22 August	Car bomb exploded in Newry
29 August	Bomb found on County Down roadside near Newcastle
4 September	Four-man Independent Monitoring Commission set up to scrutinise paramilitary ceasefires; parties engaged in exploratory talks about restoration of devolution
16 September	Threats to members of policing partnership cause a resignation
17–19 September	Intimidation of members of district policing partnerships results in further resignations
11 October	130-pound car bomb found outside Rosslea police station, County Fermanagh
14 October	Bomb attack on Belfast police station
14 October	30-pound gas cylinder car bomb left outside a church in north Belfast, detonated by controlled explosion
18 November	45-pound bomb found in Newcastle, County Down; attempt to lure police to scene with a hoax device then detonate real bomb
24 November	Bomb injures two police officers at army base in Dungannon, County Tyrone; in a separate attack shots are fired at police headquarters in Armagh city
26 November	Despite protests from Trimble about the need first for more movement from PIRA, assembly election takes place: DUP and SF replace UUP and SDLP as the largest parties. The assembly would never meet
28 November	Police seize several million cigarettes in County Louth
15 December	Five men arrested by Gardaí in Cork and Limerick, accused of RIRA membership. The five, Ciarán O'Dwyer (Limerick), John Murphy (Cork), Ultan Larkin (Limerick), Aidan O'Driscoll (Cork) and Gerard Varian (Cork), were jailed in 2005

2004

14 January	Independent Catholic member of Armagh DPP is targeted in arson attack on her car in Tandragee

19 January	Home of independent member of Cookstown DPP in County Tyrone isattacked with a pipe bomb
4 February	Controlled explosion of lunchbox-type bomb attached to a bin, at Shackleton barracks in Ballykelly, County Londonderry. RIRA claims responsibility and pledges to carry out further attacks
13 February	Explosives discovery and arrest in Limerick
24 February	Secretary of state asks IMC to investigate the abduction with apparent intent to murder by PIRA members of Bobby Tohill, an alleged dissident republican
19 April	Letter bombs sent to DUP deputy leader Peter Robinson and Alex Attwood of SDLP; no-one hurt
21 April	Police seize a bolt-action sniper rifle in south Armagh
23 April	The civil action against the five men accused of responsibility for Omagh begins in Belfast – unprecedented move in British jurisdiction. Initially only McKevitt and Campbell offered defences – part of which was a denial of Real IRA involvement in Omagh
29 April	Bomb-making base found in Strabane, County Tyrone, together with six fully primed incendiary devices
4 May	Bullets sent in post to SDLP assembly member P.J. Bradley
24 May	Liam Campbell found guilty on membership charges; jailed for eight years with eighteen months suspended (and dated from 2001 when arrested). In February 2005 an appeal was rejected
14 June	70-pound bomb explodes at golf club, Lurgan, County Armagh
1 July	Belfast rush hour halted by bomb hoaxes; claimed by RIRA in protest at conditions in Maghaberry
13 July	CIRA designated by US government as foreign terrorist organisation, along with RSF
20 July	Punishment shooting in Strabane; victim ordered to leave the country by the RIRA
8 September	Three days of intensive all-party talks at Leeds Castle, Kent, end with the only agreement being to have more talks; DUP demands visible decommissioning of PIRA weapons; RIRA gun attack on Derry's Strand Road police station

14 September	Derry home of SDLP MLA Pat Ramsey attacked with petrol bombs – the fifth attack over the course of several months
17 September	Explosives and ammunition seized in west Belfast; three men arrested and charged
17 November	After two months of negotiations, governments put proposals to DUP and SF; parties agree to consult memberships; main stumbling blocks are visible decommissioning and Paisley's call for PIRA to 'wear sackcloth and ashes'; controlled explosion of firebomb in Belfast shop in city centre – RIRA admit planting the device
19 November	Two more incendiary devices are found at shops in Belfast
20 November	Firebomb in Belfast city centre store ignites; no-one injured
24 November	Another live incendiary device found in central Belfast; made safe by army bomb experts
December	Further incendiary attacks in Newtownabbey, Ballymena, Newry, Derry and Lisburn take the total number to at least sixteen. RIRA say they are attacks on 'the North's false economy and normalisation process' and pledge that they will continue: 'we are braced as never before to prevent the sell-out of our republican ideals of a united Ireland'
5 December	Police arrest three men and seize what are believed to be bomb components in County Longford
21 December	After several intensive meetings between Blair, Ahern and SF, an armed gang steals £26.6 million from Belfast Northern Bank

2005

1 January	Taxi driver forced to drive firebomb to Belfast police station; later claimed by CIRA
7 January	PSNI Chief Constable says PIRA carried out the Northern Bank robbery; Ahern says trust and confidence in the peace process has been damaged
9 January	Blast-bomb attack on Lurgan PSNI station
20 January	Pipe-bomb under van in Dublin
22 January	Agricultural supplies shop in Strabane destroyed by RIRA

incendiary device; police warn of new dissident republican fire-bomb campaign

30 January	Army bomb-experts defuse incendiary bomb in Strabane shop
30 January	PIRA members kill Robert McCartney in front of numerous witnesses in Belfast, which sets off a campaign by his five sisters and his partner to bring the murderers to justice
5 February	Police discover three firebombs in Ballymena, County Antrim
17 February	SDLP DPP member in Warrenpoint sent letter bomb; defused
24 February	Weapons seized and two arrested in north Belfast
12 March	Police in the Republic seize bomb-making equipment and a firearm in raids in the south and east of the country; three men arrested
20 March	Report that MI5 warning dissident threat level 'substantial'
14 April	Car bomb left at civic centre in Lisburn; described by police as 'crude but viable' and defused
8 June	Gardaí in Dublin investigating suspected RIRA activity recover a handgun from a car
9 July	Controlled explosion of pipe bomb at Coalisland police station, County Tyrone
14 July	Army defuses 'viable device' in a car near Milford, County Armagh; a coded bomb warning had claimed there were devices at fifteen other locations, but no others were found
28 July	PIRA promises henceforth to pursue an exclusively democratic and peaceful path
1 August	British government promise extensive reductions in army presence in NI, the closure of barracks, the de-fortification of police stations and repeal of counter-terrorist legislation peculiar to NI
9 August	'Crude but viable' bomb found in a taxi in Lurgan – the driver had been ordered to drive it to the police station. As the army worked to defuse the device, they were attacked by crowds throwing petrol bombs, bricks and other items; seven police officers were hurt
21 September	RIRA blamed for attack on the vice-chair of the Policing Board,

Denis Bradley, who was beaten by a masked man with a baseball bat in a public house in Derry

26 September   After a report from Father Alec Reid and the Reverend Harold Good, who have witnessed the process, the decommissioning body says PIRA has put all its weapons beyond use

2 November   2,000 people attending a UK retail conference have to be evacuated from Belfast's Waterfront Hall following a coded bomb-warning

5 November   9,000 people at Down Royal racecourse evacuated after suspect device found; RIRA blamed, though CIRA claim it

7 November   Body of Martin Conlon found near Armagh city – he had previously served a sentence in Portlaoise in relation to a RIRA training camp in Meath

27 November   Suspect bomb left outside the Derry home of SDLP MLA Pat Ramsey in the Bogside area; declared to be a hoax (eighth incident at his home)

8 December   Controlled explosion on dissident republican car bomb near Dublin – thought to be work of CIRA

16 December   Senior SF figure Denis Donaldson, one of three men against whom charges of spying at Stormont on behalf of PIRA had been dropped 'in the public interest', admits to having been a British agent but denies any republican spy ring

20 December   Man and his son shot in the leg in paramilitary-style shootings in Derry; claimed by RIRA

26 December   Down Royal racecourse again evacuated after telephone bomb warning; no device found

2006

1 February   IMC's eighth report notes the emergence of a splinter group from within CIRA going by the ONH title; based mainly around Strabane; also mentioned is SNH

9 February   'Crude' pipe bomb linked to CIRA placed under car in Dublin suburb of Kilbarrack; no-one injured

25 February   Riots in Dublin force the cancellation of a 'Love Ulster' parade; RSF play key role in leading protests, but deny instigating violence

14 March	Gardaí uncover RIRA-linked cannabis-growing operation in County Louth
21 March	Hoax device planted at the home of Pat Ramsey, MLA, bringing the number of such incidents to twelve
3 April	Murder of Denis Donaldson in County Donegal
5 April	Seven arrested in Belfast and later charged with possessing bomb-making materials
19 April	250-pound bomb seized in Lurgan, County Armagh; four arrested
1 June	Two men arrested and charged in Banbridge, County Down, with RIRA membership and smuggling cigarettes worth over £1 million
19 June	Police, working with MI5 and French police, make ten arrests in Armagh and Fermanagh and claim to have disrupted a 'potential major terrorist conspiracy'
24 June	Man charged in Craigavon, County Armagh, with RIRA membership and conspiracy to import weapons and explosives
27 June	Two men hijack a bus in north Belfast and force driver to take it to an Orange march in Glengormley, leave hoax device; RIRA later claim responsibility
2 July	Nail bomb in Bellaghy, County Derry – described as 'lethal and indiscriminate' by the police – but no-one injured
July	Pipe bomb in Strabane
13 July	Hoax device left at the home of Pat Ramsey, MLA, in the Bogside – the fourteenth such incident. Soon after, Ramsey moved out of his home
August onwards	Persistent attacks on Orange halls in counties Armagh and Antrim
9 August	RIRA firebomb attacks in Newry with nine devices cause millions of pounds of damage to several businesses. Sinn Féin MP Conor Murphy blames 'republican micro organisations' who are 'opposed to the peace process and opposed to the Good Friday Agreement', but who have 'little or no support within this community and … do not have a strategy to deliver Irish unity and independence'

12 August   RIRA claims two devices left on the Belfast–Dublin railway line near Newry. An alert also forces the closure of the main Belfast–Dublin road. During police searches, youths throw stones and petrol bombs at police

15 August   Partially detonated 70-pound bomb at site belonging to unionist peer, former senator Lord Ballyedmond, near Hackballscross in County Louth

16 August   Fires at two tyre stores in Dungannon believed to be caused by dissidents

30 August   Bomb planted at venue for DPP meeting in Newtownabbey, County Antrim; controlled explosion carried out by the army

4 October   IMC says CIRA, ONH and other dissident groups are active and RIRA a 'real threat'

7 October   Incendiary device left at B&Q retail store in Coleraine; causes £200,000 damage. Further attacks follow on outlets of the chain in south Belfast, Newtownabbey and Newry. CIRA claims responsibility, describing B&Q as a 'legitimate target' because it supplies the British army

13 October   After intensive multi-party talks at St Andrews in Scotland, governments unveil roadmap with 10 November deadline for the parties to respond and target date of 26 March for restoration of devolution; main divisive issue now SF's attitude to policing

16 October   CIRA claims responsibility for three paramilitary-style shootings of men aged seventeen to nineteen years old in Belfast over the previous month

18 October   Twenty-six-year-old man becomes the fourth man to be shot by the CIRA; a fifth man reported to have gone on the run to escape the group

27 October   Orde warns that dissidents are a major threat to latest efforts to achieve peace deal in NI

28 October   Gardaí announce major find of explosives in County Carlow

1 November   Co-ordinated firebomb attacks on Belfast retail stores cause £3 million damage. Peter Hain reveals that dissident firebombing over the previous seven months had cost some £25 million

9 November   Shots fired at PSNI station in Keady, County Armagh – IMC later attributed it to CIRA

9 November	Bomb found near Rosslea, County Fermanagh, after CIRA statement saying it had abandoned a landmine
5 December	Failed mortar attack on PSNI in Craigavon, County Armagh; bomb defused in the garden of a County Tyrone house; and 'viable device' removed from public house car park in Cloughcor, County Fermanagh
7 December	Pipe bomb at PSNI station Lurgan, County Armagh, fails to explode; later attributed by the IMC to the CIRA

2007

28 January	SF special party conference votes to support the PSNI
12 March	Fourteenth report of IMC warns dissident groups remain active and committed to terrorism, whereas PIRA has 'firmly committed' to the political path, disbanded its operational structures and not engaged in violent acts
12 March	Two former CIRA members, Ed Burns and Joe Jones, killed by ex-colleagues
25 March	It is reported that two members of RSF have received death threats from the IRLA – a group that split from CIRA – following the deaths of Burns and Jones
26 March	Ian Paisley and Gerry Adams announce power-sharing will return to NI on 8 May
9 April	32CSM-organised Easter parade in the Creggan in Derry – police are attacked with petrol bombs and bricks
8 May	Direct rule over NI by Westminster ends after four years and seven months: Paisley FM; Martin McGuinness DFM
31 May	SF takes seats on the Policing Board
15 July	Two bombs in Newry fail to injure army unit
7 August	400 pounds of explosives recovered by police in Craigavon; police come under sustained attack from crowd throwing stones, petrol bombs and other missiles in aftermath
23 August	Gun attack on the home of a former deputy mayor of Derry, independent nationalist councillor Liam Bradley

20 October   Paul Quinn from south Armagh beaten to death at a farm in County Monaghan; his family blame the Provisional IRA

8 November   Police officer Constable Jim Doherty shot and injured in Derry. RIRA claims attack, warning the police 'might not be so lucky the next time'. Speaking afterwards, Martin McGuinness declares, 'It is sad, almost pathetic, that a tiny, tiny microgroup believe that this attack was in the interest of Derry or Ireland. They are totally disconnected from the people of Derry who have bought into the peace process ... These people are living in the past and need to wake up to themselves and desist from this sort of action ... Those who are still wrapped up in selfish bitterness need to grow up and stop'

11 November   RIRA claims small 'grenade-style' device that exploded in ceremonial canon in Newry on Remembrance Sunday

12 November   Police officer Constable Paul Musgrave shot and badly injured by RIRA in Dungannon, County Tyrone

27 November   RIRA promises to launch more attacks against the police: 'We will continue to target Crown forces at a time and place of our choosing'

15 December   Pipe bomb thrown at PSNI station in Strabane, County Tyrone fails to explode but described as 'viable'

16 December   It is reported that police have carried out raids in Fermanagh and west Belfast and arrested two people, believed to be linked to imminent attacks on the PSNI

2008

5 January   CIRA fires shots over the grave of Dan Keating in County Mayo

22 January   Michael Campbell, brother of Liam, arrested in Vilnius in 'sting' operation, allegedly trying to buy arms

7 February   RIRA announces it intends to 'go back to war' by launching new offensive against 'legitimate targets'. In the aftermath, the police reintroduce VCPs in parts of Derry, south Down and south Armagh

12 February   Murder of Andrew Burns, former RIRA member, in Castlefin, County Donegal; later attributed by the IMC to the 'ONH' that had splintered from CIRA. The group was said to have only around twenty members and be based around Strabane

18 March	Senior republican Frank 'Bap' McGreevy is beaten to death in Belfast; thousands attend the funeral at which Gerry Adams speaks of 'the failure of the PSNI to respond properly to criminality in our community'
1 May	IMC report notes the existence of at least two clear factions within the RIRA. One of these would become increasingly associated with the label ONH (and the earlier group utilising that label effectively became moribund)
8 May	RIRA leave hoax device on Belfast–Dublin railway line at Poyntzpass, County Armagh; coincides with high-profile US international investment conference in Belfast
9 May	Incendiary device left in toy store in Cookstown, County Tyrone, believed to be work of ONH
12 May	Catholic police officer Constable Ryan Crozier is badly injured near Castlederg, County Tyrone, by bomb underneath his car
21 May	Two incendiary devices found in McDonald's in Cookstown, County Tyrone
26 May	Punishment shooting of man alleged by RIRA to be a drug dealer in Armagh city; incendiary device placed in Belfast store
5 June	Peter Robinson succeeds Paisley as first minister
14 June	Two PSNI officers lured to site of 150-pound landmine bomb near Rosslea, County Fermanagh; the officers escape when the device malfunctions and only partially explodes
19 June	Northern Irish Executive meets for the last time before impasse over the devolution of policing and justice powers deadlocks business
24 June	Emmett Shiels, a pizza delivery man, is shot dead in the Creggan area of Derry; INLA later blamed
16 August	Attack on PSNI foot patrol in Lisnaskea, County Fermanagh, sees two officers slightly injured; rocket-propelled grenade, powered by Semtex, fails to fire
26 August	Rioting in the Tullygally and Drumbeg estates of Craigavon, County Armagh. PSNI officers are attacked with stones and petrol bombs, followed by a gun attack. It is subsequently reported that 'veterans of the Provisional IRA's North Armagh brigade' were responsible for orchestrating the violence, having defected from the Provisionals

11 September	Car bomb mistakenly targeted at a school teacher in Ballyskeagh, Lisburn, fails to detonate
12 September	Éamonn Hughes, a former republican, is stabbed to death by youths in Dungannon
13 September	220-pound bomb found in hedge in Jonesborough, south Armagh
16 September	Gun attack on Belfast house
25 September	Alleged drug dealer shot and injured in Donegal
4 October	Bomb found near Newtownbutler, County Fermanagh
23 October	Serious rioting in Craigavon, County Armagh
18 November	It is announced that a deal has been reached to resolve the stalemate over the devolution of policing and justice; the Executive meets two days later, ending a 152-day hiatus in its operation

2009

4 January	Five people are arrested in Dublin in connection with ongoing dissident republican activity; seven guns and ammunition are also recovered
29 January	Two men are arrested and a gun seized by police investigating dissident republican activity in Dublin
31 January	300-pound car bomb found in Castlewellan, County Down after telephone warning; it is believed to have been destined for Ballykinler army base
5 March	RIRA faction utilising the name ONH claims responsibility for a paramilitary-style shooting in west Belfast – the fifth such attack since the start of 2009
6 March	Sir Hugh Orde says the threat posed by dissident republicans is at a 'critical' level and the highest since he became Chief Constable in 2002. Orde announces that he has requested the deployment of members of the Special Reconnaissance Regiment in Fermanagh
7 March	Sappers Mark Quinsey and Patrick Azimcar are murdered in a dissident republican attack on Massereene army barracks in County Antrim; two other soldiers and two pizza delivery men are seriously injured; the attack is later claimed by the 'South Antrim Brigade of the Real IRA'

9 March	PSNI Constable Stephen Carroll is murdered in a gun attack in Craigavon, County Armagh; CIRA claim responsibility
10 March	Martin McGuinness, standing alongside Sir Hugh Orde and Peter Robinson, condemns those responsible for the murders, describing them as 'traitors to the island of Ireland'
14 March	Colin Duffy, a prominent republican from Lurgan, is arrested in connection with the Massereene barracks murders; he would later be charged in connection with the attack
30 March	Series of co-ordinated security alerts in Belfast because of hoax devices left near various police stations and prominent roads; a man is the victim of a paramilitary-style 'punishment' shooting in Derry
31 March	A gang of masked men attack and attempt to hijack seven vehicles over a nine-hour period in Lurgan
1 April	One man shot in Belfast and another in Derry in a further spate of paramilitary-style attacks
3 April	Bomb alert near Rosslea, County Fermanagh – turns out to be an elaborate hoax; IMC later attributes it to CIRA
6 April	Home of Mitchel McLaughlin, SF MLA, attacked in Derry
9 April	Another man is shot in Belfast in paramilitary-style attack
9 April	Easter edition of *An Phoblacht*, for the first time, does not contain an Easter statement from the IRA; instead it merely carries a 'Sinn Féin leadership Easter statement'
12 April	SF office in Derry shopping centre damaged in arson attack
12 April	RIRA statement on Easter Sunday in Derry; in an interview with the *Sunday Tribune* RIRA claims responsibility for the 2006 murder of Denis Donaldson, threatens members of the PSNI and ex-IRA informers and pledges to carry out attacks in Britain
24 April	It is reported that Martin McGuinness has been warned by the PSNI of a threat to his life from dissident republicans; also that employees of Belfast City Council have received death threats and bullets in the post from dissident republicans operating under the name 'North Belfast Republican Brigade'
27 April	Home of SF MLA Daithí McKay (also a member of the Policing Board) attacked in the village of Rasharkin, County Antrim

7 May	Latest report from the IMC describes the dissidents as being 'highly dangerous', though also notes they did not yet have the 'capacity to mount a consistent and substantial campaign'
11 May	At a rally in Derry, Martin McGuinness calls on the 32CSM to condemn attacks on the home of Sinn Féin politician Mitchel McLaughlin
12 May	A spokesman for the 32CSM condemns the attack on Mitchel McLaughlin's home
22 May	Attack on Rasharkin Orange Hall – repeated on 24 May
23 May	The car of Bobby Storey, a senior republican in west Belfast (and chairman of Belfast Sinn Féin), is destroyed
2 June	Séamus Brady of west Belfast is shot in both knees in a paramilitary-style attack, claimed by RIRA/ONH
4 June	Two cars are set alight outside the home of Conor Murphy, Sinn Féin MP and minister in the Northern Ireland Executive; that evening another man is shot in the ankles and wrists in a paramilitary attack in west Belfast
5 June	Orange hall is burnt down in Keady, County Armagh; halls in Newtownhamilton and Newcastle had also been targeted over the previous two weeks
15 June	Semtex device left at Strand Road PSNI station in Derry
15 June	A DPP meeting in east Belfast is attacked by republican protestors, believed to be linked to the IRSP. Reports hold that prominent republican Bobby Storey remonstrated with the protestors
28 June	RAAD claim responsibility for shooting a man in the legs in the Rosemount area of Derry; in the aftermath, Criminal Justice Minister Paul Goggins admits there is 'no end in sight' to dissident republican violence
3 July	Dissident republicans claim an explosive device that had been left in Newtownbutler
10 July	A series of hoax bomb alerts in Belfast and Derry cause widespread commuter disruption
13 July	Serious rioting breaks out in Ardoyne, north Belfast, during an Orange parade, and continues for three nights. Shots are fired at the police. Sinn Féin's Gerry Kelly criticises those behind the

Ardoyne rioting, while RNU and éirígí members are noted to have been present in support of the rioters. Elsewhere, disturbances occur in Rasharkin (where an Orange hall is targeted), Wattlebridge near Newtownbutler (where another Orange lodge is attacked) and Derry

14 July	An Orange lodge is attacked with a petrol bomb in Dunloy, near Ballymoney – the latest in a series of attacks on the premises
15 July	Gerry Kelly says that police have warned him of a dissident threat against his life
20 July	RAAD tells the *Derry Journal* that an alleged drug dealer will be 'executed on sight' when they find him
21 July	Five men are jailed by the Special Criminal Court in Dublin for INLA-related activity
23 July	Brian Shivers, a former éirígí member from Maghera, is charged in connection with the Massereene attack
31 July	RIRA admits to sending six bullets in an envelope to relatives of police officers working in a bank in Derry; DPP meeting in Derry is called off due to protests from 32CSM
19 August	INLA shoot man in the leg in Derry's Waterside
21 August	Armed and masked men set up road block in Meigh, near Newry in south Armagh and distribute leaflets warning people not to co-operate with the police or Sinn Féin. A police patrol that approaches the block withdraws rather than force a confrontation
8 September	600-pound roadside bomb with command wire running across the border into the Republic is discovered near Forkhill in south Armagh; attributed to RIRA/ONH
11 September	RIRA in Derry claims responsibility for leaving pipe bombs at the homes of the relatives of a PSNI officer from the Shantallow area. The group also claims a punishment shooting in the Hazelbank area
16 September	Three men from Lurgan, linked to CIRA, are jailed for fifteen years each in connection with a mortar-bomb plot to kill police officers earlier that year. Their sentences lead to serious rioting in the Kilwilkie Estate, which sees the hijacking of vehicles which are then placed on the Belfast–Dublin railway line (closing it for thirty-eight hours); that same day a hoax alert in Rosslea, Fermanagh, forces fifteen families out of their homes

18 September	PSNI in the Greater Belfast region launch Operation Descent – involving mobile vehicle checkpoints and increased security measures in an effort to combat a feared dissident 'spectacular' to mark the impending arrival of Matt Baggott as the new Chief Constable
19 September	Sectarian attacks on Orange halls in Ballymoney and Rasharkin in County Antrim
22 September	Bomb defused outside Lavin Orange Hall in Armoy, north Antrim
23 September	Meeting of the Derry DPP disrupted by protestors from the 32CSM and RNU
29 September	Dissident republicans blamed for shooting a man five times in Twinbrook in west Belfast
8 October	Man shot in the leg in paramilitary attack in the Bogside in Derry; police investigating the incident are attacked by a crowd throwing stones and other missiles. In Strabane shots are fired by masked men over the coffin of John Brady, a former member of the PIRA suspected of dissident involvement, who had died while in police custody the previous weekend
16 October	Bomb explodes under the car of a woman in east Belfast; intended target believed to be her partner, a PSNI dog handler; attack later claimed by RIRA/ONH
17 October	RAAD shoot a 17-year-old in the legs in the Waterside area of Derry, accusing him of being 'heavily involved' in anti-social behaviour
22 October	Bomb explodes inside a Territorial Army base in north Belfast; later claimed by RIRA
31 October	Youths in Crossmaglen attack the local PSNI station with petrol bombs and paint containers
3 November	RAAD shoot a man in the Creggan area of Derry
8 November	A Remembrance Day parade in Bellaghy, County Londonderry, is cancelled after police receive a warning that a viable device had been planted
9 November	It is reported that dozens of judges in Northern Ireland have had 24-hour security restored after coming under threat from dissident republicans
18 November	The army makes safe a 'horizontal mortar', designed to kill police officers, in the Friary Road area of Armagh

20 November	A man is shot in the leg in Beechmount Crescent in west Belfast; CIRA later claim responsibility
21 November	400-pound car bomb partially explodes outside the Policing Board's headquarters in Belfast; elsewhere, the security forces successfully prevent a dissident attack on a police officer in Garrison, County Fermanagh. Four men are arrested by undercover police, acting on information supplied by the Special Reconnaissance Regiment
23 November	Elaborate hoax device causes disruption in Armagh
30 November	Pipe bomb is thrown at Strabane police station, but fails to explode
6 December	Police responding to two pipe bomb attacks in the Creggan in Derry are attacked by a crowd throwing petrol bombs, bricks and stones. Three other pipe bombs were planted that evening, all of which were later claimed by RAAD
7 December	Two hoax devices are left outside banks in south Belfast
11 December	Two men are shot in the legs by RAAD in the Creggan area of Derry. Police trying to help the victims are attacked by youths throwing missiles.
17 December	A man is shot in the hands, ankles, knees and calves in west Belfast
30 December	Shots fired at Crossmaglen PSNI station

2010

7 January	Man is shot in the leg by masked men in Armagh
8 January	Car bomb attack near Randalstown, County Antrim critically injures Constable Peadar Heffron, an Irish-language specialist for the PSNI and captain of the PSNI GAA team
12 January	Masked gunmen shoot a man in the legs in west Belfast
18 January	Man shot in the leg in Lurgan in paramilitary attack
20 January	Alleged drug dealer Gerard 'Topper' Staunton is shot dead in Cork. The 32CSM later release a statement from the RIRA claiming responsibility and promising to take further action against drug dealers

24 January	Gun attack on Crossmaglen police station
27 January	RAAD shoot and seriously injure man who owns a shop selling legal highs in Derry
29 January	Two INLA members, arrested in Dublin in September 2008 in possession of explosive materials, are sentenced to nine years in jail
31 January	RIRA gun attack on Bessbrook PSNI station
3 February	Pipe-bomb attack on Old Park police station in north Belfast, claimed by the 'Real IRA Belfast Brigade'; police foil suspected dissident attack when they stop a car near Stranorlar in County Donegal
8 February	Statement announces that INLA has decommissioned its weaponry – comes after November 2009 statement confirming that its armed struggle was over
9 February	Dissolution of the IICD
19 February	Mortar bomb left outside Keady PSNI station
22 February	250-pound car bomb in Newry detonates outside the court house
23 February	Hoax bomb alert in Lurgan; 29-year-old man is shot in both legs by RAAD in the Creggan area of Derry
24 February	Real IRA admits responsibility for murdering Kieran Doherty, 31, in Derry
26 February	Hoax device in north Belfast causes major traffic disruption
27 February	Hoax device used to draw police officers and then a suspected mortar bomb is fired at Brownlow PSNI station in Craigavon; the incident is followed by serious rioting in the Drumbeg and Meadowbrook estates of the town
1 March	Police vehicles attacked with petrol bombs in west Belfast
19 March	RIRA claims four devices left around Derry, causing security alerts (notably outside Strand Road police station and Bishop Street courthouse); a series of hoax alerts in Belfast bring traffic and railway lines to standstill in afternoon rush hour
20 March	'Viable device' is discovered in Magherafelt and destroyed by a controlled explosion; suspicious device left on the railway line in

	Newry and police are shot at while investigating the incident (later declared to be a hoax)
28 March	Four masked men claiming to be RIRA members hijack a van on the Coshquin Road in Derry and then abandon it in Bridgend – leading to a security alert; RAAD claims two pipe-bombs left in vehicles in the Creggan area of Derry
29 March	RAAD leaves pipe-bomb planted outside a shop selling legal highs in Letterkenny, County Donegal; it also raids a house in Dungiven and warns a man to 'cease' his activities
2 April	Man attacked in paramilitary assault in north Belfast
3 April	Car bomb left outside PSNI station in Crossmaglen
3–5 April	Easter commemorations held across Ireland by dissident groups

Bibliography

INTERVIEWS CARRIED OUT BY THE AUTHOR

Tony Catney, Belfast, 22 June 2009
Brian Leeson, Dublin, 24 June 2009
Breandán Mac Cionnaith, Portadown, 22 June 2009
Anthony McIntyre, 30 October 2009
Danny Morrison, London, 12 March 2005
Ruairí Ó Brádaigh, Dublin, 24 June 2009
Sean O'Callaghan, London, 12 December 2009
Richard Walsh, Belfast, 23 June 2009

NEWSPAPERS, NEWSLETTERS AND MAGAZINES

An Phoblacht
An Phoblacht/Republican News
Andersonstown News
Beir Bua: The Honest Voice of Republicanism
Belfast Telegraph
Daily Ireland
Daily Mail
Daily Record (Scotland)
Daily Telegraph
Derry Journal
Derry News
éirígí Newsletter
Financial Times
Fortnight
Forum Magazine
Fourthwrite

Galway City Tribune
Guardian
Impartial Reporter
Ireland on Sunday
Irish Echo
Irish Examiner
Irish Independent
Irish News
Irish Republican Information Service
Irish Republican News
Irish Times
Londonderry Sentinel
Magill
Nenagh Guardian
Newry Democrat
News Letter
Parliamentary Brief
Saoirse – Irish Freedom: The Voice of the Republican Movement
Scotland on Sunday
Sunday Business Post
Sunday Independent
Sunday Life
Sunday Mirror
Sunday Telegraph
Sunday Times
Sunday Times (Irish edition)
Sunday Tribune
Sunday World
The Cambridge Student
The Independent
The Irish World
The Observer
The Sovereign Nation
The Times
Toronto Globe and Mail
Tyrone Times
Ulster Herald
Village Magazine

MEMOIRS, PARTY PAPERS, OFFICIAL DOCUMENTS AND OTHER
PRIMARY MATERIAL

32 County Sovereignty Movement Press Releases

32 County Sovereignty Movement, *Suspension of Stormont: Suspension of Democracy?* (32CSM Educational Department, n.d.)

32 County Sovereignty Movement, *Sovereignty and Sectarianism* (32CSM Educational Department, n.d.)

32 County Sovereignty Movement, *80 Years Under Attack: Who Still Stands by the Republic?* (32 CSM Educational Department, 2003)

An Address to the People of Ireland from Republican Sinn Féin Poblachtach (Dublin: Republican Sinn Féin, 2003)

An Historical Analysis of the IRSP; Its Past Role, Root Cause of its Problems and Proposals for the Future, IRSP Information Sheet (n.d.)

Beir Bua: The Thread of the Irish Republican Movement from the United Irishmen Through to Today (Dublin: Republican Sinn Féin, n.d.)

Bloody Sunday 2008: Truth and Lies (pamphlet available at http://www.serve.com/pfc/cases/bs/bs2008.pdf)

Cabhair Testimonial Journal (Dublin, 1999)

Charlie Kerins: 50th Anniversary (Dublin: Republican Sinn Féin, 1994)

Collins, É. *Killing Rage* (London: Granta, 1997)

Constitution of the 32 County Sovereignty Movement

Éire Nua: A New Democracy (Dublin: Republican Sinn Féin, March 2000)

Independent Monitoring Commission Reports (one to twenty-three)

Irish Republican Prisoners Welfare Association (IRPWA) Press Releases

Maghaberry Prison Protest, Leaflet (Republican Sinn Féin, 2006)

McIntyre, A. *Good Friday: The Death of Irish Republicanism* (New York: Ausubo, 2008)

Ó Brádaigh, R. *Dílseacht: The Story of Comdt. Gen. Tom Maguire and the Second (All-Ireland) Dáil* (Dublin: Irish Freedom Press, 1997)

O'Callaghan, S. *The Informer* (London: Bantam, 1998)

O'Rawe, R. *Blanketmen: An Untold Story of the H-Block Hunger Strike* (Dublin: New Island Books, 2005)

Powell, J. *Great Hatred, Little Room: Making Peace in Northern Ireland* (London: The Bodley Head, 2008)

Proclamation of the Irish Republic (1916)

Programme of Motions for RSF Árd Fheis/National Conference, 2000

Programme of Motions for RSF Árd Fheis/National Conference, 13–14 October 2001

Programme of Motions for RSF Árd Fheis/National Conference, 19–20 October 2002

Protest against US State Department, Leaflet (Republican Sinn Féin, n.d.)

Republican Resistance Calendar 2009

Republican Sinn Féin, *Elections and Abstentionism: Republican Education 3* (Dublin, 2000)

Republican Sinn Féin, *Where We Stand: Republican Education 1* (Dublin, 2000)

Republican Sinn Féin, *Youth in Republican Sinn Féin: Republican Education 5* (Dublin, 2000)

Saol Nua: A New Way of Life (Dublin: Republican Sinn Féin, 2004)

Sinn Féin, *The Politics of Revolution: The Main Speeches and Debates from the 1986 Sinn Féin Árd Fheis* (Dublin, 1986)

Speech of Des Long on Motion 16, Dublin, 31 November 1996 (Republican Sinn Féin, 1996)

Stormont Election Manifesto, 2007 (Republican Sinn Féin, February 2007)

Support Crossan: The POW Candidate: Spoil Your Vote for Political Status, Leaflet (Republican Sinn Féin, 2001)

'The Ballad of Ronan MacLochlainn'

Towards a Lasting Peace in Ireland (Dublin: Sinn Féin, 1992)

Transcript of Interview Between Damien Okado-Gough and Member of RIRA Army Council, January 2003 (available in Linenhall Library Northern Ireland Political Collection)

SPEECHES

Martin Galvin, *Speech to IRPWA Meeting*, Belfast, 18 August 2000

Martin McGuinness, *Oration to Annual Wolfe Tone Commemoration*, Bodenstown, 22 June 1986

Anthony McIntyre, *Speech Made to Sinn Féin Internal Conference*, the RDS, Dublin, 30 September 1995

Ruairí Ó Brádaigh, *Address on Behalf of the National Executive to the 83rd Árd Fheis of Sinn Féin in the Spa Hotel, Lucan, County Dublin, October 24 and 25, 1987*

Ruairí Ó Brádaigh, *A Permanent Peace Depends on Ending British Rule, Not Updating It: Presidential Address to the 93rd Árd Fheis of Sinn Féin Poblachtach*, Dublin, 9 November 1997

Ruairí Ó Brádaigh, *Participation in Partition Parliament Denial of Sovereignty: Wolfe Tone Commemoration 2006*, Bodenstown, 11 June 2006

Ruairí Ó Brádaigh, *Stormont an Obstacle to Realising Ideals of 1916: Speech Given at the GPO*, Dublin, Easter Monday, 9 April 2007

S. Murphy, *Address Given at Bundoran Hunger Strike Commemoration, August 2000* (Dublin: Republican Sinn Féin, 2000)

Sean Ó Brádaigh, *Oration at Bodenstown, 15 June 2003* (Dublin: Republican Sinn Féin, 2003)

Marian Price, *Speech to 32CSM Árd Fheis 2000*, Carrickarnon, County Louth, 24 June 2000

Marian Price, *Funeral Oration for Joseph O'Connor*, Belfast, 18 October 2000

Marian Price, *Voice of the Lark Speech: Legacy of the Hunger Strikes: Lessons Learned, Lessons Forgotten*, Conway Mill, Belfast 31 January 2001

INTERNET RESOURCES

32 County Sovereignty Movement Derry, http://www.derry32csm.com

32 County Sovereignty Movement Tyrone, http://www.32csmtyrone.com/aboutus.htm

ARK Northern Ireland Elections Website, http://www.ark.ac.uk

BBC News online, http://news.bbc.co.uk

Brendan 'Darkie' Hughes, 1948–2008 RIP, http://dorcha.webs.com

CAIN (Conflict Archive in Northern Ireland), http://cain.ulst.ac.uk

Centre for Public Inquiry, http://www.publicinquiry.ie

Dáil Éireann Parliamentary Debates, http://historical-debates.oireachtas.ie

eirígí, http://www.eirigi.org

Elections Ireland, http://electionsireland.org

Electoral Office for Northern Ireland, http://www.eoni.org.uk

Gerry McGeough Blog, http://gerrymcgeough.blogspot.com

Hansard: House of Commons Northern Ireland Select Committee Evidence, http://www.parliament.the-stationery-office.co.uk

Hansard: House of Commons Written Answers, http://www.publications.parliament.uk/pa/cm199900/cmhansrd

Hansard: House of Lords Debates, http://www.parliament.the-stationery-office.co.uk/pa/ld/ldhansrd.htm

Irish Republican Socialist Movement, http://irsm.org

New Republican Forum, http://www.newrepublicanforum.ie [available via web archive]
Northern Ireland Office, http://www.nio.gov.uk
Ógra Shinn Féin, http://ograshinnfein.blogspot.com
Omagh Bomb Digital Archive, http://hq-obda-01.welbni.org/Osshg.html
Republican Network for Unity, http://www.republicannetwork.ie
Republican Sinn Féin, http://www.rsf.ie/intro.htm
RTÉ News, http://www.rte.ie/news
Slugger O'Toole, http://sluggerotoole.com
The Blanket, http://lark.phoblacht.net [and archived at http://indiamond6.ulib.iupui.edu:81/]
The Pensive Quill, http://thepensivequill.am
Traditional Unionist Voice, http://www.tuv.org.uk
Uncovering the Truth About the 1981 Hunger Strike, http://www.longkesh.info

TELEVISION PROGRAMMES

'Leargas: The Brookeborough Raid', RTÉ, 9 July 2006
'Newsnight', BBC Two, 28 November 2007
'On the Record', BBC One, 21 January 2001
'Panorama: Who Bombed Omagh?', BBC One, 9 October 2000.
'Prime Time: Leaders' Debate', RTÉ, 16 May 2007

SECONDARY SOURCES

Alonso, R. *The IRA and Armed Struggle* (London: Routledge, 2007)
Bew, J., Frampton, M. and Gurruchaga, I. *Talking to Terrorists: Making Peace in Northern Ireland and the Basque Country* (London: Hurst & Co., 2009)
Bew, P., Gibbon, P. and Patterson, H. *Northern Ireland 1921–2001: Political Forces and Social Classes* (London: Serif, 2002)
Bew, P. *Ireland: The Politics of Enmity, 1789–2006* (Oxford: Oxford University Press, 2007)
Bew, P. *The Making and Remaking of the Good Friday Agreement* (Dublin: Liffey Press, 2007)
Bishop, P. and Mallie, E. *The Provisional IRA* (London: Corgi, 1988)

Bourke, R. *Peace in Ireland: The War of Ideas* (London: Pimlico, 2003)

Bowman-Grieve, L. 'Irish Republicanism and the Internet: Support for the New Wave of Dissidents', *Perspectives on Terrorism*, 4, 2 (May 2010)

Bowyer Bell, J. *The Secret Army: The IRA, 1916–1979* (Dublin: Academy Press, 1979)

Bowyer Bell, J. *The IRA, 1968–2000* (London: Frank Cass Publishers, 2000)

Collins, É. *Killing Rage* (London: Granta, 1997)

Coogan, T.P. *The IRA* (London: HarperCollins, 2000)

Cruise O'Brien, C. *States of Ireland* (London: Hutchinson, 1972)

Dudley Edwards, R. *The Faithful Tribe: An Intimate Portrait of the Loyal Institutions* (London: HarperCollins, 2000)

Dudley Edwards, R. *Patrick Pearse: The Triumph of Failure*, 2nd edition (Dublin: Irish Academic Press, 2006)

Dudley Edwards, R. *Aftermath: The Omagh Bombing and the Families' Pursuit of Justice* (London: Harvill Secker, 2009)

Dunphy, R. *The Making of Fianna Fáil Power in Ireland, 1923–1948* (Oxford: Clarendon Press, 1995)

English, R. *Radicals and the Republic: Socialist Republicanism in the Irish Free State, 1925–1937* (Oxford: The Clarendon Press, 1994)

English, R. *Armed Struggle: A History of the IRA* (London: Macmillan, 2003)

English, R. *Irish Freedom: The History of Nationalism in Ireland* (London: Macmillan, 2006)

Foley, C. *Legion of the Rearguard: The IRA and the Modern Irish State* (London: Pluto Press, 1992)

Foster, R.F. *Modern Ireland, 1600–1972* (London: Allen Lane, 1988)

Frampton, M. *The Long March: The Political Strategy of Sinn Féin, 1981–2007* (Basingstoke: Palgrave Macmillan, 2009)

Garvin, T. *Nationalist Revolutionaries in Ireland, 1858–1928* (Dublin: Gill & Macmillan, 2005)

Godson, D. *Himself Alone: David Trimble and the Ordeal of Unionism* (London: HarperCollins, 2004)

Hanley, B. *The IRA, 1926–1936* (Dublin: Four Courts Press, 2002)

Hanley, B. and Millar, S. *The Lost Revolution: The Story of the Official IRA and the Workers' Party* (Dublin: Penguin Ireland, 2009)

Harnden, T. *'Bandit Country': The IRA and South Armagh* (London: Hodder & Stoughton, 1999)

Hart, P. *The IRA at War, 1916–1923* (Oxford: Oxford University Press, 2003)

Hennessey, T. *The Northern Ireland Peace Process: Ending the Troubles?* (Dublin: Gill & Macmillan, 2000)

Hennessey, T. *The Evolution of the Troubles, 1970–2* (Dublin: Irish Academic Press, 2007)

Holland, J. and McDonald, H. *INLA: Deadly Divisions* (Dublin: Torc, 1994)

Holland, J. and Phoenix, S. *Phoenix: Policing the Shadows: The Secret War Against Terrorism in Northern Ireland* (London: Hodder & Stoughton, 1996)

Lee, J.J. *Ireland, 1912–1985* (Cambridge: Cambridge University Press, 1989)

Lynn, B. 'Tactic or Principle? The Evolution of Republican Thinking on Abstentionism in Ireland, 1970–1998', *Irish Political Studies*, 17, 2 (2002)

Mac Eoin, U. *The IRA in the Twilight Years, 1923–1948* (Dublin: Argenta Publications, 1997)

McIntyre, A. 'Modern Irish Republicanism: The Product of British State Strategies', *Irish Political Studies*, 10, 1 (1995)

McMahon, P. *British Spies and Irish Rebels: British Intelligence and Ireland, 1916–1945* (Woodbridge: Boydell Press, 2008)

Maillot, A. *New Sinn Féin: Irish Republicanism in the Twenty-First Century* (London: Routledge, 2004)

Mallie, E. and McKittrick, D. *Endgame in Ireland* (London: Hodder & Stoughton, 2001)

Millar, F. *David Trimble: The Price of Peace* (Dublin: The Liffey Press, 2004)

Moloney, E. *A Secret History of the IRA* (London: Allen Lane, 2002)

Mooney J. and O'Toole, M. *Black Operations: The Secret War against the Real IRA* (Ashbourne, Co. Meath: Maverick House, 2003).

Murray, G. and Tonge, J. *Sinn Féin and the SDLP: From Alienation to Participation* (London: C. Hurst & Co., 2005)

Myers, K. *Watching the Door: A Memoir, 1971–1978* (Dublin: Lilliput Press, 2006)

Neumann, P. *Britain's Long War: British Strategy in the Northern Ireland Conflict, 1969–98* (London, 2003)

Ó Broin, E. *Sinn Féin and the Politics of Left Republicanism* (London: Pluto Press, 2009)

O'Doherty, M. *The Trouble with Guns: Republican Strategy and the Provisional IRA* (Belfast: Blackstaff Press, 1998)

O'Halpin, E. *Defending Ireland: The Irish State and its Enemies since 1922* (Oxford: Oxford University Press, 2000)

Patterson, H. *The Politics of Illusion: A Political History of the IRA* (London: Serif, 1997)

Patterson, H. 'Sinn Féin and the Peace Process: The End of the Republican Project?' (unpublished seminar paper given to the Cambridge University, Irish Studies Group, 13 May 2003)

Smith, M.L.R. *Fighting for Ireland? The Military Strategy of the Irish Republican Movement* (London: Routledge, 1997)

Tonge, J. '"They Haven't Gone Away You Know": Irish Republican Dissidents and "Armed Struggle"', *Terrorism and Political Violence*, 16, 3 (2004), pp.671–93

Toolis, K. *Rebel Hearts: Journeys within the IRA's Soul* (London: Picador, 1995)

Townshend, C. *Political Violence in Ireland: Government and Resistance since 1848* (Oxford: The Clarendon Press, 1983)

Townshend, C. *Easter 1916: The Irish Rebellion* (London: Allen Lane, 2005)

Walsh, P. *Irish Republicanism and Socialism: The Politics of the Republican Movement, 1905–1994* (Belfast: Athol Books, 1994)

White, R. *Provisional Irish Republicans: An Oral and Interpretive History* (London: Greenwood Press, 1993)

White, R. *Ruairí Ó Brádaigh: The Life and Politics of an Irish Revolutionary* (Bloomington, IN: Indiana University Press, 2006)

Index

32 County Sovereignty Movement (32CSM), 97–106, 121–32, 142, 159
2002-2006 period, 163, 182–90, 192, 193, 202, 208, 209, 211–12, 215–16, 285
2007-10 period, 212–18, 221–4, 246, 251, 253, 260, 261, 264, 266, 279–80, 281, 286–7
'advice centres' and branches, 186, 214–15, 259
armed struggle and, 98, 99, 100–1, 121–3, 129–36, 139–40, 143, 163, 217, 281, 286–7
The Blanket and, 162–3
designated as terrorist organisation in USA, 135–6
electoral politics and, 186
Irish Democracy: A Framework for Unity (2005), 186–7
Omagh bombing and, 104–5, 106
OSSHG and, 133, 134
other dissident groups and, 82, 221, 222–4
policing and, 183, 184, 208, 209, 213, 215–16, 223, 261
Marian Price and, 57, 98, 99–100, 101, 124–6, 131, 133, 159, 163, 186, 212, 279
Real IRA and, 97, 100–6, 113–14, 121–4, 128–36, 140, 183, 185, 187, 202, 217, 281
republican ideology and, 182–4, 280, 281
republican prisoners and, 127–8, 187–90 213
social issues and, 213, 214–15
The Sovereign Nation, 123, 124, 137, 182, 184, 213–14, 217
UN initiative, 101–3, 126, 186
Abernathy, Thomas Noel, 113
Adams, Gerry
abstentionism and, 47–50, 51, 52, 114
on alleged PIRA crimes, 252, 253
'appeal' to IRA (2005), 4, 5, 57
armed struggle and, 3–4, 252, 282
criticism of leadership *see* Provisional republicanism, criticism of Adams-McGuinness leadership
criticism of within party, 225–6, 227–9, 264
dual approach and, 47–50, 51
electoral politics and, 69, 225–6
hunger strikes and, 164–5, 267
on March 2009 killings, 249–50, 263–4
'modernisation' of Provisional movement, 47–53, 54, 59–60, 114
Official IRA and, 50, 124–5, 171, 202
peace process and, 3–4, 38, 75, 90–1, 116, 124, 139, 265
policing and, 206, 207
Real IRA and, 107, 116, 138, 139, 178

'republican veto' and, 94
scandals and accusations (2009-10 periods), 229
Ahern, Bertie, 14, 103, 105, 106, 132, 213
Ahern, Dermot, 258
Aiken, Frank, 23
Allister, Jim, 7
al-Qaeda, 120, 167, 214
Amazon website, 133
Andersonstown News, 178–9, 187
Anglo-Irish Treaty (December 1921), 15–16, 17, 23, 46, 55–6, 61, 102, 175, 183
Ardoyne rioting (July 2009), 263
'Armed Forces Day' in Northern Ireland, 235
armed struggle and violence
1926–36 period, 21, 25
1996–2000 period, 74, 108, 109, 117–22, 140, 142, 147
2001–2006 period, 138, 141, 142–5, 147–8, 162, 173, 176, 177–8, 179, 181, 192
2006-10 period, 1, 67, 76–7, 217, 219, 240, 243–51, 253–63, 279–82, 284, 286
2006–10 period as potential 'tipping point', 266–7
32CSM and, 98, 99, 100–1, 121–3, 129–36, 139–40, 143, 163, 217, 281, 286–7
Gerry Adams and, 3–4, 252, 282
Belfast Agreement's inability to end, 6
border campaign (1956-62), 32–3, 34, 45, 71, 84, 148
Continuity IRA and, 80, 281
see also under Continuity IRA (CIRA), violence éirígí and, 239–43, 263–4, 282
'England Campaign' (1939-40), 26–9, 148
INLA violence (1970s-80s), 92
insurrectionist violence of 1916 and, 14
Irish-American republican groups and, 111–13, 114
Martin McGuinness, 49, 252, 282
Omagh bombing as 'defining moment', 104, 106–7, 147, 157, 162
PIRA and, 38, 47, 48, 49, 54–5, 139–40, 252, 282, 283
PIRA's official end of (2005), 5, 178, 184, 191, 193–4, 201–3, 267
post-2002 support for, 181–92
Real IRA and *see also under* Real IRA (RIRA), violence, 91–2, 93, 95–6, 103, 118–22, 172–3, 174–6, 177–8, 179, 181
RSF and, 54–5, 57, 73, 75–7, 79, 80, 287
army, British, deployment in Northern Ireland (1969), 37

Azimcar, Patrick, 1

Balkan wars (1990s), 110–11
Banbridge bombing (1 August 1998), 93, 96
Barker, Victor, 132
Barnes, Peter, 28, 39
Basque militants, 110
BBC *Panorama* programme on Omagh bombing (October 2000), 141
BBC Television Centre bombing (March 2001), 141, 285
Behal, Richard, 54
Beir Bua (32CSM newsletter), 214–15
Belfast rioting (1970), 37
Bell, John Bowyer, 16, 26
Bennett, Jack, 34
Bew, Paul, 15
Blair, Tony, 3, 4–5, 6, 43, 106, 120
The Blanket (online journal), 160–6, 181, 189, 192, 193, 194, 201, 208–9, 210, 221, 264, 286
Bloody Sunday (January 1972), 37
Bloody Sunday (November 1920), 15
blueshirt movement, 30
Bodenstown 'Unity Commemorations', 222–3
Boland, Gerald, 25–6
Boland, Kevin, 4
border campaign, IRA (1956-62), 32–3, 34, 45, 71, 84, 148
Bradley, Denis, 178, 217
Breen, Suzanne, 262
Breslin, Séamus, 213
British state
    Anglo-Irish Treaty and, 15
    anti-terrorist legislation, 28, 105, 106
    nformers and agents in Provisional movement, 162, 184, 254–5, 267
    mistakes at start of Troubles, 37–8
    oath of allegiance to, 17, 21, 22
    peace process and, 3, 4–5, 43, 161, 171, 184–5
    policing in Northern Ireland and, 206, 208, 216
    proposed visit to Ireland of queen, 215
    Real IRA and, 134–5, 136
Brookeborough raid (1 January 1957), 32
Burke, Christy, 227, 228
Burke, Michael, 98
Burke, Pascal, 91
Burns, Matthew, murder of (February 2002), 143
Byrne, Pat, 287

Cabhair (prisoner organisation), 57, 112
Cahill, Joe, 36, 283
Caldwell, David, murder of (August 2002), 143, 144, 145
Callanan, Daniel, 226
Campbell, Liam, 91, 109, 116, 133, 134, 136, 138, 141, 144, 146, 176, 244
car bombs, 94, 95, 96, 104, 115–16, 118–19, 120, 142, 143, 247–8, 249, 257
Carlingford Lough gun boat, 120
Carroll, Declan, 172–3
Carroll, Stephen, murder of (Craigavon, 10 March 2009), 1, 6, 241, 247, 249, 250, 253–4
Carson, Paul, 262–3
Carty, Packy, 191
Catholic Church, 19, 24, 59, 63
Catney, Tony, 209, 219–21, 223, 230, 234, 284
Celtic Tiger, 215
Centre for Public Inquiry, 233
Chechen militants, 110
civil rights movement in Northern Ireland, 35
Civil War, Irish (1922-23), 15–16, 17, 284
Clinton, Bill, 43

Coalition of Irish Republican Women, 221
Cole, Roger, 232
Cole, USS, al-Qaeda assault on (September 2000), 120
Collins, Éamon, 125
Collins, Michael, 4
Columbian PIRA arrests (2001), 160
Communist Party of Ireland, 232
Concerned Families Against Drugs (CFAD), 262–3
'Concerned Republicans' movement, 208–11, 216, 218, 222
Connolly, James, 18, 39, 51, 237, 242, 280
Connolly, John, 188
constitution, Irish (1937), 23, 58, 213, 220
Continuity IRA (CIRA)
    Army Council, 74, 75
    County Fermanagh and, 109, 256–7, 262
        founding of (1986), 73–4, 92
        hoax alerts as tactic, 177, 243
        ideology and, 108, 181
        IFC and, 121
        IMC on, 177, 181, 243, 244, 262
        March 2009 killings, 1, 6, 76–7
        MI5 security service and, 201
        Omagh bombing and, 104, 105, 114, 115
        ONH splinter group (Strabane), 180, 244
        PIRA and, 202
        prisoners, 69, 188
        Real IRA and, 94, 104, 113, 114–15, 117–18, 180
        republican legitimacy of, 73, 74–5
        RSF and, 69, 73, 74–6, 94, 191, 281
        split (late 2006-7), 244
        violence, 7, 80, 281
        1996–2000 period, 74, 93–4, 108, 109, 117–18
        2002-2005 period, 173, 176, 177, 178, 179, 181, 192
        2006-2010 period, 1, 6, 76–7, 243–4, 246, 255
        warnings on by Sir Hugh Orde (2008/2009), 6, 249
        weakness in 2003-5 period, 148, 285
Costello, Séamus, 34, 92
Coughlan, Anthony, 34
Coventry bombing (August 1939), 28
credit crisis, global, 284
criminal justice system in Northern Ireland, 126, 256
Criminal Justice (Terrorism and Conspiracy) Act, British (1998), 105
Cronin, Sean, 32
Crossan, James, 71
Crossan, Tommy, 69, 71
Crozier, Ryan, 246
Cruise O'Brien, Conor, 38
Cumann na mBan, 99
Cumann na nGaedheal, 17, 22, 23
Cumann Poblachta na hÉireann, 20
Cunningham, Martin, 163, 165
Cypriots, radical, 110

Dalton, Des, 67–8, 78, 79, 80, 81–2
Daly, Séamus, 133, 134
Davis, Thomas, 12
de Brún, Bairbre, 225
de Chastelain, John, 161
de Rossa, Prionsias, 4
de Valera, Éamon, 3–4, 15–16, 17, 20–4, 175, 246, 283, 284
    formation of Fianna Fáil (1926), 17, 30
    government of (from 1932), 22–4, 25–6, 28–9
    IRA and, 20–2, 23, 25–6, 28–9, 30
    Second World War and, 24, 28
decommissioning of weapons, 5, 76, 108, 116–17, 119, 123, 124, 161, 171, 201–2, 206, 229, 282

INLA and, 174, 258
inspection process, 119, 123, 161
Democratic Unionist Party (DUP), 5, 7, 70–1, 193, 203, 204–5, 207, 211, 220, 266
Dillon, Joe, 98, 99, 103, 113, 142, 221
dissident republicanism
  academic neglect of, 2–3
  'Concerned Republicans' platform (2007 election), 209–11, 216
  control over key republican districts (2008–10 period), 247–8, 258–61, 262–3
  conventional wisdom on, 284–5
  co-operation between groups, 92, 93–4, 104, 180, 221–4, 247
  deaths of Brendan Hughes and Brian Keenan as 'watershed moment', 264–6, 267
  definition of, 8
  fluid boundaries between groups, 246–7
  fragmentation and discord (2002-6), 173, 177, 178, 179–81, 192
  IMC on, 177, 178, 179–80, 181
  the internet and, 78, 133, 211, 214, 218, 220–1, 232, 234–5
  March 2009 killings, 1, 6, 67, 76–7, 219, 240–1, 249–51, 253–4, 280
  policing and, 208–9, 210, 218, 220, 221, 223
  see also under Police Service of Northern Ireland (PSNI)
  prevailing peace process narratives and, 3, 167, 254
  Provisionals' intimidation/brutality towards, 136–7, 163–5, 178, 203–4
  warnings on by Sir Hugh Orde (2008/2009), 6, 249
  see also under entries for individual organisations
Dodds, Diane, 211
Doherty, Constable Jim, 245, 256
Doherty, Kieran, 146, 260
Donaldson, Denis, 162, 184, 254–5, 267
Donnelly, Gary, 217, 286–7
Donnelly, Mickey, 165
Dougan, Geraldine, 231
Dougan, Rory, 98, 103, 139
Down Royal race course hoax (November 2005), 243
Downes, Brenda, 238
Downes, Sean, 238
Doyle, Paul, 189
Droppin' Well Bar bombing (December 1982), 92
drugs, 180, 213, 214, 248, 260–1, 262–3
Drumcree dispute, 215, 236
Duffy, Colin, 236, 240
Duffy, John, 71
Duffy, Martin, 248
Dwyer, Ciarán, 98
Dwyer, John, 228

Ealing Broadway bombing (August 2001), 142
Easter Rising (April 1916), 11–14, 46, 57, 67, 82, 131, 142, 190, 214, 281–2
Ebrington barracks bombings (2000, 2001), 119, 141
economic war (1930s), 22, 23
Edwards, Ruth Dudley, 2, 14
Egan, John, 25
éirígí, 7, 194, 221, 230–43, 263–4, 266, 279–80, 282
electoral politics
  abstentionism *see* republican ideology, abstentionism
dissident republicanism and, 68–71, 79, 186, 235
elections
  British general elections, 7, 34, 69, 71, 193, 225
  Dáil general elections (1920s/30s), 17, 18,

21, 22, 23
  Dáil general elections (1950s onwards), 32, 45, 48, 193, 225–6, 231
European elections, 7, 193, 225
Irish local government, 68, 79, 226–7
  Northern Ireland, 31, 32, 68–9
  Northern Ireland Assembly (2003), 186, 192, 193
  Northern Ireland Assembly (2007), 69–71, 209–11, 216, 225
  IRA and (to 1964), 17–18, 20, 21, 22, 34
  Sinn Féin and *see* Sinn Féin, electoral politics
  unionist rejectionists and, 7
Emergency Powers Act (1940 amendment), 28–9
Emmet, Robert, 67
English, Richard, 12, 24, 30, 35, 157
European Union (EU), 58, 61, 64, 66

Falls curfew (July 1970), 37
Federal Bureau of Investigation, American (FBI), 2, 100, 110
Felsted (Essex), 32
Fenianism, 67, 82, 214, 241
Ferris, Toireasa, 227–8
Na Fianna Éireann, 78
Fianna Fáil, 4, 17, 19, 30, 31, 48
  government of (from 1932), 22–4, 25–6, 28–9, 36
  IRA and, 20–3, 24, 25–6, 30, 253
Fine Gael, 253
Fisherwick estate, Ballymena, 248
Fitzgerald, David, 19
Fitzpatrick, Michael, 19
Flanagan, Ronnie, 105, 141
Flannery, Michael, 111
Fleming, Gary, 223
Fleming, Paddy, 31
Foley, Gerard, 228
Forde, Killian, 228
Forum magazine, 146, 167, 168–71, 172
Fox, Bernard, 233, 236
Fox, Paddy, 110, 136, 165, 176

Gallagher, Felix, 226
Gallagher, Michael, 132, 133
Galvin, Martin, 112, 124, 131, 133, 135
Gardaí, 25, 30, 95, 135, 136, 144, 233–4, 287
Garvin, Tom, 63
Gaughran, Liam, 80, 81
Gibney, Jim, 49
Gilmore, George, 19, 20
Glynn, Frank, 54
Godson, Dean, 107, 206
Good Friday (Belfast) Agreement (April 1998), 6–7
  Tony Blair and, 4–5, 6, 43
  dissident republican rejection of, 7–8, 95, 96, 222
  32CSM, 101–3, 122–3, 126–7, 182, 186–7, 213, 216, 217, 223–4
  Blanket/NRF, 158, 166, 167, 168–9
  INLA, 7, 107, 173–4
  RIRA, 146, 174, 175
  RNU, 220, 221, 223
  RSF, 43–4, 61, 72
  historical comparisons, 13, 44, 61, 122, 158, 175, 183
  institutions created by *see* Northern Ireland Executive and Assembly
  referendum on, 43, 95, 107, 174, 175
  as 'the end of history', 3, 8, 43

Gorman, Tommy, 137, 157, 165
Goss, Richard, 80, 81
Goulding, Cathal, 32, 34, 35–6, 45, 50, 73, 171, 202
governor-general, British, 23
Grogan, Liam, 96, 127
Groogan, Patsy, 226
Guerrine, Darren, 260

Hain, Peter, 207
Hamas, 212
Hammersmith Bridge bombing (1 June 2000), 119
Hanley, Brian, 20, 24, 31, 35
Harrington, Maura, 235
Harrison, George, 111
Hartley, Tom, 49, 51
Haughey, Charles, 33, 48
Hayden, Josephine, 78
Hayes, Stephen, 29–30
Heffron, Peadar, 258
Hendon sorting office bombings (2001), 142
Hennessey, Thomas, 37
Holy Cross primary school dispute (2001), 126
Hughes, Brendan, 123, 137, 157, 159–60, 165, 229
    death of (February 2008), 264–5, 267
Hughes, Éamon, 259, 267
Hughes, Francis, 70, 226
Hughes, Oliver, 226
Hughes, Sean, 252–3
Hulme, Aiden, 188–9, 232
Hunger (Steve McQueen film, 2008), 233
hunger strikes (1940s), 29, 30
hunger strikes (1981), 48, 66–7, 70, 72, 114, 130, 164–5,
    185, 188, 233, 267
Hyland, Anthony, 96, 127

Independent International Commission on Decommission-
    ing (IICD), 5
Independent Monitoring Commission (IMC), 5, 177, 178,
    179–80, 181, 204, 243, 244, 245, 252, 258, 261–2
informers and British agents in Provisional movement,
    162, 184, 254–5, 267
Ingram, Adam, 129
International Human Rights Association of American
    Minorities, 122
international law, 102, 103
the internet, 78, 133, 211, 214, 218, 220–1, 232, 234–5
internment
    border campaign, 32
    the Troubles, 37
Iraq, 64, 167, 214
Irish Citizen Army, 11, 241
Irish Freedom Committee (IFC), 111–13, 121, 221
Irish language, 59, 61
Irish National Liberation Army (INLA), 7, 92–3, 94, 107,
    130, 173–4, 188, 258, 260
Irish People's Liberation Organisation (IPLO), 92, 179
Irish Press, 31
Irish Republican Army (IRA)
    1916–23 period, 14–15
    1923–39 period, 16–29
    1940s period, 29–31, 45–6, 66, 80
    1945–62 period, 31–3, 34
    army council, 20, 27, 45, 56
    border campaign (1956–62), 32–3, 34, 45, 71, 84, 148
    ceasefire (1972), 92
    'England Campaign' (1939–40), 26–9, 148
    leftist politics and, 16, 18–21, 24, 25, 34
    'northern campaign' (1940s), 30, 31
    PIRA and, 124–5

Sinn Féin and, 17–18, 22, 31
    split (1969), 35–7, 45, 50, 53, 56, 73
    'Sticks' label, 50, 124–5, 165, 171, 202
    see also Provisional republicanism
Irish Republican Brotherhood (IRB), 11
Irish Republican Liberation Army (IRLA), 180, 246
Irish Republican Prisoners Welfare Association (IRPWA),
    112, 121–2, 127–8, 133, 135, 136, 143, 186, 188–9,
    213, 214
Irish Republican Socialist Party (IRSP), 82, 92, 128, 168,
    221, 222, 223, 251
Irish Republican Writers' Group (IRWG), 160–6, 181, 193
Irish state
    anti-Partition campaign (1950s), 31
    anti-terrorist legislation, 28–9, 105, 106
    constitution (1937), 23, 58, 213, 220
    de Valera's views on legitimacy of Free
        State, 15–16, 21–2
    dissident republicanism and, 103–4, 132, 134, 135–6
    militant republicanism and (1923-45 period), 15–31
    military tribunals (during border
        campaign), 33
    proposed visit of British queen, 215
    romantic violent tradition and, 13, 14, 15–16
    Irish Volunteers, 11

Jackson, Jake, 233
Jackson, Rab, 241–2, 243
James Connolly Debating Society, 232
Johnston, Roy, 34
journalism, 2, 9
jurors, IRA targeting of, 25

Kearney, Declan, 208, 258
Keating, Dan, 80
Keenan, Brian, death of (May 2008), 265–6, 267
Keenan, Sean, 67, 80
Kehoe, Nicky, 226
Kelly, Gerry, 137, 138, 139, 219, 263, 265
Kelly, John, 165, 209, 221
Kerins, Charlie, 30, 66, 281
'Kilmichael ambush' (November 1920), 15
Kilwilkie estate (Lurgan), 247–8, 255
King, Peter, 103, 106

Lalor, Fintan, 12
land annuities, 19, 23
Leeson, Brian, 230–1, 232, 234–5, 236, 238–41, 242,
    243, 263, 282, 283, 284
Lemass, Sean, 17
Libya, 110
Lisbon Treaty, 212–13, 234
Little, Paul, 208
London, 28, 96, 99, 115, 116, 119, 120, 121, 127, 142,
    201
Long, Des, 52, 54, 68, 74, 75, 78, 82
Loughman, Ann, 135
loyalist paramilitary groups, 93, 126
Lynagh, Jim, 83

Mac an Mháistir, Daithí, 231
Mac Cionnaith, Breandán, 236–7, 238, 240, 241, 284
Mac Coitir, Pádraic, 279–80
Mac Giolla, Tomás, 4, 34
Mac Lochlainn, Ciarán, 172
Mac Niallais, Donncha, 236
Mac Stíofáin, Seán, 32, 36
MacBride, Sean, 101–2
MacCurtain, Tomás, 31

Mackey, Francie, 98–9, 102–3, 130–1, 132, 182, 186–7, 211, 223, 232, 281
  armed struggle and, 99, 129–30, 183, 216–17
  'Concerned Republicans' movement and, 208, 209, 216
  Omagh bombing and, 106
  on Provisional republicanism, 123, 183–4, 185, 215, 222, 246
MacLochlainn, Ronan, 95–6, 99
MacManais, Éamann, 241
Magan, Tony, 31
Maghaberry prison, 72, 127–8, 187, 188, 189, 190, 213, 248, 256
Maguire, Sean, 191
Maguire, Tom, 36, 73, 74–5, 191
Maillot, Agnes, 36, 38
Mallon, Kevin, 52
Mallon, Séamus, 101, 206
Maloney, John, 144
Mandelson, Peter, 134–5
Mansergh, Martin, 103, 109, 132, 284
Martin, Leo, 53
Maskey, Alex, 250
Mason, Peter, 143
Massereene barracks assault (8 March 2009), 1, 6, 219, 240, 249, 251, 253–4, 280
McAllister, Jim, 253
McBrearty, Danny, 221
McCall, George, 178
McCartan, Eugene, 232
McCartney, Raymond, 251
McCartney, Robert, murder of (2005), 164, 202, 203, 204, 206, 253
McCaughey, Sean, 29–30
McConville, Jean, murder of (1972), 229
McCrory, Alex, 238
McCusker, John Joe, 83
McDermott, Tommy, 45–6
McDonagh, John, 159
McDonald, Joanne, 231
McDonald, Mary Lou, 225, 231
McDonald, Michael, 144
McFadden, Brian, 222, 261
McGarrigle, Eddie, 209
McGeough, Gerry, 208, 209
McGirl, John Joe, 32, 53
McGlinchey, Dominic, 92, 209
McGlinchey, Dominic (Jnr), 208, 240
McGlinchey, Paul, 209
McGonigle, Michael, 70
McGrane, Séamus, 90, 91, 115, 117, 244
McGreevy, Frank, 259, 263, 267
McGuinness, Martin, 38, 47, 50, 51–2, 54, 55, 107, 162, 261
  armed struggle and, 49, 252, 282
  criticism of leadership of *see* Provisional republicanism, criticism of Adams-McGuinness leadership
  as deputy first minister, 5, 210
  electoral politics and, 70–1, 210, 225
  hunger strikes and, 164–5
  on March 2009 killings, 67, 250, 253, 254–5, 280
  peace process and, 90–1, 116, 124
  Real IRA and, 138, 139, 143
McGuirk, Cathleen Knowles, 78
McGurk, Daniel, murder of (August 2003), 162, 177, 178, 179
McHugh, Gerry, 226
McInerney, Denis, 54
McIntyre, Anthony, 37–8, 189, 209, 211,
221, 252, 265
  on armed struggle, 137, 140, 145, 162, 163, 253, 282
  The Blanket and, 161–5, 189, 194, 264
  criticism of Adams-McGuinness leadership, 157, 160–5, 205, 253, 265, 283
  criticism of Provisional republicanism, 137, 140, 157, 158–9, 160–5, 194, 203, 205
  on Real IRA, 137, 145, 162, 253, 282
  'three Ds' of, 37, 53
McIvor, Michael, 140
McKay, Daithi, 257
McKearney, Tommy, 157, 165, 232
McKee, Billy, 53
McKenna, Séamus, 133, 134
McKevitt, Michael, 52, 90, 91, 94, 95, 104, 105, 106, 188
  arrest/trial and prison sentence, 109, 110, 141–2, 144, 162, 185, 244
  civil action against (2008-9), 133, 134
  Ruairí Ó Brádaigh and, 114
  Provisionals and, 138, 139, 171, 283
  Real IRA post-Omagh and, 109–18, 119–22, 124, 131–2, 133, 135, 136, 138, 139, 140, 141
  Real IRA split (2002) and, 146, 147, 176
  David Rupert and, 100, 104, 109–18, 119–20, 121, 131–2, 136, 138, 141–2, 148, 185
McLaughlin, Brendan, 70
McLaughlin, Mitchel, 138, 139, 189
McLogan, Pádraig, 31
McManus, Michael, 70, 76
McManus, Patrick, 71
McPhilips, Tony, 209
Meehan, Martin, 263, 265
Meehan, Martin Óg, 262–3
Meigh Bridge railway bombing (2000), 120, 138
Mellows, Liam, 18
Menary, Stephen, 141
MI5 security service, 104, 110, 133–4, 185, 201, 219, 258
MI6 headquarters grenade attack (20 September 2000), 120
Millar, S., 31, 34, 35
Minihan, Louise, 228, 231
Mitchel, John, 12
Mitchell Principles, 90–1, 97, 98–9, 220, 282
Moloney, Ed, 59, 90
Monteith, Barry, 236
Mooney, John, *Black Operations: The Secret War Against the Real IRA* (with Michael O'Toole, 2003), 2, 91, 94, 103, 109
Moore, Stephen, 178
Morgan, Mr Justice, 134
Morris, Séamus, 228–9
Morrison, Danny, 48, 51, 52, 59–60, 205, 216
Moyne, Ronan, 263
Mulholland, Darren, 96, 127, 168
Mulligan, Sean, 168
Murphy, Colm, 133, 134, 136
Murphy, Conor, 138, 139, 252–3
Murphy, Thomas, 252
Musgrave, Constable Paul, 245
Myers, Kevin, 143

Napoli (Italy), 214
Nazi Germany, 29
Neave, Airey, murder of (March 1979), 92
Nelson, Rosemary, 126
New Republican Forum, 7, 146, 166–73, 181, 189, 192, 193, 194, 201, 286
Newry car bomb (February 2010), 257

Ní Chathmhaoil, Líta, 78
'No More Lies' campaign (from May 2004), 165–6
NORAID, 111, 112
Norman invasion of Ireland (1169), 12
Northern Bank robbery (December 2004), 202, 203, 204, 206, 253
Northern Ireland Executive and Assembly, 266
  suspension of (February 2000), 118, 123
  suspension of (October 2002), 182, 192, 203, 284
  re-establishment (2007), 5

Ó Brádaigh, Ruairí, 43–7
  abstentionism and, 45, 50, 52, 54, 55, 56–7, 114
  armed struggle and, 4, 45, 57, 66, 75, 76, 181, 248, 255
  attitudes toward Provisionals, 44, 50, 54–5, 57, 67, 70, 75, 79, 81, 192, 202, 283
  Comhar na gComharsan and, 62–3
  Continuity IRA and, 74, 75, 76, 255
  Éire Nua (policy document, 1971–2) and, 59–60, 65
  electoral politics and, 32, 70, 79
  Michael McKevitt and, 114
  as President of Provisional Sinn Féin, 45, 48, 52–3, 59, 60
  republican ideology and, 43–7, 49–52, 54–7, 64–7, 75, 79–80, 82, 84–5, 181, 192, 281, 287
  split of 1969 and, 35–6, 45, 56
  split of 1986 and, 4, 49–53, 54–5, 56, 57, 81
  steps down as RSF president (2009), 78
Ó Brádaigh, Ruairí Óg, 114
Ó Brádaigh, Sean, 54, 65
Ó Brolcháin, Ciarán, 232
Ó Conaill, Daithí, 35–6, 53, 59, 60, 81
Ó Curraoin, Tomás, 79
Ó hAnnain, Peadar, 130
Ó Muilleoir, Máirtín, 178–9
Ó Ruairc, Liam, 168
O'Brien, Denis, 30
O'Callaghan, Sean, 74, 265–6
O'Connor, Gareth, 178
O'Connor, Joseph, murder of (October 2000), 137–8, 139, 164, 178, 203–4
O'Connor, Rory, 137
O'Doherty, Malachi, 252
O'Donnell, Peadar, 18, 19, 20
O'Donoghue, John, 134–5
O'Donovan, Séamus, 29
O'Driscoll, Donal, 231
O'Farrell, Fintan, 144
O'Ferrell, Richard More, 25
Offences against the State Act (June 1939), 28, 105
Óglaigh na hÉireann (ONH), 7, 100–1, 108, 118, 143, 174, 217, 248, 280
  CIRA splinter group in Strabane, 180, 244
  RIRA group, 109, 183, 245, 255–6, 258, 260–1, 262, 263
  see also Continuity IRA (CIRA); Real IRA (RIRA)
O'Hanlon, Eineachan, 32
O'Hanlon, Fergal, 32, 39, 45
O'Hara, Patsy, 210
O'Hara, Peggy, 208, 210
O'Higgins, Kevin, 21, 25
Okado-Gough, Damien, 174
O'Kane, Séamus, 180
Omagh bombing (15 August 1998), 2, 104–7, 114, 115, 132, 133–4, 147, 157, 162
  BBC *Panorama* programme (October 2000), 141
  civil action (2008-9), 110, 133–4

criminal trials, 136, 185
Omagh Support and Self-Help Group (OSSHG), 132–4, 135
O'Neill, Joe, 52, 54, 70
O'Neill, Laurence, 208
Orange Order parades, 177, 215, 220, 236, 263
O'Rawe, Richard, *Blanketmen* (2005), 164, 267
Orde, Sir Hugh, 6, 204, 215, 246, 249, 250, 254, 256, 285
O'Reilly, John, 92
O'Sullivan, Tom, 54, 74
O'Toole, Michael, *Black Operations: The Secret War Against the Real IRA* (with John Mooney, 2003), 2, 91, 94, 103, 109

Paisley, Ian, 5, 70–1, 193, 203, 204–5, 215, 220
Palestine, 110, 167, 212
partition, 14, 15–16, 31, 39, 46, 54–5, 216, 280, 287
Patten report on policing, 127, 176
Patterson, Henry, 18, 63
Patterson brothers (Kenneth and Alan), 144
Peace and Neutrality Alliance, 232
peace process
  32CSM and, 97–9, 101
  British state and, 3, 4–5, 43, 161, 171, 184–5
  'entrenchment' of sectarianism and, 182–3
  liberal principles of, 6–7
  McGuinness and, 90–1, 116, 124
  'No More Lies' campaign (from May 2004), 165–6
  policing and, 126–7, 176–8, 183, 205–9, 218, 221, 223, 229, 266, 282
  see also Police Service of Northern Ireland (PSNI),
  Sinn Féin and prevailing narratives of, 3, 167, 254
Provisional republicanism and, 67–8, 75, 168–72, 182–5, 191–2, 230–1, 282–6
  Adams and, 3–4, 38, 75, 90–1, 116, 124, 139, 231, 265, 283
  McGuinness and, 38, 90–1, 116, 124, 265, 283
  PIRA and, 122–6, 139–40, 159, 168–72, 174, 183, 184, 230–1, 282–6
  PIRA ceasefires, 38, 44, 66, 74, 90, 93, 96, 97, 112, 220, 282
  PIRA decommissioning of weapons, 5, 76, 108, 116–17, 119, 123, 124, 161, 171, 201–2, 206, 229, 282
  Sinn Féin, 3–4, 44, 72, 91, 101, 122–6, 139–40, 157–9, 168–72, 182–5, 282–6
  Sinn Féin and electoral popularity, 84, 192–3, 203, 224–5, 285
  Sinn Féin as primary vehicle, 38
  Sinn Féin defections (2006-10), 219, 220, 226, 228, 230–1, 236, 284
  Sinn Féin negotiations with DUP (from 2004), 203, 204, 205, 206, 207, 266
  split (1997), 90–1, 100–1
  as successful endeavour, 5–6
  suspension of Executive and Assembly (February 2000), 118, 123
  suspension of Executive and Assembly (October 2002), 182, 192, 203, 284
  unionist rejectionists, 7
Pearse, Patrick, 14, 18, 39, 58, 84, 95, 118, 176, 185, 191, 242, 279, 280, 286–7
  four pamphlets of, 12–13, 67
Perry, Kevin, 178
An Phoblacht, 18–19, 107, 204–5, 227, 250, 261
Police Federation, 256
Police Service of Northern Ireland (PSNI), 79, 142–3, 183, 204, 210, 256–7

casualties, 1, 6, 245, 246, 247, 248, 249, 250, 256, 258
'Concerned Republicans' movement and, 208–10, 218
dissident targeting of, 1, 6, 142–3, 177, 246, 254, 257–8, 261
attacks on police officers, 1, 6, 244, 245, 246, 247–8, 249, 250, 251, 255, 258
attacks on police stations, 76, 173, 243, 244, 245, 255, 257
District Policing Partnerships (DPPs), 176–8, 226, 228
dissident targeting of, 176–8, 180, 244, 255
referred to as 'RUC' by dissidents, 64, 71, 77
Sinn Féin and, 171, 180, 182, 184, 205–9, 215–16, 218, 221, 223, 229, 266, 282
Anthony McIntyre on, 161
defections/resignations over, 209, 220, 226, 228, 231
March 2009 killings, 250–1
Popular Front for the Liberation of Palestine (PFLP), 110
Portlaoise prison, 128, 145, 174, 188, 189, 190
Powell, Jonathan, 4, 6, 107, 139
Power, Thomas, 92–3
Prevention of Violence Act (Temporary Provisions), British (1939), 28
Price, Dolours, 75, 99–100, 166
Price, Marian, 137, 158, 159, 223, 286
32CSM and, 57, 98, 99–100, 101, 124–6, 131, 133, 159, 163, 186, 212, 279
armed struggle and, 99–100, 101, 125–6, 130, 163, 279
RSF and, 57–8, 75, 99–100
traditional republican ideology and, 57–8, 99–100, 101, 124, 125–6, 130, 131, 163
Price, Michael, 19, 20
Pringle, Thomas, 226
prisoners, republican, 187–90, 219, 232
32CSM/IRPWA and, 112, 121–2, 127–8, 133, 187–90, 213
Continuity IRA and, 69, 188
Real IRA and, 112, 121–2, 123, 127, 145–7, 166, 172–3, 174, 188
Republican Sinn Féin and, 66, 69, 71–2, 73, 128, 190
Proclamation (Easter 1916), 11–13, 18, 27, 58, 66, 101, 129, 183–4, 190, 213, 215, 231–2, 242–3
Provisional IRA (PIRA)
Adams' 'appeal' to (2005), 4, 5, 57
army council, 45, 90
ceasefires (1994, 1997), 38, 44, 66, 74, 90, 93, 96, 97, 112, 220, 282
Columbian arrests (2001), 160
decommissioning and, 5, 76, 108, 116–17, 119, 123, 124, 161, 171, 201–2, 206, 229, 282
defections from to dissident groups (2006–10 period), 261–2
formation of (December 1969), 35–7, 56, 73
London bombings (1973), 99
'Loughgall martyrs', 83
official end of armed struggle (2005), 5, 178, 184, 191, 193–4, 201–3, 267
radicalising of Catholic community in Northern Ireland, 37–8
truce (mid-1970s), 49
violence (1996–97), 74
Provisional republicanism
abstentionism, 38, 49–51, 52, 54, 67, 73, 80–1, 114, 282
academic studies of, 3
Adams' 'modernisation' of, 47–53, 54, 59–60, 114

alleged involvement in crime/violence (2000–10 period), 137–8, 139, 164, 170, 178, 202–4, 206, 252–3
armed struggle and, 3–4, 38, 47, 48, 49, 54–5, 139–40, 252, 282, 283
'backlash' against in republican districts, 259
criticism of Adams-McGuinness leadership, 124–6, 159, 160–6, 169–71, 175, 183–5, 202, 218–20, 222–3, 231, 283–4
by Anthony McIntyre, 157, 160–5, 205, 253, 265, 283
dual approach and, 47–50, 51, 201–2
legitimacy of PIRA's violent campaign, 139–40, 251, 252, 282, 283
loss of support/control in republican districts, 258–9, 261–5, 267
Francie Mackey on, 123, 183–4, 185, 215, 222, 246
March 2009 killings and, 249–51, 264
Anthony McIntyre's criticism of, 137, 140, 157, 158–9, 160–5, 194, 203, 205
Mitchell Principles and, 90–1
Ruairí Ó Brádaigh and, 44, 50, 54–5, 57, 67, 70, 75, 79, 81, 192, 202, 283
Official IRA and, 124–5
peace process and *see* peace process, Provisional republicanism and Real IRA and, 107, 116–17, 119, 121–4, 136–40, 178–9
reorganisation (late 1970s), 47
republican ideology and, 37, 38, 47–51, 52, 54, 67, 73, 80–1, 114, 139–40, 224, 282–3
Republican Sinn Féin and, 44, 54–5, 66–8, 75, 76, 81–3, 191–2
responses to dissident violence, 138, 143, 178–9, 250–2, 253, 254–5, 263–4, 280
Sinn Féin and PIRA relationship, 106
social control and use of intimidation/ostracism, 137, 139, 163–5, 178, 203–4, 267
split (1986), 49–55, 56, 57, 67, 73, 80–1, 82–3, 114
split (1997), 90–1, 100–1
see also Provisional IRA (PIRA); Sinn Féin
Public Safety Act (1931), 19, 22
'punishment attacks', 243, 262

Qadhaffi, Colonel, 110
Quinn, Paul, 252
Quinsey, Mark, 1

Radio Free Éireann, 97, 159
Rafferty, Declan, 144
Raytheon arms company (Derry), 212
Real IRA (RIRA)
32CSM and, 97, 100–6, 113–14, 121–4, 128–36, 140, 183, 185, 187, 202, 217, 281
army council, 109, 113, 174
arrests of major personnel, 117, 136, 141–2, 144, 244
cessation of violence (18 August 1998), 106–7, 108, 109, 132
civil action against (2008-9), 133–4
claims of responsibility and, 6, 115, 134, 143
Continuity IRA and, 94, 104, 113, 114–15, 117–18, 180
designated as terrorist organisation in USA, 135–6
failure of (2000-2005 period), 144–8, 172, 192
founding of (October 1997), 91–2, 97
hoax alerts as tactic, 119, 120, 142, 148, 177
IMC on, 177, 179, 181, 262
international links and contacts, 94, 110–13, 121, 122, 132, 135

Irish Freedom Committee and, 111, 112–13, 121
mainland bombings (2000-2001), 119, 120, 141, 142–3
New Republican Forum and, 146, 166–73
Omagh bombing and, 104–5, 106–7, 114, 115, 133–4, 147
ONH group, 183, 245, 255–6, 258, 260–1, 262, 263
OSSHG and, 132–4, 135
other dissident groups and, 94, 104, 112, 113–15, 117–18, 121–2, 180, 222
peace process and, 95–6, 116–18
policing of 'crimes against the community', 259–61, 262
prisoners, 127, 145–7, 166, 172–3, 174
Provisionals and, 107, 116–17, 119, 121–4, 136–40, 178–9, 188, 202, 254–5
'renewed offensive' declared (February 2008), 245–6
second campaign/re-establishment of (post-Omagh), 109–22, 131–2, 138, 141–2, 147–8, 192
security services and, 201
David Rupert, 2, 100, 104, 109–18, 119–20, 121, 131–2, 136, 138, 141–2, 148, 185
southern-based membership, 91
split (2002), 145–7, 148, 172, 173, 174–6, 177, 192, 244, 285
vigilantism south of the border, 260–1
violence, 7, 91–2, 93, 95–6, 103, 172–3, 174–6, 177–8, 179, 181
2000-2002 period, 117–22, 138, 140–1, 142–5, 147–8, 162
2003-2005 period, 176, 177–8, 179, 192
2006-10 period, 1, 6, 217, 219, 245, 246, 251, 253, 255–6, 258, 260–1, 262, 263
warnings on by Sir Hugh Orde (2008/2009), 6, 249
'Reclaim the Republic' campaign, éirígí, 231–2, 233
Redmond, Thomas, 146
Reid, Fr Alec, 103, 132
Reid, John, 284–5
Reiss, Mitchell, 207
Republican Action Against Drugs (RAAD), 246, 260
Republican Congress, 19–20
Republican Defence Army (RDA), 180, 246
Republican Forum for Unity (RFU), 223–4
republican history and tradition
Éamon de Valera and, 15–16, 21–2, 175
Declaration of Independence, 128–9
'First Dáil' (1919), 36, 55, 56, 67, 129
legitimacy, 8, 15–16, 21–2, 28, 38, 39, 52, 139–40, 251, 252, 282, 283
of elite minority violence, 8, 11, 12, 13, 14, 15, 25, 38–9, 100, 101, 131, 175, 181, 281–2
line of succession/inheritance, 16, 21, 38, 55–6, 58, 175–6, 280
32CSM and, 122–3, 183–4, 216–17, 280
'England Campaign' (1939-40) and, 26–8
Provisional republicanism and, 36
RSF and, 55–6, 61, 67, 73, 74–5, 82, 84, 190–1, 280
NRF and, 167
Ruairí Ó Brádaigh and, 43–4, 52, 54, 55–7, 63, 66, 67, 75, 84, 181, 287
partition and, 14, 15–16, 31, 39, 46, 54–5, 216, 280, 287
post-1923/post-1998 parallels, 16–17

romantic nationalism of 1916 and, 11–14, 38–40, 51–2, 57–8, 63, 66, 67, 131, 183–4, 190–1, 280
éirígí and, 232, 242–3, 282
violence and, 12, 13, 14, 15–16, 39, 129, 281–2
see also armed struggle and violence
RSF and, 66, 67, 82, 84, 281
'Second Dáil' (1921), 27, 36, 55–6, 73
violence and, 12, 13, 14, 15–16, 39, 129, 241–2, 281–2
see also armed struggle and violence
republican ideology, 193, 279–82
32CSM and, 97–101, 122–6, 128–31, 139–40, 163, 182–7, 193, 279, 280, 281, 286–7
abstentionism
éirígí and, 235
Ruairí Ó Brádaigh and, 45, 50, 52, 54, 55, 56–7, 114
Provisional republicanism and, 38, 47–51, 52, 54, 67, 73, 80–1, 114, 282
RSF and, 53, 54, 55, 56–7, 68–9, 73, 80–1, 114, 280–1
Sinn Féin (pre-1964), 17, 18, 22, 31, 34, 36, 45, 55
aim of united 32 county republic, 8, 14, 15, 36, 40, 46, 54–5, 92–3, 108, 128–9, 191, 280
éirígí and, 279, 280, 282
illegitimacy of 1921 Treaty, 46, 55–6, 61, 67, 175, 183
legitimacy of elite minority violence, 8, 11, 12, 13, 14, 15, 25, 38–9, 100, 101, 131, 175, 181, 281–2
'no compromise', 14, 15, 39, 45–7, 57, 66, 67, 79, 176, 191
Ruairí Ó Brádaigh and, 43–7, 49–52, 54–7, 64–7, 75, 79–80, 82, 84–5, 181, 192, 281, 287
Patrick Pearse and, 12–13, 14, 58, 67, 176, 185, 191, 279, 280, 286
Marian Price and, 57–8, 99–100, 101, 124, 125–6, 130, 131, 163, 279
Provisional republicanism and, 37, 51, 139–40, 224, 282–3
RSF and, 61, 64–5, 66, 67–8, 79–80, 81–2, 83–4, 191–2, 193, 280–1
violence and, 25, 26–8
Republican Network for Unity (RNU), 7, 218–24, 251, 263, 264, 266, 280, 282
Republican Prisoners Action Committee, 128
Republican Prisoners Action Group (RPAG), 190
Republican Sinn Féin (RSF), 53–63
abstentionism, 53, 54, 55, 56–7, 68–9, 73, 80–1, 114, 280–1
attitudes toward Provisionals, 44, 54–5, 66–8, 75, 76, 81–3, 191–2
Tony Catney on, 221
Comhar na gComharsan, 62–3
Continuity IRA and, 69, 73, 74–6, 94, 191, 281
Éire Nua (policy document, 1971-2) and, 59, 60–1, 63, 65, 69, 71, 79, 281
electoral politics and, 68–71, 79
founding of (1986), 53–4
international 'solidarity' and, 64
Irish Freedom Committee and, 111–12
'line of succession' to, 55–6, 58, 61, 67, 73, 74–5, 190–1, 280
north Armagh and, 248
other dissident groups and, 113–15, 122, 128, 190, 266
peace process and, 61, 66–8, 81

political platform/principles, 58–61, 63–6, 68, 71–2, 78–80
post-2002 decline, 182, 285
Price sisters and, 75, 99–100
profile of membership, 53–4, 69–70, 77–8
republican prisoners and, 66, 69, 71–2, 73, 190
Saoirse (newspaper), 71, 76, 80, 81, 248
Saol Nua ('social and economic programme', 1992), 61–3, 65, 79
'Shell to Sea' protests and, 71, 234
traditional republican ideology and, 46–7, 54–7, 61, 66, 68, 79–80, 81–2, 83–5, 191–2, 193, 281, 286
violence and, 54–5, 57, 73, 75–7, 79, 80, 181, 287
revolutionary period, Irish (1913-23), 11–16, 17
Rice, Brendan, 164, 178
Rice, Gerard, 236
Rice, John Joe, 32
Richards, James, 28
Robinson, Peter, 5, 207
Rogers, Keith, 178
Rossa, Jeremiah O'Donovan, 191
Royal Irish Regiment 'homecoming' parade (November 2008), 221, 237–8
Royal Ulster Constabulary (RUC), 32, 64, 77, 93, 105, 109, 126–7, 135, 142, 161, 248
Royal Victoria Hospital, Belfast, 176
RTÉ, The Brookeborough Raid (television documentary, 2006), 57
Ruane, Tony, 54
Ruddy, Gerry, 168, 232
Rupert, David, 2, 100, 104, 109–18, 119–20, 121, 131–2, 136, 138, 141–2, 148, 185
Russell, Sean, 26–7, 29
Ryan, Frank, 19

Sands, Bobby, 39, 77, 97–8, 233
Sands, Marcella, 162
Sands-McKevitt, Bernadette, 97–8, 99, 102, 103, 104, 105, 106, 109, 113, 127, 131, 141
Saoirse na hÉireann, 180, 246
Saor Éire, 19, 20, 221
Scappaticci, Freddie, 162, 184, 255, 267
Second World War, 24, 28, 29–30
security services, 2, 104, 110, 133–4, 185, 201, 219, 258
see also Rupert, David
Semtex, 140
senate, Irish, 23
Serious and Organised Crime Agency (SOCA), 252–3
Shackleton barracks bombing (25 February 2000), 118
Shannon, Brendan, 164, 178
Shannon airport, 212
Shell, 71, 233–4
'Shell to Sea' protests, 71, 215, 234, 235
Shiels, Emmett, 217
Shivers, Brian, 240
Sinn Féin
    32CSM and, 97, 98, 99, 101
    abstentionism (pre-1964), 17, 18, 22, 31, 34, 36, 45, 55
    Civil War defeat and, 15–16, 284
    defections from (2006-10 period), 219, 220, 226, 228, 230–1, 236, 284
    Éire Nua (policy document, 1971-2), 59–60
    éirígí and, 236, 237, 238
    electoral politics, 69, 70–1, 84, 186, 192–3, 203, 210–11, 224–5, 285
    1923-64 period, 17, 22, 31, 32, 34
    failure to break through in South (2007–9), 225–7, 230, 231, 266, 283, 286
    the Troubles and, 251–2

internal divisions/unrest (2006-10 period), 226–30
internal party criticism of Adams, 225–6, 227–9, 264
IRA and (pre-1969), 17–18, 22, 31
legitimacy of PIRA's violent campaign, 139–40, 251, 252, 282, 283
negotiations with DUP (from 2004), 203, 204, 205, 206, 207, 266
November 1986 árd-fheis, 49–53
Ruairí Ó Brádaigh as president, 45, 48, 52–3, 59, 60
peace process and *see under* peace process, Provisional republicanism and
PIRA 'criminality' (2000-10) and, 137, 164, 202–4, 206, 225, 252–3
policing and *see* Police Service of Northern Ireland (PSNI), Sinn Féin and
political apex/triumph of (2002-5), 84, 192–3, 203, 224–5, 285
power-sharing arrangement, 70–1
'Shell to Sea' protests and, 234
split (January 1970), 36
Smith, M.L.R., 33
Social Democratic and Labour Party (SDLP), 186, 193, 225, 253, 285
socialism, 16, 18–21, 24, 25, 34, 60, 92–3, 264
    éirígí and, 230, 232, 233–4, 237, 239, 242, 279
    RSF and, 58, 62–3
Socialist Environmental Alliance (SEA), 223
Somerville, Henry Boyle, 25
South, Sean, 32, 39, 45, 96, 281
Sovereign Nation, 137
Special Reconnaissance Regiment (SRR), 249, 250, 257
Spence, Terry, 256
Spriggs, Denis, 216
St Andrews Agreement (October 2006), 205, 207–8
The Starry Plough (IRSP-INLA publication), 221
Staunton, Gerard, 261
Stewartstown police station bombing (2000), 120, 138
Storey, Bobby, 263
Strabane (County Tyrone), 180
Straw, Jack, 127
strike, bus and tram (Dublin, March 1935), 20, 25
Sunningdale Agreement (1973-4), 44, 125
Swift, Bernice, 226, 235

Tamil Tigers, 110
Taylor, Geraldine, 70
Tidey, Don, 98
Tohill, Bobby, 170, 178, 204
Toman, Barry, 70
Tone, Wolfe, 12, 51, 67, 191
Tonge, Jonathan, 2, 69, 148
Toolis, Kevin, 95
Townshend, Charles, 11
Traditional Unionist Voice (TUV), 7
transport infrastructure, attacks on, 96, 120, 138, 142, 255
'Treaty ports', 23
Trimble, David, 107, 117, 206
the Troubles, 3, 35, 37–8, 60, 92, 204, 251–2
'Truth and Lies' event, RNU (2008), 223
Twomey, Maurice, 20, 25
Tyrell, Áine, 229

Uí Cathain, Poilín, 226
Ulster Unionist Party (UUP), 117, 206
unionism, 5, 7, 70–1, 203, 204–5, 206, 211, 220, 266, 285
    backlash against civil rights movement, 35
    dissident republican views of, 60–1, 175, 186–7

United Irishman, 31
United Irishmen Rebellion (1798), 43, 67, 82, 241
United Nations (UN), 101–3, 126, 186
United States of America, 12, 102–3, 106, 132, 134–5,
     167, 185, 206–7, 212
Irish-American republican groups, 111–13, 114, 121, 135

Volunteer Reserve (formed 1934), 23, 24

Walsh, Richard, 60–1, 67, 76–7, 78, 79, 248
War of Independence, Irish (1919-21), 14–15
Ward, Pat, 52

Ware, John, 141
Weber, Max, 26
White, Robert, 45, 53
Whyte, Richard, 144
Wolfe Tone Society, 34
Woodward, Shaun, 267
Workers Party of New Zealand, 239
Wright, Billy, murder of (1997), 93

Yates, Chris, 256
Young Irelander Rebellion (1848), 67, 241